THE ENCHANTMENT OF WORDS

The Enchantment of Words

of Words

Wittgenstein's *Tractatus Logico-Philosophicus*

DENIS McMANUS

CLARENDON PRESS · OXFORD

OXFORD

UNIVERSITY PRESS

Great Clarendon Street, Oxford OX2 6DP

Oxford University Press is a department of the University of Oxford.
It furthers the University's objective of excellence in research, scholarship,
and education by publishing worldwide in

Oxford New York

Auckland Cape Town Dar es Salaam Hong Kong Karachi
Kuala Lumpur Madrid Melbourne Mexico City Nairobi
New Delhi Shanghai Taipei Toronto

With offices in

Argentina Austria Brazil Chile Czech Republic France Greece
Guatemala Hungary Italy Japan Poland Portugal Singapore
South Korea Switzerland Thailand Turkey Ukraine Vietnam

Oxford is a registered trade mark of Oxford University Press
in the UK and in certain other countries

Published in the United States
by Oxford University Press Inc., New York

© Denis McManus 2006

The moral rights of the author have been asserted
Database right Oxford University Press (maker)

First published 2006

British Library Cataloguing in Publication Data

Data available

Library of Congress Cataloging in Publication Data
McManus, Denis, 1967–
The enchantment of words : Wittgenstein's Tractatus
logico-philosophicus / Denis McManus.
p. cm.
Includes bibliographical references (p.   ) and index.
ISBN-13: 978–0–19–928802–1 (alk. paper)
ISBN-10: 0–19–928802–X (alk. paper)
1. Wittgenstein, Ludwig, 1889–1951. Tractatus logico-philosophicus.
2. Logic, Symbolic and mathematical. 3. Language and languages—Philosophy. I. Title.
B3376.W563T7344 2006   192–dc22   2006009853

Typeset by Laserwords Private Limited, Chennai, India
Printed in Great Britain
on acid-free paper by
Biddles Ltd., King's Lynn, Norfolk

ISBN 0–19–928802–X   978–0–19–928802–1

1 3 5 7 9 10 8 6 4 2

Dedicated to my mother and to the memory of my father

Preface

It has taken me a long time to write this book, and there are many people I would like to thank for helping me over the years. Anita Avramides first introduced me to the work of Wittgenstein when I was an undergraduate student; Renford Bambrough and Jane Heal supervised my Ph.D. on the development of that work; in their very different ways, all three taught me a great deal about what it is to think seriously about philosophical problems. Towards the end of my Ph.D., I was fortunate enough to spend a year as a Herchel Smith Visiting Fellow at Harvard University; my time with that group of scholars and students revitalized me, and I want to thank here Stanley Cavell, Warren Goldfarb, David Macarthur, Ian Proops, Jérôme Sackur, and Ori Simchen. An unanticipated bonus that that year brought were trips across the river to Burt Dreben's seminars at Boston University, which were a marvellous experience; it was also there that I met Matt Ostrow, who has been a good friend to me since. After my Ph.D., I came to teach at Southampton University; on this occasion, I would like to thank, in particular, Tony Palmer, who, I still suspect, played a major part in getting me the job in the first place. But all of my colleagues have helped me, and they provide a friendly and supportive environment in which excellent teaching and research persists despite all attempts to 'assure the quality' of the former and 'assess' the latter.

For helpful comments on earlier versions of some of the material presented here, I would like to thank, in addition to many of those mentioned above, Maria Alvarez, Anne-Marie Christensen, James Conant, John Divers, Paulo Faria, Sebastian Gardner, Simon Glendinning, Martin Gustafson, Peter Hacker, Cressida Heyes, Andrea Kern, Sandra Laugier, John McDowell, Marie McGinn, Joanna McManus, Ray Monk, Adrian Moore, Daniele Moyal-Sharrock, David Owen, Dawn Phillips, John Preston, Rupert Read, Aaron Ridley, Richard Sørli, Graham Stevens, James Tully, and in particular, Stephen Mulhall and Genia Schönbaumsfeld. Apologies to anyone I may have forgotten. I would like to thank Arne Delfs and Sylvia Hilken for their help with translations, and Jean van Altena, Jenni Craig, and Peter Momtchiloff of Oxford University Press for their assistance and support.

My work has also benefited from the comments of members of audiences at the universities of Amiens, Amsterdam, Bristol, Chicago, Cambridge, Dundee, Glasgow, Hertfordshire, Leeds, New Mexico, Middlesex, Paris I, Reading, Sheffield, Southampton, Stirling, St Andrews, Saint Xavier (Chicago), and Birkbeck College, London. I would like to thank the University of Southampton for a period of research leave and the World Universities Network for an Exchange Award that allowed me to present my work on two occasions at the

Wittgenstein Archives at the University of Bergen (and thanks to Alois Pichler for helping to bring those visits about). I have also inflicted versions of the thoughts offered here on several generations of undergraduate and postgraduate students at Southampton University, and their forbearance has been much appreciated.

There are some non-professional (or should that be 'unprofessional') friends who have taken an unhealthy interest in the progress of this book. In particular, I would like to mention Richard Hindley, Danny Sullivan, 'Bernard' Sullivan, and the Fleming Park Monday Night Football boys; I hope this book goes some way to convincing the latter that 'research leave' does not mean the same as 'holiday'; but I doubt it. There is also a tradition of sorts in my department of thanking pubs in the prefaces of books; I would like to mention the Clarendon Arms in Cambridge, the Black Bull in Reeth, and the Volunteer in Ventnor, Isle of Wight, in each of which, believe it or not, 'research was conducted'.

My wife, Joanna, has helped me no end in getting this book completed; not only has she has put up with my extended absences but also, when work was driving me mad, she was the one who noticed and helped me escape. She has brought a little bit of normality and a lot of love into my life.

The book is dedicated to my mother and to the memory of my father; despite, I think, not always being too sure where it was all going to lead, they supported me all the way.

A word or two about the content of the book. One thing on which commentators on the *Tractatus* agree is that it is a difficult work to understand, and I certainly cannot claim to know that the interpretation that I offer here is correct. I also suspect that there are many ways through the *Tractatus*, and my reading certainly highlights particular aspects of it at the expense of others. I myself have other ideas about it that are incompatible with the ones presented here, ideas to which I may return some day. But I hope that readers of the present book will find something of use in the presentation here of an interpretation that, it seems to me, is philosophically interesting, is reasonably consistent, and fits—at least prima facie—what Wittgenstein says.

Contents

List of Abbreviations

BB   *The Blue and Brown Books*, Oxford: Blackwell, 1969.

CL   *Ludwig Wittgenstein: Cambridge Letters*, ed. B. F. McGuinness and G. H. von Wright, Oxford: Blackwell, 1995.

CV   *Culture and Value*, ed. G. H. von Wright, trans. P. Winch, rev. 2nd edn. ed. A. Pichler, Oxford: Blackwell, 1998.

GT   *Geheime Tagebücher 1914–16*, ed. W. Baum, Vienna: Turia und Kant, 1992.

LE   'A Lecture on Ethics', repr. as *PO* ch. 5.

L I   *Wittgenstein's Lectures Cambridge 1930–32*, ed. D. Lee, Oxford: Blackwell, 1980.

L II   *Wittgenstein's Lectures Cambridge 1932–35*, ed. A. Ambrose, Oxford: Blackwell, 1979.

LO   *Letters to C. K. Ogden*, ed. G. H. von Wright, Oxford: Blackwell; London: Routledge & Kegan Paul, 1973.

LPE   P. Engelmann, *Letters from Ludwig Wittgenstein, with a Memoir*, ed. B. F. McGuinness, trans. L. Furtmüller, Oxford: Blackwell, 1967.

LW I   *Last Writings on the Philosophy of Psychology*, vol. 1, ed. G. H. von Wright and H. Nyman, trans. G. C. Luckhardt and M. A. E. Aue, Oxford: Blackwell, 1982.

M   G. E. Moore, 'Wittgenstein's Lectures in 1930–33', repr. as *PO* ch. 6.

MS   A *Nachlass* manuscript, published in *Wittgenstein's Nachlass*, the Wittgenstein Archives at the University of Bergen/Oxford University Press, 1998.

NB   *Notebooks 1914–16*, ed. G. H. von Wright and G. E. M. Anscombe, trans. G. E. M. Anscombe, Oxford: Blackwell, 1979.

NFL   'Notes for Lectures on "Private Experience" and "Sense Data" ', ed. R. Rhees, repr. as *PO* ch. 10.

OC   *On Certainty*, ed. G. E. M. Anscombe and G. H. von Wright, trans. D. Paul and G. E. M. Anscombe, Oxford: Blackwell, 1974.

PG   *Philosophical Grammar*, ed. R. Rhees, trans. A. Kenny, Oxford: Blackwell, 1974.

Ph   'Philosophy: Sections 86–93 (pp. 405–35) of the so-called Big Typescript (Catalog Number 213)', ed. H. Nyman, trans. C. G. Luckhardt and M. A. E. Aue, repr. as *PO* ch. 9.

PI   *Philosophical Investigations*, ed. G. E. M. Anscombe and R. Rhees, trans. G. E. M. Anscombe, Oxford: Blackwell, 1967.

PO   *Philosophical Occasions*, ed. J. Klagge and A. Nordmann, Indianapolis: Hackett, 1993.

PPO   *Public and Private Occasions*, ed. J. C. Klagge and A. Nordmann, New York: Rowman & Littlefield, 2003.

PR   *Philosophical Remarks*, ed. R. Rhees, trans. R. Hargreaves and R. White, Oxford: Blackwell, 1975.

PT   *Prototractatus—An Early Version of Tractatus Logico-Philosophicus*, ed. B. F. McGuinness, T. Nyberg, and G. H. von Wright, trans. D. F. Pears and B. F. McGuinness, London: Routledge & Kegan Paul, 1971.

RFM   *Remarks on the Foundations of Mathematics*, ed. G. H. von Wright, R. Rhees, and G. E. M. Anscombe, trans. G. E. M. Anscombe, 3rd edn., Oxford: Blackwell, 1978.

RLF   'Some Remarks on Logical Form', repr. as *PO* ch. 4.

RPP I   *Remarks on the Philosophy of Psychology*, vol. 1, ed. G. E. M. Anscombe and G. H. von Wright, trans. G. E. M. Anscombe, Oxford: Blackwell, 1980.

TLP   *Tractatus Logico-Philosophicus*, trans. C. K. Ogden, London: Routledge & Kegan Paul, 1922. Another translation by D. F. Pears and B. F. McGuinness (London: Routledge & Kegan Paul, 1961) is also sometimes used in this book.

TS   A *Nachlass* typescript, published in the *Wittgenstein's Nachlass*, the Wittgenstein Archives at the University of Bergen/Oxford University Press, 1998.

VC   *Wittgenstein and the Vienna Circle*, shorthand notes recorded by F. Waismann, ed. B. F. McGuinness, trans. J. Schulte and B. F. McGuinness, Oxford: Blackwell, 1979.

Z   *Zettel*, ed. G. E. M. Anscombe and G. H. von Wright, trans. G. E. M. Anscombe, Oxford: Blackwell, 1981.

References are to page numbers with the following exceptions: (i) *PT* and *TLP*, where numbers refer to proposition or paragraph numbers; (ii) MS and TS, where the first number gives the manuscript or typescript number, the second the page number, and the parenthetical third the (sometimes approximate) date (details of the cataloguing of the *Nachlass* are given in von Wright (1969)); (iii) *CV* and *PPO*, for which, since *CV* is made up of MS and TS remarks spanning 1914–51, and *PPO* includes diary remarks from 1930–2 and 1936–7, references also include the date of the remarks to which reference is made when the context has not already made the date clear.

[I]t is a task of philosophy to break the power of words over the human mind.

Frege 1879, p. vi

1

Introduction

Wittgenstein's early masterpiece, the *Tractatus Logico-Philosophicus*, has had a profound effect on philosophy since it was published in 1922.[1] It is a short but intimidating work, made up of seventy or so pages of numbered remarks, many of which are, as David Pears puts it, 'plainly enigmatic' (1997, p. 602). The *Tractatus* is a work for which its author has stratospheric ambitions: he claims that its 'definitive' and 'unassailable' truths provide 'on all essential points, the final solution' to the problems of philosophy (*TLP* preface). But Wittgenstein also claims that those who understand him will recognize that the book's propositions are actually nonsensical. What I offer here is an interpretation of this deeply puzzling book.

I argue that the *Tractatus* elucidates a conception of what it is for thought to be intelligible and for language to be meaningful; Wittgenstein demonstrates how thought, language, and the world that they represent must be for that conception to make sense, but with the ultimate purpose of showing us that it doesn't, as well as why we come to think that it does. Working through his analogy between propositions and pictures, we come to see that the 'intelligibility of thought' and the 'meaningfulness of language', which logical truths would delimit and which metaphysics and the philosophy of mind and language would explain, are issues constituted by confusions, and that Wittgenstein's own propositions are a working through of the pseudo-logic of the addled thinking that these confusions inspire. What is exposed is a mirage of a kind of self-consciousness, a misperception of the ways in which we happen to think, talk, and act as reasons why we ought to think, talk, and act as we do. The root of that misperception is our confusedly endowing words with a life of their own: we enchant, and are enchanted by, words, colluding in a confusion that transposes on to them, and on to the world which we then see them as 'fitting', burdens that are actually ours to bear. Such words promise to spare us the trouble, not only of thinking, but of living.

---

[1] References to the *Tractatus* are given in the text by proposition or paragraph number; in contexts in which it might not be clear that I am referring to that particular book, these numbers are prefaced by *TLP*. Other works by Wittgenstein are referred to using abbreviations given in the prelims. I have used both Ogden's and Pears and McGuinness's translations of passages from the *Tractatus* and, on occasion, my own.

1.1 THE PUZZLE OF THE *TRACTATUS* AND ITS FOUR 'KEYS'

The present section will set out some of the most obviously puzzling features of the *Tractatus*.

The early pages of the book seem to set out a view of the metaphysical constitution of reality. Quite what the view is, and what basis it is meant to have, is unclear. It invites (and has received) a realist interpretation, a setting out of how the world is independently of those who may think about it. But, in the same work, we also read the seemingly idealist slogan, 'I am my world' (5.63), and Wittgenstein declares that 'what solipsism *means*, is quite correct, only it cannot be *said*, but shows itself' (5.62). It is not at all clear that this view—whatever it is, and whatever basis it is meant to have—is consistent with the apparent realism of the book's opening. And in any case, solipsism is surely a hopeless view, irrespective of whether it is being meant, said, or shown (not that it is obvious what Wittgenstein has in mind in distinguishing those terms here either).

But it is also unclear how Wittgenstein can be offering a metaphysical theory of any sort, realist, solipsist, or otherwise. Elsewhere in the book, he declares that '[t]here is no *a priori* order of things' (5.634); at 5.5542, Wittgenstein poses the question, 'Has the question sense: what must there *be* in order that anything can be the case?', and in comments to Ogden on the translation of 5.5542, he insists that '[t]he correct answer to this question would be, that we may NOT!' (*LO* 33–4). So what *kind* of message is one to extract from the *Tractatus*? This challenge is given a further twist in the book's infamous, penultimate paragraph:

> My propositions are elucidatory in this way: he who understands me finally recognizes them as nonsensical [*unsinnig*], when he has climbed out through them, on them, over them. (He must so to speak throw away the ladder, after he has climbed up on it.)
> He must surmount these propositions; then he sees the world rightly. (6.54)

If—perhaps by having just arrived from another philosophical planet—it were possible today to read the *Tractatus* without knowing in advance what its penultimate paragraph says, one would, in all likelihood, be shocked by it. Just as we reach its end, we find that the whole status of this work, this 'elucidatory' piece of writing, is thrown into doubt: we are made uncertain about just what kind of book it is that we have read, and just what it is to have read it.

Towards the end of the *Tractatus* one finds remarks on ethics. These remarks are few in number, and are among the most obscure in this book of obscure remarks, and some commentators have questioned whether they connect, at any deep level, with the themes with which the rest of the book is concerned;[2]

---

[2] Cf., e.g., Hacker 1986, p. 105, and Glock 1996, p. 108.

but, famously, Wittgenstein wrote to Ludwig von Ficker that 'the point of [the *Tractatus*] is ethical'. He elaborated the point as follows

[T]he Ethical is delimited from within, as it were, by my book; and I'm convinced that, *strictly* speaking, it can ONLY be delimited in this way. In brief, I think: All of that which *many* are *babbling* today, I have defined in my book by remaining silent about it.[3]

If tempted to take these remarks lightly, we seem to confront here a rather uncharacteristic attempt on Wittgenstein's part to 'sell' his work. (Ficker was at the time a potential publisher of the *Tractatus*.) I believe, however, that we can take these remarks seriously.

But in doing so, we also need to address the prima facie problem that Wittgenstein identified *several* 'keys' to his early work. A second emerges when the preface of the *Tractatus* declares that 'its whole meaning could be summed up somewhat as follows: What can be said at all can be said clearly; and whereof one cannot speak [*reden*] thereof one must be silent'; with one small alteration ('*sprechen*' for '*reden*') the latter clause also makes up the book's 'conclusion', its final proposition. A third 'key' is Wittgenstein's declaration, at 4.0312, that his fundamental thought, his '*Grundgedanke*', is 'that the "logical constants" do not represent': 'the *logic* of the facts cannot be represented'. And a fourth key is Wittgenstein's insistence, in a letter to Russell, that his 'main contention' is 'the theory of what can be expressed (*gesagt*) by prop[osition]s ... and what can not be expressed by prop[osition]s, but only shown (*gezeigt*)', which he declares is 'the cardinal problem of philosophy' (*CL* 124). Ideally, an interpretation of the *Tractatus* will find a single lock which these apparently rather different keys—'the point' of the book, its 'whole meaning', its author's 'fundamental thought', and his 'main contention'—all fit.

1.2 PART 1 OF A SKETCH OF THE PRESENT BOOK

Chapter 2 begins the book proper, setting out some themes from the work of Frege and Russell, the philosophers whom Wittgenstein describes as providing 'in large measure the stimulation of [his] thoughts' (*TLP* preface). In their work can be traced, first, the roots of a conception of philosophical problems as confusions generated by our being misled by the 'surface grammar' of our ordinary language, and, secondly, a conception of useful philosophical work as analysis of that language pursued with the aim of undermining the perceived need for philosophical theories that will solve (what we would then recognize as unreal) philosophical problems. It is these conceptions that Wittgenstein inherits and to which he gives a radical twist.[4]

---

[3] Quoted in Monk 1990, p. 178.
[4] I make no claim for novelty in my reading of the work of Frege and Russell, the main purpose of Ch. 2 being to document the presence in that work of these two conceptions; those familiar with that work could probably get away with reading Sects. 2.4 and 2.7 and skimming the rest of that chapter.

Wittgenstein proposes that 'the whole of philosophy is full' of confusions that arise when we conflate what he calls 'signs' and 'symbols': roughly speaking, the 'mere' 'dead' signs are the noises that we emit and the marks that we make on paper, whereas 'symbols' are signs considered in their 'significant use' (3.326). Many very different symbols are expressed by very similar-looking or -sounding signs, and this leads us, confusedly, to assimilate the uses to which those signs are put. Wittgenstein's bold metaphilosophical hypothesis is that this is the root of philosophical confusion. If it were true, such confusions would be prevented by introducing notations that did not feature the kinds of 'surface-grammatical' similarities that confuse us. By expressing ourselves using such an ideal notation, philosophical problems would not arise. My own reading of the *Tractatus* places these concerns at its heart and argues that this implausible-sounding diagnosis of philosophical confusion, and its complementary but equally implausible-sounding prescription for how that confusion might be prevented, actually has some power.

The particular philosophical problem that provides the immediate stimulus to Wittgenstein's most important early work is also inherited from Frege and Russell: the problem of the nature of the laws of logic. There is a difficulty in regarding logical truth as a form of truth at all; to assert an ordinary truth like 'It is raining outside' is to say how things are, and to rule out another way things might be, the ways things are when 'It is not raining outside' is true; but with logical truths, nothing seems to correspond to this second aspect: logical impossibilities are specifically not ways things might be, and hence logical truths cannot be seen as ruling out ways things might be. Similarly, if we were to interpret the laws of logic as determining what is conceivable, what they would rule out would be inconceivable: we could not grasp what they would rule out. Wittgenstein's early work can be seen as attempting to resolve these difficulties by demonstrating that, in a sense, there are no such laws of logic. Wittgenstein's case can be seen as coming in two parts. One is his presentation of logical truths as tautologies, and logical falsehoods as contradictions. The second part is his attempt to expose as confused what I will call a 'con-formist' conception of the intelligibility of thought and language.

1.3 INTELLIGIBILITY AS CON-FORMITY

Post-Cartesian philosophy has characteristically taken its bearings by sceptical questions concerning whether we have real knowledge of the external world, other minds, the past, etc. But there is reason to believe that when we worry that our thoughts about the external world, say, might be false, we presuppose an answer to the following question: how must our thoughts and that world be constituted for it to be possible for the former to represent, or indeed misrepresent, the latter?

One of the most basic thoughts of philosophy can be seen as an answer to that question: that thoughts and the world share 'forms', with the 'intelligibility' of thought imagined as something like a fit, an isomorphism, between the 'form of thought' and the 'form of the world'. The latter refers not to the particular way in which, as a matter of contingent fact, the world happens to be: its being, for instance, one in which there happens to be a blue pen on the table in front of me, the 'form of the world' to which the thought 'There is a blue pen on the table in front of me' could be said to correspond in the sense of 'being *true* of', while the thought 'There is a black pen on the table in front of me' could not. Instead, the 'form of the world' refers to something that might also be called the world's 'logical' or 'metaphysical possibilities': the objects that happen to exist within it, as well as those that could happen to exist in it, belonging to certain fundamental kinds, possessing certain very fundamental or essential properties, and standing to one another in certain very fundamental or essential relations. In the relevant senses of 'form' and 'correspondence', the 'form' of the thought 'There is a black pen on the table in front of me' would 'correspond' to the 'form' of the world in which there happens to be a blue pen on the table in front of me, in that that thought embodies a false but none the less intelligible claim about that world, articulating another way in which the world might have been and reflecting, in some sense, the kinds of objects that might be found in that world, the kinds of properties that those objects might be found to have, and the kinds of relation in which they might be found to stand. It is this conception of intelligibility that I will call 'intelligibility as con-formity'. To ask how exactly one ought to understand the key notions it involves—'contingency', 'logical' and 'metaphysical possibility', 'kind', 'being fundamental', and 'being essential'—is obviously to raise large, and fundamental, philosophical questions. For now, I take it that anyone familiar with a little philosophy has a rough sense of how these notions are meant to be understood here.

A question that the conception of intelligibility as con-formity naturally raises is how thought and world come to have common forms, a question I will call the 'question of acquired con-formity'. The question is not one of how a thought comes to be true of a particular fact, but of how a thought comes to be the kind of thing that is capable of being true or false of a particular fact. What we seek is an account of the seemingly manifest fact that we *can* think about the world, this feat understood as the existence of a con-formity between our thoughts and the world.

Answers to the 'question of acquired con-formity' come in two very broad kinds: those I will call 'realist views', which state that the form of the world (somehow) dictates that of thought, and those I will call 'idealist views', which state that the form of thought (somehow) dictates that of the world. To illustrate the latter option, in a world that a god has created, ideas do not represent a peculiar mark of thinkers, as unthinking objects too were created to instantiate particular ideas that that god possessed. The notion that there might be a correspondence between thought and object is now given sense by the fact that they are both 'informed by' ideas: objects by the creator god's ideas, but ideas none the less to which the thinker's ideas might then be suited to correspond. As the realization of certain thoughts, the objects we think about are formed in a way that makes them, one might say, 'ready' or 'suited for' thought.

One reason why philosophers sometimes embrace the characteristic metaphysical extravagance of idealism is realism's inability to solve what I will call 'the problem of concept acquisition'. If the con-formity of thought and world is what allows the former to embody intelligible claims about the latter, then that con-formity is a necessary presupposition of, and thus cannot be brought about through, observation of the contents of that world. So, for example, an understanding of what it is for something to be a table cannot be gathered a posteriori through observing tables. As Sellars puts it:

[I]nstead of coming to have a concept of something because we have noticed that sort of thing, to have the ability to notice a sort of thing is already to have the concept of that sort of thing, and cannot account for it. (Sellars 1956, § 10)

I leave aside here two important questions. First, how do these forms of realism and idealism relate to the diverse other views to which philosophy has given those same labels? Secondly, how have these forms of realism and idealism manifested themselves in the thinking of particular philosophers? As a matter of fact, I do think that it is plausible to suggest that these con-formist issues are at the heart of much philosophical discussion of realism and idealism and, hence, that the Wittgensteinian attack on these issues is at the same time an attack on that discussion.[5] I introduce the idea of con-formism primarily to help provide that attack with some kind of definition, one which 'an attack on realism and idealism' would not have. But demonstrating that any particular 'realist' or 'idealist' is indeed a 'con-formist' would still have to be done on a case-by-case basis.[6]

1.4 PART 2 OF A SKETCH OF THE PRESENT BOOK

The notion that our thoughts 'work', are coherent, when the 'form' of those thoughts matches the 'form' of reality promises us an explanation of what an intelligible thought is and, if the laws of logic delimit the boundary between intelligible and unintelligible thinking, an explanation of why that boundary lies where it does and what kind of boundary it is. (Such an explanation, supplemented by a parallel story about the form of 'language', would answer corresponding questions about the boundary between meaningful talk and nonsensical

---

[5] In my (2004a) I use this same map in presenting a reading of the early Wittgenstein's understanding of scepticism, and in my forthcoming I use it to shed light on Heidegger's relationship to realism and idealism.

[6] Ch. 10 n. 1 discusses a related issue in connection with some of Russell's reflections on intentionality.

talk.) If, however, we are confused in thinking that there are substantial 'laws of logic', then beliefs of ours that would entail that there are must be confused too. In this way, a critique of the idea of 'logical truth' would expand into a critique of metaphysical reflection on the 'form' of language, thought, and world: 'Theories which make a proposition of logic appear substantial are always false' (6.111). Beginning in Chapter 3, I argue that Wittgenstein offers just such a broad critique.

I argue that Wittgenstein's remarks on the nature of language, thought, and world represent a working through of the demands of con-formism. For example, a con-formist might imagine objects and the possible facts that they may figure within as determining why we talk as we do, in that the names that are the ultimate components of the propositions we use have the form that they do because of the form of the objects that they represent, and the propositions we use have the form that they do because of the form of the facts that they represent; a name of an object must be combined with other names to form propositions in ways that mirror the ways in which that object is combined with objects to make up the facts in which it figures. If so, objects must meet certain explanatory obligations, and hence must take a certain form. Wittgenstein sets out that form, arguing that we will arrive at the conclusion that these objects must be characterized by a particular set of 'internal properties'; these are properties which 'it is unthinkable that its object does not possess' (4.123) and the holding of which 'cannot ... be asserted by propositions' (4.122).[7] I argue, however, that this working through of the demands of con-formism is intended to help us see that it is only confusion that gives those demands their apparent sense.

Though a new notation would prevent philosophical problems arising, what will prevent may not also 'cure', and the core work of the *Tractatus* is the latter: a working through of the confused logic of philosophical concerns that are already 'at large', with the aim of helping us recognize that confusion. Chapter 4 adds to the sign/symbol metaphilosophical hypothesis the other basic commitments that inform my reading of the *Tractatus*. These are, first, what has become known as 'resolution'; second, an understanding of what it is to 'elucidate nonsense', and third, an understanding (as themselves moves within such elucidation) of Wittgenstein's remarks mentioning 'internal properties' and 'internal relations'.

Quite what it is for a reading of the *Tractatus* to be 'resolute' is a controversial issue; but I take a central element to be a commitment to reading the book not as defending a particular metaphysics and a particular philosophy of mind and language. To think that it does is the most natural, initial response to the opening pages of the *Tractatus*, and for this reason alone the 'resolute' approach would

---

[7] Since I will argue that there is something inherently problematic about the notions of 'internal property' and 'internal relation', I will on occasion use scare-quotes for these expressions. But, as with 'object' (cf. Ch. 3 n. 3), I follow no consistent policy other than using scare-quotes when it will help and not when it won't.

have its critics. That those opening pages encourage such an initial reaction is, however, to be expected on my understanding of what it is for Wittgenstein's propositions to be 'elucidatory' (6.54). Wittgenstein works through the confused pseudo-logic of our con-formist commitments, and the 'claims' that he makes elaborate on, extend, the nonsense that those confusions prompt us to talk; thus Wittgenstein's own claims are, as *TLP* 6.54 indicates, nonsensical; but their value is in leading us to see that our philosophical talk is itself already nonsensical. To follow through the pseudo-logic of this confusion is to see how one claim it prompts us to make appears to entail another; such an exploration of such commitments thus takes on the form of an argument; but it is an argument designed to show us that those commitments are confused, and I argue that to understand Wittgenstein's talk of 'internal properties', 'internal relations', 'the inexpressible', 'showing', and 'the transcendental' is to recognize that the thinking that leads us to it is informed by confusion.[8] The 'insights' that this talk expresses bring us to the point of recognizing and being able to reject confusions *within which* these 'insights' emerge. What one is left with is an understanding of the nonsense that one previously unwittingly talked.

Wittgenstein's analogy between pictures and propositions plays a crucial part in helping us see how this account can fit his 'claims' about the internal properties and internal relations characterizing language, thought, and world. The analogy that initially struck Wittgenstein was one not between a proposition and a conventional picture, but between a proposition and a model (using toys to represent the events in a car accident) and, at 3.1431, he suggests that we reflect on models 'made up of spatial objects (such as tables, chairs, books) instead of written signs'. A central element of the present book is an exploration, beginning in Chapter 5, of where following that advice leads us. Thinking through what is involved in understanding such a model serves to bring out a certain truth in the internal properties and internal relations that Wittgenstein identifies. But it also makes apparent that these 'properties' and 'relations' do not, as the con-formist expects, represent a basis for an explanation of how words are used with meaning. Their 'discovery' is itself a move within a confusion, but one which indicates that that is what it is, along with why the explanation alluded to does not make sense.

For example, according to the con-formist thought that a name and the object it names must have combinatorial possibilities that 'correspond', 'the illogical' would be produced when names are combined in ways that violate these requirements: what such combinations of names would say is incoherent because the objects that they represent cannot be combined to form facts. But thinking through the picture analogy makes clear how the truth of the internal relations identified is that 'illogical combinations' simply have no meaning within the systems of representation involved. Moving a pepper-pot across a folded napkin

---

[8] I concentrate my attention on the first two of these expressions, though the broader moral for the other three is addressed explicitly in Sects. 14.5–14.10, 15.1–15.4, and 8.5–8.6, respectively.

may represent Frank crossing a road, but what is wrong with a napkin being placed on top of the pepper-pot is not that the possibility depicted is, in some sense, 'illogical'; rather, this combination of signs has been given no meaning in that system of representation. What we misperceive as a distinction between two kinds of situation or two kinds of thought—'the logical' and 'the illogical'—is the difference between signs to which a sense has been assigned and signs to which it hasn't. Getting clear about the latter distinction—which the picture analogy helps us to do in the same way that Wittgenstein's imagined ideal notation would, namely, by breaking the associations between the familiar signs we use in English, say, and the use that that language makes of them—will eliminate the felt need for an explanation of the former distinction, a need which our con-formist metaphysical speculation is meant to meet.

Undoing the appeal of such speculation thus lies in a 'disenchanting' of the signs we use. Chapter 6 shows how this understanding of the spur to that speculation underpins Wittgenstein's notion that arriving at a notation that could not be so 'enchanted' could lead to our 'do[ing] away with' philosophical theories that divide the contents of the world into different ontological types.[9] In line with the understanding of 'the illogical' set out above, contexts in which, for example, numbers and colours are brought into comparison with one another, including precisely those in which they might be declared to belong to *different* ontological types, are themselves cases of word-play which the ideal notation would render impossible. I argue that this view has some plausibility.

Part of the power of the picture analogy is to show that a certain truth is captured in the assertions about internal properties and internal relations to which Wittgenstein's elucidation of con-formism leads us. There is also a certain truth to how we are led to them: the arguments in the text that this elucidation follows shows, as one might put it, that no propositions are 'left' with which one might describe how, for example, the referents of the ultimate analyses of our propositions can be combined in order to make up facts: it is an 'internal property' of such an 'object', it is 'essential' to it, 'that it can be a constituent part of [the possible facts]' of which it can be part (2.011). Chapter 5 shows how the picture analogy reveals deeper truths to such claims and to the arguments that lead to them, and Chapter 7 extends that treatment to the idea that there is an 'internal relation of depicting' between objects and the 'names' that refer to them, between possible facts and the propositions that describe them. When we imagine the intelligibility of a name as lying in its 'con-formity' with the object that it denotes, we have indeed failed to assign sense to the 'possibilities' that we imagine here as the name's being used intelligibly and its being used unintelligibly. The illusion that we have got hold of a substantial issue here arises out of another sign/symbol conflation, our alternating between two different uses of the word 'object'.

---

[9] Cf. *CL* 25, quoted in Sect. 6.1.

How the realizations described ought to feed back into our philosophical reflection on thought and thinkers is the concern of Chapter 8. A truth behind the internal relatedness of a thinker and the world it thinks about is explained, as is the way in which that truth naturally expresses itself in solipsistic terms, in the impossibility of making sense of a certain distance between thinker and world, which might, for example, be imagined as crossed when the thinker comes to master concepts: the impossibility of our ultimately being '*told how* the proposition represents' seems to reveal that instead propositions must simply 'show their sense' (*NB* 25; *TLP* 4.022) and with it the world they describe. But again the ultimate upshot is a recognition of how we are in the grip of a confused con-formist notion of what it is for thought to be intelligible, to 'work', and for a pupil's thought to 'come to work'. The metaphysical claims about the nature of language, thought, and world that the *Tractatus* lays out are claims that must be made if we are to make sense of the first two con-forming to the third; this is how they must 'look' if one believes that the notion of intelligibility upon which it draws makes sense; but Wittgenstein's ultimate intent is to show that it doesn't. Chapter 9 shows how this insight informs Wittgenstein's other proposals about objects. (Chapter 10 returns to some of the methodological proposals made in Chapter 4 in order to bring out further aspects of those proposals in the light of having seen them 'in action'.)

Chapters 11 and 12 turn to the second part of Wittgenstein's attack on the idea of substantial 'logical truths'. The obvious fact that some deductive infer-ences are valid and others are not seems to indicate that there must be such truths. Wittgenstein's response is, first, to argue that inferential relations must be internal relations if we are to avoid a 'substantial' logic and, secondly, to provide an account of propositions that allows us to see beyond those internal relations. Wittgenstein presents logical inference as, one might say, the 'unpack-ing' of what he calls 'complex propositions', propositions which are themselves the result of combining, using truth-functions, what he calls 'elementary pro-positions', propositions which are logically independent of one another. (Cru-cial here are Wittgenstein's truth-table analyses of the truth-functions, which contribute to his effort to demonstrate that 'the "logical constants" do not rep-resent' (4.0312).) Since complex propositions can possess 'overlapping' 'truth-grounds', in that they may be made up of overlapping sets of elementary propos-itions, certain combinations of propositions cannot be asserted at the same time; this, argues Wittgenstein, is the basis of deductive inference. Once again a set of internal relations—here inferential relations—turn out not to be the relations that they seem to be: a proposition that follows from another 'overlaps with', is not genuinely distinct from, that other proposition. Hence, inferential relations are not relations between genuinely distinct propositions, and our making valid inferences does not commit us to logical truths that might underpin or explain the possibility of such inferences.

Wittgenstein describes this account of the structure of propositions as revealing 'the general form of the proposition' (GFP), since that account is meant to encompass all propositions. Chapter 11 explains why Wittgenstein was tempted into believing that it did—he was later to conclude that he was mistaken—and why this GFP, while 'giv[ing] the essence of all description [and] therefore the essence of the world' (5.471–5.4711), might not have struck the early Wittgenstein as having metaphysical implications. (If it had, that would undermine a 'resolute' reading of the *Tractatus*.) Chapter 12 goes on to examine how Wittgenstein believed the GFP would subsume propositions and forms of inferential relation which do not appear to fit its requirements. Crucial to understanding how Wittgenstein deals with such propositions will be, once again, limitations on the forms that might be taken by an explanation of 'how a proposition represents'; I will offer an indication of how we might be thought to be able to survive without the explanations we crave by drawing on Chapter 6's discussion of logical types.

Chapters 13 and 14 turn to the thorny question of the early Wittgenstein's view of ethics.[10] Chapter 13 argues that a concern which profoundly marks Wittgenstein's own personal ethical reflection, a concern with 'decency' [*Anständigkeit*], and an argument that parallels Chapter 8's discussion of the notion that a proposition must 'show its sense' coincide to provide a sense for Wittgenstein's proposal that 'ethics cannot be expressed' (6.421). This proposal can be seen as pointing to a certain basic responsiveness to the world which one might articulate using concepts including 'conscience', 'good will', and 'decency', a fundamental but ineffable form of moral knowledge without which supposedly ethical utterances have no traction upon our lives.

But in line with the broader interpretation offered here, Chapter 14 argues that this supposed insight needs to be handled with care; like the internal relations discussed, the form in which this moral philosophical insight initially strikes us must be 'thrown away', and I argue that there are indications in Wittgenstein's remarks on decency that support this view. The explanatory urge which is apparently thwarted when we run into these forms of ineffable knowledge is confused; to extend the analogy with internal relations further, the striking 'insight' in question ought to signal to us precisely that the explanatory project that has led us here is confused; and to extend the analogy one more step, the root of our confusion in our moral philosophical reflection is, again, sign/symbol

---

[10] Topics that the *Tractatus* discusses but which my own book does not include mathematics and probability; I also examine only ethical aspects of its discussion of the will.

conflation. 'The sayable' that we come to feel must be supplemented by an ineffable moral knowledge is a confused hybrid of sign and symbol, supporting and supported by a confused vision of expression and teaching as the passing on of something like assertoric sentences. The 'recognition' of the 'need' for inexpressible and unteachable powers of 'conscience' emerges for those in the grip of this confusion; when we shed this confusion, we ought also to shed our belief in those 'powers' as solutions to (what we now see are unreal) problems. Another image of a problematic gap between subject and world which we come to believe must be spanned by a perplexing inexpressible insight turns out to be the product of sign/symbol conflation, of our enchanting and being enchanted by mere words.

The concluding chapter reviews how the reading I have offered places the four 'keys' to the *Tractatus*. To understand Wittgenstein's invocations of the say/show distinction—Wittgenstein's 'main contention'—is, in each case, to 'confront' an internal property or internal relation, first as an apparent answer to a philosophical question, then as a limitation on how deep our desire for philosophical explanation can delve (certain things one wishes to understand turn out to be things one must simply 'see'), and then finally as an insight into the confusion that constitutes that question, that desire for explanation. For example, the 'ineffable knowledge' embodied in 'conscience' first appears as an explanation of how moral seriousness is possible; then we see it as a limit on the extent to which that seriousness can be understood or explained; but finally, we recognize how we had conceived of 'understanding' or 'explaining' that seriousness and that such a conception draws on a confused notion of 'the effable'. The 'disappointment' that leads us to 'the *in*-effable' is one which strikes only those in the grip of that confusion, that fantasy of enchanted words. To reject that fantasy is to recognize the need for a kind of vigilance over when we express ourselves through our talk and when our talk embodies a failure to express ourselves, when our empty talk disguises the fact that *we* are saying nothing or that there is nothing more *to* say: then, the responsible, non-obfuscating response is silence. Con-formism serves to obscure the kind of achievement that this vigilance is and itself instantiates that empty talk.

Finally, I propose that we might understand our succumbing to the fantasy of 'the independent life of words'—our enchantment by, and of, words—as our desiring (madly) to be free of an identity, and that a recognition of this refusal of what Weininger calls '[t]he highest expression of all morality'[11] is the 'ethical point' of the *Tractatus*. The desire to be free of this burden, to be anonymous in this way, is at the same time a desire to live in an animistic world, one which tells us how we ought to describe it, and thus what it is about it that ought to interest us. This craving finds expression in the philosophical vision of a world with a

---

[11] Cf. Sect. 15.7.

metaphysical form of its own upon which logical facts might rest; that this vision is confused is Wittgenstein's 'fundamental thought', his '*Grundgedanke*'.[12]

[12] A couple of comments must be made on the sources upon which I draw. First, the fact that Wittgenstein's philosophical outlook underwent a radical rethink affects which textual sources one can draw upon in presenting 'a reading of the early Wittgenstein'. In this regard, uncontentious sources are, in addition to the *Tractatus* itself, *CL*, *GT*, *LO*, *LPE*, *NB*, and *PT*. (I say 'in this regard' because one might well ask how clear a picture such sources give of Wittgenstein's considered views, since these sources, unlike *TLP*, were not prepared by him for publication.) But I will also sometimes cite passages from his work in the early years of his return to philosophy (1929–31), citing some as expressing the same view as his earlier view: whether it is believed that this is indeed what they do will, of course, depend on the readers' opinion of the overall interpretation offered. Secondly, though I comment on continuities and discontinuities between Wittgenstein's early and later work (cf. esp. Sects. 11.7–11.8 and Appendix A), I have not addressed continuities and discontinuities between the different 'early' sources (such as between *TLP*, *PT*, and the different sets of notes published in *NB*); this lack of attention, though widespread among commentators, may become indefensible in years to come. (McGuinness's work ought perhaps to have already raised our scholarly standards in this regard (cf., e.g., his 2002, ch. 15); forthcoming work by Michael Potter certainly should).

2

Some Historical Preliminaries

In the preface of the *Tractatus*, Wittgenstein states:

[T]o the great works of Frege and the writings of my friend Bertrand Russell I owe in large measure the stimulation of my thoughts.

Both Frege and Russell are major philosophers in their own right; the present chapter will present a mere sketch of some of their concerns. These have been selected on the basis that they allow us a way into Wittgenstein's early work. But it must be borne in mind that this is the purpose of the account that follows, which, as a result, is anything but a comprehensive or thorough presentation of Frege's and Russell's philosophies.[1]

2.1 LOGIC AS TRUTH AND LOGIC AS LANGUAGE

The truth or falsity of certain claims seems not to depend upon the particular subject-matters of those claims. For example,

> The moon is full or there is a cup on the table if and only if it is not the case that the moon is not full and there is not a cup on the table.

This, it seems, would be true no matter what, whether the moon is full or not, and whether there is a cup on the table or not. This claim seems to instantiate a certain pattern that guarantees truth:

> (p or q) if and only if not (not p and not q).

Similarly, even if I know nothing about mammals, whales, or animals, I can still be sure that if

> All whales are mammals

and

> All mammals are animals

turn out to be true, then

> All whales are animals

---

[1] As was indicated in Ch. 1, those familiar with their work ought perhaps to read Sects. 2.4–2.7 of this chapter and skim the rest.

is true also. Again, we seem to have uncovered a certain pattern which guarantees truth:

All As are Bs.

All Bs are Cs.

Therefore,

All As are Cs.

The study of such patterns has been called the study of 'logic'. But what are these patterns and what kind of insight do they embody?

Different answers to that question have underpinned different ambitions that philosophers have harboured for logic. Logic has been seen as embodying a set of extraordinary truths that can be established a priori and hold universally. But what kind of truths are these? Logic appears to reveal to us the laws of valid inference, but what is it that it can do that? One view is that these truths articulate the laws of thought, the laws that a properly functioning mind follows irrespective of what it thinks about. Another view is that logical truths are 'super-laws-of-nature': while the laws of physics govern the physical, and the laws of biology govern the biological, the laws of logic are laws that everything must obey.

Another philosophical ambition for logic sees it as embodying a special language. 'Ordinary language' has been charged with having many flaws, with unclarity, ambiguity, and vagueness, as well as with encouraging confusions such as 'category mistakes'. Logic has been thought to promise a superior mode of expression, a language without these impediments. We have already seen, in modest forms, logic's 'linguistic reforms' at work, in the formalization of the two examples above. Only once formalized does it become obvious why the first claim must be true and why the second argument is valid. This also illustrates how the idea of logic as language and the idea of logic as truth co-operate. Logic may reveal to us certain kinds of truth, but it may be necessary to analyse or otherwise re-express our thoughts if we are to see how those truths bear on those thoughts. By the same token, to recognize in the first place that there are certain patterns that are characteristic of valid arguments may require that those arguments come in the right form, appropriately manipulated.

Opinions on the importance of logic have varied throughout the history of philosophy. For example, the belief that its truths are trivial—that all it can tell us is, for instance, that if A and B are true, then A is true—has recurrently driven logic to the periphery of philosophy. 'Logicism', on the other hand, is the name of one of the most audacious dreams for logic in the history of philosophy. Geometry provides an example of how, from simple and apparently obvious premisses, complex and unobvious conclusions can be derived; the logicist project attempts to demonstrate that arithmetical truths are really just complex logical truths, derivable in a system which takes basic logical truths as its axioms. Were this to prove successful, it would reap rich philosophical rewards, eliminating ontological and epistemological problems that arithmetic poses. If arithmetical truths are just complex logical truths, our knowledge of arithmetic and our understanding of the nature of arithmetic are as unproblematic as our knowledge of logic and our understanding of the nature of logic, and surely there is nothing problematic about truths like $(p \ \& \ (p \rightarrow q)) \rightarrow q$! Or, at least, so one might well think.

2.2 FREGE'S REVOLUTIONARY LOGIC

The German logician and philosopher Gottlob Frege pursued this logicist project and, in so doing, revolutionized logic. He developed a new logical notation, which he labelled the '*Begriffsschrift*', or 'concept-script', that seemed to provide the analytic tools necessary to develop a logicist analysis of arithmetic. A crucial innovation here was his construction of a notation for the quantifiers, the devices which we use to construct sentences such as 'All ravens are black' and 'Some swans are black'. These Frege rendered as:

$\forall x \ (Rx \rightarrow Bx)^2$

which can be read as 'For all xs, if x is a raven then x is black' and

$\exists x \ (Sx \ \& \ Bx)$

which can be read as 'For some x, x is a swan and x is black'. These renderings also introduce Frege's replacement of the subject–predicate form by an argument–function form. On the face of it, the subject of 'All ravens are black' would appear to be 'All ravens'. Yet, in Frege's rendering, there is nothing quite equivalent to 'All ravens'. Instead we have a function $(Rx \rightarrow Bx)$ which is true of all objects (including those which aren't ravens, for which Rx is false but $(Rx \rightarrow Bx)$ is still true). On this reading, one might naturally say that what 'All ravens are black' is about is the concept 'raven', rather than the collection of entities to which that concept may apply. This analysis gives more natural readings to some related, problematic propositions. For example, following the Fregean analysis, we see 'There are no white ravens' not as about a non-existent collection of birds, but as about the concepts 'white' and 'raven', as saying that the function $(Rx \ \& \ Wx)$ is true of nothing.

This analytic twist pays off for Frege in his account of the ascription of numbers to collections of objects, where he takes 'There are four horses' not as ascribing a property to the objects that we here call 'horses' (as Mill, for example, had[3]) but as saying of the concept 'Horse' that it is instantiated four times. The latter interpretation avoids many problems that the former raises—for example,

---

[2] I have not used Frege's own notation here, but that which has been widely adopted in modern logic and is used here is a stylistic variant on his.
[3] Cf. Mill 1973 [1843].

'Are four horses a kind of horse like black horses are?', 'What distinguishes these from ordinary horses?'—and provides a much more appealing interpretation of statements such as 'There is one moon' and 'The number of living dodos is zero'. In this way, by refusing to allow the subject–predicate form to dictate how we parse these perfectly familiar sentences, their intelligibility no longer appears to depend upon the existence of certain non-existent entities—dodos—or the elusive property of horses called 'Fourness'.

Frege's innovations also offer an interpretation and unification of the established logical disciplines such as the propositional and syllogistic logics that Section 2.1's opening examples illustrate.[4] Moreover, Fregean logic can handle forms of proposition and associated modes of inference which neither of these disciplines can. Of particular importance (especially for our understanding of mathematics) are propositions involving multiple forms of generality. Consider the sentence:

Somebody killed somebody.

What role does the expression 'somebody' play here? Does it name a strange amorphous person? Does it mean the same body in both cases? Consider:

Everybody envies somebody.

Here 'everybody' and 'somebody' present us not only with the problem of saying which individuals they pick out, but also with the problem of distinguishing the very different functions that these expressions seem to perform in the two different statements that this sentence can be used to make, either:

(1) There is someone that everyone envies.

or:

(2) For each person, there is somebody that he or she envies.

Despite being expressed by the same sentence, the structures of these statements are profoundly different, reflected, for example, in the role that the expression 'somebody' plays within them. In (1), it is used to pick out some particular individual; but in (2), it is used to pick out a possibly distinct particular person for each of the people picked out by the 'everybody'. But these differences are represented clearly in the Fregean analysis of these two statements:

(1) $\exists x \, \forall y \, Eyx$

(2) $\forall y \, \exists x \, Eyx$

Our earlier puzzles over what 'somebody' and 'everybody' refer to are also now solved, taking us back to the theme of needing to distinguish concept from object. The above statements have been revealed as statements about how the relation 'envies' is instantiated; by our rejecting the apparent form of the sentence, and

---

[4] For discussion, cf. Beaney 1996, ch. 2.

the temptation to treat 'everybody' and 'somebody' like noun phrases, as if they pick out particular people, the strange amorphous person, 'Somebody', vanishes.[5]

2.3 THE LOGICIST PROJECT

Multiple generality is endemic in mathematics; in a relatively simple formula such as

$$a^2 + ab + c = d$$

we already have four variables at work. Only with Frege's logic and its ability to handle multiple generality did the vague possibility that arithmetical statements might be recast as logical become a distinct possibility.

Take, for example, statements such as 'There are as many Fs as there are Gs'. Frege comments:

If a waiter wants to be sure of laying just as many knives as plates on a table, he does not need to count either of them, if he simply lays a knife right next to each plate, so that every knife on the table is located right next to a plate. The plates and knives are thus correlated one-one, by means of the same spatial relationship. (Frege 1953 [1884], § 70)

If, like Frege's, one's logic can handle multiple generality, this process can be represented in purely logical terms as follows:

$$\forall x(Fx \to \exists y[Gy\& \forall z(Rxz \leftrightarrow z = y)])$$
$$\& \forall y(Gy \to \exists x[Fx\& \forall w(Rwy \leftrightarrow w = x)])$$

This states that, for any of the Fs, there is one and only one G that it is R-related to, and that for any of the Gs, there is one and only one F that it is R-related to. Thus by correlating a plate with each knife, our innumerate waiter can check that there are as many plates as knives. 'There are as many Fs as there are Gs' uses an expression ('as many as') which may appear to be peculiarly arithmetical and non-logical. But the analysis above uses nothing but purely logical terms, and yet appears to do the same job. I will refer to this definition as a definition of equinumerosity.

The logicist project requires that we be able to reconstruct all of arithmetic using no more than logical notions and logical truths. Rival philosophies of arithmetic claim that arithmetic cannot stand on such a slender basis, and must at some point or other rely upon other kinds of judgements. In Mill's case, these are judgements of the nature of empirical reality and, in Kant's, judgements arising from what he calls the 'forms' of our intuition; he had argued that '[t]he concept of 12 is by no means already thought in merely thinking [the] union of 7 and 5':

I may analyze my concept of such a possible sum as long as I please, still I shall never find the 12 in it. (1961 [1781/1787], B15)

---

[5] For further discussion, cf. Dummett 1973, pp. 11–20.

He concluded instead that '[w]e have to go outside these concepts, and call in the aid of intuition'. For Frege, this perceived need for aid arises out of the inadequacy of the logico-analytic tools that were at Kant's disposal. Using those tools, even those who believed in the logicist thesis (such as Leibniz) could not hope to demonstrate that it was true; but using his *Begriffsschrift*, Frege thought, one might:

> So that nothing intuitive could intrude here unnoticed, everything had to depend on the chain of inferences being free of gaps. In striving to fulfil this requirement in the strictest way, I found an obstacle in the inadequacy of language: however cumbersome the expressions that arose, the more complicated the relations became, the less the precision was attained that my purpose demanded. Out of this need came the idea of the present *Begriffsschrift*. It is thus intended to serve primarily to test in the most reliable way the validity of a chain of inference and to reveal every presupposition that tends to slip in unnoticed, so that its origin can be investigated. (Frege 1967 [1879], pp. 5–6)[6]

Frege developed the *Begriffsschrift* with these particular 'scientific purposes' in mind (p. 6), hoping to show that, in arriving at the conclusion that $7 + 5 = 12$, for example, 'nothing intuitive' would *need* to 'intrude here', as 'the chain of inferences'—that leads us from '$7 + 5$' to '12'—would be 'free of gaps'. Like a microscope, this 'system of symbols from which every ambiguity is banned' (1972 [1882], p. 86) would enable us to perform tasks which we would find impossible were we to rely merely on our humble, ordinary tools—in this case, ordinary language.

But even supposing we do now have a language adequate for such a demonstration, from what will the truths of arithmetic be derived? The *Begriffsschrift* system has nine fundamental logical axioms, including

$$p \rightarrow (q \rightarrow p) \qquad p \rightarrow \neg\neg p$$
$$a = a \qquad \forall x\, Fx \rightarrow Fa$$
$$\neg\neg p \rightarrow p^7$$

But just what kind of truths are these? Of one thing, Frege was convinced: namely, that they could not be understood as psychological laws; if logic captures the laws of valid inference, they cannot be equated with the natural laws which govern our reasoning because we sometimes make invalid inferences: what it is right to do cannot be read off what people do happen to do, any more in the study of valid inference than in ethics.[8] But if logical laws are not psychological laws, what are they? Frege's understanding of logic is difficult to pin down,[9] but

---

6 The translation used here is that provided by Beaney (1997).

7 As is discussed briefly below, he requires (unfortunately, for Frege) a little extra help upon which his logicism subsequently founders.

8 Cf. Sluga 1980, chs. 1–2, for a discussion of the influence of such 'psychologism' on nineteenth- and early twentieth-century philosophy.

9 For a discussion of Frege's conception of logic, cf. Conant 1991*a*.

a salient theme is that these laws are the laws of truth in general, having nothing to do with specific subject areas or particular types of entity: unlike physical laws which are true of physical objects, and geometrical laws which are true of spatially intuitable objects, logic is true of all objects. Sciences such as physics and geometry reveal particular types of truth, physical truths and geometrical truths. '[I]t falls to logic', on the other hand, 'to discern the laws of truth' (1997 [1919], p. 325), of truth as such, rather than the truths of some particular domain. Logic captures that which 'holds with the utmost generality for all thinking, whatever its subject-matter', and '[c]onsequently we can also say: logic is the science of the most general laws of truth' (1997 [1897], p. 128).[10] Hence, the attempt to show that arithmetical truths can be deduced solely from logical truths was an effort 'to ascertain how far one could proceed in arithmetic by inferences alone, with the sole support of those laws of thought that transcend all particulars' (1967 [1879], p. 5).

2.4 PHILOSOPHICAL PROBLEMS AND LOGICAL ANALYSIS

For Frege, the *Begriffsschrift* was to allow us to recognize the 'conceptual content' of the propositions that we use (1967 [1879], p. 5), which is obscured by the merely superficial features that the grammar of our ordinary language projects on to those propositions. Thus it turns out that 'Somebody' does not refer to a mysterious hazy person, or 'four' in 'four horses' to an elusive feature of certain animals. In the case of arithmetic, the *Begriffsschrift* was to undermine the belief that at some point we must rely on some peculiarly arithmetical insight, empirical or otherwise; instead, arithmetical truths are merely consequences of 'the laws of thought that transcend all particulars' (1967 [1879], p. 5). In this way, the logicist project would undo the need for a certain kind of philosophy of arithmetic: it would show that there are no philosophical problems peculiar to arithmetic, in that arithmetic's epistemology and ontology are merely the epistemology and ontology of logical truth.

A certain metaphilosophical hope can emerge here, the hope that logical analysis of propositions will eliminate philosophical problems, showing that they arise out of failure to understand how our propositions really work. Whether Frege ever harboured this general, and hence, grand, ambition is doubtful.[11]

---

[10] Compare Russell's proposal that 'logic may be defined as (1) the study of what can be said of *everything*, i.e. of the propositions which hold of all entities, together with (2) the study of the constants which occur in true propositions concerning everything' (1901 draft of ch. 1 of Russell 1937 [1903], p. 187).

[11] Frege retained belief in the need for synthetic a priori truth (in geometry, e.g.), was not tempted to try to 'eliminate' numbers understood as some kind of object (cf. Sect. 2.5), and, though Frege's later work addressed broader philosophical issues, it did so still under the controlling

Russell, however, came to champion just such a programmatic role for logical analysis:

> [E]very philosophical problem, when it is subjected to the necessary analysis and purification, is found either to be not really philosophical at all, or else to be . . . logical. (Russell 1929 [1914*b*], p. 35)

Russell saw logical analysis as making possible a revolution in philosophy. In this new age, philosophical problems would be seen to be tractable and to lack any peculiar subject-matter of their own; inasmuch as they would turn out to be more than apparent problems, they would turn out to require either scientific or logical solutions. Then the kind of solution previously attempted would turn out to be unnecessary, and indeed to represent a misapprehension of the kind of problem that philosophical problems instantiate. So, for example, Russell's own earlier philosophy of arithmetic had been Hegelian in spirit, a species of idealism that was driven by belief in seeming contradictions in arithmetic. Russell saw his later logicism as showing that such contradictions were merely apparent, and as they vanished, so too did the need for a kind of 'higher synthesis' that his younger self had thought necessary.[12]

Much of Russell's philosophical work in the years immediately prior to his meeting with Wittgenstein can be seen to have a similar motivation. The meaningfulness of certain propositions would seem to demand the reality of certain entities which intuitively strike us as unreal or even impossible; such propositions include expressions that seem to refer to entities that are not, or cannot be, real. Russell's strategy is to present analyses of the propositions in which these expressions figure which will show that these expressions are 'incomplete symbols': in the ultimate analysis of these propositions there will turn out not to be any referring expression which corresponds to the expressions that caused problems. Thus, for example, when philosophers come to believe that 'queer entities' (1956 [1918], p. 270) like unicorns and even square circles must, in some sense, exist if seemingly meaningful propositions—such as 'There are no unicorns' and 'There is no such thing as a square circle'—are indeed to be meaningful, those philosophers have allowed themselves to be taken in by 'surface grammar'. Their philosophies are driven by pseudo-demands, which would be seen as such if those puzzling propositions were properly analysed. This philosophically motivated analytic project seeks to 'clear away incredible accumulations of metaphysical lumber' (1929 [1914*b*], p. 42), and drove Russell's reflections on, among other topics, definite descriptions, names, phenomenalism, and the self.

influence of his relatively narrow, real interests: the philosophy of arithmetic and, secondarily, the philosophy of logic.

[12] Cf. Hylton 1990.

The idea that logical analysis might show that philosophical problems are unreal is one to which the young Wittgenstein was deeply receptive[13] and to which he gave a radicalizing twist. He saw Frege and Russell as insufficiently radical adherents to this project, and extended their 'eliminativist' vision even to the very truths to which they, as logicists, had claimed arithmetical propositions are reducible: namely, logical truths. Wittgenstein argued that there are no such things and, in doing so, hoped to eliminate the philosophical problems associated with those truths too. But the idea that drove the logicist project, and which Wittgenstein retained, is that philosophical claims are made because we misunderstand propositions: 'the method of formulating' [*die Fragestellung*] the problems of philosophy 'rests on the misunderstanding of the logic of our language' (*TLP* preface). Indeed, the notion of intelligibility as con-formity rests, I will argue, upon a failure to respect the sign/symbol distinction. But before reaching that general topic, what is philosophically problematic about the idea of logical truth anyway? To answer that question, I will complete my brief and partial survey of the early history of the logicist project.

2.5 FREGE'S DEFINITION OF NUMBER

Building on the definition of equinumerosity specified above, Frege ultimately identifies numbers with certain classes. From this identification, one can go on to derive many of the well-known properties of numbers.[14] The numbers are identified in the following way:

   0 is the class of concepts equinumerous with the concept 'thing not identical with itself' —which has no instances

   1 is the class of concepts equinumerous with the concept 'thing identical with zero' —which has one instance

   2 is the class of concepts equinumerous with the concept 'thing identical with zero or one' —which has two instances

   And so on.[15]

From a post-Wittgensteinian perspective, it can seem surprising that Frege insisted on providing a definition of the numbers, rather than trying to 'eliminate' them too. But for complex and disputed reasons,[16] Frege insists on numbers being objects of some sort, and that 'Just as many . . .' propositions are statements of

[13] The idea that our most intractable puzzles would vanish if we could express our propositions more clearly is also an important theme in the work of Hertz and Boltzmann, authors that the young Wittgenstein read and admired. Cf. Hacker 1986, pp. 2–5.
[14] For discussion, cf. Currie 1982, pp. 55–7.
[15] Frege actually uses the term 'extension' instead of 'class', the 'extension' of a concept being made up of those things that fall under it. I ignore this complication in what follows.
[16] For discussion, cf. Beaney 1996, pp. 192–200; Dummett 1991, chs. 9 and 11; Kenny 1995, ch. 5.

identity. Such statements inform us that the object which we have got hold of under one description, 'the number of Fs', is one and the same object as that which we have got hold of under another, 'the number of Gs'. Frege's definition of equinumerosity tells us that when the 'Just as many . . .' propositions are true, then so is the following:

The class of Fs is equinumerous with the class of Gs.

An identity statement that this suggests is:

The class of concepts that are equinumerous to the concept F is identical with the class of concepts that are equinumerous to the concept G.

If such statements tell us that a particular object (which we call a 'number') has been uncovered in two different ways, which object might it be? The class of concepts that are equinumerous with the concept F is the same as the class of concepts that are equinumerous with the concept G; and the same class of concepts is picked out by the concept 'equinumerous with the concept H' if there are as many Fs as Hs; thus, if we wish to pick out an object which is apparently picked out in different ways in all such cases, the class of concepts which is the class of concepts that are equinumerous with the concept F, equinumerous with the concept G, equinumerous with the concept H, and so on is an obvious candidate. Thus we have a case for identifying these collections, these classes, with the numbers.

So far, we have seen how, when we say that a particular number belongs to a particular concept, we are saying that that concept belongs to a certain class of concepts, 'those equinumerous with F'. In order to achieve the logicist aim, there must be an F for every number, and F must be defined only by reference to logical notions. It is Frege's search for such a set of concepts that leads him to what might seem his outlandish invocation of the concepts 'thing not identical with itself' and 'thing identical with zero'.

There are plenty of concepts with which we associate particular numbers—'apostles of Jesus', for example. But that concept is not defined purely in logical terms and, if 12 is to be understood in purely logical terms, it must not end up being defined by reference to Jesus and his apostles. The concept of 'things not identical with themselves' is defined solely in logical terms ('thing' and 'identity'), and can be known on purely logical grounds to have no instances. All concepts that have no instances are equinumerous with the concept 'things not identical with themselves', and thus Frege identifies 0 with that class of concepts equinumerous with 'things not identical with themselves'.[17] Frege then arrives at the concept used to define 1 by drawing upon his definition of 0; there is only

---

[17] Frege's response to the worry that such a concept may not make sense in the first place, for what it's worth, is: 'All that can be demanded of a concept from the point of view of logic and with an eye to rigour of proof is only that the limits to its application be sharp, that it should be determined, with regard to every object whether it falls under that concept or not' (1953 [1884], §74).

one class of concepts 'equinumerous with the concept "things not identical with themselves" ', so 1 can be defined by drawing upon that purely logical fact: we have here a class which can definitely play the role we need in defining 1 as a class of concepts equinumerous with a particular concept. Once that identification has been achieved, we can then draw upon it in defining 2. And so on. Crucially, there will be a class of this purely logically defined form for all of the numbers, irrespective, as one might put it, of the way that the world turns out to be, there being, for example, a certain number of apostles or planets or species of butterfly.

2.6 RUSSELL'S PARADOX AND THEORIES OF TYPES

However, it is out of these definitions that Russell's Paradox emerges. Russell came upon Frege's logicist account having developed one of his own which was, in many respects, importantly similar. But Russell came to realize that certain contradictions could be derived from the resources upon which this form of logicism was based, the most famous being the paradox that now bears his name.

Common sense suggests that some classes are members of themselves (e.g., the class of all classes), while others are not (e.g., the class of cats). Let us label 'R' the class whose membership consists of exactly those classes of this latter sort: that is, those that are not members of themselves. Now, is R a member of itself? If we suppose it *is*, then it is a member of the class of all classes that are *not* members of themselves, and hence it *is not* a member of itself! If we suppose instead that R *is not* a member of itself, then, since it is a class that is not a member of itself, it now satisfies its own membership conditions, and hence it *is* a member of itself after all! So either supposition leads to contradiction. This suggested to Frege that there is a logical incoherence at the heart of the concept 'class' upon which the above definitions draw: there appear to be certain classes of which we can make no sense, since there are certain entities of which we can say that they neither are nor are not members of certain classes. Frege offered various responses to this problem, but all had unacceptable consequences, leading to bizarre conclusions, such as that there can be no more than two distinct objects.[18]

There are, however, more general anxieties that Russell's Paradox raises and it is these that provide an important stimulus for Wittgenstein's early work. These are best introduced through an examination of one of Russell's attempts to resolve the paradox, his Theory of Types.[19] The core claim of this theory was that the logical universe is 'stratified', forming a regimented hierarchy of types (see table 2.1).

---

[18] For discussion, cf. Beaney 1996, pp. 196–200.

[19] The account I offer here differs from Russell's initial sketch in [1903], App. B, and glosses over a range of interpretative issues (cf. Stevens 2005, chs. 2–3); indeed, it should be borne in mind throughout this chapter that the picture it presents of the work of Frege and Russell is one heavily influenced by Wittgenstein's understanding of that work.

Table 2.1 The 'stratified' universe of Russell's Theory of Types

Type 0	Objects	
Type 1	Concepts	Classes of objects
Type 2	Second-order concepts	Classes of classes of objects
Type 3	Third-order concepts	Classes of classes of classes of objects
etc.		

From this perspective, the source of the paradox appears as the mistaken assumption that classes and their members form a single, homogeneous logical type. The Theory of Types states that the members of a given class must all be drawn from a single logical type n, and the class itself must reside in the next higher type $n + 1$. Since the members of a class must all be of the same logical type, there is no such class as the class of classes that are not members of themselves, whose definition would cut across all types. For each type n, there will be a class R, of all non-self-membered classes of that particular type. But the question of whether R is a member of itself does not arise, because R is itself of type $n + 1$. Hence, the paradox breaks down.

Wittgenstein argues, however, that this success comes at an unacceptably high price, as there is an inconsistency at the heart of the idea of a Theory of Types:

Types can never be distinguished from each other by saying (as is often done) that one has these *but* the other has those properties, for this presupposes that there is a *meaning* in asserting all these properties of both types. (*NB* 101)

Stating Russell's Theory of Types requires us to violate its prescriptions: if one takes some set of 'entities' that one is going to divide up into objects, concepts, second-order concepts, etc., in specifying which are which, one will have to use a predicate that can be meaningfully applied to objects, concepts, second-order concepts, etc.; but such predicates are precisely the kind that the Theory of Types was to rule out. Saying, for example, that one set of entities 'are objects' and denying that another set of entities 'are objects' requires 'is an object' to be a predicate ascribable across the logical categories. In specifying the rules as to which predicates can be ascribed to which things, the predicates that one uses oneself seem necessarily to violate those rules.[20]

---

[20] One of the reasons why the paradox arises within Frege's system is his dogged adherence to the superficially unappealing claim that every genuine concept must be defined for all objects. (Cf. n. 16 above and, for further discussion, Beaney 1996, ch. 7.) So, e.g., he demands that definitions of number provide a straightforward answer to questions such as whether Julius Caesar is a number. But Frege's adherence to this claim in the face of its odd consequences may indicate that he was alive to the inadequacies of a Theory of Types: to reject that claim would be to state that only over certain domains need a concept be defined; unfortunately, specifying such domains requires one to use concepts that apply beyond these ranges anyway, specifying some property that those that fall within the range possess and those outside it don't. This issue is related to that which Sect. 12.3 discusses.

Frege encounters a similar difficulty in his efforts to explain the rules governing his *Begriffsschrift*. The kind of restriction that the paradox demands bring into focus just the kinds of restriction that those very rules would 'state', and Frege had already recognized that he faced some kind of problem in explaining them. He wished to insist, for instance, that a term for a concept cannot occupy the place of a term for an object in an intelligible proposition. Unfortunately for Frege, his attempts to state this stricture simultaneously violate it. What characterizes a concept are the locations within a proposition that it can take up, and hence the very term 'concept' is misleading, because it may take up locations from which terms for concepts are banned. (Similarly, the term 'object' is misleading when it occurs in the predicate 'is an object'.) Thus, strictly speaking, 'the concept *horse* is not a concept': '[b]y the very act of calling it a [concept], we deprive it of this property' (1892, p. 197 n.).[21] Frege seems to see this problem as the result of no more than 'a certain inappropriateness of linguistic expression' (1892, p. 205), 'an awkwardness of language' (p. 196):

By a kind of necessity of language, my expressions, taken literally, sometimes miss my thought ... [I]n such cases I was relying upon a reader who would be ready to meet me half-way—who does not begrudge a pinch of salt [*mit einem Körnchen Salz nicht spart*]. (p. 204)

He insists that he can merely give 'hints', blaming this predicament upon the fundamental simplicity of what he must explain (pp. 182–3, 185, 194). But we should not underestimate the difficulty here. It arises not just because in our everyday language we can construct sentences featuring expressions like 'the concept *horse*'. Rather, it seems that whatever medium one uses in stating the difference between a concept and an object, one will need to ascribe to one of these items certain features and to deny those same features of the other item; the difficulty is that Frege denies that it makes sense to ascribe or deny the same features of these items.[22]

2.7 THE NATURE OF LOGIC

The underlying problem surfacing in these different contexts in the work of Frege and Russell concerns the nature of logical truth, and this problem and its ramifications are the focus of the early work of Wittgenstein. Axioms of the *Begriffsschrift*, rules for the combination of different types of expression in the *Begriffsschrift*, principles of a Theory of Types, and principles of deductive

---

[21] Page numbers are those of the German original.

[22] For discussion, cf. Diamond 1991, chs. 4 and 6. Some commentators (in particular, Weiner 1990) have argued that Frege himself was fully aware that such explanations were literally nonsensical, and that he recognized their character as 'elucidations', forerunners of the propositions of Wittgenstein's *Tractatus* that must be, in some sense, 'climbed up over' and then 'thrown away'.

inference all appear superficially to embody 'claims' about the way the world is. Yet, when we come to fill out this comparison with 'ordinary claims', we seem to run into difficulties.

Consider how we are to understand what logical truths rule out. If we take the assertion that one cannot form a fact from two concepts alone, what are we saying about the situation ruled out? What is the force of this 'cannot'? The excluded 'situations' are, we may say, 'impossible'. But what is the force of this 'impossibility'? It is not a physical impossibility, comparable to my jumping to the moon. It seems to be a different order of impossibility, and a popular way of characterizing it is to propose that the excluded 'situations' are unthinkable, inconceivable, or unimaginable. But this view leaves unclear what fundamental difference there is (if any) between these situations and those of which we might come to conceive—think, grasp—merely by broadening our imagination or by having minds broader than our mere human minds. (This worry informs Frege's attack on such psychologistic philosophies of logic.) Moreover, there is something odd about saying that 'This', whatever it might be, 'does not make sense', 'cannot be thought', or 'cannot be grasped'. What is it that cannot be grasped? What is it that does not make sense? To make the claim that these 'situations' are inconceivable or ungraspable seems to involve a grasp of those situations—in which case they cannot be ungraspable, after all. It is on these grounds that Wittgenstein argues that we cannot understand logic as distinguishing what is, as a matter of 'logical fact', possible or thinkable from what is, in the relevant senses, impossible and unthinkable; since we cannot grasp that which would be excluded, it seems to make no sense to try to draw such 'bounds of sense':

[I]n order to be able to draw a limit to thought, we should have to find both sides of the limit thinkable (i.e. we should have to be able to think what cannot be thought). (*TLP* preface)

It seems to be impossible to stand in judgement on a 'logical possibility' in that way; in judging something to be unthinkable, one would be thinking it.

Indeed, the very image of 'logical truths' as *truths* appears suspect. Obviously, 'logical truths' cannot merely happen to turn out to be true: if there was another way that things could have stood logically, but which our candidate 'logical truths' rule out, then we know that we have not got hold of '*logical* truths'. 'Logical truths' cannot represent 'hypotheses', since the possibilities represented by the truth *and* falsity of a hypothesis are both possibilities, and as such must be 'dealt with' by logic:

Nothing in the province of logic can be merely possible [*Etwas Logisches kann nicht nur-möglich sein*].
Logic deals with every possibility and all possibilities are its facts. (2.0121)

But even if we insist explicitly that a logical truth is a necessary truth, then—to adapt the words of Diamond—'[e]ven in thinking of it as true in all possible worlds, . . . we think of it as itself *the case*; our thought contrasts it with as it were a different set of necessities' (1991, p. 195).

It is in Wittgenstein's work that the puzzling notion of logical truth is most thoroughly worked through, and its implications traced. His early work can be seen as attempting to defuse all efforts to draw the bounds of sense, as attempting to expose as illusions anything that 'would give logic an impossible reality' (*NB* 48):

Theories which make a proposition of logic appear substantial are always false. (6.111)

Yet in philosophy we are surrounded by such theories. Many see metaphysical theories as delimiting what can and cannot sensibly be said or thought, revealing super-laws that govern the fundamental elements of reality and the basic combinations into which they may enter. This 'super-science' of objects, properties, and relations can reveal to us what any sensible thought or utterance must ultimately be about. For example, a metaphysician might insist that sensible claims about reality must resolve themselves into claims that ascribe properties to objects or identify a relation between two or more objects, etc. There may be any number of particular points of detail which the sciences may go on to fill in; but the most basic, metaphysical characteristics of reality dictate that all such details will fit certain basic, metaphysical patterns. Such a body of truths renders what it makes sense to say or think a consequence of how the world happens to be constituted metaphysically. But '[i]n logic nothing is accidental', and 'there can *never* be surprises' (2.012, 6.1251). So how can this be? How can we anticipate the substantial truths that logic embodies? Wittgenstein's answer is that we can't, but that we don't need to because it doesn't! Anything that would seem to set the bounds of sense, to give 'substance' to the laws of logic, is an illusion, Wittgenstein argues. Making good on this claim is a task for the *Tractatus*.

3

Objects, Names, Facts, and Propositions

Although Wittgenstein wrote a preface for the *Tractatus*, he wrote no introduction.[1] One of the most baffling things about the book is the manner in which it launches into a series of claims the nature and direction of which are undeclared. Yet it opens with a discussion that anyone familiar with Western philosophy will have some sort of feel for, even if they are unclear about precisely how Wittgenstein means these propositions to be understood and precisely what basis he has for offering these propositions seemingly as truths. The opening of the book reads like a treatise on the metaphysical constitution of reality, stating that the world is the totality of facts, and that ultimately such facts are made up of combinations of objects. He goes on to ascribe particular features to these objects, doing so on the grounds that only by their possessing those features might we avoid rendering logic 'accidental'. Parallel to this account runs a story about the nature of the proposition, proposing that a proposition and the possible fact that it represents must share a logical form, which is itself a matter of the names that are combined in that proposition and the objects whose combination would be the holding of that possible fact themselves having corresponding logical forms.

3.1 OBJECTS AND FACTS

In his wartime notebooks, Wittgenstein remarks:

The great problem round which everything that I write turns is: Is there an order in the world *a priori*, and if so what does it consist in? (*NB* 53)

The opening pages of the *Tractatus* appear to answer the first question affirmatively and set out the detail of an answer to the second. Ultimately, I will argue that such a reading distorts the fundamental intent of the book, but the dialectic that this reading suggests is important to that intent none the less.

A desire to know the a priori structure of reality would be a desire to know what must be the case irrespective of which facts happen to hold or not to hold. One apparent constant is the set of propositions which are true or false depending on which possible world we happen to be in.[2] Though their truth or falsity will

---

[1] Wittgenstein saw in Russell's introduction little more than 'superficiality and misunderstanding' (*CL* 154).

[2] Sect. 9.1 raises some doubts about this 'constant'.

vary, their meaningfulness would be a constant. Hence, if there are certain conditions that must hold if these propositions are to be meaningful, they would hold irrespective of which facts happen to hold or not to hold: they would constitute an a priori ordering of the world. So what might such conditions be? A picture naturally suggests itself when we consider an example like 'The cat is on the mat'. Whether the cat is on the mat is clearly a contingent matter, but our using such a sentence to assert a truth or a falsehood appears to assume certain things about the world, such as that there are a cat and a mat to be talked about. We clearly don't want to claim that the existence of cats and mats forms part of the a priori order of things, since 'There are cats' and 'There are mats' express what are obviously contingent matters of fact; so before the a priori order of things will reveal itself, we will need to do some analytic work.

We imagine ourselves now working down, so to speak, through language, exposing, for example, what is meant by the more basic claims that we see as presupposed by the meaningfulness of our ordinary everyday claims, presuppositions such as that there are cats and mats. Our initial example imagined the work of a proposition to be that of stating how the elements of reality that are referred to by the elements that constitute the proposition are themselves combined in reality. Extending this picture to 'There are cats' is plausible if we bear in mind the rather gory image of what happens when a cat turns into a non-cat. That is to say, 'There are cats' too might be understood as a claim about how certain elements of reality are organized or not, into cats or into non-cats. As we continue this process, through claims about cat parts down to claims about the elements which, when combined, constitute those parts, down to talk of molecules, atoms, subatomic particles, and so on, a certain familiar terminus looms: the atomist view that at some point this analysis must end, and that there we would be confronted by the elements the combination of which constitutes the holding of any possible fact.

The opening of the *Tractatus* seems to echo this kind of dialectic, in describing the world as dividing up into facts, claiming that the holding of these facts is a matter of the existence of certain 'atomic facts', and that those facts are 'combinations of objects' (1.2, 2, 2.01). But what will these ultimate existents look like? They can't be the atoms of chemistry, for example, as we now know that these are also complex entities which can be split and re-formed. Might then they be sense data? If so, the most basic propositions could be understood as stating that certain combinations of perceptual impressions have presented themselves. But can't we talk about a particular sense datum 'happening' or not, existing or not? If so, they do not seem to fit the bill as the elements about which the most basic propositions talk either; there will be more basic propositions like 'Sense datum *a* exists'. Wittgenstein does not seem to confront such issues at all in the *Tractatus*, but none the less goes on to describe the objects of which he speaks. His basis in doing so seems to be that we can know certain things about how these objects must be merely from the role that we envisage them playing and from the claim that '[i]n logic nothing is accidental' (2.012). This is the fundamental premiss that drives Wittgenstein's deduction of the internal properties of objects, facts, names, and propositions, a premiss which (as discussed in Chapter 2) emerges out of his reflections on the failure of Frege and Russell to present a coherent philosophy of logic.

If we imagine ourselves talking about the ultimate constituents of reality to which the *ultimate* components of our propositions refer, there cannot be any mere fact of the matter about these constituents which would make any difference to which propositions make sense and which do not, as 'whether a proposition had sense would depend on whether another proposition was true' (2.0211), another, impossibly '*more* ultimate' proposition. Moreover, if the basic features of 'objects' and the existence of certain kinds of 'objects' dictate which combinations of 'objects' can form and, hence, which facts are possible and, hence, which propositions make sense, then, if the relevant features of objects were features that they merely *happened* to possess, logic would, *per impossibile*, be 'accidental'.[3] So instead, those features must be 'internal properties', properties 'it is unthinkable its object does not possess' (4.123). (Their 'external properties' are their forming particular combinations with other objects, the existence of these combinations being the holding of particular contingent facts.) Wittgenstein identifies, and demonstrates, why such objects must possess three internal properties. First,

(O-S) Objects are simple.[4]

Objects cannot be complex, as propositions about complexes can be further analysed into propositions about their constituent parts and propositions which completely describe the complexes (2.02–2.021). There can be no such 'deeper' propositions concerning the composition of the entities referred to by the component parts of fully analysed propositions; there is no such room here for the further analysis that the complexity of objects would make possible. Secondly,

(O-E) Objects are indestructible.

If there were meaning in statements which asserted or denied the existence of objects, these statements would state that certain component—'sub-objectual'—elements were or were not so arranged as to make up these objects. But if so, the 'objects' we had taken to be the ultimate constituents of reality would be shown not to be, since there would be yet more basic constituents

---

[3] Since Wittgenstein's remarks on 'objects' often serve to articulate a particular 'technical' sense for that word, I did consider the policy of using scare-quotes for all such uses; but this blanket policy seemed on occasion to introduce more confusion than it would eliminate; as a result, I do not follow any such consistent policy in what follows, but instead hope that the different senses in which this term is used here are clear in the contexts in question (and, to that end, I will *sometimes* use scare-quotes).

[4] For ease of reference, Appendix B provides a list of all abbreviations used to refer to particular 'theses' of the *Tractatus*.

of reality. Moreover, the intelligibility of propositions that include names of these false 'objects' would depend on a matter of contingent fact, and hence would be (impossibly) 'accidental'. Thus, it can make no sense to say that objects—the *true* objects—exist or not. Instead, '[o]bjects form the substance of the world', '[s]ubstance [being] what exists independently of what is the case' (2.021, 2.024). Finally,

(O-F) An object's identity is internally related to the possible facts in which it can occur.

Objects must be 'internally related' to the other objects with which they may combine, because it makes no sense to say that they can or cannot be combined in this way or that with these or any other objects. We cannot grasp an object *and then discover that* it can occur in this possible fact, that possible fact, etc.:

It is essential to a thing that it can be a constituent part of an atomic fact.

In logic nothing is accidental: if a thing *can* occur in an atomic fact the possibility of that atomic fact must already be prejudged in the thing.

It would, so to speak, appear as an accident, when to a thing that could exist alone on its own account, subsequently a state of affairs could be made to fit.

If things can occur in atomic facts, this possibility must already lie in them. (2.011–2.0121)

If objects were externally related to the facts in which they figured, then there would be deeper facts, described by 'deeper' propositions, describing which facts these objects happened to be capable of figuring in and those in which they could not. Instead, within a state of affairs, objects 'fit into one another like the links in a chain' (2.03), meaning '*that there isn't anything third* that connects the links but the links *themselves* make connexion with one another' (*LO* 23).[5]

My suggestion is that Wittgenstein is here working out the minimal form that a con-formist theory of intelligibility could take, exploring the demands that must be met by the metaphysics that such a theory involves. Hence, the crucial demand that dominates his articulation of the metaphysics of objects is the requirement that their characteristics which will determine which propositions make sense and which do not must not leave logic 'accidental'. There must be no room left for us to say that, had these objects been different, different propositions would have made sense: if they could make sense, they too must be accounted for by the characteristics of objects, since '[l]ogic deals with every possibility' (2.0121). Or, put another way, we would have discovered that what we thought were objects—the ultimate constituents of reality—are not, since the entities that we had latched on to could have been otherwise, opening up other possible ways in which the world could be. These possibilities would then need to

---

[5] This also provides a sense for why '[t]he world is the totality of facts not of things' (*TLP* 1.1). If instead the world was the totality of things, which facts were possible could be seen as an 'external feature' of those things.

be accounted for as the existence of certain configurations of yet deeper entities, which, if they turned out to be simple, indestructible, and internally related to the possible facts in which they could figure, might be the true objects we seek.

3.2 NAMES AND PROPOSITIONS

Parallel to this story about objects runs a story in the 3.2–3.4s about the expressions which refer to objects, which Wittgenstein labels 'names', and the propositions within which they figure. He identifies three internal properties corresponding to the (O)s. First,

(N-S) Names are simple.

As the end-points of analysis, names themselves cannot be analysed: they are 'primitive signs' (3.26). If, *per impossibile*, an object were divisible, the expression denoting it would be 'divisible' into simpler components. But as such, this expression would not be a 'name', 'an end-product of analysis':

The sense of the proposition must appear in the proposition as divided into its simple components—. And these parts are then actually indivisible, for further divided they just would not be THESE. (*NB* 63)

Secondly,

(N-E) Names allow us to speak *of* objects, not to say *what* or *that* they are.

Co-ordinate with the senselessness of the talk of objects existing or not, names, the expressions that refer to objects, serve only to name that to which they refer:

Objects I can only *name*. Signs represent them. I can only speak *of* them [*von ihnen sprechen*]. I cannot *assert* [*aussprechen*] them. A proposition can only say *how* a thing is, not *what* it is. (3.221)

One can say *how* objects are, in that one can describe how they happen, as a matter of contingent fact, to be arranged—one can describe their external properties—but not *that* they are or *what* they are—one cannot describe their internal properties. If one could, this would again open up an impossible space of possibilities the reality of which would show that what we thought were our ultimate constituents, our true objects, are not. Given the role that objects and names are meant to play, there are no facts left, so to speak, to characterize those objects—objects are 'colourless' (2.0232)—and no propositions left to represent those (impossible) facts. This imposes on names a corresponding inarticulacy, so to speak. By using names, one can talk about objects, and by using propositions, one can say something about the objects named. Propositions have sense, 'resembl[ing] arrows', whereas names resemble 'points' (3.144); they do not *sprechen* the objects that they name *aus*, variously translated as 'assert them' (by Ogden), 'express them' (by Anscombe in her translation of *NB* 51, the *NB* source of *TLP* 3.221), and 'put them into words' (by Pears and McGuinness).

Finally,

(N-P) A name's identity is internally related to the propositions in which it can occur.

Corresponding to the connection of objects to 'one another like the links in a chain' (2.03), 'only in the context of a proposition has a name meaning' (3.3). Were there facts that expressed how objects could be combined with one another, these 'objects' would not be true objects, 'objects in the original sense' (*NB* 63). There would then be a substantial body of knowledge about how their names could and could not be combined in order to say something meaningful, and logic would therefore merely happen to be a particular way: it would be accidental. Since it cannot be, there can be no such body of knowledge, and thus genuine names must be 'internally related' to the propositions in which they figure: it is not that such a name happens to participate in the formation of propositions; rather, its being the name that it is its participation in the formation of the propositions in which it figures.

3.3 THE INTERNAL RELATION OF DEPICTING

From the impossibility of an accidental logic, Wittgenstein deduces that objects and possible facts are internally related, as are names and propositions. He goes on to declare that there is an 'internal relation of depicting that holds between language and the world' (4.014), articulating what sounds very much like a conformist account of the meaningfulness of language. In the 2.1s, Wittgenstein introduces his comparison of propositions with pictures. He declares:

What the picture must have in common with reality in order to be able to represent it after its manner—rightly or wrongly—is its form of representation. (2.17)

What is this 'form of representation'?

That the elements of the picture are combined with one another in a definite way represents that the things are so combined with one another.

This connection of the elements of the picture is called its structure, and the possibility of this structure is called the form of representation of the picture. (2.15)

This structure and this form correspond to the structure and form of a possible fact:

The way in which objects hang together in the atomic fact is the structure of the atomic fact.[6]

The form is the possibility of the structure. (2.032–2.3)

Indeed, the 'form of reality' and the 'form of representation' of the proposition that represents that reality are identical (2.16–18), and this is reflected in

---

[6] Ch. 11 explains the significance of the important qualification 'atomic'.

the names that make up propositions and the objects which those names name (objects which combine in facts) having a common form (3.2, 3.21).

Why, then, must the depicting relation be an internal relation? Why not an external relation of correspondence between the form of the proposition and the form of the possible fact? One reason is that there is not, it would seem, room for such an external relation because of how the corresponding forms themselves are constituted. To take the case of an object and its name, it is potentially confusing to speak of the combinatorial possibilities that an object has, because its 'possessing' those possibilities is an internal property of that object: were it not to possess those particular possibilities, it would not be *it*! The same is true of a name and its combinatorial possibilities. Thus a correspondence between a name and an object is a matter not of *how* the name and object are, but of *what* they are. Talk of corresponding possibilities suggests that there are two possible situations, one in which an object's possibilities correspond to a name's possibilities and one in which they do not. But this cannot be the case, since we would be talking about two different objects in the two situations. In other words, an object's being isomorphic with a name is an internal property of that object:

(O-N) Objects are internally related to the names that name them.

And to this corresponds,

(F-P) Facts are internally related to the propositions that represent them.

These proposals express the 'internal relation of depicting'.

As Chapter 8 will explain, to these claims about language and world, Wittgenstein also adds a set of claims about thought and subjectivity, a parallel set of claims about the internal relatedness of components of thoughts, those components and the thoughts they make up, those components and the objects to which they 'refer', thoughts and the possible facts whose possibility we entertain when we entertain those thoughts, and indeed the subject who thinks these thoughts and the world of possible facts about which it thinks.

3.4 AN INEXPRESSIBLE CON-FORMISM?

So what is Wittgenstein trying to do in setting out the proposals that I have identified so far in this chapter? Though not articulated in the terms I have used above, that the *Tractatus* addresses something like the question of intelligibility set out in Section 1.3 is a widely held view, as is the notion that Wittgenstein offers an account of intelligibility designed to answer that question:

What makes sense in language and thought is dependent on and derived from the nature of the objects. . . . What makes sense in language is based on the possible combinations of the simple elements of reality. (Malcolm 1986, p. 14)[7]

[7] Cf. also Pears 1987, p. 8: 'Language enjoys certain options on the surface, but deeper down it is founded on the intrinsic nature of objects, which is not our creation but is set over against

Depending on whether the proposed answer is what I call 'idealist' or (like Malcolm's) 'realist', commentators then disagree over just what it is that needs explaining: so, for example, Black sees Wittgenstein as asking the question, 'Given that this is what the world must be, what *must* language be, in order to be capable of representing the world adequately?' (Black 1964, p. 72), whereas Mounce sees the *Tractatus*'s opening 'metaphysics' as 'statements about how the world has to be if there is to be sense, if there are to be propositions' (Mounce 1981, p. 19). But that the *Tractatus* offers us some kind of 'con-formism' is an opinion that cuts across such differences, and does indeed give a natural construal for the assertions set out in Sections 3.1–3.3; read in that way, they embody an account of how the form of components of thoughts and propositions and of components of facts (that those thoughts and propositions are to represent) must be if those thoughts and propositions are indeed to be intelligible.

But another point on which there is a wide consensus is that Wittgenstein reveals that con-formism must be given a radical twist: its insights, supposing that that is what they are, are 'inexpressible'; they cannot be 'said', but instead 'show themselves'. The say/show distinction has been a subject of controversy since the *Tractatus* was published; Pears has famously labelled it 'a baffling doctrine bafflingly presented' (1987, p. 143).[8] One of its most baffling aspects is that Wittgenstein himself seems to state a variety of the truths which he tells us cannot be 'said'. For example, the assertions upon which we have concentrated in this chapter assert that certain entities have certain internal properties, and that certain internal relations hold; but the possession of internal properties and the holding of internal relations, the *Tractatus* tells us, 'shows itself' and 'cannot be asserted by propositions' (4.122).

Nevertheless, Sections 3.1–3.3's presentation of the arguments that support the assertions in question reveals a reason why this should be so: for example, (O-S) was arrived at on the grounds that there can be no 'deeper' propositions concerning the composition of the entities referred to by the component parts of fully analysed propositions. There are no propositions left, so to speak, to articulate 'how objects are constituted'.

But Wittgenstein's definition of 'internal properties', as properties 'it is unthinkable its object does not possess' (4.123), points us to another sense in

---

us in mysterious independence.' I cannot do justice here to the complexities of the views of the commentators that I quote here, but several aspects of Hacker's interpretation, which shares some important features with Malcolm's and Pears', are discussed in detail (cf. Sects. 4.9, 6.4, 7.1, and 8.2).

    [8] There are actually two words that translators have rendered as 'show' in the *Tractatus*, '*zeigen*' and '*aufweisen*' (the latter occurring only twice). Ogden and Pears and McGuinness translate *zeigen* as 'show'; Pears and McGuinness translate *aufweisen* as 'display'; Ogden translates *aufweisen* at 2.172 as 'show forth' and at 4.121 as 'exhibit'. Despite these complexities, 4.121 suggests that Wittgenstein sees the terms as near synonyms. (Cf. also *PT* 4.103.) A word which it is tempting to assimilate to 'show' is *erläutern*, which has been translated by Ogden and by Pears and McGuinness as 'elucidate'; the temptation arises because it too seems to denote a conveying of something that is not a matter of saying something. Sects. 4.3–4.8 discuss elucidation at length.

which one might understand the truth of the assertions in question as something that one must simply *see*. To take internal relations, one has no grasp of the relata, nor then of the sense of the 'assertion' that those relata are so related, if one has not already recognized the 'truth' of this 'assertion'; one must already appreciate what the 'assertion' says if one is to understand which entities the 'assertion' describes. Correspondingly, if we attempt to imagine someone learning what such an 'assertion' 'asserts', by virtue of being someone who is yet to 'learn of' the 'asserted' relationship, then we must recognize that such a person could not have had an understanding of the entities in the first place, or, therefore, of this 'assertion' about them.[9] In this way, there is something misleading in the image of the holding of an internal relation as something expressible through a statement *about* the relata and the relation; one might suggest instead that to learn that an internal relation holds is to learn *of* its relata and *of* the relation. One cannot seek to establish—or inform someone of—whether such a relation holds, because the moment one learns *that* the relation holds is the moment one learns *of* the relation itself and *of* what it relates: one must come to *see* all of these 'elements' (the relation, its relata, and its holding) in one fell swoop.[10]

Yet the *Tractatus* does seem to assert that various internal properties are possessed by various things and that various internal relations hold. Is this just a rather shocking inconsistency on Wittgenstein's part? Do the claims that he has advanced require that we cannot make sense of anyone arriving at those very claims? A popular way of avoiding this outcome is to propose that, for Wittgenstein, these 'claims' are only '*strictly speaking* inexpressible', but can still be intimated in some other way; that, it is sometimes suggested, is just what their 'showing' is.

This is not my view. I agree with the commentators cited above that the *Tractatus* can be read as working through the vision of thought as intelligible by virtue of con-formity with reality, revealing internal properties and internal relations that must characterize the vehicles and objects of our thought if the con-formist vision is to have any prospect of making sense; but I believe that, ultimately, it doesn't, and that that is what this 'working through' is meant to reveal. We emerge not with a novel con-formist theory, but with the realization that we have not assigned any sense to our con-formist concerns; those concerns are the product of particular confusions of which we are unaware. Wittgenstein 'elucidates', follows through the pseudo-logic of, those confusions, leading us to the conclusion that the crucial 'claims' that articulate con-formism must take a certain form; but, in doing so, he is trying to bring us to see that those 'claims' are actually nonsensical. The challenge, then, is to see how, given Wittgenstein's

---

[9] *TLP*'s discussion of identity statements (cf. 5.5303 and 6.2322–6.2323) may provide an illuminating parallel here.

[10] Sect. 4.9 reassesses the morals drawn in this paragraph and the one that precedes it.

understanding of nonsense, that could possibly be the case. The final section of this chapter introduces that understanding, in the course of setting out an argument that helps reveal, in a simplified form, the kind of incoherence that the *Tractatus* exposes in intelligibility as con-formity.[11] It is not an argument that one will find in the *Tractatus*, but it will provide a scaffold using which we can reconstruct what can be found there: my first such use of it will be to show how the confusion that intelligibility as con-formity involves can be understood as arising through the form of confusion 'of which', Wittgenstein declares, 'the whole of philosophy is full' (3.324), the conflation of what he calls 'signs' and 'symbols'.

3.5 WITTGENSTEIN ON SIGNS, SYMBOLS, AND INTELLIGIBILITY AS CON-FORMITY

Part of what a realist story of acquired con-formity involves is the notion that metaphysical characteristics of the world serve as a standard to which the 'form' of meaningful talk is answerable, the other element of such a realist story being an explanation of how that con-formity comes about. Without worrying here about the latter, let us consider just what kind of success or failure the match or mismatch envisaged is meant to embody.[12] One possible interpretation is that the ways in which we use colour vocabulary, for example, is subject to a kind of external discipline; for instance, our never describing anything as 'red and green all over' might be said to reflect the fact that there are no possible facts corresponding to that combination of words. Our uses of colour vocabulary would then be seen as meaningful by virtue of their conformity with the world's possibilities.

But there are confusions at work here which, I will suggest, Wittgenstein wants to expose, and which underpin the notion of intelligibility as con-formity. Consider for a moment 'sound vocabulary' or 'length vocabulary'. Do the forms of propositions constructed using these other collections of words — 'sound propositions' and 'length propositions' — correspond to those of possible colour facts? The natural reaction for the con-formist here is to say, 'Of course not. Why on earth should they?!' But why, then, when we imagine the forms of such propositions as *lacking* an isomorphism with the forms of these possible facts, do we see these *failures* of fit as no *threat* to their meaningful use? In thinking of a proposition's being used meaningfully as a matter of its con-formity with that of a possible fact, it seems that we must, at the same time, discount the notion that this proposition is subject to the external discipline of conforming to an

---

[11] What it is to 'elucidate' nonsense, and why one ought to think of 'internal property/relation' remarks as part of such an elucidation are questions addressed in the next chapter.

[12] I ignore here issues that arise out of the particular details of Wittgenstein's ontology of 'objects' and 'atomic facts' and his notions of 'names' and 'elementary propositions'.

indefinite number of other possible facts: we must not end up declaring our sound propositions confused by their failure to con-form with, for example, possible colour facts.

The natural response for the con-formist now is to say that these propositions were never meant to represent these other kinds of possible fact; their forms are simply irrelevant to the meaningfulness of those propositions. But is this natural response available to him? Note some of the expressions just used—'propositions that were never *meant* to describe such and such', 'forms that simply aren't *relevant* to such and such a proposition'. But how does one determine what the proposition is *meant* to describe, which possible facts have forms that are *relevant* to it? Only, I suggest, by presupposing the meaning of the propositions in question; we have taken for granted what it is that they apply to and what they do not apply to, and thus also the 'meaningfulness' that we were meant to be investigating, the question of whether and how they 'can' indeed be applied.[13] In contemplating the goodness of a proposition's con-formity with the world's possibilities, which possibilities are relevant must already be determined. But what determines that is precisely the sense of the proposition. Our thinking runs then in a circle. We must somehow overlook this embarrassing fact when we imagine this con-formity or its absence as imposing an external discipline on the ways in which we talk.

In the preface of the *Tractatus*, Wittgenstein claims that 'the problems of philosophy' and their 'method of formulation [*Fragestellung*]' rest 'on the misunderstanding of the logic of our language'. At 3.324, he proposes that 'the most fundamental confusions (of which the whole of philosophy is full)' arise out of a failure to respect the distinction between what he labels 'signs' and 'symbols':

The sign is the part of the symbol perceptible by the senses.

Two different symbols can therefore have the same sign (the written sign or the sound sign) in common—they then signify in different ways.

It can never indicate the common characteristic of two objects that we symbolize them with the same signs but by different *methods of symbolizing*. For the sign is arbitrary. We could therefore equally well choose two different signs and where then would be what was common in the symbolisation? (3.32–3.322)

While '[i]n order to recognize the symbol in the sign we must consider the significant use' (3.326), 'sign' denotes, roughly speaking, the mere 'dead' sign, the physical mark on paper or sound in the air.

This distinction can help articulate the confusion behind the con-formist story sketched above. No one thinks that one might discover rules for the use of signs, rules regarding how a physical mark on a page ought to figure in or as a proposition: 'the sign is arbitrary' (3.22). Such 'dead' signs can be used how so ever one

---

[13] Regarding the use of scare-quotes here, see Sect. 8.6.

wants, and thus '[w]e cannot give a sign the wrong sense' (5.4732). If instead we are contemplating a string of signs with a particular meaning—a symbol—then there is a set of possible facts which they serve to articulate, and their meaningful use is a matter of their being used in that way. But this is no *external* determination of how these words *ought* to be used, as we are only considering—are only led to—those particular possible facts because we have taken for granted how these words *are* actually used. When considered as symbols, we take for granted how the words in question ought to be used; consequently, that cannot be seen as a matter *to be determined* by reference to some con-formity between their use and the form of possible facts.[14] The 'external discipline' to which we imagined our propositions were to be subjected is an illusion which looms before us only if we take the meaning, and hence 'meaningfulness',[15] of those propositions for granted. We generate the illusion by disconnecting words from their customary use while at the same time keeping that use at the back of our minds. In other words, we treat these words simultaneously as signs and as symbols. Such 'enchanted words' provide the *Fragestellung* of our con-formist *Fragen*.

I will end this section by discussing three ways in which the argument set out might be misconstrued. First, does it imply that we never intelligibly say 'That's nonsense'? No. Although the argument does show that there is something confused in a certain philosophical vision of a proposition making sense or not making sense, there clearly are facts about whether certain *sentences* make sense or not, facts about existing languages. These are facts about *signs*. Wittgenstein is asking whether it makes sense to imagine facts about *symbols*, about whether certain propositions make sense and others don't, where these are propositions that might be expressed in *any* language. The con-formist vision suggests that we can, but the argument I have set out suggests that that vision is confused. Secondly, does the argument imply that one cannot talk nonsense? No. But it does imply that 'talking nonsense' is not something one does by using symbols in ways that are incompatible with facts of some sort that determine which combinations of symbols make sense: there are no such facts. But that does not prevent

---

[14] What we miss here is a reason (a) for comparing our use of a particular proposition with the form of a particular possible fact which (b) functions independently of the way in which this proposition is used. If a 'mental act' of some sort 'assigned' in some way a proposition to a possible fact, then our failing to talk intelligibly with that proposition could then perhaps be understood as a matter of an inconsistency of some sort between the way in which that proposition is used and the form of the particular possible fact to which the relevant mental act assigns that proposition. Sect. 8.2 criticizes a related view, but we can at least see why it is a natural partner for a realism that sees the form of language as answerable to—as needing to be brought into con-formity with—that of reality.

[15] Cf. n. 13 above.

the possibility that a given string of *signs* has no use, expresses no thought in a particular language. In a 1914 notebook, we read:

Let us remember the explanation why 'Socrates is Plato' is nonsense. That is, because *we* have not made an arbitrary specification, NOT because a sign is, shall we say, illegitimate in itself! (*NB* 1)[16]

Thirdly, is the point of the argument *epistemological*? No. But we can identify why it might appear so. Consider the following misleading gloss:

We cannot justify the claim that a proposition, p, makes sense by pointing out that it corresponds to a possible fact, f. Why not? The reason is that, since we must rely upon the proposition in articulating the content-determining fact, we cannot know that the proposition is actually meaningful even if that is the conclusion at which we arrive. We cannot possibly know if our conclusion is reliable as we must rely upon the very 'tool' we are evaluating.[17]

We imagine here someone somehow standing outside us—a god perhaps—being able to discern the elusive fact of the matter that links our proposition to a fact, but we users of the proposition being unable to do so. But this misrepresents the problem that the argument reveals. First, the argument does not presuppose that advocates of a conception of intelligibility as con-formity think that someone might read off from reality how a proposition ought to be used; the core claim, and the claim that the argument attacks, is that the intelligibility of a proposition is constituted (at least partly) by its form corresponding to that of part of reality. Secondly, the problem that the argument identifies is not that we cannot know that our proposition is intelligible, but that it is undetermined *what* test the intelligible proposition passes. *What* should the imagined god test? Whether this thought successfully maps on to this fact?

---

[16] It is interesting that in the remarks in the *Tractatus* (5.473) which are clearly descendants of the notebook remarks quoted here, Wittgenstein has substituted 'symbol' for 'sign'. If the distinction is as important as I suggest, it might seem unlikely that Wittgenstein can make such a substitution and still produce a sentence he wants to assert. The reason he can is that a philosophically interesting distinction between 'the logical' and 'the illogical' emerges only if we conflate sign and symbol, as Ch. 5 will explain in greater detail. No one wittingly searches for a delimitation of signs that are 'nonsensical in themselves', because 'the sign is arbitrary' and can always be assigned a sense; no one wittingly searches for a delimitation of symbols that are 'nonsensical in themselves', because to identify a symbol is to identify its 'significant use' (3.326). Thus, one can draw attention to the philosopher's confused notion of what it is to judge a proposition 'nonsensical' by pointing out that he must wish this judgement to concern neither signs nor symbols; instead, he confusedly wants it to concern a hybrid of both.

[17] Child formulates (but does not endorse) something like this argument in his 2001, p. 84. (I have doubts about whether the argument can be found in Wittgenstein where Child suggests it can (viz., in *PG* 185–7).)

Why think of this thought as *about* this fact? The problem that the argument exposes is not that we cannot answer our question; rather, which question we ought to ask is undetermined. The 'epistemological gloss' suggests that the perspective from which the fit of a proposition to the world might be described is one which the user of the proposition cannot occupy. But the deeper point that that gloss overlooks is that the perspective does not make sense, that there is no such perspective.

4

The Method of the *Tractatus*

One of the basic ideas informing my reading of the *Tractatus* is that Wittgenstein believed he could make good on the claim that philosophical problems emerge out of sign/symbol confusions; that idea was introduced and illustrated in Section 3.5, will be elaborated on in Chapter 6's discussion of what Wittgenstein believes notations can do for us philosophically, and will be returned to repeatedly throughout the rest of the book. This chapter will set out some of the other basic ideas that inform my reading. These include an understanding of what it is to elucidate nonsense (Sects. 4.3–4.8) and an understanding of what is at stake in Wittgenstein's talk of 'internal properties' and 'internal relations' (Sects. 4.9–4.10). But I will look first at that cluster of commitments that have become known as 'resolution'.

4.1 RESOLUTION: AN INITIAL SKETCH

Given the range of literary forms that philosophy has employed over the centuries, the *Tractatus* is not *that* strange; certainly we recognize it as a philosophical text, presenting perplexing but recognizably philosophical claims. Consequently, 6.54's claim that Wittgenstein's propositions ought to be recognized as nonsense seems to run counter to our entire experience of engaging with the book: 'How can the book that I have just *read* be nonsense?' The view of the *Tractatus* which has been, certainly until recently, most popular (developed by, for example, Norman Malcolm and Peter Hacker) deals with this problem by suggesting that when Wittgenstein talks of that work's propositions as 'nonsense', his point is that his philosophical 'message' is one 'which *strictu sensu* cannot be said' (Hacker 2001*a*, p. 19). That message can still be thought of as embodying a set of metaphysical views, for example, but part of that message is that these views are, somehow, inexpressible.

This view has acquired the labels 'traditional' and 'orthodox' in recent years due to the promotion of an alternative view by, in particular, Cora Diamond and James Conant.[1] An early criticism of the *Tractatus*, understood 'traditionally',

---

[1] Cf., e.g., Diamond 1991, chs. 1–6, 2000*a*, and 2000*b*; Conant 1991*a*, 1991*b*, 1993, 2000, and 2002; Conant and Diamond 2004. While the present and following sections indicate some of what I take from Conant and Diamond's work, I am sure that their influence on my reading extends further, though in ways it is hard for me to pin down. I do not know what a considered and comprehensive picture of the *Tractatus* would be like for them and I strongly suspect it would

was made by Frank Ramsey: 'what we can't say, we can't say, and we can't whistle it either'.[2] Conant and Diamond maintain that Wittgenstein recognized that, and renounced as unintelligible the idea of *views* which '*strictu sensu* cannot be said'. In arguing that when Wittgenstein said that we should come to recognize his propositions as nonsense, he meant 'real nonsense, plain nonsense, which we are not in the end to think of as corresponding to an ineffable truth' (Diamond 1991, p. 181),[3] this view styles itself as 'resolute', as refusing to 'chicken out': 'when Wittgenstein calls something nonsensical he implies that it has really and truly got no articulable content' (Diamond 2000*b*, p. 155).[4] Rather than trying to intimate ineffable metaphysical truths, the *Tractatus* does no more than reveal our susceptibility to certain illusions:

[W]e are drawn into the illusion of occupying a certain sort of perspective. . . . From this perspective, we take ourselves to be able to survey the possibilities which undergird how things are with us, holding our necessities in place. From this perspective, we contemplate the laws of logic as they are, as well as the possibility of their being otherwise. We take ourselves to be occupying a perspective from which we can view the laws of logic from sideways on. The only 'insight' the work imparts therefore is one about the reader himself: that he is prone to such illusions. (Conant 1991*a*, p. 157) [5]

Critics of this approach believe that only a kind of wilfulness or self-deception on the part of resolute readers allows them to believe that they can make sense of the proposal that Wittgenstein's propositions are nonsensical in just the same way as pure gibberish—such as 'piggle wiggle tiggle' (Diamond 2000*b*, p. 151)—is. Criticism of resolution can be seen to condense around four main charges.[6]

First, traditionalists claim that resolute readings of the *Tractatus* are incompatible with so many claims that its author makes that it cannot possibly capture the meaning of that book. Resolute readers respond that, in a work that is

be importantly different from the picture I offer here; indeed a sympathetic reader for another press asked why I associated my own reading with theirs. I do sometimes criticise their views in what follows, but I still think that their work remains the most important influence on my own thought on the *Tractatus*.

  [2] Quoted in Hacker 2000, p. 355.
  [3] Cf. also Conant 1993, p. 216.
  [4] The reading in question has also been labelled 'therapeutic' (McGinn 1999), 'deconstructive' (Hacker 2000), simply 'American' (Hacker 2003), and, in the light of Crary and Read's 2000 collection, simply 'new' (though Crary and Read themselves use that term to denote a broader approach which also takes in Wittgenstein's later work).
  [5] There is debate over quite who can claim to be the originator of the 'resolute' interpretation; pieces of work which are clearly important, either as anticipations or as forerunners, include Ishiguro 1969; McGuinness 1981; Winch 1987; Goldfarb, unpublished *a* (for discussion of these pieces, cf. Goldfarb, unpublished *b*); Burton Dreben was also an important influence on the development of this view through his teaching at Harvard and Boston universities. Other significant contributions to the 'resolute' literature include Floyd 1998 and 2002; Friedlander 2001; Goldfarb 1997*a*; Kremer 2001, 2002, and 2004; Ostrow 2002; Ricketts 1985 and 1996; Witherspoon 2000; and other pieces included in Crary and Read 2000.
  [6] There are others, and I will address some of them below (cf., e.g., n. 11 below, Sect. 4.9, and Ch. 10 n. 16 and Sect. A.10); but the ones I present here are, I think, the most important.

to be 'thrown away' having been seen to be made up of propositions that are nonsensical, 'the claims that its author makes' have to be viewed with circumspection: some—perhaps many—of these claims are *meant* to be 'thrown away'.[7] Critics have, in turn, responded by pointing also to remarks of Wittgenstein's which seem to articulate the views of the author of the *Tractatus* and to embody substantial metaphysical claims but which are made *outside* the 'frame' that 6.54 provides; most of these have come in the form of retrospective comments that Wittgenstein makes.[8] Resolute readers have responded by arguing that these remarks are cases of Wittgenstein subsequently recognizing that he had particular philosophical commitments;[9] thus the claim that the *Tractatus* was not designed to impart any substantial metaphysical message may yet be harmonized with Wittgenstein's later remarks about having held metaphysical commitments when he wrote that book: the proposal is that these commitments were unwitting commitments of the early Wittgenstein that he later recognized as such.

Needless to say, neither of the resolute rejoinders set out in the preceding paragraph are adequate as they stand: both need to be made good through a detailed reading of the relevant texts. I present my own attempt to do that in what follows.[10]

Secondly, there is the undeniable 'phenomenological' fact that reading the *Tractatus* is not at all like reading a book of meaningless gibberish. This complaint is superficially the easiest for resolute readers to respond to. Although resolute readers insist that nonsensical philosophical propositions are actually strings of signs to which no content has been assigned and are, in this respect, no different from gibberish, their interpretation positively *requires* that the phenomenology of reading the *Tractatus* not be that of reading gibberish. Their point is that, on reading the work, our confusions conjure up a pseudo-understanding; a person who is philosophically confused succumbs to an *illusion* of understanding, and, as a result, reading philosophical propositions (Wittgenstein's included) does *not feel* like reading 'piggle wiggle tiggle'.

None the less, what I think this criticism rightly points to is a failure on the part of the resolute to give a detailed account of just what reading the *Tractatus* does involve. This failure also prompts the third complaint, which McGinn captures well: 'if the ladder . . . turns out to be an illusion, how have we got anywhere by climbing it?' (1999, p. 496). An aspect of that question might be developed by asking, in particular, how strings of pure nonsense can constitute a chain of reasoning, how they can constitute a 'ladder' that is 'climbed' by thinking through arguments. To deny that that is crucial to what reading the *Tractatus* involves would seem to require that the book is a body of squiggles that merely *causes* the philosopher to stop saying what he says, something that acts on us, as

---

7 Cf., e.g., Conant 2000, p. 215.
8 Hacker 2000 and Proops 2001 have both followed this path.
9 Cf. Conant and Diamond 2004, sect. 5.
10 The second rejoinder comes to the fore in Sects. 9.4 and 11.9 and Appendix A.

Sullivan puts it, 'like a blow on the head' (2003, p. 196). Sections 4.3–4.8 will set out the basis of a response to this third complaint, and throw new light on the second.

Finally, there is the worry that Hacker expresses when he declares that the resolute perspective 'dismiss[es] the philosophical insights' of 'this great book' (Hacker 2000, p. 359). One often encounters the view that resolute readings are ingenious and fit well some of the book's 'framing' metaphilosophical remarks (6.54, in particular), but that they leave much of the rest of the book—the '*content*' of the book—unilluminated.[11] Resolute readings are often depicted as unsatisfactorily *thin*, as very abstract, 'strategic' accounts of how the book ought to work, as opposed to detailed readings of the text as we find it. So Sullivan, for example, sums up his reaction to the core ideas of this reading as 'Well, yes, so far. And now . . . ?' (2002, p. 44). Perhaps in response to this pressure from Sullivan, Conant and Diamond have recently stated:

To be a resolute reader is to be committed at most to a certain programmatic conception of the lines along which [the details of the book] are to be worked out. (Conant and Diamond 2004, p. 47)

The viability of that programmatic conception will depend on the possibility of those details being worked out. My book presents one way in which this might be attempted. In case it needs stating, my aim is not resolution for resolution's sake; rather, I believe that the reading that emerges is broadly in line with what Wittgenstein says and does, and is of philosophical interest.

4.2 RESOLUTION: A SHARPER SPECIFICATION

One effect of the controversy that resolute readings have sparked has been an effort to delimit more precisely just what a resolute reading of the *Tractatus* is. Sullivan (2002) has suggested that, to the extent that there is a unifying core to resolution, it is constituted by two particular commitments. The first is an 'austere' conception of nonsense, according to which 'nonsense is a failure to make sense [and not] a matter of making the *wrong kind* of sense' (p. 45): to say that a string of signs is 'nonsensical' is to say that 'no meaning has been given to one or more of the component signs as they occur in that string . . . and *not*, as one might be tempted to think, that the meanings that *have* been assigned to the various components of the string will not cohere' (p. 45). The second commitment is 'a "full-hearted recognition" that when Wittgenstein describes his own

[11] Another criticism I will mention here is that, by presenting the *Tractatus* as 'real nonsense, plain nonsense', the resolute 'surprisingly disregard the fact that in the preface Wittgenstein speaks of *the thoughts* expressed in the book [and] asserts that their *truth* is "unassailable and definitive"' (Hacker 2000, p. 360). This complaint strikes me as placing inordinate weight on turns of phrase that can easily be interpreted differently: on my own (broadly resolute) view, Wittgenstein certainly has a view—'thoughts'—about philosophy that he thinks is right—that those thoughts 'are true'.

propositions as "nonsense" [he means] that they fail to make sense' (p. 45). A 'full-hearted recognition' contrasts with 'half-hearted' views that would depict those propositions as making the 'wrong kind of sense'. As illustrations of what the resolute think that 'half-heartedness' looks like, Sullivan quotes (at p. 45) Kremer and Goldfarb: half-heartedness might be a matter of seeing Wittgenstein's propositions as 'something like propositions', as 'quasi-truths' (Kremer 2001, p. 41) or as sentences which, 'while nonsensical, somehow gesture at something that is going on, some inexpressible state of affairs or true but inexpressible thought' (Goldfarb 1997*a*, p. 61).

According to Conant and Diamond, on the other hand, the following two other 'interrelated features . . . suffice to make a reading "resolute" ':

The first is that it does not take those propositions of the *Tractatus* about which Wittgenstein said, at 6.54, that they are to be recognized as 'nonsensical' to convey ineffable insights. The second feature is a rejection of the idea that what such recognition requires on the part of a reader of the *Tractatus* is the application of a theory of meaning that has been advanced in the body of the work—a theory that specifies the conditions under which a sentence makes sense and the conditions under which it does not. (2004, p. 47)

To indicate roughly how these taxonomic claims relate, Conant and Diamond's first feature illustrates Sullivan's second, and his first (at least, according to Conant and Diamond (p. 48)) is a corollary of their second.

But neither of these characterizations seems quite adequate to me. These attempts to find the 'core', the 'heart', of what motivates resolute readings seem to leave out another hazily specified concern: namely, their sense that the early Wittgenstein shared the later Wittgenstein's view that philosophical problems ought to be dissolved rather than solved, that the appropriate response to a philosophical problem is *not* the formulation of a substantial philosophical theory about the nature of the world, thought, or language, but instead an identification of *confusions* that have left us facing this apparent—but *only apparent*— problem.[12]

I take my own reading to have both of Conant and Diamond's features, the first of the commitments that Sullivan picks out, and the 'hazy' commitment that I have suggested needs to figure somewhere in an account of 'resolution'. The situation is less straightforward, however, with the second commitment that Sullivan picks out: I do not see Wittgenstein's propositions as gesturing at 'some inexpressible state of affairs or true but inexpressible thought' (and thus my reading has the first of Conant and Diamond's features), but I do take them to be 'something like propositions', as 'somehow gesturing at something that is going on', and even as 'quasi-truths'. Having said that, I take my position to be in the spirit of the resolute approach, and my willingness to use the formulations just

---

[12] Conant has recently made clear in conversation that he sees the omission of this broader commitment as a mistake. Sullivan's reason for doing so is, I suspect, the belief that resolution's 'core' commitments are actually compatible with the idea that the *Tractatus* 'presents a philosophical system of the world, and thought about the world' (Sullivan 2004, p. 32).

mentioned is one which, I will argue, the resolute can share if they broaden their diet of examples of nonsense; Sections 4.3–4.8 explore the crucial issues here.

Why embrace these commitments? Again, rather then summarize the whole resolute literature, I will make a few comments here, and point in the direction of some further support to be found elsewhere in the book.

An argument in favour of Conant and Diamond's first commitment that has received a lot of attention seems to be less than convincing. This is the argument that there is something hopelessly confused in the idea of ineffable truths: 'traditionalist' readers are taken to say something of the form, 'Wittgenstein conveys to us that *p* and that *p* is unsayable', and such a reading treats Wittgenstein, as Kremer puts it, 'as a bumbling fool' (2001, p. 45). Proops (2001) and Sullivan (2002) have both argued recently that the recognition of ineffable *truths* does not exhaust the possible range of 'insights' that might be thought ineffable but conveyed through the *Tractatus* or through the revision of our symbolism that it envisages: the argument presented, for example, would not bear on insight into 'features of a proposition, of a state of affairs, of language, of reality, the world' (Sullivan 2002, p. 50).[13]

I will offer my own account of why the notion of the ineffable is to be 'thrown away': it is not because 'the unsayable' is, in some way, an inherently confused notion; rather, in the particular cases in which we resort to this notion, we do so out of confusion. I do, none the less, think that Wittgenstein's use of the notion of 'the unsayable' is meant to unsettle us, to make us wonder about the route that has led us to the point at which we believe we run into 'the unsayable'. I will argue that Wittgenstein's demonstration of how we come to reach for 'the unsayable' is something that is meant to help us see the confusion in whose grip we are thinking.

There are two principal reasons why Conant and Diamond's second commitment appeals to me. First, I know of no theory of meaning that has been proposed as articulated within the *Tractatus*, and as providing the reason why Wittgenstein's own 'propositions' and those of other philosophers are nonsensical, that strikes me as plausible—as, for instance, resting on premises that are more compelling than our own initial conviction that those apparent 'propositions' make sense. (Many theories have been offered, and I cannot examine all of them here. I will, however, examine an example in Sect. 4.9.) Secondly, I believe that I am offering here a sensible story about the *Tractatus* that does not need to ascribe to it such a theory of meaning.

Turning to the features that Sullivan picks out, if one embraces the first, then there is a clear case for embracing the second, it being an application of the

---

[13] Conant and Diamond have recently insisted that their view 'need not require throwing away the idea of showing *per se*' (2004, p. 65); this leaves open the possibility that some species of say/show distinction might be preserved and, with it perhaps, some notion of 'the ineffable'; but what they have in mind is not clear to me. I make explicit my own view of this distinction in Sects. 15.1–15.3.

austere conception of nonsense to Wittgenstein's own supposedly nonsensical 'propositions' (though I will argue below that we must be careful quite how we interpret this second feature). As for the first, it appeals because Wittgenstein does seem to go out of his way to defend such a view of nonsense.[14] A trickier question is: Can Wittgenstein endorse this view without recourse to a substantive philosophical theory of meaning? While Sullivan argues that it is 'an immediate consequence of [a] contextualism about meaning' (p. 45), I am inclined to agree with Kremer that this 'view' is a 'pre-theoretical, common-sense' notion (2001, p. 43): when one talks nonsense, one produces signs but says nothing. My commitment to Sullivan's first feature is a matter of trying to demonstrate that, for Wittgenstein, we invoke other, less 'common-sensical' 'forms of nonsense' only when confused.

My added 'hazy' commitment seems to me to be consistent with Wittgenstein's rejection of an '*a priori* order of things' (5.634, quoted in Sect. 1.1) and to be a corollary of the combination of the austere conception of nonsense and Wittgenstein's claim in 4.003:

Most propositions and questions, that have been written about philosophical matters, are not false, but nonsensical.

He continues: 'We cannot ... answer questions of this kind at all'; if such 'questions' don't actually pose questions, then there are no questions there to be answered; these 'deepest problems are really *no* problems'.

4.3 ELUCIDATING NONSENSE

Don't *for heaven's sake*, be afraid of talking nonsense! But you must pay attention to your nonsense.

(*CV* 64 (1947))

The different specifications of 'resolution' that the previous section examined all present 'resolution' as not only a programmatic 'conception' of how to read the *Tractatus*, but also as essentially a conception of how *not* to read the book. So what are the other basic notions upon which my positive reading draws?

In the light of *TLP* 4.003, and 6.54's laying down of the further challenge of understanding how Wittgenstein's own propositions can be nonsensical too, any reading needs to consider carefully what Wittgenstein understands 'nonsense' to be. According to the 'austere conception', nonsense is an absence of sense, rather than the presence of the 'wrong kind of sense'. But Wittgenstein tells us more

---

[14] Cf. *TLP* 5.473 and *NB* 1, quoted in Sect. 3.5.

about the particular kind of nonsense to which philosophers are given: conflations of sign and symbol give rise to 'the most fundamental confusions (of which
the whole of philosophy is full)' (3.324). I will argue that this metaphilosophical claim, which was introduced above in Sect. 3.5, can be taken seriously: if
we follow Wittgenstein's guidance, we can see how fundamental philosophical
concerns arise out of sign/symbol conflation and how Wittgenstein's own propositions 'elucidate' confusions with their roots in such conflations. This brings
or to another basic 'plank' in my account, namely, an understanding of what such
an 'elucidation of nonsense' involves.

Every reader of the *Tractatus* faces the question of what it is to understand a
book whose contents are supposedly nonsensical. For example, Conant asks of
'traditional readers': 'how is nonsense able to convey an insight into ineffable features of reality?' (1991*a*, p. 153). But the 'resolute' approach faces the third traditionalist criticism set out in Section 4.1; Hacker echoes McGinn's sentiment:

[W]e can hardly claim that a 'ladder' consisting of mere gibberish can lead anywhere.
(Hacker 2001*a*, pp. 15–16)[15]

And how can such a 'ladder' be 'climbed' by thinking through arguments, as the
Tractatus surely is?

Conant claims that 'the elucidatory strategy of the *Tractatus* depends on the
reader's provisionally taking himself to be participating in the traditional philosophical activity of establishing theses through a procedure of reasoned argument', though the reader must ultimately ' "recognize" that he has only been
going through the motions of "inferring" (apparent) conclusions from (apparent) "premises" ' (2000, pp. 196–7). The challenge for the resolute is twofold:
first, to give a sense to the 'successful' going through of those motions (to be con-
trasted with that in which I nod my head as I move my finger down the page,
muttering 'Yes, I see', when in fact I have no idea what is going on) without
going back on either the belief that 'entailment is a relation between sentences
only in so far as they are meaningful' (Witherspoon 2000, p. 348)[16] or the claim
that the 'premises' and 'conclusions' 'really and truly [have] no articulable content'; secondly, to explain why 'going through' such 'motions' might get one
somewhere!

For Wittgenstein, nonsense is a failure to recognize when we have conflated
different symbols as a result of similarity between the signs that express them. But
talking nonsense is not always something that leads to perdition, or something
that one does without the possibility of control. In explaining this view, I will
explain a corollary of the sign/symbol conflation view of nonsense that resolute

---

[15] As Stephen Mulhall has formulated the point, 'If there's nothing there, how can it bear even
provisional weight?' (private communication). Cf. also Reid 1998, pp. 107–8.

[16] Cf. also Diamond 2000*a*, p. 273: 'Any grasp which I have of [sentences'] logical relations is
inseparable from my grasp of the sentences themselves, of each as a sentence saying that such-and-
such is the case. . . . *If I can take a sentence to stand in logical relations to other sentences, then I can
understand that sentence.*'

readers have either overlooked or mistakenly taken to lead to irresolution; it is that, in a perfectly reasonable sense, items of nonsense have an identity and a logic. If anything, their problem is having *too much* of both. And in another sense, of course, it is not '*their* problem' at all. One can 'cross' propositions to generate nonsense in this way if one wants to: for example, as we will see, Lewis Carroll does it. But one thing that does distinguish the production of philosophical nonsense is that the 'crossing' of propositions that it involves is carried out *unwittingly*. I will suggest that Wittgenstein wittingly follows out the pseudo-logic of these confusions in order to reveal that that is indeed what they are.

The debate over how to read this nonsensical book with understanding has been conspicuously short of examples; I will offer a series of examples, drawn from Carroll, which demonstrate that there are varieties of nonsense with which that debate has failed to reckon. Such items of nonsense can, in recognizable ways, be understood and form steps in arguments that are, in recognizable ways, valid; but neither of these feats turns on our thinking of these items of nonsense as intimating ineffable claims of some sort. It is the work of the rest of the book to show how, by analogy, these examples, and the conception of 'the elucidation of nonsense' that they suggest, might help us understand what it is to understand the *Tractatus*.

4.4 BROADENING OUR 'DIET OF EXAMPLES'

It is not unusual for the name of Lewis Carroll to come up in discussions of the *Tractatus*; *Jabberwocky* is clearly one of our favourite examples of nonsense.[17] But it is not the kind of example at which I want to look.[18]

When Alice passes through the looking-glass, she is surprised to find that the flowers there talk. But the 'explanation' is simple:

'In most gardens,' the Tiger-lily said, 'they make the beds so soft—so that the flowers are always asleep.' (1992 [1872], p. 120)

Now in one sense this is a simple play on words, a pun on 'beds'. But what is funny about this, what makes it a joke that one can 'get', is that we can understand Carroll's extrapolation: if we imagine (if that is the word) flowers in their beds as like people in theirs, the reason that the flowers don't talk must be because they are asleep. In one sense, Carroll presents us with nonsense. But it is nonsense with a logic in the sense that it can be followed—someone who has understood the preceding few sentences has done just that—and indeed elaborated upon: for example, bed-wetting is clearly applauded among plants ... To understand such nonsense—to get the joke—is to be able to follow the pseudo-logic of such nonsense.

---

[17] Cf., e.g., Kremer 2001, p. 39.
[18] Pitcher (1967) does look at the kinds of examples I will consider, though without connecting them to Wittgenstein's early philosophy.

Other examples require analysis before one can see what is happening (not, thankfully, before one can enjoy them). In the course of her strange day in Wonderland, Alice remarks:

How queer everything is to-day! And yesterday things went on just as usual. I wonder if I've been changed in the night? Let me think: was I the same when I got up this morning? I almost think I can remember feeling a little different. But if I'm not the same, the next question is, Who in the world am I? Ah, *that's* the great puzzle! (1992 [1865], p. 11)

At this point, Carroll tells us:

[Alice] began thinking over all the children she knew that were of the same age as herself, to see if she could have been changed into any of them.
'I'm sure I'm not Ada,' she said, 'for her hair goes in such long ringlets, and mine doesn't go in ringlets at all; and I'm sure I can't be Mabel, for I know all sorts of things, and she, oh! she knows such a very little. ... I'll try if I know all the things I used to know.'

Alice proceeds to test herself, gets answers that she is sure are wrong, sadly concludes 'I must be Mabel after all', and then resolves:

[I]f I'm Mabel, I'll stay down here! It'll be no use their putting their heads down here and saying 'Come up again, dear!' I shall only look up and say 'Who am I then? Tell me that first, and then, if I like being that person, I'll come up; if not, I'll stay down here till I'm somebody else.

Alice's words here are both nonsensical and comprehensible. We can make explicit our understanding—the understanding that we have by virtue of having 'got' the humour of the passage—by analysing what she says through the borrowings and conflations of sense that make up the fabric of her utterances, the borrowings and conflations appreciated by those who 'get' Carroll's humour. What Alice says runs together two senses of 'being a different person'. On the one hand, she notes that she feels different; on the other, she knows a number of other people (such as Ada and Mabel), a number of 'different people'. At this point, two perfectly good lines of reasoning merge courtesy of a common sign, 'different person': '[I]f I'm not the same, the next question is, Who in the world am I?'

'Different person' figures in two more or less distinct sets of claims: on the one hand, 'I am the same person I always was', 'He's a different person now', etc.; on the other, 'Is that the same person in these two pictures?', 'These books are both by someone called Lewis but they were two different people', etc. These sets of claims themselves feature in two more or less distinct sets of chains of reasoning. Carroll's humour makes vivid the fact that these two sets don't coincide, in that there seems to be a sense in which being 'a different person' does not make one 'a different person'! Getting the joke is seeing this and following the extrapolation: if I imagine (again that may not be the word we want, but it will do) my way into Alice's confusion, I can ask myself 'How *would* one try to determine whether one had changed into someone else?'. I continue my extrapolation when I conclude, 'Well, one would see if one had their most salient features', and ask 'How old am I and how old are they?', 'Is my hair like theirs?', and 'Do I know what they know?' These are all 'intelligible questions' in the sense that we know of contexts in which their being posed can be understood. But, of course, in those contexts, our asking of these questions might lead us to the conclusion, 'I'm very *like* Mabel'. In Wonderland, it can lead us to conclude 'I *am* Mabel'!!

4.5 UNDERSTANDING NONSENSE AND ITS LOGIC

Carroll's work is full of examples like these. The guests at the Mad Hatter's Tea Party are trapped at 6 o'clock because he and Time are no longer on good terms after the Mad Hatter 'murdered the time' when singing a song (1992 [1865], p. 61). And this makes a kind of sense: after all, how would *you* react if someone tried to murder you? Again, an overlap of signs (here embedded within a broader culture of personifying Time—'Time has been cruel to him', for example) allows Carroll to give us a nonsense with a logic, a nonsense which one can, in a recognizable sense, understand and which, in a recognizable sense, is capable of being inferred from other items of nonsense.

Such items of nonsense possess these features by virtue of borrowing sense from elsewhere. Part of what that borrowing is is their standing in pseudo-logical relations with other nonsensical 'propositions' that borrow their sense from corresponding sources. An aspect of what it would be for someone not to get Carroll's humour would be their failure to see how conclusions that his characters draw 'follow' from their premisses, despite the fact that the arguments in question are also nonsensical—patently so to those who *do* understand. As a result, one can offer reasons why certain nonsensical claims should naturally 'follow' from others. Consider one more example. The White King marvels at Alice's eye-sight when she tells him that she saw nobody on the road: 'Why, it's as much as I can do to see real people, by this light!' (1992 [1872], p. 165). When the Messenger is next to arrive, the King concludes that 'Nobody walks slower than you':

'I do my best,' the Messenger said in a sullen tone. 'I'm sure nobody walks much faster than I do!'
'He can't do that,' said the King, 'or else he'd have been here first.' (pp. 166–7)

There is an obvious sense in which the White King is *right* when he draws this conclusion: it follows in that it would follow if 'Nobody' figured in these propositions as a name; the humour—and the confusion—arises because that is not what 'Nobody' is in English, though its surface grammar can suggest to us that it is. (An important point to which Sect. 5.4 will return is that though the White King's response to the Messenger is, in a recognizable sense, right, it remains, in a recognizable sense, nonsense: it is an elaboration on—the talking of *more*—nonsense.)

In this example too, a confusion arises out of an overlapping of signs, though of a different sort from that of our earlier examples. Our earlier examples featured different symbols being expressed by a common sign ('bed', 'different person', and 'murder'). In the case of 'Nobody', the root of our confusion—and of the joke—is that we have very different kinds of symbol being expressed by signs that look similar and look to play similar roles in sentences. 'Nobody' *looks like* a referring expression; one can substitute it for 'the man' in the sentence 'The man jumped into the water' and generate a meaningful sentence. As a result, we may then find ourselves asking, 'To what does "Nobody" refer?'

The significance of the examples that I have presented in this and the preceding sections is that they combine features that the debate over nonsense in the *Tractatus* has taken to be incompatible. In each example, we confront, it seems to me, something that can perfectly reasonably be described as 'nonsensical', as capable of being 'understood', as capable of figuring in 'arguments', and hence as 'possessing a logic'; but at the same time, these items of nonsense can perfectly reasonably be described as 'real nonsense, plain nonsense, which we are not in the end to think of'—and, crucially, which no one, when they recognize what they have before them, is likely to be tempted to think of—'as corresponding to an ineffable truth' (Diamond 1991, p. 181).

4.6 AN INTERLUDE: 'UNDERSTANDING' AND UNDERSTANDING, 'LOGIC' AND LOGIC

In the preceding sections, I have sometimes used scare-quotes for terms like 'follow' when used in connection with the Carrollian examples of nonsense; but I have also talked of the White King being *right* when he draws his nonsensical conclusion and have done so without using scare-quotes; similarly, I have sometimes talked of these examples as having a logic and sometimes a pseudo-logic. A form of what I take to be an unwarranted 'hyper-resolution' would see these 'inconsistencies' as problematic, and as symptomatic of a failure on my part to recognize that it is 'irresolute' to believe in forms of nonsense that are not 'pure gibberish'. This section will explain why I think such 'hyper-resolution' is mistaken.

There is clearly a point to asking of the forms of 'comprehensibility' and 'logic' illustrated by the items of nonsense that I have presented, 'But is it *real* comprehensibility?' and 'Is it *real* logic?' My response to these questions is that, in clear, distinct senses, we should answer them 'Yes' and 'No'. One would deny that the King's conclusion followed if one thought that someone might believe that the King was saying something unconfused within which a particular inferential step can be made; but one would affirm that it followed if one was helping someone to see how the confusion and the humour involved works. For example, one might spell out the premises from which 'Nobody walks slower than the Messenger' *would* follow if 'Nobody' were a name, and from which 'Nobody walks *faster* than the Messenger' *wouldn't*.

Consider the question, 'Is it *real* nonsense?' In the face of the apparent patterns of inference just considered, hyper-resolution might drive one to insist that these items of supposed nonsense must have a sense after all. But again, I think we should answer our strident either/or question 'Yes and no'. One would deny that someone had understood these items if he took them not to involve any confusion; there is no such thing as understanding them if that is what 'understanding them' involves. But one might assert that one can indeed understand them if confronted with someone who does not recognize the kinds of understanding which the previous paragraph illustrated. In the light of the sense that there is to be made of these items of nonsense, not only hyper-resolution, but also the not unreasonable policy that 'sense' and 'understanding' are correlate notions, might prompt one to insist that these particular items of 'nonsense' actually do have a sense; but a remaining, good reason for shying away from such a conclusion is how different the relevant forms of understanding are. In the above examples, it is a matter of getting the joke; it differs from our ordinary grasp of a proposition as much as someone who 'gets' Carroll's remarks on 'sleeping flowers' differs from someone who hears them as an explanation of plant behaviour.

To be reminded of the forms of nonsense discussed here is to see why one ought to feel pulled in both directions in the face of questions like 'Is it *real* comprehensibility?', '*real* logic?' or '*real* nonsense?' My point is that, when we look at particular cases, our sense that these questions must have straight forward 'Yes' or 'No' answers fades. The challenge set out in Section 4.3, and upon which those questions elaborate, rests on black-and-white, either/or intuitions about sense, nonsense, understanding, inference, and logic which have not been seriously tested by examples. In the face of the sensitivity to case and context I have described, I will continue to use scare-quotes for 'following' (and the like) sometimes and sometimes not, to speak of logic sometimes and sometimes of pseudo-logic, in the hope that my choice on each occasion helps.

4.7 SIGN/SYMBOL CONFLATION AND PHILOSOPHICAL CONFUSION

The examples that I have given combine properties that the recent debate over the *Tractatus* has tended to treat as incompatible. But one might still wonder what those kinds of example have to do with philosophy.

The White King case will ring bells with anyone familiar with Frege's work: part of his achievement was to let us see how expressions like 'Something', 'Nobody', and 'Anywhere' differ from referring expressions.[19] No one has ever seriously thought that 'Somebody' refers to a strange person. It would be almost as crude a thought that leads us to say that 'Something' refers to a fuzzy thing, 'Anywhere' a fuzzy place, and 'Nobody' a person-shaped hole. But the notion that the right question to ask—if one wants to understand how such expressions 'work'—is 'To what do these expressions refer?' has proved far more popular; the history of logic prior to Frege provides us with a set of sophisticated responses to this very question.[20] Though a lot less funny than Carroll, they exploit the same conflation of senses by treating as a referring expression what is in fact the 'name' of a variable; where the tradition in question differs from Carroll is in 'exploiting' this conflation *unwittingly*; for him, it yields a joke; for them, it reveals a problem, a possible research programme.

The notion that something akin to confusions of this sort informs philosophical thinking more broadly is not such an outlandish one. To take an example, philosophers may not have thought, with the Mad Hatter, that 'time' referred to a *person*; but the same 'power of language to make everything look the same' that makes that 'thought' possible (*CV* 19 (1931)) may perhaps allow more subtle absurdities to enter in to our thinking in the form of the presumption that 'time'—and perhaps 'space' too—refers to a *thing*. (A first bulwark against the absurdity of the notion is the acknowledgement that they are rather special or unusual things.[21]) What also helps, no doubt, is the place that the word 'thing' has in remarks such as 'There is no such thing as . . .', from which one can generate the question 'Are you saying that there is no such thing as time?' We don't want to say 'Yes', but does that mean that time *is* indeed a *thing*? Similarly, part of the fabric of scepticism about the external world is, arguably, a treating of 'the world' as if it referred to a (very, very large) thing: by generalizing particular doubts about our knowledge of particular 'external objects', we generate doubts about our knowledge of 'the realm of external objects' and come to imagine ourselves reaching out for, and failing to lay our hands on, that realm in the way we may reach out for, and fail to lay our hands on, an object within that realm. So it doesn't seem wildly implausible to suggest that some of philosophy's problems are profoundly informed, perhaps even *constituted*, by certain such images, images that those in the grip of those problems do not recognize.

But has anyone ever believed that philosophy as a whole could be marked by such confusions? The answer is 'Yes', that someone being the author of the *Tractatus*, who believed that conflating sign and symbol gives rise to 'the most fundamental confusions' and that 'the whole of philosophy is full' of precisely such

---

[19] Cf. Sect. 2.2.
[20] Russell's 'denoting concepts', e.g., could be seen as standing in this tradition (cf. Russell 1937 [1903], § 56), as could some of the debate over abstract ideas in the empiricist tradition.
[21] Cf. Sect. 5.2's discussion of the 'direction' of time's 'flow'.

confusions (3.324). My interpretation uses this opinion as a guiding principle in reading the *Tractatus*.

4.8 THE *TRACTATUS* AS ELUCIDATING NONSENSE

I will argue that the *Tractatus* 'elucidates' a con-formist image of language, thought, and world; like Carroll's humour, what such 'elucidations' do is work through what is in fact a confused logic, a double-think that characterizes this confused image's borrowings of sense;[22] these elucidations demonstrate how we must look at language, thought, and world in order for the con-formist image to *seem* to make sense, but with the ultimate intent of demonstrating that it doesn't. Wittgenstein presents his own philosophy as 'not a theory but an activity', its result being 'not a number of "philosophical propositions", but to make propositions clear' (4.112); we cannot answer our philosophical questions because they are nonsensical; instead, all we can do is 'establish [*feststellen*] their nonsensicality', and the activity by which we do that is, I suggest, that of elucidation as set out here.

The particular form of confusion that Wittgenstein focuses on in his early work is one which creates an illusion of bodies of fact: facts about how objects and possible facts relate, how names and objects relate, how the subject and the world relate, etc. He argues that, if we are to avoid an 'accidental' logic, these 'relations' must be 'internal'. This is an odd turn of phrase. In one sense, it doesn't sound like the denial of the existence of a body of facts at all; rather, it sounds like the noting of a different *kind* of fact. But the intent of the qualification 'internal' seems to be that it taketh away what the word 'relation' giveth.

The con-formist image demands, for example, that the 'substance of the world' (2.021) be 'objects' characterized by certain internal properties and internal relations. To offer up an explanation of the sort we desire, an explanation of *how* and *why* the propositions that make sense *do* make sense, that these objects possess such properties and relations, must constitute a body of facts. But, at the same time, that explanation must not leave the 'intelligibility' of particular items of thought and talk a mere contingent matter of fact that could have been otherwise, because '[i]n logic nothing is accidental' (2.012): 'Nothing in the province of logic can be merely possible' (2.0121). That the relevant properties and relations are 'internal' sums up the required squaring of that circle. What these 'conclusions' flag is that con-formism requires us to bounce between two incompatible

---

[22] Just in case this needs saying, I see no more than an analogy between the work of Carroll and that of Wittgenstein; I do recognize significant differences: e.g., despite Wittgenstein's later proposal that it ought to be possible to write 'a serious and good philosophical work . . . that would consist entirely of jokes' (Malcolm 1984, p. 29), one has to concede that, no matter how good a mood one is in, the *Tractatus* is not that funny. (For braver souls who are inclined to push the analogy further, *PI* § 111's connection of the 'depth of philosophy' with the depth of 'grammatical jokes' might perhaps be a starting-point.)

perspectives: its explanatory pretensions require a body of facts whose happening to hold explains which propositions make sense; but the requirement that that set of propositions not be 'accidentally' so means that their intelligibility cannot depend on a body of facts.

To extend our analogy with Carrollian nonsense, imagine trying to convince the White King that he is confused. Suppose we say to him, 'Nobody is in the wood behind us'. If that is true, would that mean that Alice was wrong in saying that she saw 'Nobody on the road'? No, because 'Nobody is on the road' would also still be true. So what would our two claims being true reveal? We *might* conclude that Nobody is a very special person: unlike the rest of us, but like some saints apparently,[23] he can be in more than one place at a time. But arriving at such a conclusion might also awaken suspicion that, at some point, we have confused ourselves.

My suggestion, which the next section will explain, is that Wittgenstein's 'deduction' of 'internal properties'—properties that are unlike properties—and 'internal relations'—relations that are unlike relations (4.122)—is meant to perform a similar signalling function. The ultimate point of 'deducing' such claims is not to tell us how the things in question are related—how matters stand with the supposedly intelligible issues under consideration—but to reveal confusions that make us think that we have got a hold of intelligible issues, about these 'things' being 'related' in any way or indeed 'not related' at all. Building on my discussion of elucidation, I will suggest that such assertions are part of an elucidation of nonsense, following through its pseudo-logic and helping us to recognize it as nonsense.

4.9 THE QUESTIONABLE STATUS OF ASSERTIONS ABOUT INTERNAL RELATIONS

But what reasons are there for thinking that the *Tractatus*'s assertions that invoke internal relations and internal properties are indeed moves *within* confused thinking? The concluding sections of this chapter will set out my answer to that question. (In what follows, I take the points I make about 'internal relations' to hold also of 'internal properties', and vice versa.)

It is deeply implausible to think that when, in 6.54, Wittgenstein declares that 'my propositions' are nonsensical, he means every proposition in the book. Hacker has argued that resolute approaches to the *Tractatus* face a peculiar problem here, that such approaches 'cherry-pick' some propositions of the book as to be 'thrown away' while treating others as straightforwardly meant, and that this 'cherry-picking' is somehow problematic (2000, p. 360). But it seems to me that *any* interpretation that takes some of the book's propositions as nonsensical will

---

[23] On the phenomenon of 'bilocation', cf. Gray 2004.

have to make such choices, because some of the *Tractatus*'s claims seem to be straightforwardly empirical,[24] and no commentator has suggested that Wittgenstein saw claims of that kind as nonsensical.[25]

So some kind of distinction must be drawn. Hacker himself seems to draw such a distinction, and to some extent, I would endorse the way he draws it: I think he is right that the propositions that invoke internal relations are central cases of those that are to be 'thrown away'. But I will argue that his reasons for coming to this conclusion are the wrong reasons.

Hacker argues that, in 'exclud[ing] ascriptions of internal properties and relations from well-formed propositions with a sense', Wittgenstein 'rel[ies] upon the principle of bipolarity' (2001*a*, p. 19). This is the proposal 'that it is of the essence of a proposition with sense ... to be capable of being true *and* capable of being false' (p. 16; cf. also, e.g., 1996*b*, p. 28, and 2000, p. 355). Hacker's view here strikes me as problematic. The bipolarity principle is a cataclysmic claim for philosophers to accept, since, if one accepts it, one must immediately rule out the possibility of necessary truth and necessary falsehood,[26] the specific forms of truth and falsehood that philosophers have taken to distinguish their professional area of interest. Presented with a principle that rules out such forms, it must surely be tempting for philosophers to think, 'So much the worse for that principle'.[27] If such a dismissal is to be avoided, the bipolarity principle had better be well-grounded. But according to Hacker, the principle 'was rooted in *Wesensschau*' (1996*a*, p. 19), an intuition about the essence of propositions and what they represent. Setting aside the obvious worry that what we intuit here is itself presumably a necessary truth, and hence not bipolar, on Hacker's construal, one has been given the core of Wittgenstein's case for perhaps his most distinctive and most contentious claim—that philosophical claims are nonsensical—when one has been presented with the seemingly question-begging bipolarity principle and invited to experience the intuition that that principle is true. This seems implausible.[28] I will offer a different interpretation.

[24] Cf., e.g., the first sentence of 3.031, the second sentence of 3.323, the second sentence of 4.002, the first paragraph of 4.003, and the third and the last two sentences of 5.02.

[25] Sects. 10.2–10.3 will comment on why, on my broadly resolute reading, it is perfectly natural for nonsensical elucidations to be interwoven with perfectly 'sensical' observations.

[26] Cf. Hacker 2001*a*, p. 27.

[27] In his 2001*a*, Hacker acknowledges that if we are to be persuaded that the bipolarity principle does reveal necessary truths to be 'illegitimate pseudo-propositions', rather than their 'simply [being] counter-examples to the bipolarity principle, [then] reasons must be given for their illegitimacy' (p. 18). But in the next-but-one paragraph in which we are told to expect to find a reason why ascriptions of internal relations are not 'simply counter-examples', I can find no reason given other than the bipolarity principle itself.

[28] It is true that this is not the whole case as Hacker understands it: e.g., the *Tractatus*'s account of logical truths and logical falsehoods shows that the impression that they constitute counter-examples to that principle is only superficial. The crucial cases that remain, however, are philosophical propositions; Hacker tells us that these attempt to say what can only be shown; but the reason he gives for why the matters in question cannot be said is, again, the bipolarity principle.

If, as I have suggested, our arrival at 'internal relation' assertions is meant to signal to us that all is not quite well with our thinking, then we would have to believe that all is not quite well with such assertions. At *TLP* 4.122, Wittgenstein defines 'internal relations' through a contrast with 'proper (external) relations'; so what is 'improper' about 'internal relations'? I will pick out five considerations that suggest that Wittgenstein's remarks about 'internal relations' are problematic, that they are, as it were, asking to be 'thrown away'.[29]

The first two we have already met in Section 3.4: the arguments set out in Sections 3.1–3.3 turn on the notion that there are, so to speak, no more propositions left using which the holding of internal relations could, in principle, be expressed, and there is something misleading in the image of the holding of an internal relation as something expressible through a statement *about* the relata and the relation, since one has no grasp of the relata or relation, nor indeed of the sense of the 'assertion' that those relata are so related, if one has not already recognized the 'truth' of this 'assertion'. Section 3.4 discussed these considerations as possible grounds for thinking that the holding of internal relations must 'show itself'. I want to suggest instead that they also provide grounds for thinking that, in reaching these 'conclusions', our thinking has somehow gone awry. To take the first, let us simply remind ourselves that the *Tractatus* itself seems to *state* these 'facts' for the stating of which there are supposedly no more propositions. The second requires that one is confused if one thinks that one knows what objects, say, are *and then* learns from Wittgenstein that they are internally related to the facts in which they can figure; what is problematic about that is that this is indeed, I think, how we do initially read the remarks in question, as *telling us something about* objects; we take ourselves to have already some rough sense of what those are.

---

[29] Conant resists the idea that one can give a criterion by reference to which one can declare certain propositions *unsinnig* (2000, pp. 216–17): on the face of it, the austere conception of nonsense alone implies that one cannot be given a reason why propositions of a particular form—say, 'those that assert that something possesses an internal property'—are nonsensical, because that would require that one be able to identify what such a proposition says in order to then rule it out as lacking sense. Conant goes on to suggest that the status of a remark in the *Tractatus* depends on 'the sort(s) of aspects it presents to [the reader], and that will depend on *her*—on the use(s) to which she is drawn to put it in the course of her ascent [of the ladder]' (p. 217). This strikes me as only a half-truth. Certainly, one cannot declare that a *sentence* is in itself *unsinnig* or not because as a mere sign—'the sign is arbitrary'—it can always be assigned a sense. But we can say something about how particular remarks are designed to explore, and perhaps invite us further into, what are, in fact, confusions; the considerations I am about to offer above are reasons for thinking that this is what Wittgenstein's remarks about 'internal relations' do. Now the effect that such remarks can have (and can be expected by Wittgenstein to have) depends upon their reader being able to follow the pseudo-logic that they articulate and being susceptible to the sign/symbol confusions thus elucidated; what this requires is that the reader speak a certain language with particular sign/symbol associations. (Cf. Sect. 10.4 for further discussion of this point.) But insisting on the kind of radical relativity of the status of Tractarian remarks to particular readers, upon which Conant wants to insist, strikes me, following up on my analogy with Carroll, as analogous to insisting that one cannot say which passages of the *Alice* books are meant to be funny because, in other languages, those same sentences could be used to express other, unfunny thoughts.

The third consideration is a historical one: Wittgenstein was working in a philosophical climate in which the notion of 'internal relations' was being criticized on all sides. An important feature of the break that Moore and Russell attempted to make from their idealist predecessors was a disagreement over the nature of relations. In the course of that controversy, Moore offered in *Principia Ethica* (which we know Wittgenstein read at least in part (*CL* 13)) an argument concerning 'organic wholes' that was intended to undermine the notion of 'internal relations':

When we think of the part *itself*, we mean just *that which* we assert, in this case, to *have* the predicate that it is part of the whole; and the mere assertion that *it* is a part of the whole involves that it should itself be distinct from that which we assert of it. Otherwise we contradict ourselves since we assert that, not *it*, but something else—namely it together with that which we assert of it—has the predicate which we assert of it. (G. E. Moore 1903, p. 33)

Quite what the import of this argument is, is not a straightforward matter,[30] though its guiding thought overlaps, I am sure, the thoughts I set out below; I cite it here simply to show that doubts about whether one can make sense of the notion of an internal relation would have been familiar to Wittgenstein. Indeed, these were shared by the idealists whom Moore took himself, in advancing this argument, to be criticizing. Bradley, for example, denied the reality of *all* relations, internal and external.[31] What sympathy he had for talk of internal relations—they are 'truer by far than "external" relations' (1914, p. 312)—lay in their *manifest* instability: 'internal relations . . . point towards a higher consummation beyond themselves' (pp. 239–40), a 'pointing' to which I will return.

Our fourth consideration turns, like the second above and the fifth to come, on how Wittgenstein himself defines internal relations, as those in which it is 'unthinkable' their relata might not stand (4.123): the very idiom of 'object', 'property', and 'relation' seems to impose upon its subject-matter a 'logical space' with which *internal* properties and *internal* relations are incompatible: so, for example, what 'the relation' giveth, the qualifying 'internal' taketh away. Wittgenstein observes:

Here to the shifting use of the words 'property' and 'relation' there corresponds the shifting use of the word 'object'. (4.123)

One might gloss a claim like 'Object *a* has property *p*' as saying that the possibility that *a* might not have *p* is not realized. But when *p* is an internal property of *a*, 'Object *a* has property *p*' cannot be understood as saying that 'the possibility that *a* might not have *p* is not realized' because *there is no such other possibility*. To say that it is raining is to deny that it is not raining. But when *p* is an

---

[30] Cf. Baldwin 1990, pp. 23–4; Hylton 1990, pp. 122–3.
[31] Cf. Bradley 1897, p. 513, and 1914, pp. 239–40.

internal property of *a*, 'Object *a* has property *p*' does *not* deny that 'Object *a* does not have property *p*', because the latter 'sentence' makes no sense. (As Sect. 2.7 discussed, 'logical truths' have the same puzzling feature.)

Finally, and perhaps most importantly, 4.123's definition uses the notion of the 'unthinkable' in a now familiarly problematic way: we are *told what* is 'unthinkable': namely, that the relata of such a relation might not stand in that relation to one another (4.123). Similarly, what one is saying when one says that a property is 'internal' is that something makes no sense: *namely* (!), its bearer lacking that property. At 3.031, we read: 'The truth is, we could not say of an "unlogical" world how it would look.' But if that is so, then we cannot say what it is that a property's being 'internal' rules out; yet it is by reference to what is ruled out that this 'internal property' has been defined: to grasp the 'internality' of a property is to grasp that a particular state of affairs—that in which the bearer does not bear that property—is ungraspable.

So what is someone who, like Wittgenstein, asserts the holding of an internal relation doing? I will develop a proposal that emerges from our second and third considerations, that such assertions would represent an item of news for the confused: the person who hears an 'internal relation' assertion as telling him something has to be confused, and that is what someone who asserts such assertions is getting at.[32] These assertions are moves *within* a person's confusion, Carrollian elaborations or elucidations of those confusions designed to draw that person's attention to those confusions as such.

4.10 THE ASSERTION OF THE HOLDING OF INTERNAL RELATIONS AS A MOVE WITHIN CONFUSIONS

Consider some examples of what I want to suggest the assertion of the holding of internal relations might be like. In the *Wizard of Oz*, the Straw Man imagines being able to tell us 'why the ocean's near the shore'. Is there something here that he needs to learn? There is, but it is not what he thinks it is. What he really needs to learn—what 'getting a brain' might let him see—is that there isn't a why—and not because it's a *mystery* or because the ocean sometimes *isn't* near the shore! Consider the 'researcher' who, having spent many hours down by the track investigating why it is that the Russians so often win a race, goes on to try to answer using the same methods the similar-sounding question, 'Why does the person who crosses the line first *always* win?'[33] Finally, a similar example from Searle:

[32] There is a sense in which someone who was not themselves confused might 'learn from the assertion of an internal relation': what they would learn, though, would be something about how people can be confused. They would learn not 'what the assertion says', but of a confusion to which it stands as a response (not a question to which it stands as an answer). They might say: 'I hadn't thought of people confusing themselves in that way.'

[33] In McManus 2004a I develop this example further.

If you are told that a scientific study has shown that touchdowns actually only count 5.999999999 points, you know that somebody is seriously confused. (1992, p. 62)

It would be misleading to say that the confusion here is that the 'scientists' in question got the wrong answer; rather, they have confused themselves into imagining that there is a question here that might be answered scientifically; not that it is somehow *beyond* the powers of science to understand 'such matters'; rather, one might instead say that there are no 'such matters', because the 'issue' that our 'scientists' wish to explore is itself unreal: it—and they—are confused. One might imagine someone arriving at the answer, 'On average, 30', to the question, 'How many points do New England score each time Tom Brady plays?'. But that does not mean that there is a comparable issue to be investigated expressed by the similar-sounding sentence, 'How many points do New England score each time they score a touchdown?'

One might say that our 'scientists' have mistakenly taken the relation between scoring a touchdown and getting six points as an *external* relation. One might then correct them by saying that that relation is instead an internal one. But they (and we) must take such an assertion in the right way: to understand the point of asserting the 'holding' of this 'internal relation' is to be able to see the confusion to which this assertion responds. Otherwise such an assertion may suggest that the scientists have answered a question incorrectly, that the wrong answer is that a particular external relation holds when the right answer is that a particular internal relation holds. But their root problem is their asking their question in the first place. They need to learn not 'how things are' (externally *or* internally, one might say), but how a misunderstanding brought them to imagine that they dimly saw 'how things are', a matter on which one might hold views, correct or incorrect. And the assertion that these matters are 'internally related' is first and foremost not a statement about 'how the things in question are', but an indication of a confusion on the part of the person who wants to know.

My proposal does not presuppose that a sensible question must be a scientific question or a question of contingent fact. What is crucial to my proposal is that those who might be addressed by asserting that an internal relation holds have *conflated* questions of different kinds. Relatedly, one might well say that it is a matter of external relation that a touchdown is worth six points, because the rule might be changed to make them worth more or less. But Searle's 'scientists' are confused, in that when they consider 'the possibility that a touchdown might not be worth six points', they imagine something changing on the field of play, not in the rule book, something that players might bring about, rather than administrators. Inasmuch as there are views one could hold on an issue that might be expressed in the same terms, Searle's 'scientists' do not recognize the *kind* of views they are. There is certainly nothing nonsensical about 'investigating', 'making discoveries about', or 'stating' the rules of a game; the confusion of Searle's 'scientists' is that they don't realize that this is, at best, what they are doing. One might say that 'what they need to learn' lies not out on the football field but in the rule book; but it is the nature of their confusion that they would regard anything that one might find in the rule book as simply irrelevant to their issue (just as, to anticipate a little, philosophers who puzzle over metaphysical issues would never take 'what they need to learn' to lie in the ways we use words). What Searle's 'scientists' really need to learn is that and how they are confused. Going by their confused understanding of what an 'answer' to their 'question' looks like, might be arrived at and defended, there is no 'answer'; nor does our supposed 'answer' (invoking 'internal relations') answer that 'question'.[34]

The next chapter begins the process of showing how this understanding of what someone might be doing in asserting the holding of internal relations can be applied to the author of the *Tractatus*.

---

[34] My examples might be seen as conflating rules with facts; but there is a corresponding possibility that one might mistake a fact for a rule: imagine someone emerging from confusion with the words 'Oh, I thought referees weren't *allowed* to award penalties against Manchester United!'

5

The Picture Analogy

The solution of philosophical problems can be compared with a gift in a fairy tale: in the magic castle it appears enchanted and if you look at it outside in daylight it is nothing but an ordinary bit of iron.

(*CV* 13–14 (1931))

As his initial remarks on objects and facts come to a close, Wittgenstein declares: '[w]e make to ourselves pictures of facts' (2.1). Subsumed by this claim is another, which has been taken as the basis of a 'picture theory of the proposition': '[t]he proposition is a picture of reality' (4.01). Prima facie, such a theory is not very appealing. If we are puzzled by how language represents, will our puzzles be solved by the proposal that language represents in the same way that pictures represent? There are two obvious objections. First of all, how alike are linguistic and pictorial representation anyway? Secondly, and more worryingly, how does pictorial representation work in the first place? Pictorial representation is not philosophically unproblematic either, facing problems that parallel those concerning linguistic representation that may initially have inspired hope for 'a picture theory of representation'. If so, Wittgenstein may simply seem to be seeking to assimilate one problematic form of representation to another.[1]

Ascribing a 'picture theory' of representation to the *Tractatus* is, I believe, a mistake anyway. My view is that Wittgenstein uses the analogy between pictures and propositions not as part of an explanation of how meaning or thought is possible, but rather in questioning whether we have assigned sense to that very 'possibility', whether we really understand what it is that we think needs to be 'accounted for' here, the supposed philosophical problem that needs to be 'solved'. By thinking through the analogy, we will see emerge some of the internal relations whose deduction in the *Tractatus* Chapter 3 explained. But as the oxymoronic quality of 'internal relation' suggests, we need to see beyond these claims; the picture analogy also helps us to do that, and thus to see what this 'seeing beyond' amounts to. What we see is our confusion in believing that we have assigned a sense to the idea of representation 'being possible' in the first place, as well as the sign/symbol conflations that create that confusion.

---

[1] These general remarks cannot, and are not meant to, substitute for a proper evaluation of 'picture theories' that have been ascribed to the *Tractatus*; that is a task for another occasion.

5.1 PICTURES AND THEIR PARTS

Wittgenstein reported that the picture analogy came to him when reading about how a car crash had been represented in a Parisian court room using dolls and toy cars.[2] What is immediately striking about this is that such a representation is not what most people would immediately think of as an example of a picture. This same predilection for, instead, the image of a model can be found in the *Tractatus*:

The essential nature of the propositional sign becomes very clear when we imagine it made up of spatial objects (such as tables, chairs, books) instead of written signs.
    The mutual spatial position of these things then expresses the sense of the proposition. (3.1431)

The model envisaged here is even less 'picture-like', in that its 'elements' are physically or visually dissimilar to what they are to represent. The German word translated as 'picture' is '*Bild*', which is used of both pictures and models; but it is difficult to make much of this fact (for instance, by suggesting that 'model' might be a better translation), since Wittgenstein himself endorsed the Ogden translation, and there seems no reason to think that he did so as a result of a poor grasp of English. Nevertheless, I will argue that there is much to be learnt by following the detail of Wittgenstein's advice.

    Let us consider how one might represent a road accident on a kitchen table, with cups, napkins, and a pepper-pot. Let us imagine the roads are represented by folded napkins, the cars involved by cups, and the unfortunate pedestrian, who I will call 'Frank', by the pepper-pot. Consider first what we must have understood to have grasped what each element represents. To grasp how the pepper-pot can represent a person is to grasp how moving it here and there upon the table, into different places relative to the napkins and the cups, is to describe different things that can have happened to that person: for example, to see how the pepper-pot's movement across this napkin is the person's crossing a road.

    Note what is involved in this achievement: to grasp how this particular 'name' represents is to see how other 'names' represent. To understand what the pepper-pot represents is to see how it can be used in telling stories in which cups represent cars and napkins represent roads. Note also how the analogy presents the project of 'constructing a proposition'. In particular, note that we do not construct the proposition out of already understood elements; rather, we understand the elements when we understand how they can be used to construct propositions. To see this pepper-pot as this person is to see it as used in a context that will itself have meaning and will be populated by other entities having meaning—a context which is here a particular range of spatial locations and the other entities

[2] Cf. von Wright 1954, p. 8, and *NB* 7.

being cars and roads. We may say, 'Let's say that this is Frank, that cup is Bert's car, this cup is . . .'. But we do not first grasp that the pepper-pot is Frank, then that the cup is a car, etc., and then finally grasp how they can be used to tell stories about Frank, a car, etc. We do not understand how indeed 'this' 'is Frank' until we see how 'this' and 'that' will be used to tell stories about Frank and Bert's car, how this combination of kitchenalia can be the car, the road, the traffic lights, etc., how the movement of the pepper-pot across the napkin can be Frank crossing the road (as opposed to the rise of a stock price or a gas's density increasing, say, which that same movement of that same pepper-pot could represent in a different system of representation).

Imagine what it would be like to be told, having been presented with the pepper-pot, that 'This is Frank', followed by . . . nothing. There is no further 'This is Bert's car, this is the red car, and . . .' Instead we are simply told 'This is Frank'. Now what are we in a position to do? We can't *place* Frank anyway, because no system for representing location has been explained to us. But neither has any system for explaining *any* 'logical space' (age, star sign, favourite holiday venue, etc., etc.). In other words, there is nothing for us to say about Frank. We find ourselves wondering not so much what to do with our new 'sign', but more what it was that the person we took to be explaining a new sign was trying to do.[3]

This dependence of the representational characteristics of a name on its place within articulated propositions which draw on other names can also be seen in conventional, 'representational' pictures. Suppose one finds a piece of paper on which is drawn a picture of a cat next to a dog. Note straight away that this very description already prejudges many issues: one is that this is a picture of a-cat-next-to-a-dog, as opposed to a-picture-of-a-cat next to a-picture-of-a-dog: Are we looking at a picture of two animals, or two separate pictures, each of one animal? Are the cat and the dog meant to be represented as living in the same 'space'? If not, to adapt remarks of Anscombe's about a parallel example, then 'although of course there is a relation between [these two figures] — they are, say, a certain distance apart on a single leaf — this relation is non-significant' (Anscombe 1959, p. 67);[4] for example, the dog cannot step in front of the cat. What we see here is that how the particular part of the picture represents depends on how it relates to

---

[3] Cf. Anscombe 1959, pp. 66–7: 'Suppose I said: "That door stands for Dante and that table for Bertrand Russell". My audience would, if anything, look at me enquiringly and say: "Well?" And here "Well?" means "Do something to shew the point of this"; and *that* means "Let something else come into such a relationship with this door, or again with this table, that the terms in relation represent something." We could say: "Only in the connections that make up the picture can the elements of the picture stand for objects." ' Cf. also *NB* 9: '[H]ow CAN a SINGLE *word* be true or false? At any rate it cannot express the *thought* that agrees or does not agree with reality. That *must* be articulated.'

[4] Similarly, when I attempt to introduce a sign by picking up the pepper-pot and saying 'This is Frank', the pupil must understand which aspect of this object symbolizes and which aspects don't: for instance, that it is this particular pepper-pot that represents Frank, not whatever I happen to have in my hand, not this pepper-pot *when* held at this angle, and not another pepper-pot that someone might put on the table. Sect. 7.1 returns to this topic.

the other representing elements within the picture, including the 'space' within which the part stands (the space itself having a representational job to do), and whether two items even belong to the same picture is something to be resolved by examining how they are used.

Thus the picture analogy makes clear that grasping how one particular name—one particular element of such a picture/model—represents involves grasping how other names represent, along with the propositions within which they figure. To grasp names is to understand how they can be used together in telling stories, and there is no prior grasp of any of these distinguishable facets of our story-telling. In other words, we have seen a truth in (N-P). But the picture analogy also helps us to see how we must now look beyond this 'internal relation', as the next section will explain.[5]

5.2 'THE ILLOGICAL'

Logic *precedes* every experience—that something is *so*.
It is before the How, not before the What.

(5.552)

Seven is darker than your hat. Whatever the preceding string of signs amounts to, we can recognize that it causes us problems that the following does not: Your coat is darker than your hat. One way to characterize the difference is to say that the latter expresses a logical possibility, while the former does not: your coat may or may not be darker than your hat, but seven could not be darker than, as dark as, or lighter than, your hat. As the history of logic illustrates, one could elaborate this proposal in different ways, for example, as a remark about a set of entities, saying of them that they cannot be combined to make up a state of affairs in the way suggested, or as a remark about a set of ideas and the thoughts which they can be combined to form. But why can't these entities or ideas be so combined? What looms now is a body of facts about the possible combination of these elements: certain elements can 'fit together', whereas others cannot, resulting in certain combinations being possible, and certain others impossible. Moreover, we know something else about these supposed bodies of fact: what they identify must be *internal* properties of the elements in question, since it is not that it just *happens* to be the case that seven could not be darker than, as dark as, or lighter than, your hat, though things could have been otherwise. The facts that we postulate, these laws of logic, are, then, not merely natural laws.

[5] As the quotations given from Anscombe (including that in n. 3) show, there certainly are 'non-resolute' readers of the *Tractatus* who would agree with much of my exposition of the picture analogy thus far. It is from here on that dissent might be expected to emerge.

The picture analogy throws into question the line of thought set out in the preceding paragraph. The picture analogy's exposure of the 'claim' of (N-P) also exposes what one might call 'the myth of the independent life of names'; in doing so, it casts a new light on the idea of 'laws of logic', the domain of quasi-facts whose pursuit motivates our interest in 'how names can be combined'.

To see this, consider 'where' 'the illogical' might be thought to be found in the model described above, what an 'illogical claim' 'made' using the elements of that model might look like. Consider what we would say if, for example, the pepper-pot were picked up and put back in the cupboard. What, one might ask, would this say of Frank now? Only if we understand what the cupboard and the pepper-pot's being placed inside the cupboard are to represent, do we have any sense of what would then be being said about Frank, and indeed whether this pepper-pot is still representing Frank, instead of representing something else or nothing at all. Or suppose someone said 'What if *this* happens?' and placed two napkins on top of each other. What is the force of our saying now 'That cannot happen'? The answer that the picture analogy suggests is not that the presented state of affairs is physically or logically impossible (or indeed unthinkable or indescribable). Rather, the response that comes to mind is: 'Well, what is that meant to repre-sent?' We do not judge 'this'—'this' referring to 'the depicted situation'—to be physically or logically impossible; rather, we wonder what 'this'—'this' referring to this combination of signs—is meant to mean, what situation this arrangement is meant to depict. Prior to the envisaged question, 'Is this logically possible?', is the question, 'What is *this* meant to be?' Prior to our philosophical 'How?' question is a sobering 'What?' question.

What the picture analogy serves to remind us of here is that our signs have as much life as our use of them gives them. But when the elements of our repres-entation are familiar words or elements which, as in conventional, non-abstract pictures, have some visual similarity to what they represent, it is easier to fall into thinking of such elements as possessing lives of their own, as it were. We may then arrange them in ways that are expressive within other, but superficially similar, actual or possible modes of representation, and then ask 'Is this logically possible?', untroubled by the prior question of whether 'this' has been assigned a sense. The philosopher's 'possibility' question need not then be expressive of an unusual but admirable rigour or imagination. Rather, to come to understand the signs is to understand which aspects of them and their combinations represent, *and* which do not, which are, to use Wittgenstein's terms, their 'essential' features and their 'accidental' features (3.34). To understand this is not to be tempted by the philosopher's question.

If we fail to be clear about which systems of representation are in play—if we unwittingly switch from seeing a sign as expressing at one moment one symbol and at another moment another—then we may come to 'see' 'new (impossible) possibilities' lying 'around', so to speak, the things we do (as we confusedly come to think of it) happen to say, among which we may find 'possibilities' that we would feel forced to say are '*impossible* possibilities'. If we placed two napkins on top of each other and were tempted by the question, 'Might what these things represent really happen?', the picture analogy reminds us that we would first need to ask: 'But what do "these things" represent?' We *might* perhaps be envisaging a landslide: landslides are not physically impossible, and it's unclear why one might say that they were logically impossible. We might be representing how roads from a millennium ago map on to existing roads, showing in this particular case that there was a road then that followed the same course as a road does now. But the physical or logical possibility of landslides or of roads being destroyed, maintained, or rebuilt is not the reason why we might 'allow this proposition'. We 'allow' it when we can see a new way in which our signs could be used. It is not that we have seen that the 'this' of 'What if this happens?' makes sense; we haven't evaluated a 'candidate possibility', and declared it a 'possible possibility' rather than an 'impossible possibility'. The relevant insight is not into the state of affairs that the combination of signs represents—initially we don't understand it as representing *anything*—but into how that combination of signs can be used to represent some state of affairs.

Thus, the picture analogy helps us to see that 'illogical combinations' (putting a cup under a napkin, or two napkins on top of each other) are problematic just because we haven't given those combinations any sense yet, any role to play in our systems of representation: 'because *we* have not made an arbitrary specification, NOT because [such] a sign is, shall we say, illegitimate in itself!' (*NB* 1).[6] To take these combinations as 'logical impossibilities' presupposes our first knowing what these combinations of elements would represent, and then realizing that these states of affairs are logically impossible. The picture analogy suggests that this is confused, and that we are discovering not new possibilities for the world, or 'impossible possibilities'—which we had hitherto ignored or somehow ruled out—but 'dead space' within our forms of representation which, nevertheless, looks superficially like 'live space'.

We may hear such failures to say something in several different ways, of which I will mention three. First, if, having arranged elements in a way which does not say anything within our system of representation (but perhaps could in some other), someone still in the midst of learning our system asks, 'So what does this say?', we would hear that question as an indication that he has not yet mastered that system. Secondly, we can hear these 'sentences' as *jokes*: a (coarser) Lewis Carroll knocks over the pepper-pot, points to the spilt pepper, and shouts, 'Oh, how disgusting! Frank's been sick!' Or compare the following passage from Flann O'Brien, reminiscent of the moving napkins in our kitchen table example:

---

6 Cf. *TLP* 5.473. This is also a point of continuity with Wittgenstein's later thought; cf. *PI* §500: 'When a sentence is called senseless, it is not as it were its sense that is senseless. But a combination of words is being excluded from the language, withdrawn from circulation.'

Ahead of us went the road, running swiftly across the flat land and pausing slightly to climb slowly up a hill that was waiting for it in a place where there was tall grass, grey boulders and rank stunted trees. (O'Brien 1988, pp. 88–9)[7]

But there is also a third possibility, which Wittgenstein sets out in a 1931 remark:

Philosophers often behave like little children who scribble some marks on a piece of paper at random and then ask the grown-up 'What's that?'—It happened like this: the grown-up had drawn pictures for the child several times and said: 'this is a man', 'this is a house', etc. And then the child makes some marks too and asks: what's *this* then? (*CV* 24)

For Wittgenstein, allowing signs a life of their own provides us with the method of formulating philosophy's problems, their *Fragestellung*; such sign/symbol confusions are the 'fundamental confusions' of which philosophy is 'full' (3.324). In its full, unconscious development, the philosophical error asks not 'What does that say?', but 'Might that happen?', followed by 'Why not?' and 'How do you know?' In some cases, the joke is obvious, as when someone, on hearing that Frank left with haste and with the money in his bag, asks whether his haste was in the bag too. But then there are cases that we don't regard as jokes and which perplex us, such as the possibility of reversing the flow of time: time flows, and so do rivers; one can reverse the flow of a river; so might the flow of time reverse?[8] For the early Wittgenstein, this kind of word-play, when enacted unwittingly—in other words, when words play tricks *on us*—is the way in which we endow metaphysical claims with pseudo-content. I explore this possibility in detail throughout the rest of the book.

5.3 'THE LOGICAL'

Following through Wittgenstein's picture analogy, 'the illogical possibilities' that perplex and worry philosophers emerge as mirages. The fence we thought we were interested in identifying and understanding fences off nothing; 'the laws of logic' hold back nothing at all, in that the monsters that dwell beyond them are combinations of signs that do not represent in our systems of representation; to use an expression from his later work, these are merely 'grammatical monsters' (NFL 283). The distinction that troubled us, and that we articulated through an opposition of 'logical' and 'illogical combinations', is at best a misperception of a distinction concerning signs, between those strings of signs that have a sense in a particular system of representation and those that don't. The philosopher who took 'the distinction between the logical and the illogical' to be something that might be explained by constructing a theory about the metaphysics of the objects

---

[7] O'Brien 1988, pp. 83 and 137, presents other examples of Carrollesque sign/symbol play. Another source is the work of Spike Milligan.

[8] Cf. Sect. 6.5.

we talk about or the form that our ideas take now appears like the Straw Man examining the shoreline or Searle's 'scientist' poring over video of football games. The 'danger of falling into illogical thought' is not at all the danger we thought it was, not at all a danger to be addressed in the way the philosopher in us imagines.

That assessment finds expression in Wittgenstein's ambitions for innovations in the notations that we use. The course of action necessary if we are to keep ourselves from talking nonsense is not the formulation of a theory of sense—of how world and language, picture, or thought must be for us to make intelligible claims—but instead the elimination of the source of confusion that can give rise to 'illogical combinations'. That is done by 'employ[ing] a symbolism which excludes them, by not applying the same sign in different symbols and by not applying signs in the same way which signify in different ways' (3.325); in such a symbolism, 'different kinds of symbols . . . *cannot* possibly be substituted in one another's places' (*CL* 25). I will discuss this proposal and its implications in detail in the next chapter.

Though it has often been remarked that the construction of a new notation does not seem to be the philosophical method that the *Tractatus* itself employs,[9] the picture analogy itself works—to help us see the truth and the confusion in (N-P), for example—in a remarkably similar way to that in which the envisaged notation ought to work: it undermines philosophical illusions by 'disenchanting' words. By asking us to think about models that are 'made up of spatial objects (such as tables, chairs, books) instead of written signs', Wittgenstein introduces a (short-lived) 'notational reform' that breaks up the familiar sign/symbol associations upon which our philosophical confusions feed: the 'expressions' used no longer even seem to carry their meanings outside the uses in which they represent in the particular systems of representation in which they figure, and the temptation to see confusing illusions of meaning in non-representing combinations—in 'illogical combinations'—is dissipated. We no longer seek to understand the difference between 'logical impossibilities' (such as 'Seven is darker than your hat') and sentences with sense (like 'My coat is darker than your hat') as that between 'impermissible' and 'permissible' combinations of objects or ideas.

The philosophical reflection in which we have engaged fits several of the claims that Wittgenstein makes for his kind of philosophy. Faced with the philosophical problems in question, what we need is not a theory about what can be said, but clarity about what we are saying: lacking the latter is what leads us to believe that we understand a need for the former. 'The result' of Wittgenstein's philosophy is 'mak[ing] propositions clear'; clarity about what we are saying makes clear in our example where we have strayed into talking nonsense: in this sense, we have 'limit[ed] the unthinkable from within through the thinkable' (4.114). We have engaged in a 'critique of language' (4.0031), not so much in displaying the limit

---

[9] Sect. 10.1 will explore this issue.

of what language *can* do, but rather by getting clear about what it *does* do; this is a delimitation not of thinking as such, but of the 'expression of thoughts', making clear where the signs we use to express thoughts are used without sense; and what is beyond that limit is 'simply nonsense' (*TLP* preface). The next section will explain how our reflection gives sense to the most mysterious of Wittgenstein's metaphilosophical claims, explaining how and why, on my reading, (N-P) constitutes a 'rung' of a 'ladder' that is to be 'climbed' and then 'thrown away'. My proposal is that we should hear that 'claim' as we hear our efforts to 'correct' the Straw Man and Searle's 'scientists'.

5.4 'THROWING AWAY THE LADDER'

On what one might call first reading, the *Tractatus* leads us—on the grounds that there is no logical room, so to speak, for them to be otherwise—to the conclusion that names and propositions are internally related. This conclusion may seem to hold out the promise of contributing to an explanation—in terms of 'how' certain 'internal relations' 'are'—of how and why certain combinations of names yield descriptions of 'logically possible' situations, while others do not: in other words, why the 'logical/illogical' boundary lies where it does, and just what kind of boundary it is. But then we run into 6.54, and we must begin our second reading of the book, one which must make sense of how Wittgenstein's propositions—such as the conclusion ('conclusion'?) that names and propositions are internally related—can be nonsensical.

The preceding sections have shown that the picture analogy, if followed through, helps us to see a truth in the conclusion that we arrived at on first reading—in that there is indeed no sense to the notion of first grasping what a name represents and then learning how that name relates to the propositions in which it figures—but also that when we arrive at such a conclusion—at such an internal relation—we are one step away from recognizing that the questions which it might appear to help answer are pseudo-questions, themselves combinations of signs that merely look like questions, but to which we have not assigned sense.[10] So the picture analogy shows us, for example, that 'the illogical' is a mirage, and that the difference that, on first reading, we may have taken 'internal relations' between name and proposition to explain is a difference between 'the logical' and ... nothing. What initially sounds like an explanation of that difference indicates instead that we did not understand what we were trying to explain. What sounded at first like an answer to our question indicates instead that we don't understand the 'difference' we wanted to explain, and that our 'question' about that 'difference' lacks sense; that 'answer'—these 'internal relations'—can now be discarded along with that 'question'.

[10] To echo Bradley (cf. Sect. 4.9), this is the 'higher consummation' to which these conclusions point.

There is a real enough, but philosophically uninteresting, question of which combinations of signs, as a matter of contingent fact, have sense assigned to them in particular languages, and which do not. For our philosophically interesting 'issue' of 'how names can be combined to form propositions' to emerge, must we then be considering these names as symbols? But the picture analogy shows that such names—names understood as symbols—come into view, and hence our question can seem to have its philosophical sense, only once we have an understanding of how they figure in propositions: 'Names and propositions are internally related,' one might say. But what this indicates is that, on this construal too, our 'question' is confused: here, posing it presupposes its 'answer'. To have identified a name—understood as a symbol—one must already know how it figures in propositions.

Thus the assertion 'Names and propositions are internally related', which at first sounds like an identification of what determines how names can be combined to form propositions, actually indicates why there is no such thing as a philosophically interesting explanation of how names can be combined to form propositions. The impression that there is arises only through confusedly treating these 'names' upon which we are reflecting simultaneously as signs and as symbols: we take the possibility of producing novel combinations of names—understood as *signs*—and the fact that these combinations (of signs) misfire (the fact that they have no role in any of our systems of representation) to show the need for an explanation of how names—understood as *symbols*—can be combined, a need which sets us off in pursuit of, for example, an explanation of what it is about numbers that means that they 'cannot' be darker than, lighter than, or as dark as, physical objects. By conflating our thoughts about two different things that we label in English with the same sign, 'name', we have conjured up philosophical puzzles.

Just as when we point out 'internal relations' to the Straw Man and Searle's 'scientists', Wittgenstein draws our attention to our confusions by leading us to formulations which, in our confusion, we may hear as alternative solutions to the puzzles by which we were perplexed; but they are also formulations which retain an air of the oxymoronic, which, with what remains of our good sense, we can detect. To understand Wittgenstein is to see through his 'alternative solutions' to the confusions that are our puzzles; we can now turn away from those puzzles and 'throw away' what we had taken to be Wittgenstein's 'alternative solutions'.

Sections 4.4–4.5's examples of nonsense suggest that this too is to be expected: there is a clear sense in which successful elucidations of items of nonsense are themselves nonsense. Like the White King's conclusion that 'Nobody walks slower than the Messenger', which we can see as, in recognizable senses, both right and nonsensical, Wittgenstein elucidates nonsense by talking more of what we come to recognize as nonsense, bringing us to what are recognizably the 'right' pseudo-conclusions (such as that names and propositions are 'internally related'), in order to help us discard them along with the explanatory needs they 'meet' (such as explaining the difference between 'the logical' and 'the illogical'). The final step is to recognize that what these 'deductions' elucidate is confused, and—as 6.54 requires—that they, as elucidations of nonsense, are nonsensical too. In other words, Wittgenstein himself talks nonsense. Unlike the philosopher, however, Wittgenstein knows he is doing it; he is doing it with understanding and at will.

Carrollian nonsense follows out the logic of a confusion, its power to amuse lying in the fact that it does so in ways that we can follow too. But ultimately it is recognizably nonsensical; it is a move within a confused game, a move which amuses us because, for a fraction of a second, it takes us in;[11] when we see that it is nonsense, we laugh; we recognize as mirages the characters—such as the White King's Nobody—that populate Carroll's tales and can see the 'logic' of the sign/symbol conflations by which we were fooled. Similarly, Wittgensteinian nonsense follows out the logic of philosophical confusions, its power to enlighten lying in the fact that it does so in ways that we can follow too. But ultimately it is recognizably nonsensical; it represents moves within already existing, confused, philosophical games; these moves themselves initially take us in as more legitimate moves within those games, and they do indeed correctly follow through the pseudo-logic of those games; but when, shocked by 6.54, we go back through the book to try and see how its own moves could be nonsensical, we see—if we follow the route suggested by Wittgenstein's remarks on nonsense, his invocation of internal properties and internal relations, and his proposed construal of the picture analogy—just how the games that these moves elaborate are confused, and how those moves too are indeed nonsensical. Just as we might try to show the Straw Man that the ocean and the shore are 'internally related', or Searle's confused scientists that scoring a touchdown and getting six points are 'internally related', Wittgenstein, through his own nonsensical elucidations, enters into our confusions to help us see that there is no puzzle of the sort we envisage to be solved. When we recognize this, we learn; we recognize as mirages the characters—such as 'the illogical'—that populate these games and the 'logic' of the sign/symbol conflations which fooled us. At the end of this process, we emerge not with answers to the philosophical questions with which we arrived, but instead with a recognition that those were not real questions after all.

---

[11] Do Carroll's examples really 'take us in'? They do in that only someone who can experience the confusion that they trade on, the feeling for a fraction of a second that some fantastic possibility has been expressed, can 'get' the joke. One would not if, e.g., one's initial reaction was instead: 'The person speaking is producing combinations of words to which no sense has been assigned, although there are some surface-grammatical similarities between those combinations and combinations to which sense has been assigned.' A natural continuation here would be 'Earthlings speak of such empty combinations as "humorous"'.

6

Logical and Ontological Types

This chapter will examine how the insights of Chapter 5 ought to feed back into our understanding of ontology. According to a con-formist conception of intelligibility, the difference between sensical and nonsensical talk lies in a conformity of the former with the world. But the picture analogy suggests that the former distinction is one between signs to which sense has been assigned and signs to which it hasn't; the philosophically interesting distinction, for which a con-formist theory would account, is a myth. How, then, does this insight feed back into our understanding of ontological theories? If they were meant to contribute to a con-formist story by articulating bodies of metaphysical fact that would make possible an explanation of how a particular distinction—the logical/illogical—ought to be drawn, and we then discover that that distinction is confused, it would seem that we have reason to reassess whether we really understand such ontological theories, because it now appears that we don't understand what it is that we want them to do for us here, for example, in substantiating an understanding of intelligibility as con-formity.

6.1 AMBITIONS FOR NOTATION

Russell envisaged Theories of Types as delimiting what *can* be said: one can construct propositions from only certain combinations of types of expression. One can, for example, form a proposition from a referring expression and a predicate, but not from two predicates: 'The King is bald' makes sense, but 'Is bald is fat' doesn't. A body of knowledge seems to loom about which combinations of which types of expression form intelligible propositions. Having explored the picture analogy, suspicion now falls on these images of a fit, of round pegs fitting—and square pegs failing to fit—round holes. In the case of putting names together to form propositions, we have seen how fixing what names represent is one and the same thing as fixing what their arrangement (propositions) represent. One might be tempted to say that we fix the logical form of the parts and the whole all in one go, or that the name's 'logical form' and the proposition's 'logical form' are 'internally related'. But again we can see beyond these oxymoronic formulations. There is no longer any substance to notions of a match between expressions of different 'logical form'. There is no description or explanation to be had of how or why these names *can be* used together to form propositions. Prior to seeing how they 'can be combined', they are mere physical marks, sounds, or tokens. They are a cup, a pepper-pot, and a napkin, which 'can be combined' in any number of ways to say any number of different things.

Efforts to 'draw the bounds of sense', to 'delimit what can be said', heap confusion on confusion. Recall what 'the illogical' has turned out to be: combinations of signs that may look like propositions with sense, but which haven't been given a sense. The danger is not 'ill-formed propositions', expressions combined in ways in which they cannot be 'legitimately combined'. Rather, it is our failure to be clear about when we are using different symbols. We need to make the differences between symbols apparent:

Frege says: Every legitimately constructed proposition must have a sense; and I say: Every possible proposition is legitimately constructed, and if it has no sense this can only be because we have given no *meaning* to some of its constituent parts.

(Even if we believe that we have done so.)

Thus 'Socrates is identical' says nothing, because we have given *no* meaning to the word 'identical' as *adjective*. For when it occurs as the sign of equality it symbolizes in an entirely different way—the symbolizing relation is another—therefore the symbol is in the two cases entirely different; the two symbols have the sign in common with one another only by accident. (5.4733)[1]

To prevent our arriving at 'illogical combinations', we need a symbolism, a notation, which, for example, bars the use of the same sign to express different symbols:

In order to avoid these errors, we must employ a symbolism which excludes them, by not applying the same sign in different symbols and by applying signs in the same way which signify in different ways. (3.325)

Wittgenstein sees the development of such a symbolism as an alternative to the formulation of Theories of Types. In an early letter to Russell, Wittgenstein writes:

[A]ll theory of types must be done away with by a theory of symbolism showing that what seem to be *different kinds of things* are symbolized by different kinds of symbols which *cannot* possibly be substituted in one another's places. (*CL* 25)

That we should simply strive to make more apparent the difference between different symbols, rather than (*per impossibile*) stating *what* the difference between the symbols is (for instance, by discussing the different kinds of things to which they refer), helps explain another of Wittgenstein's more obscure critical comments about Russell:

In logical syntax the meaning of a sign ought never to play a role; it must admit of being established without mention being thereby made of the *meaning* of a sign; it ought to presuppose *only* the description of the expressions.

---

[1] Cf. also 3.323.

From this observation we get a further view—into Russell's *Theory of Types*. Russell's error is shown by the fact that in drawing up his symbolic rules he has to speak about the things his signs mean. (3.33–3.331)

The best we can do when 'faced with the illogical' is point out that the combinations of signs in question do not represent anything. This is an utterly different business from that which we might imagine as showing that what these combinations do represent is somehow impossible. These combinations are not distinguished from those that do represent by reference to differences between what these two kinds of combination represent, because the first kind do not represent anything.

If a specification of how an expression can be used is a specification of what it means, there is no room for a body of doctrine about how 'symbols of this type' should be used, and no room for an explanation of the 'facts' that such a doctrine seeks to offer. As early as his notes dictated to Moore, Wittgenstein observes of what he describes as 'the nonsensical assertion', 'Symbols like this are of a certain type':

This you can't say, because in order to say it you must first know what the symbol is; and in knowing this you *see* the type and therefore also [the] type of [what is] symbolised. I.e. in knowing *what* symbolises, you know all that is to be known; you can't *say* anything *about* the symbol. (*NB* 110)[2]

Understanding a particular sign—a cup, say—as representing a car is understanding how moving it here and there upon the table, into different places relative to the napkins and the pepper-pot, is to describe different things that may have happened to that car: its reversing round a corner, stopping at the lights, etc. In other words, saying what you can say with this sign, saying how one can combine it with other signs, is saying what this sign means; saying 'what a sign *can* be used to say' is saying what it *does* say, what the relevant symbol is.[3] If, following our explanation of the above use of the cup, someone says, 'Ah, so you cannot represent how many people are in the car by the level of the tea in it, then?', the appropriate answer is 'Well, it's not that you *can't*, it's just that, in this system, this sign *doesn't* represent that; but you could use this cup in that way if you wanted to represent how many people are in cars.' Hence, 'that which one cannot do' does not represent a limitation on this use of the sign, on the relevant symbol. What we are doing in setting out 'that which one cannot do'—say, by talking

---

[2] Cf. *NB* 109, where Wittgenstein suggests that we replace a statement to the effect that 'this symbol is of this type' by one to the effect that 'this symbolizes and this doesn't'.

[3] Cf. *NB* 130–1: 'You cannot prescribe to a symbol what it *may* be used to express. All that a symbol *can* express, it *may* express.' This is a comment on the following remark made by Russell: 'The theory of types, in my view, is a theory of correct symbolism: a simple symbol must not be used to express anything complex: more generally, a symbol must have the same structure as its meaning.'

about how the level of tea in the cup is not representationally significant—is distinguishing the present use of the sign from *other* uses that one might make of this sign. To specify what one can use signs to say is to specify what they happen to mean; thus to hear 'what one can say with this sign' as a restriction is to be confused: it is to be disappointed over the fact that our word does not . . . mean something else! There are rules that describe which combinations of particular signs in particular systems of representation say something. But 'beyond' those 'restrictions', as the picture analogy shows, we find not 'logical monsters' but the napkins heaped up in a pile, the cups placed in the sink, and the pepper-pot put back in the cupboard. These 'restrictions' give the signs meaning, and when we throw off the rules of that conversation, it is only because it has ended.

6.2 ONTOLOGICAL DISTINCTIONS

The view set out in the previous section is that ontological issues 'emerge' when 'surface grammar' takes an unrecognized hold of our thinking, and that notational reform is needed to close off that road to misunderstanding.[4] The problem could be described as there being two superficially different descriptive 'routes' to one and the same phenomenon—those things that we describe as 'coloured' and those we describe as 'lighter than' or 'darker than' one another. Since the sentence 'Three is darker than four' looks like a grammatical sentence, and our susceptible imagination happily sets us off thinking about whether this (nonsense) might be true or false (while at the same time another part of our mind tells us that this no 'issue' at all), it may seem that the 'connection' between those things that we describe as 'coloured' and those things that we describe as 'lighter than' or 'darker than' one another has some kind of substance: something about the ontology of coloured objects and numbers means that it makes no sense to ask whether three is darker than four. But this 'solution' heaps confusion on confusion. It is not that three being darker than four is logically impossible or unthinkable; rather 'it' is a grammatical monster. It is a piece of dead space in our symbolism that looks like live space. What we need is not an ontology of coloured objects and numbers, but a notation that doesn't allow talk of 'coloured objects' and talk of 'lighter than' and 'darker than' to become detached from one another in a way that the surface grammar of English happens to allow. As a matter of 'mechanical' fact, so to speak, the 'holes' either side of 'darker than' and the terms that refer to coloured objects ought to be so shaped that only the latter terms can fit the former 'holes'.[5], [6]

---

[4] For an earlier discussion of some of these themes, cf. McManus 2002.

[5] Another source of inspiration for belief in logical and ontological types presents them as necessary in explaining the 'scope' of general propositions. Ch. 12 explores how a 'mechanical' dissolution of the apparent reality of types might be extended to deal with this source also.

[6] It is tempting to ask how, without an ontology of colour, one can tell which items are coloured so as to be able to construct one's appropriate notation. Wittgenstein would have two things, I

To echo 6.53, the envisaged replacement of a substantial Theory of Types with a notation that invites fewer confusions arising from superficial similarities between signs will seem unsatisfying to the philosopher in the grip of the powerful and plausible notion that we speak the way we do because this reflects the character of reality and who has sought a view regarding the metaphysical landscape upon which the 'laws of sense' might be imagined to rest. A system in which different symbols are expressed through different signs seems to leave unaddressed the question of what the difference between different symbols consists in. There is a powerful urge to suggest that the difference between symbols of different logical classes lies in their denoting different kinds of thing—names denote objects, predicates denote properties, etc. Are these not explanations, explanations which Wittgenstein appears to have ruled out as impossible? And how could the refinement of our symbolism have anything to do with addressing these issues? Surely that couldn't teach us anything about metaphysics or the philosophy of language. And how can one really deny that we have knowledge of different ontological types: for example, that which we express when we say that 'space' and 'physical objects' are 'different kinds of thing'? To see some plausibility in Wittgenstein's critical proposals, we must ask what the 'knowledge' claimed amounts to.

Let us consider the picture analogy and our kitchen table example again. One might feel the need to be able to explain the different roles played by the different elements in our model on the grounds that they denote different kinds of thing. To make the case striking, let us take the cups and the kitchen table surface itself. The latter (or most of it) plays the role of helping to specify the location of particular objects and particular features of the landscape, whereas the former pick out particular physical objects. Isn't this an example of the kind of explanation ruled out above, an explanation of how names function by reference to the different kinds of thing to which they refer? If we press on, we will see that perhaps it isn't.

A symbol which allows us to describe the spatial location of physical objects seems to represent in a very different way from that in which the name of a physical object represents. But can we say *what* this difference consists in? What we have done so far is merely *note* the difference. What, then, about the difference between the pepper-pot and the cups? The former denotes a person, and the latter, cars. But what is 'the difference' between a car and a person? One might say

think, to say in reply. First, he would see this problem as ultimately unreal, as itself a legacy of confusing notations that conjure up talk of coloured objects and numbers, say, as 'different kinds of things'. This is not to deny, however, that the process of producing an appropriate notation, a process which may demand a good deal of thought, may be hindered by deep-seated philosophical temptations of this form. But it does rule out a certain kind of solution to that problem. Secondly, our capacity to classify things cannot rest ultimately on our applying an ontological theory of what those things are. The application of such a theory would require that we be able to apply its concepts to things without the further mediation of an ontological theory of the things to which those concepts apply; if it did, we would begin an unstoppable regress. Cf. Sect. 8.3.

of the cups and the kitchen surface that physical objects can change their physical locations, whereas it is their relation to physical locations that change when physical objects move. But does this description tell us 'the difference' between these kinds of symbol, or does it merely *reiterate* it? Such an explanation would, after all, seem to draw upon a grasp of the distinction we are trying to draw.[7]

Let us broaden our set of examples. Consider signs that are used to denote a colour, a season, a note, a burial practice, a tree, and a mental activity. Consider now some odd-sounding questions: 'What is the difference between purple and winter?'; 'What is the difference between middle-C and mummification?'; 'What is the difference between an oak and persuasion?' The natural answer to all of these questions is: 'All the difference in the world'. But what is 'the difference' in each case? In particular, can we state the difference without relying on another distinction about which we experience a similar inarticulacy? One might say that purple is a colour, whereas winter is a season. But what is 'the difference' between colours and seasons? One might say that colours are sensory qualities, and seasons are periods of time. But then what is 'the difference' between those yet more general categories? Are we getting any closer to being able to point towards what we would be happy to call 'the difference'? Similarly, one might say that an oak is a plant, whereas persuasion is a mental activity. But what is 'the difference' between plants and mental activities? Do we have a framework within which they represent 'different kinds of thing', different in some determinate, identifiable way?

An obvious problem arises if one believes that there must be 'a difference' to be grasped—something to be thought—whenever a distinction is drawn in thought: that thought will itself draw on further distinctions if, as it must, it depicts things as like this . . . on one side of the distinction to be grounded and like that . . . on the other. Such a second-order framework raises the question of the third-order framework we use to articulate the distinctions on which the second-order framework draws. And must there be a fourth-order framework in which is articulated the distinctions on which the third-order framework draws? Clearly this hierarchy has no end, and if the notion of what it is to grasp a distinction that it invokes is correct, then such a grasp seems to lie at the 'end' of this infinitely extending hierarchy.

The suggestion I have taken from Wittgenstein is that the notion of what it is to grasp a distinction is mistaken, or at least, that in some of the cases in which we are tempted to apply it, we are succumbing to a myth of a kind of self-consciousness. Instead, 'the differences' that we may imagine an ontology articulates arise out of a confused word-play: like the children in *CV* 24 (quoted in Sect. 5.2), we take expressions used in different frameworks, combine them in ways to which none of the frameworks assign sense, and then wonder what we have said using this new combination of signs. Are, then, the 'things' that the

---

[7] Sect. 14.6 discusses how the notion of 'parts of speech' can give rise to an idea of 'logical types'; but it is one which, again, does not yield the philosophical rewards we might seek.

different frameworks pick out different? If one answers 'Yes', one must at least recognize the character of the understanding that one claims for oneself in saying so. In particular, we 'explain' the 'difference' by using one of the frameworks, stopping, and then using the other, not by articulating 'the difference'. What corresponds to ontological insight is a recognition that the questions of 'sameness' and 'difference' have been given no sense; we demonstrate our 'mastery of these differences' not by knowing (however implicitly) the answers to these questions of difference, but by recognizing them as pseudo-questions, dead space 'around' our systems of representation that merely *looks like* live space 'within' one of them. When we reply to these 'questions', 'All the difference in the world', we express not an answer to the question, but bemusement at the questioner's posing of it.

Within our systems of representation, there are combinations of signs that may look like they represent but don't; to treat the latter 'issues' as daft and to be ignored is an aspect of what it is to understand the things we say. Thus it would show a lack of understanding of our kitchen table system of representation, rather than original and audacious insight, to ask our interlocutors 'But what if this had happened?', laying, as we say this, the newspaper on top of the cups. No one had 'considered' that 'possibility', but not through lack of imagination; rather, it was through an understanding of the system of representation, of where it begins and where it ends, as it were. The problematic 'samenesses' and 'differences' we encountered above illustrate, I am suggesting, failure of this same kind of understanding.

6.3 UTTER DIFFERENCES AND 'AN INFALLIBLE PARADIGM OF IDENTITY'

The suggestion that the 'questions' considered are without sense invites some obvious but, I think, flawed, responses which the next two sections will examine. One such response is: 'So you are saying that there's *no* difference between middle-C and mummification? That they're one and the same thing??' This clearly isn't what we want to say either. Our incapacity to find something to say about this supposed 'difference' does not imply that we will feel that there is indeed sense in saying 'there is no difference'. Suggesting that we have nothing to say about 'the difference between an oak and persuasion' does not imply that 'Nothing' is the answer to the question 'What is the difference?'; the framework of 'sameness' *and* 'difference' seems without sense here. No less than any other question we might pose, these questions need a system of representation within which they mean something, and the fact that one can construct a sentence which looks similar to sentences which are meaningful in other systems of representation does not imply that there is some system of representation within which this newly constructed sentence means something.

Accepting an amorphous difference between two kinds of expression does seem more natural than accepting an amorphous sameness. But I would suggest that this reflects another philosophical confusion: namely, that we have a 'context-transcendent' understanding of identity, of sameness, a notion of which Wittgenstein was critical, early and late.

We seem to have an infallible paradigm of identity in the identity of a thing with itself. I feel like saying: "Here at any rate there can't be a variety of interpretations. If you are seeing a thing you are seeing identity too."

Then are two things the same when they are what *one* thing is? And how am I to apply what the *one* thing shows me to the case of two things? (*PI* § 215)

Roughly speaking: to say of *two* things that they are identical is nonsense, and to say of *one* thing that it is identical with itself is to say nothing. (5.5303)

The 'useless proposition', 'A thing is identical with itself', 'is connected with a certain play of the imagination', as if 'we put a thing into its own shape and saw that it fitted' (*PI* § 216). This 'play' provides deceptive comfort when faced with questions about differences where we 'don't know what game [our interlocutor is] playing' (*BB* 134). Our confusion over what 'the difference' is meant to be, coupled with our illusory clarity over 'sameness', leaves us happy to deny sameness when what we thereby assert remains indeterminate.

6.4 SHOWN DIFFERENCES AND INTERNAL RELATIONS

Someone familiar with the *Tractatus* and the history of its interpretation may well suggest one of two further related possible responses that I will address now: first, that these differences are matters of 'internal relation', and secondly, that the problematic differences are shown rather than said.

First let me introduce another kind of example: 'What is the difference between purple and pink?'; 'What is the difference between middle-C and top-C?' What these cases share with the earlier cases is that it is unclear whether one can set out these differences without presupposing an answer to the question we are trying to answer. For example, one might say that top-C is higher than middle-C, but an appreciation of what top-C is would surely presuppose an understanding that it is higher than the likes of middle-C. Saying that middle-C and top-C, for example, are 'internally related' may now seem to articulate a reason why we cannot say what the difference between them is without relying on some other distinction which itself is grasped only by those who grasp, for example, the difference between middle-C and top-C: namely, that to grasp the one is to grasp the other, and we cannot then grasp the difference that 'happens' to distinguish them. Now to say that 'they' are then 'internally related' could be harmless. But it also may tempt us to conclude that we *have* really answered our question, that we have not merely rejected the request for a statement of 'the difference' but *met* it.[8] Similarly, one might say that an oak and persuasion are *in a way* internally related too, inasmuch as a person who might claim to have grasped one must have no tendency to confuse it with the other! But in doing so, *what* has he grasped? 'It' would seem to be expressed not by his having the answers to certain real questions, but by his not putting certain signs together in ways that may *look* like questions but, to which in fact, no sense is assigned. If he wished to articulate 'what he knows', he might say, 'Well, you can say this with this and that with that', but again the listener would 'not have the feeling' that the person was 'teaching him philosophy'.

I allude here to the method that Wittgenstein recommends as what 'would be' the correct method in philosophy (6.53). One would talk about what an oak is and what persuasion is, and hope that this brings the person to see that his was a daft question. This will be 'unsatisfying to the other', as he wouldn't feel as if he were learning an answer to his question, 'that we were teaching him philosophy'. He might well stop one in one's 'explanations' and say, 'Yes, that's all very well, but what *is* the *difference?*' But the point is not to answer his question, but to see that 'he had given no meaning to certain signs in his propositions', in our case, 'the difference between'. I return to these methodological questions (including that of why the *Tractatus* itself does not employ what 'would be the only strictly correct method' of philosophy (6.53)) in Chapter 10.

The second response takes our saying nothing or our rehearsing the mundane things that one can say about oaks and persuasion as revealing that 'the difference' cannot be expressed, that it is there, but beyond our meagre expressive resources, *shown* to us in some sense. But to regard these differences as 'unsayable' is to return to the questions that ask for a statement of these 'differences' a respectability that I hope to have weakened. We may be bounced into insisting on 'differences' between what different kinds of propositions are about, struggle to articulate them, and then declare them to be unsayable. (Remember the reaction, 'What, you are saying there is no difference??') But the fault lies with the 'questions' we find ourselves 'answering'. Faced with these strange questions of 'sameness' and 'difference', we will reach a point at which we just say, 'Don't you see it?'. But this does not show that there *is* an 'it' of which we have a grasp. This response is despair, not an answer; exasperation, not information; a final *uncomprehending* response to a question with which we can do nothing.

---

[8] Compare the following later remarks from *BB* 134 and *PG* 208, respectively: 'Now what should we answer to the question "What do light blue and dark blue have in common?"? At first sight the answer seems obvious: "They are both shades of blue". But this is really a tautology. So let us ask "What do these colours I am pointing to have in common?" (Suppose one is light blue, the other dark blue.) The answer to this really ought to be "I don't know what game you are playing". And it depends upon this game whether I should say that they had anything in common, and what I should say they had in common.' 'When asked "what is the difference between blue and red?" we feel like answering: one is blue and the other is red. But of course that means nothing and in reality what we are thinking of is the distinction between the surfaces or places that have these colours. For otherwise the question makes no sense at all.'

Let us illustrate this response and how it may confuse us. Hacker has claimed that for Wittgenstein, revealing inexpressible, logical distinctions is the job of a *Begriffsschrift*; with 'an adequate conceptual notation', 'what philosophers mis-guidedly endeavour to say will be shown by features of the notation' (1986, p. 22):

When the forms of language are laid bare in a proper conceptual notation, then the essence of the world, which philosophy has always striven to describe, though unutterable, will be lying upon the surface in full view. (p. 24)

A pressing question for Hacker (and, as I indicate below, others too) is: how can a mere notation do this? In particular, the possibility of the 'essence of the world' 'lying upon the surface in full view' would surely depend in large measure on who is doing the viewing. To obtain the insight in question, the viewer needs more than the set of (arbitrary) signs, since, presumably, he also needs to use the notation correctly. If so, this capacity seems to be what matters, and it is not clear why correct use of our ordinary notations would not then 'show logical distinctions' just as well as correct use of a 'proper conceptual notation'. In which case, what contribution does the 'proper conceptual notation' make?

My view, to adapt an expression Wittgenstein uses of proof that a proposition is a tautology or a contradiction, is that the *Begriffsschrift* is a 'mechanical expedient' (6.1263).[9] The 'proper conceptual notation' merely makes it 'mechanically' impossible to formulate 'pseudo-sentences'; but with that view comes a view very different from Hacker's of what ontological distinctions are, and what it is for them to 'show'. From my point of view, ontological distinctions are now shown simply in that 'they' are shown up for what they are: namely, the confused product of word-play. A *Begriffsschrift* can indeed help us, but not, as Hacker would have it, by *showing* rather than saying the differences. Instead, such a notation prevents 'mechanically' the formulation of those meaningless strings of signs which we confusedly come to call 'ontological questions'. In a *Begriffsschrift* in which, for example, quantifiers do not even *look like* proper names, and second-order properties do not even *look like* first-order properties, we would not find ourselves confused into formulating puzzling 'questions' about how 'they' differ. But that does not mean that the *Begriffsschrift* shows us the *answers* to those 'questions'.

My interpretation also seems to differ here from Conant and Diamond's. When Diamond (1991, p. 183) proposes that the *Begriffsschrift* 'make[s] logical similarities and differences clear', or when Conant proposes that '[t]he difference between an ideal logical symbolism and ordinary language, for the *Tractatus*, is

[9] This is not such a way-out view; though he might well not agree with the way in which I have developed it, McGuinness does talk of 'the importance [for Wittgenstein] of finding a formulation for logic in which it would be simply impossible to write down a nonsense ... one in which it would be excluded mechanically' (2002, p. 174). The example from Heal (in n. 12) is also compatible with the view I have offered.

that in the former—unlike the latter—one is able to read the symbol directly off the sign' (2001, p. 45), the question that occurs to me is one analogous to that which I posed to Hacker: how can a symbolism do this? From my perspective, the *Begriffsschrift* prevents the formulation of 'questions' which the identification of 'logical similarities and differences' is thought to answer. These are not questions whose answers must be seen instead of said; rather, they are daft questions, the product of a word-play that the *Begriffsschrift* will prevent.[10] The answer to a daft question, to a pseudo-question, is not unsayable, any more than the 'situation' represented by a 'proposition' to which no sense has been given is logically (or otherwise) impossible. Wittgenstein's suggestion that 'misunderstanding logical distinctions' is something that would be prevented by an improved symbolism can certainly seem philosophically disappointing: to adapt 6.53, we don't have the feeling that this will teach us any philosophy. But this is the way that it should feel: what these differences are has been neither said nor shown; at best, they have been shown up, and we are led away from such talk, from such pseudo-topics.

A certain blunt question no doubt retains some appeal: 'Is your Wittgenstein saying that there are no logical distinctions?' The Wittgenstein I am presenting wants to undermine the way of thinking that presents us with 'logical distinctions' and with the notion of their 'existing' or 'not existing'. In that 'world', for example, does the denial of the existence of logical distinctions make everything 'logically the same'? Clearly not. Rather, these 'samenesses' and 'differences', along with the issue of their 'existence' and 'non-existence', are to be seen through. Denying the reality of 'the illogical' suggests that every proposition 'is logical'—that 'proposition' and 'logicality' are internally related—only as an interim conclusion; the next step is to ask what this 'logicality' amounts to. Similarly, denying logical differences serves not to declare a universal logical monism (as Russell considered at certain times[11]), but to question whether 'logical sameness' and 'logical difference' are clear concepts. To use a formulation I introduced earlier, Wittgenstein wants not to show us what logical distinctions are, but rather to show them up for what they are.

The difference becomes perhaps most vivid if we substitute for our blunt question—the question of whether 'they exist'—the question of what is involved in 'grasping them'. Those who 'know the differences' show this by not posing the problematic 'questions', by knowing that these combinations of signs do not represent in our systems of representation. According to this understanding of 'understanding logical distinctions', those 'with understanding' don't raise the 'questions' which those 'without understanding' do. In this sense, 'logical distinctions' are 'things' which we can only misunderstand. What corresponds to understanding them is seeing through 'them' as grammatical monsters spawned by

---

[10] For this reason, I believe that my view escapes the criticism that Sullivan makes of Diamond (Sullivan 2002, pp. 46–9).

[11] Cf. the discussion of Russell's 'doctrine of the unrestricted variable' in Stevens 2005, chs. 1–2.

particular sign systems which we happen to use merely as a matter of contingent fact. An appropriate notation would allow 'logical distinctions to show themselves', in that they would show themselves not to be obscured by, but instead the very result of, language playing tricks on us.

Perhaps the clearest way of coming to see the mythical character of the kind of 'understanding of logical distinctions' that I have been questioning is to think about the kind of '*mis*understanding' that is being feared. One might panic, for example, and say that no item of knowledge would then protect us from going awry in our thinking about winter and purple. Put bluntly, what we fear here is the possibility that we might come to confuse winter and purple. But do we even know what that would be like? Does this 'possible error' itself have a sense? What, for example, would it be like to '*treat as* purple what is, in fact, winter'? Just as the item of possible knowledge that we believed we understood was a myth, so are the calamities from which we felt it protected us. 'Since there is no fact of the matter about how mummification and middle-C differ, we might end up treating mummification as middle-C!' Just as the antecedent 'refers' to something that merely *sounds like* something we might know (sounding like 'the distance between Southampton and Sunderland'), so the consequent 'refers' to something that merely sounds like something we might mistakenly do (sounds like 'run out of petrol'). Just as certain 'facts' have turned out to be chimeras, so too does what we may have envisaged as 'a proper appreciation of those facts', the species of 'understanding' that those who 'acknowledge' those 'facts' were imagined to possess.

6.5 BORROWING SENSE AND THE *FRAGESTELLUNG* OF PHILOSOPHICAL PROBLEMS

From this perspective, theories of logical or ontological types and descriptions of the logical or ontological landscape are confused pseudo-responses to confused pseudo-questions. That we do not formulate certain seeming claims may not be an indication that we grasp their sense and have judged that what they say is false or incoherent. It may instead express an understanding that the combinations of signs that 'constitute' these 'claims' do not represent in our systems of representation. To combat the temptation to formulate such claims, we want not a demonstration that these 'claims' are false or incoherent, as in both cases the problem is that there is nothing to grasp to then judge in that way. All there is is a combination of signs and our confusion. The best response, according to the early Wittgenstein, is a new set of signs that will not confuse us, one in which, for example, the expressions that denote mental activities, seasons, and plants cannot be substituted for one another in sentences to yield new sentences that still sound grammatically well-formed. In such a symbolism in which mental activities, seasons, and plants do not *sound* like 'different kinds of things', 'what seem [in our ordinary symbolism] to be *different kinds of things* are symbolized [in our ideal symbolism] by different kinds of symbols which *cannot* possibly be substituted in one another's places' (*CL* 25).[12] We would then not formulate these 'problematic claims', wonder about their truth or intelligibility, or construct Theories of Types or other logical or metaphysical doctrines that would account for why 'what they say' is somehow not possible. A 'perfect notation' will 'prevent the formation of such nonsensical constructions' (RLF 171).

But what, then, is happening to us when we feel we do glimpse before our mind's eye 'the difference between an oak and persuasion'? To arrive at one possible answer, note that one might, of course, say something like 'an oak is solid and dependable, whereas persuasion is tricky and manipulative', or that 'purple is warm and luscious, whereas winter is cold and unwelcoming'. Faced with something looking like a question, we have *gone looking for* a sense for it; having given it a sense of sorts, we can provide an answer of sorts. As a result, we may feel as if we are on our way to 'the real answer', an answer to be found at the end of a long process of (possibly philosophical) labour. But what we have done in our two examples is *borrow* sense from elsewhere, using differences between people as a basis for describing the difference between a plant and a mental phenomenon and the difference between embraces to describe the difference between a colour and a season. Borrowing a sense for these words may give us the impression that we have grasped a unique and novel 'issue' here. But still the borrowed sense remains inadequate: if met with the same straight-faced attitude that originally posed the question, 'What's the difference . . . ?', we might hear, 'Oh, so oaks and persuasion are kinds of people!'—which isn't what we meant either. One might still feel compelled to say that, surely, we have identified *some* sort of difference here, because we said *something* when we said that 'an oak is solid and dependable, whereas persuasion is tricky and manipulative'. And surely we did. But to understand the claim in question is to understand that it *is* metaphorical, that there is no matter here about which the 'straight question' that seemed to be posed can be posed or about which there might be a 'straight answer' formulated. We come to understand that our question wasn't the *kind* of question we thought it was.

One obvious response to my earlier remarks about the genesis of metaphysical issues in novel combinations of signs that 'have no sense assigned to them' is that this is how poetic discourse happens: do I want to rule that out? Obviously not. I do not want to explore here the difficult issues in aesthetics that this response raises, including the question of whether such novel combinations 'have no sense' (which seems deeply implausible in the poetic case). But what I will say is that this response would provide no comfort for the vast majority of metaphysicians:

[12] Compare the following example from Heal 1998, sect. 3: '[T]here could be a language in which properties are attributed to people by writing their names in different colours. If, for example, we could claim that Socrates is wise only by writing "Socrates" in red letters then we could never formulate any analogue to " 'is wise' is wise" because we could not take the redness of "Socrates" and make it red.'

for them, the proposal that their mode of thought and talk does have a meaning because it has the kind of meaning that poetry has would be just as maddening and depressing as the proposal that, in that mode, we think and say nothing.

What we feel we need is what we might call a 'neutral' framework of similarities and differences: one which is not constituted by the similarities and differences between colours, those between seasons, those between mental activities or any of the other 'spheres' we wish to understand. What we seek are *just* similarities and differences. The Wittgensteinian perspective developed here suggests that we 'derive' these neutral distinctions by *unwittingly* borrowing sense. We look at one sphere through an analogy with another and, crucially, do so without realizing it. In various respects the analogy will not carry over, and here we 'find' the neutral, ontological distinctions that characterize different spheres of being. Time and its ontology provide an example.

The puzzles about time are due to the analogy between time and motion. There is an analogy, but we press it too far; we are tempted by it to talk nonsense. We say time 'flows', and then ask where to and where from, and so on. (*L I* 60)[13]

Similarly, philosophical problems have arisen because '[m]emories have been called pictures'. I can go and check a picture against its original in order to confirm its accuracy, '[b]ut can I go into the past?' (*VC* 48). We conclude that 'I can *merely* remember', '[a]s if there were some other way and memory not the *only* source from which we draw' (*VC* 48). Through this crossing of frameworks, 'statements which previously had had a sense now lose it and others which had had no sense in the first way of speaking now acquire one' (*PR* 267). We glimpse here a new sphere of truths which ordinary conversation never broaches: 'it is as if we had now seen something lying *beneath* the surface' (*Z* § 444). Here philosophy's essential, ontological truths emerge, unrecognized analogies providing the very substance of philosophical dispute: 'the method of formulating [*die Fragestellung*]' the problems of philosophy 'rests on the misunderstanding of the logic of our language' (*TLP* preface). In philosophizing, we encounter, then, not facts, not even unsayable facts, but rather pseudo-claims, answering 'questions' 'of the same kind as the question whether the Good is more or less identical than the Beautiful' (4.003). As pseudo-claims, they cannot be confirmed, refuted, or demonstrated to be confused. What a *Begriffsschrift* would do for us is, instead, help us simply to *avoid* these 'claims' by eliminating the temptation to believe that they say something.

---

[13] Wittgenstein also explores this topic at *TLP* 6.3611 and *NB* 84.

7

The Supposed 'Con-formity' of Language and World

Chapter 6 explored how the insights of Chapter 5 ought to feed back into how we understand ontological theories. This chapter will continue that process, offering an understanding of how we succumb to the illusion of a 'con-formity' between language and world. I will argue that Wittgenstein leads us to that understanding through his 'deduction' of the holding of certain internal relations. Wittgenstein may seem to be a classic con-formist, proposing that names with a particular logical form can be used to represent objects with particular ontological forms, and propositions with particular logical forms can be used to describe facts with particular ontological forms; the internal relations (O-N) and (F-P), understood within the con-formist framework, would then represent substantial requirements for sense to be possible. I will suggest that, when thought through, they do not. Having developed an understanding of (O-F), I will argue that the 'internal relation of depicting between language and world' does not articulate a novel con-formist theory, but instead points to why such a theory makes no sense.

An obvious objection that one might make to the argument I am offering, an objection which earlier interpretations of the *Tractatus* might suggest, is to say that this notion of con-formity does indeed make no sense, but that this is something that Wittgenstein recognized only later. My point, however, is to show how naturally the anti-con-formist thoughts set out above express themselves in the very terms that Wittgenstein uses (in particular, in terms of the particular 'internal properties' and 'relations' that he 'deduces'), that the picture analogy that he suggests to us also helps us to see precisely that, and that the construal of con-formism that emerges fits exactly the account of what philosophical problems are that Wittgenstein offers: it is a product of sign/symbol confusion.[1]

---

[1] A second objection, which I will not consider until Sect. 8.5 is that, even if Wittgenstein does give us reason to deny that we can talk intelligibly about the conditions of con-formity that a name must meet, this does not show that he did not believe that there are such conditions. The objection might continue: 'Such conditions are inexpressible, ineffable, and that is why, for Wittgenstein, "[l]ogic is transcendental"' (6.13).

7.1 ON FINDING A FIT

The notion that one might answer the question 'What form must a name take in order to be able to represent that object?' by examining the object, and thereby arriving at substantial con-formist requirements on talk about that object is intuitively appealing: we look over at Frank and say to ourselves that we need a sign that can be used to represent an object in a variety of spatial relations to other objects. We might pick up a pepper-pot and say, 'Something of that form would do it', moving it across a napkin to illustrate its use—'Frank crosses the road'. Frank standing on the road and a pepper-pot standing on a napkin could be said to 'con-form' in such a way that, for example, we might establish a system of representation in which we use the pepper-pot as a name for Frank. The pepper-pot seems to 'have possibilities', one might say, that mirror Frank's. Moreover, the mirroring in question does not seem to be an incidental feature of the pepper-pot and Frank. It would seem to be unthinkable for these entities to lose the 'forms' by virtue of which this mirroring holds and still be the entities that they are. Thus, their possessing mirroring forms would seem to be a matter of their being 'internally related' to one another. Perhaps we see here that there must be 'an internal relation between the logical form of a name and that of the object that it names'. And perhaps that captures a substantial condition that a particular part of the world imposes on how representations of it must be 'formed'.

But we give ourselves that impression only, I will argue, if we allow ourselves to forget how we have helped ourselves to the 'forms' in question: that is, only by already conceiving of the object under a particular aspect and already having at the back of our mind a particular use for the name. We see our sign as a pepper-pot that we placed on a napkin, and do not consider it as a gift from Aunt Maude, a green object, and a collection-of-pepper-pot-parts-within-ten-metres-of-a-collection-of-napkin-parts; we do not see how we have already distinguished for 'the sign' its 'essential' and 'accidental' features, the former being aspects that symbolize within some presupposed system of representation, and the latter being aspects that don't. Similarly, we see Frank as located in a particular spatial location rather than some other, and do not consider him as a man-as-opposed-to-a-woman, a Sagittarian-as-opposed-to-someone-of-another-star-sign, a 45-year-old-rather-than-someone-younger-or-older, a mammal-rather-than-a-vegetable-or-a-mineral, or a relative-of-mine-as-opposed-to-a-relative-of-yours. Through these forms of inattention, we may come to feel that we *find* an object and a name whose 'forms' 'correspond'; but this 'discovery' emerges only as a result of 'the object' and 'the name' having had the same kind of 'logical space' projected on to them, a 'space' which neither 'demanded', a space which is not simply 'there to be found'—naturally occurring—around either.

One might respond by saying that the competing conceptualizations alluded to actually pick out quite different objects. But this takes us to the crux: the impression that there is the basis here for a con-formist explanation of sensible representation by reference to characteristics of the represented object turns, I would suggest, on a certain equivocation over the word 'object'. First, we conceive of 'the object' as an independently constituted entity whose characteristics we read off, rather than decide, and which we pick out as '*that*', with a pointing finger perhaps. But, secondly, we also conceive of 'the object' as a person-in-a-particular-spatial-location-as-opposed-to-another-spatial-location, rather than as a man-as-opposed-to-a-woman, and so on. We can attach no sense to our pepper-pot 'corresponding' to the 'object' understood in the first sense, and the 'object' understood in the second sense fails to provide an *independent* determinant of the dimension in which we ought to speak or think. The con-formist philosopher's 'solution' is to overlook the difference between these two 'objects'—invoking the person-in-a-particular-spatial-location when he wants to demonstrate the 'correspondence' of name to object and the formless *that* when he wishes to demonstrate that what is on offer is a genuinely independent determinant of how the words ought to be used.

In the above discussion, we have seen (O-F) emerge, along with (N-P) once again. To think we have observed how the sign in question happens to be logically formed is to fail to see that, as (N-P) requires, the different logical forms set out 'belong to' different 'signs in question': a piece-of-pottery-on-a-piece-of-paper, as opposed to a gift-from-Aunt-Maude-as-opposed-to-a-gift-from-Aunt-Tess, a collection-of-pepper-pot-parts-within-ten-metres-of-a-collection-of-napkin-parts, etc., etc.[2] Until one has resolved in which facts the object in question can stand, one has yet to identify the object: a Sagittarian-as-opposed-to-someone-of-another-star-sign, a mammal-rather-than-a-vegetable-or-a-mineral, etc., etc. With each different 'logical space', our same pointing gesture picks out a different object. So what we were taking in was not which logical form the object happens to have, because, as (O-F) indeed requires, each different form belongs to a different object. We have not identified how what we picked out happens to be logically formed as much as identified what we picked out, specified its identity, rather than described one of its properties. To grasp an object is to grasp it 'in its possibilities', as constituted by its possibilities; these possibilities 'must already lie in', 'prejudged in', the

---

[2] This helps explain Wittgenstein's insistence that the propositional sign is a fact: to understand a name, we need to see *how* it is within a propositional sign. Such a sign is a particular arrangement of names, rather than one of a particular determinate range of other arrangements; it is so, rather than so, or so, or so: 'The propositional sign consists in the fact that its elements, the words, are combined in it in a definite way' (3.14). Cf. also *NB* 97 and *TLP* 3.1432: 'We must not say, "The complex sign '*aRb*' says '*a* stands in relation *R* to *b*' "; but we must say, "*That* '*a*' stands in a certain relation to '*b*' says *that aRb*".'

object (2.0121, 2.012), and one cannot think 'of the object without the space' that these possibilities constitute (2.013).

When first encountered, (O-F) and (N-P) sounded like the basis for a conformist answer to the 'question of intelligibility set out in Section 1.3'. We have now come to hear them as articulating why such a story makes no sense. Pointing to how an object is internally related to the facts in which it figures might sound like the identification of the basis on which that object imposes a certain demand on any sign that would name it: any such sign must stand to the propositions in which it figures in a manner that is isomorphic, con-formist. Indeed, the entities in our example certainly *can* be said to correspond, in that, for example, there is a perfectly natural 'projective relation' between a person on a road and a pepper-pot on a napkin, mapping these parts of the picture on to those parts of the pictured. But 'the same sign' might be used to describe 'the same entity' in quite different ways: the pepper-pot being on this napkin might represent Frank's being 45 years old, if we then imaginatively fill in a neighbouring position in which we would place the pepper-pot to represent his being 46. Indeed, there seems then to be an indefinite number of ways in which these entities might be said to 'correspond'.

Crucially, then, when we imagined a way in which these physical objects might be used in a particular representational system, we did not witness anything that could be called a determination of how the picturing elements *ought* to be used.[3] No particular organization of the picture and the pictured is 'naturally occurring'; the impression that there is such an organization arose because we had already settled on a way of 'decomposing' the entities in question; they 'presented' these particular 'parts' in these particular patterns because we had already adopted a particular, but implicit, description of the signified object and selected a particular, but implicit, use of the 'signs'.[4]

Hacker has glossed the idea of 'the logical syntax of language' being 'answerable to the logical form of the world' as follows:

[A name] must admit of the very same range of combinatorial possibilities in syntax as the object which is its meaning in reality. Hence a two-place predicate *cannot* represent a three-place relation—there is no such thing, and the two-place predicate in question either means a certain two-place relation or nothing at all. (Hacker 1999, p. 119)[5]

[3] Wittgenstein states explicitly in *PT* that the identification of a sign's 'projective relation' identifies how it *is* used: 'The method of projection is the manner of applying the propositional sign [*die Art und Weise der Anwendung des Satzzeichens*]' (*PT* 3.12). (Cf. *NB* 82: 'The way in which language signifies is mirrored [*spiegelt sich*] in its use.')
[4] As Ostrow puts it, 'the picture ... is in a certain sense an abstraction from the process of picturing' (2002, p. 37). Though approaching these topics from rather different directions, this is just one of a number of points on which my own discussion of picturing and Ostrow's agree.
[5] Cf. also Glock 1996, p. 347: '[T]he rules of symbolism are not arbitrary. Once we have laid down that a certain sign is to stand for a certain object, the combinatorial rules of the former are determined by the logical form of the latter.'

I would be happy to endorse the quoted claims, but I do not think that they commit one to a substantial form of 'answerability', a substantial '(metaphysical) condition of the possibility of representation' (p. 120). Pulling that particular rabbit out of the hat is meant to be made possible by adding the following further claim:

The logical (metaphysical) forms of states of affairs are language independent—*de re* possibilities do not depend upon our descriptions of them. (p. 120)

My reason for believing that projective relations cannot be seen as *dictated* by the depicted (or indeed by the picture) is that it is only relative to a particular 'projective relation' that entities present as making up particular determinate arrangements and as having particular determinate parts. We may imagine asking ourselves how an arrangement of four cars could be represented using an arrangement of three cups, and conclude that it couldn't. But it is only once one has adopted a particular description of the signified and the sign that they 'have a form', and to the indeterminate number of other possible descriptions that we could have used, there corresponds an indeterminate number of other possible forms. Suppose, for example, that our four cars are also 30,000 kg of matter; now we have an immediate sense of how our three cups might be used to represent them/it.

This realization undermines the proposal that we speak as we do—that our systems of representation are 'formed' as they are—because of how the world we talk about is 'formed'; we imagine that we are being offered an explanation here, because we think that the proposal implies that, had the world been 'formed' differently, we would speak differently. The problem is that the world *is* 'formed differently': Frank is in the road, but he is also 93 million miles from the Sun, hungry, the youngest of three brothers, etc. 'That object' possesses a myriad different 'logical forms', and demands description using propositions with many different 'forms'.

This discussion suggests a reading of 4.12:

Propositions can represent the whole reality, but they cannot represent what they must have in common with reality in order to be able to represent it—the logical form.

To be able to represent the logical form, we should have to be able to put ourselves with the propositions outside logic, that is outside the world.

When we imagine ourselves identifying a logical form that a proposition must possess in order to represent a particular possible fact, we can only latch on to something that might impose a superficially intelligible (pseudo-) requirement by staying 'within logic': that is, by using a proposition that picks out the thus-and-so of the imagined logical form—an object's being in a particular spatial location, say. But such an identification takes for granted that we understand how this state of affairs must be represented, that its logical form is such that it must be represented using a proposition that captures an object's being spatially located. But now the 'requirement' exposed is that possible facts that are characterized like this must be ... characterized like this. Our quest for a genuine requirement must drive us, it seems, 'outside logic', and with it, outside any presupposed frame of reference with which to characterize the world. Our 'indication' of the logical form now becomes an inarticulate pointing at a bare *that*, about which we now find that we cannot ask the sort of question of con-formity which we set out to ask. The truly independent object—the mere *that*—is formless, and so imposes no determinate requirement on names; the formed object, on the other hand, is an indeterminate number of different objects imposing an indeterminate number of different requirements on how language must be formed. What determines which is relevant is one's choice of which name one is using—the name of a person-in-this-particular-spatial-location-rather-than-any-other, a Sagittarian-as-opposed-to-someone-of-another-star-sign, a mammal-rather-than-a-vegetable-or-a-mineral, etc., etc.

7.2 'THE METHOD OF COMPARISON MUST BE GIVEN ME BEFORE I CAN MAKE THE COMPARISON'

The root confusion that creates the illusion of a necessary, substantial isomorphism is that, when we contemplate Frank standing in the road and the pepper-pot standing on the napkin, we are not contemplating bases which may yet allow a correlation between the two to emerge, but rather, two *products* of a method of correlation, of projection; in this case, it is spatial location. Frank, spatially located, can be seen as closer to, or further from, the pepper-pot, spatially located; Frank can be the same distance from the car as the pepper-pot is from the kitchen door, and so on. Similarly, Frank can be older than, younger than, or the same age as the pepper-pot; and Frank can be older than Irene by the same number of years as the pepper-pot is older than the tea-pot. Our belief in 'the form of an object' as the basis for an explanation of how it must be represented was weakened by our realization that any object has an indefinite number of 'forms'. That belief should be destroyed when we realize that to single out one of those forms is to adopt a method of projection, to place the object in a space of similarities and differences. When we see object and name matching in form, what we see before us is not something which will *allow* the two to be correlated, but rather the *output* of a correlation that has already been enacted.[6]

Having adopted a method of comparison, a framework within which entities can be placed as thus-and-so, we see determinate correlations and failures of correlation between entities, and such entities might then be used to represent one another. Such entities between which a depicting relation might stand

---

[6] Cf. Ostrow 2002, p. 41: '[T]he essential possibilities of combination common to the pictorial elements and the objects are given, as it were, after the fact, precisely *through* the projection of the picture on to reality.'

will indeed be 'internally related', in that they will all be, say, spatially located and spatially organized entities, as opposed to temporally located and temporally organized entities, coloured entities, possessions, etc. But this is no discovery, and no 'requirement' that these entities might have turned out not to meet; rather, it is only because the particular method of comparison that has been adopted has indeed been adopted that *these* entities emerge before us, why the world as we look around ourselves presents itself as made up of spatially located and spatially organized entities, as opposed to contemplating it as temporally located and temporally organized entities, etc., etc.

To echo *PI* § 308, earlier moves in the conjuring trick which escape our notice may place the entities we are contemplating within a framework, and thereby determine for them an organization, a 'way that they are'. Within that framework, we can correlate entities. Outside that framework, our talk of correlation or correspondence has no sense: we would have no particular reason for seeing the entities as 'formed', 'composed', or 'organized' in any one particular way,[7] and would have no sense of how we might *try* to correlate them. Having such a framework in place is to have a method of comparison in place, and crucially, that one has this cannot itself be something established by comparing entities. A match does not make a comparison possible; rather, the matching *presupposes* that a comparison is possible: our seeing that the items match presupposes that we know how to compare them. If one decides instead not to single out *a* form for the object and one for the name, then one is faced with correlating a 'this' with a 'that', and correlating them, crucially, not in any *particular respect*: this, I suggest, is no correlation at all.

In *NB*, Wittgenstein observes:

The method of portrayal must be completely determinate before we can compare reality with the proposition at all in order to see whether it is true or false. The method of comparison must be given me before I can make the comparison. (*NB* 23)

This passage has a moral for con-formism's invitation to us to imagine the meaningfulness of names and propositions as a kind of fit with objects and possible facts, respectively. A proposition can itself be thought of as a yardstick that we compare with reality,[8] its matching being its being true, and its failing to match its being false. This true–false matching, according to con-formism, is made possible by a deeper meaningful–meaningless match between the 'forms' of proposition and possible fact. But this deeper match or mismatch must itself presuppose a 'method of comparison', not merely in order for us to be able to test *whether* the match holds, but in order for what it is for the match to hold or not hold to be a determinate matter: only if the method is given, is it settled just what the test in question is.

---

[7] We see here again the significance of propositional signs being themselves facts (3.14): the signs are arranged *thus-and-so*.

[8] Cf. *TLP* 2.1512 and *PR* 77–8.

So the problem is not just that I need the method in order to establish if this similarity exists; rather, settling on the method is settling on what the relevant kind of similarity and dissimilarity is. Consider an analogy with an argument that Wittgenstein offered in lectures in 1934. We can ask whether two objects agree with respect to their colour, weight, age, owner, etc., etc., but *not* whether they agree *full stop*:

Suppose I gave you a sample, saying "This is green", and asked you to bring me something green. If you brought me something yellow and I said it did not agree with my idea of green, *am I describing a fact of nature?* No. To say that something yellow disagrees with the green sample is to give a rule about agreement. That yellow disagrees with green does not follow from anything in the nature of green or yellow. I could instead say that what disagrees with green is something that looks nasty with green, and yellow might be said to agree with green. If something is said to agree or disagree with an idea or thought, we do not *find* it agreeing or disagreeing. What are called agreement and disagreement is something laid down as a rule. (*L II* 84)

To ask if two entities 'agree with each other' is not yet to ask a determinate question, because we need to be told which aspect of the objects to consider: 'The method of comparison must be given me before I can make the comparison.' Similarly, if I am asked whether there is an isomorphism between a name and an object, I am not yet in a position to say, as if I were simply describing some 'fact of nature'; what needs to be settled is how they are to be compared; only after that is done is one in a position to determine whether an isomorphism exists. But then an isomorphism cannot be what makes it possible for the two to be compared: their 'being isomorphic' has no sense unless a method of comparison is already in place.

Another way of bringing out this point is to consider the following. If asked whether the signs in p. 93's, 'spatial' system *failed* to correspond to the signified in p. 93's, 'age' system, we would be stumped. We wouldn't know how to even *try* to correlate them: what *might* correlate with what? But this does not show that either system of representation is confused or impossible. It shows that we need to settle on a particular projective relation before we can so much as attempt such a correlation; it is that relation that specifies the sense in which two objects might be said to correlate or not. In our bamboozling example, the problem is that we have *two* methods of comparison 'in place': the spatial framework and the age framework. We don't know how to *try* to correlate the entities, because we don't know which method to use; and to settle on one will require a reconceptualization of one of the entities to be compared.

Before ending this section, let me explain why this argument does not entail that 'logical (metaphysical) forms of states of affairs' are 'language-*dependent*'. What I take the argument to show is that we cannot make sense of the necessary notion of 'dependency' in whichever direction it is meant to run, and whether or not it is meant to hold in any particular case. One can give oneself the *impression* that one can make sense of the notion, but only by helping oneself to a particular 'organization' of 'states of affairs' which cannot itself be seen as dictated by 'the world itself'. Consequently, it remains unclear how 'the world' might impose 'its logical form' on language, how it might demand an 'answer' from language.[9]

To summarize, the notion of form that would substantiate the notion of a fit is a myth: the 'form' of entities does not dictate how they must be represented or must be used to represent, because there are no determinate 'facts of correspondence' prior to adopting a particular characterization of the pictured or a particular use of the picture. What settles the 'correspondence' of these entities is a particular projective relation that we adopt; prior to its adoption, we have no particular reason for seeing the entities as 'formed', as entities with particular determinate parts that may correspond or not. Hence, a correspondence of forms does not dictate which projective relations are possible. To think that it does is to help oneself to such a relation, to a method of comparison, and then to forget that one has done so. Only then does the con-formity necessary for comparison 'appear'.

7.3 INTERNAL RELATIONS EMERGE IN CONTEXTS OF MISUNDERSTANDING

The present and preceding chapters have shown that there is a certain truth to the assertions of the holding of internal relations the deduction of which was spelt out in Chapter 3. We have seen, for example, that there seems some basis for saying that, since names and propositions are internally related, one cannot first grasp a name and then learn how it relates to the propositions in which it figures. Instead, grasping a name is grasping the whole ensemble of name-and-propositions. Drawing on the *Tractatus*'s proposal that internal relations 'show themselves' (4.122), one might gloss this insight by saying that one must *see* the internal relation, as, unless one does so, one has no grasp of the relata. Similarly, one cannot grasp a proposition and then subsequently grasp how it relates to the fact it represents. Instead, because proposition and fact are internally related, to see a proposition before one is to see something-*in-its-relation-to*-a-fact. There is no step from a grasp of the relata of the internal relation to an appreciation that they are so related; instead, one must take in the whole that the relata with the relation make up in one go, or not at all.

But our discussion suggests a different interpretation, one which endows with sense and some credibility, first, Wittgenstein's proposal that philosophy 'is full' of confusions that arise from a failure to keep clear the sign/symbol distinction,

---

[9] If one is a certain kind of metaphysical realist, then one simply does think that the world has an organization, which might then impose demands on language. But it is noteworthy that Hacker gives no evidence for thinking that Wittgenstein is such a realist.

and secondly, his declaration in 6.54 that we understand him when we see that the propositions of the *Tractatus* are nonsensical. It also accounts for the air of the oxymoronic that lingers around the very idea of an internal relation: what the language of 'relation' and 'property' giveth, the language of 'internality' taketh away. Where we feel forced into 'seeing' internal relations, what is really to be found 'there' are pseudo-questions, questions to which we have not assigned sense; to 'see through' this talk of 'internal relations' is to see that the 'issues' such talk 'addresses' loom only as a result of misunderstanding; these are 'issues' about which only someone who was confused would have anything to say.

That we need a description of a certain form if we are to be able to describe a particular object sounds like a requirement that the world imposes on our language; but it does so only if we overlook that, in thinking of this object as formed as it is, we have already selected a particular mode of description and applied it to the object: we have already selected a way of 'placing' this object, thinking of it as a man as opposed to an animal, a volume of matter, a football player, etc. In giving our question of con-formity pseudo-sense, we have had to help ourselves to an answer, in that we have taken for granted a description of the object. When thought through, we have no clear understanding of what an answer to our question—of how language and world must be formed for the one to be able to represent the other—would even look like. We only had a sense that we did as long as we overlooked how we were considering objects already described and signs already with a use.

Similarly, that a sign can only be combined with certain others and in certain ways to construct a meaningful proposition sounds like a requirement imposed on the ways in which we can construct propositions; but it does so only if we overlook the fact that we endow these signs with 'outside edges', with a 'resistance' to being set in certain—'illogical'—combinations, only by already having a particular use for them in mind, a use which is their figuring with other signs in particular combinations to which a sense has been assigned. In giving our question of fit between constituents of propositions its pseudo-sense, we have had to help ourselves to an answer, in that we have taken for granted an understanding of names as participants in propositions. When thought through, we have no clear understanding of what an answer to our question—of how names can be combined to form propositions—would even look like. We had a sense that we did only as long as we overlooked how we were considering names already understood as participants in the construction of propositions: as signs, names can be combined however one likes; as symbols, they cannot; but that is because to grasp a name as a symbol is to grasp it, as (N-P) 'requires', in its role within propositions.[10]

---

[10] Wittgenstein's lack of concern over the so-called problem of the unity of the proposition is also now intelligible. Moore, Russell, and Frege all puzzled over the character of the connection that turns a set of terms into a proposition—'Southampton', 'London', and 'is south of' into 'Southampton

Section 4.10 suggested that the con-formist philosopher might be compared to the observer who marvels that the first across the line always wins. That may have seemed far-fetched, but it isn't. There is an instability in hearing 'Winning and crossing the line first are internally related' *as* an assertion, as revealing something about those who win (a group of people we can already identify) and those who come first (another group of people we can already identify): it turns out that . . . they are always one and the same people. But to understand that 'remarkable discovery' is to see that it comes about only as a result of overlooking how we come to describe someone as the winner: namely, precisely by seeing who crosses the line first. Similarly, to hear as a discovery that 'the ocean is *always* hear the shore' is to overlook how we come to describe something as a shore: namely, precisely by its being where the ocean ends.

Now the 'remarkable fact' that names fail to represent when combined in certain ways shows us, one might say, that names and propositions are 'internally related'. But I have argued that this directs us not to some novel kind of explanation of how names must be used in order to say something 'coherent' or 'logical'. Rather, it is understood by someone who sees that it is by confusing two superficially overlapping frameworks (featuring two different kinds of thing called 'names') that we conjure up the impression of a difference between 'logical' and 'illogical' combinations of 'names'. Similarly, the 'remarkable correspondence' of name and object arises only when we characterize them using 'corresponding' 'logical spaces'. One might then say that name and object are 'internally related'. But this directs us not to some novel kind of explanation of how the name must be used. Rather, it is understood by someone who sees that it is by confusing two superficially overlapping frameworks (featuring two different things called the 'object') that we conjure up the impression of a substantial 'con-formity' that the named imposes on anything that would name it.

To grasp what Wittgenstein is getting at when he offers such an 'elucidation' is to cease to believe or disbelieve 'what it says'; instead, what we had thought we were being offered a view on no longer looks to us like an issue at all. When he leads us to certain 'internal properties' and 'internal relations', he is not articulating perplexing answers to certain difficult questions, but indicating situations in which we face things that look like 'questions' but which we do not really understand. Thus those supposed 'answers', Wittgenstein's 'propositions', can be seen as 'rungs' of a 'ladder' to be 'climbed' and then 'thrown away'.

---

is south of London'. Wittgenstein may seem to miss this point, declaring that different expressions simply 'fit into one another like the links in a chain' (cf. 2.03). But the picture analogy undermines the temptation to believe that we have a grasp of these terms that is independent of a grasp of their role within propositions. 'How one puts them together' is a real issue only if we have a grasp of 'them' apart; we have such a grasp when 'they' are conceived of as signs, but equally we have no sense that there are restrictions on how such 'dead' signs can be combined: we have lost our sense that we understand our 'issue'.

The next chapter will apply this interpretation of what is at stake in Wittgenstein's assertions about 'internal properties' and 'internal relations' to his remarks about thought and subjectivity. The chapter after that will apply it to the other internal properties of objects identified in Chapter 3.[11]

---

[11] Sects. 15.1–15.3 summarize how this reading applies to the book's apparently disparate themes.

8

Subjectivity

Wittgenstein's reflections on language and world can be seen, first, as setting out a number of arguments against the existence of certain external relations upon which we might hope to found an explanation of the intelligibility of language; secondly, as setting out a set of corresponding claims about the existence of certain internal relations; and finally, as trying to provoke a meditation on what this talk of 'internal relations' reveals. His reflections on thought and thinkers follow a parallel path. I will examine first of all Wittgenstein's concern to identify visions of the 'constitution' of subjectivity that present us with unsustainable external relations. A subtext in Chapter 7 will come to the fore next, and will provide a key to Wittgenstein's difficult comments on the relation between thought, language, and world and his well-known but puzzling remark that 'what solipsism *means*, is quite correct, only it cannot be *said*, but shows itself' (5.62). That subtext is the apparent impossibility of making sense of the teaching or learning of language. I will argue that Wittgenstein's strategy is to think through a con-formist conception of the relationship between thinker and world; the internal relations he identifies show once again how such a conception would have to work, but serve ultimately to indicate how that conception rests on confusion. Claims such as that 'I am my world' are 'rungs' of a 'ladder' to be 'thrown away'.

8.1 THOUGHTS AND THEIR CONSTITUENTS

A set of ideas with which Wittgenstein was concerned, in the early 1910s, were those Russell explored in his 'theory of judgement', an attempt to explain how judgements are constructed which gave a central role to the work of the subject.[1] Roughly speaking, this theory proposes that the subject gathers the elements from which a judgement is to be constructed and fuses these together. Imagining the actions of a subject as constructing judgements from elements that will go on to form the component parts of judgements is to imagine those components as externally related. If so, there would be a substantive body of truths stating which constituents of thought, when combined, make up intelligible thoughts. Consequently, Wittgenstein attacks Russell for leaving open the 'possibility' of illogical thoughts, the framing of incoherent judgements:

---

[1] Cf., e.g., Russell 1984 [1913] and, for useful discussion, Hylton 1990, pp. 333–61.

The correct explanation of the form of the proposition 'A judges *p*' must show that it is impossible to judge a nonsense. (Russell's theory does not satisfy this condition.) (5.5422)

Just as con-formist explanations of why certain propositions are intelligible make room for 'wrong sense', which is an illusion, so too the Russellian explanation of why certain thoughts are thinkable makes room for 'illogical thought', which is another illusion: '[w]hat is thinkable is possible too' (3.02).[2] Just as an 'illegitimate proposition' is not the saying of something illogical, but is instead a failure to say something, so too '[w]e cannot think anything unlogical, for otherwise we should have to think unlogically' (3.03). Just as we can make no sense of the idea of pictures being constructed out of individual, independently understood signs, so too there is something potentially confusing about the idea of individual constituents of thoughts,[3] elements that represent particular things but whose combination into thoughts, into judgements, remains a subsequent, external matter of fact about those elements. 'Every right theory of judgment must make it impossible for me to judge that this table penholders the book', and 'Russell's theory does not satisfy this requirement' (*NB* 103); it, like any other account that would envisage, or indeed even allow, a substantial explanation of why certain combinations of elements go to make up coherent judgements, while other combinations do not, presents those elements as externally related.[4]

In their early discussions, Wittgenstein declares that Russell's problems 'can only be removed by a correct theory of propositions' (*NB* 122). That a theory is what we need, perhaps a 'picture theory', is not what I take to be Wittgenstein's considered view; what is is the view that Russell's account gives the subject an influence on the construction of judgements that it cannot bear if the very possibility of judging a nonsense—like a sense that is senseless—is confused. The integrity of a judgement cannot be compromised by the insinuation within its construction of any kind of 'glue', be it a Russellian subject or any other kind of subject from an examination of the activity of which one might derive a body of substantive principles of coherent thought. Such a body would ground a body of substantial principles of coherent talk which, as an 'accidental logic', would

[2] This is not to suggest that human beings can never be irrational or confused. Rather, this view challenges a particular account of that irrationality or confusion, in which the 'problem' with such a thought is that 'its sense . . . is senseless'. Cf. Sects. 3.5 and 8.5.

[3] Whatever they may be—cf. n. 26 below.

[4] In a letter of June 1913, Wittgenstein offered this criticism to Russell, leaving Russell, by his own admission, 'paralysed' (Russell 1967, p. 57): 'I can now express my objection to your theory of judgment exactly: I believe it is obvious that from the proposition "A judges that (say) *a* is in relation R to *b*", if correctly analysed, the proposition "aRb.v.¬aRb" must follow directly *without the use of any other premiss*. This condition is not fulfilled by your theory' (*NB* 122). Within the framework of Russell's theory, the elements of thought that the subject brings together (and which are thus conceived of as externally related) may or may not combine to form an intelligible thought. The fact that a subject 'entertains' this whole, this particular 'judgement', does not imply 'directly' that the judgement makes sense, that it is indeed a judgement. As Wittgenstein expresses the demand here, we must at least be able either to say that the judgement is true or to say that it is false; we cannot if the 'judgement' is 'illogical'.

endow logic with 'an impossible reality' (*NB* 48). Thus we embrace instead an analogue of (N-P), the 'internal relatedness' of the elements of judgement. Have we made here a positive discovery about the nature of thoughts and their construction? The reading of the *Tractatus* developed so far should lead us to suspect not and suggests instead the following construal of Wittgenstein's intent in asserting that this internal relation holds.

By conceiving of elements of judgements as externally related, we imagine them in a space within which certain combinations of elements can come together to form judgements, while other combinations of elements cannot. In doing so, however, we help ourselves to what we would like to imagine ourselves establishing as some matter of fact: namely, 'how these elements can combine'. In our imagining, we endow these elements with an 'outside', with a 'shape', as a result of which certain combinations can be constructed. By affirming the internal relatedness of these elements, we rule out this envisaged matter of fact and the explanation it underwrites. What gives each element the 'shape' that our imagining imagines is our already having confusedly ascribed to those elements a role within judgements, an analogue of the use that we have already unwittingly ascribed to names when we imagine matters of fact about how names can be combined to form propositions. What gives these elements their 'shape', their 'outside edge', is the use of these elements in the construction of propositions. When we then draw on those 'shapes' to explain the construction of propositions, our reasoning is circular, and an explanation seems to be revealed only as long as we fail to recognize our confusion.

As we saw with (N-P), (O-F), and the 'internal relation of depicting' ((O-N) and (F-P)), Wittgenstein's positive claims seem intended to reveal that confusion has endowed us with pseudo-questions. To understand his assertions of the holding of internal relations is to come to recognize the confusion of questions which those same assertions otherwise appear to us to be answering. The rest of this chapter will show how this reading can be extended to take in the *Tractatus*'s proposal that the subject and the world are internally related.

8.2 DOES THOUGHT BIND LANGUAGE TO THE WORLD?

The argument of Section 3.5 shows that in thinking of words' 'meaningfulness' as a matter of con-formity, we have always already taken their meaning for granted. A gloss that one might be tempted to place on this outcome is that we must take for granted that our language 'works'. Though Section 8.6 will argue that this gloss too harbours a confusion that Wittgenstein may be trying to expose, it does at least suggest one natural reading of Wittgenstein's early slogan that there is an 'internal relation of depicting that holds between language and the world'

(4.014), the suggestion being that there is no possibility of 'getting between' language and world to (somehow) 'ground' or 'understand' their relatedness. This suggestion invites two obvious objections, and in the present and following sections I will show how reflection on those leads us also to an interpretation of the proposal that 'I am my world' and Wittgenstein's apparent sympathy for solipsism.

The first objection is: 'Surely it is the subject that "makes language work"; surely *we* put the meaning into words, rather than their possessing it all by themselves.' Following this line of thought, we can find things that Wittgenstein says in which he seems to be coming to his senses. He comments that:

We use sensibly the perceptible sign (sound or written sign etc.) of the proposition as a projection of the possible state of affairs. (3.11)

This is followed by what sounds like an explanation of how that 'projection' works:

The method of projection is the thinking of the sense of the proposition.

This suggests a view about how language works, of how it has meaning: thought links language and world, endowing signs with their 'life'. Some have seen just such a view in the *Tractatus*. According to Hacker, for example, Wittgenstein believed that 'psychological processes link language to reality' (Hacker 1996*a*, p. 23):

Content is . . . injected into the constituent names of a propositional sign by mental acts of meaning, and the resultant proposition then represents a state of affairs. (p. 683)

The obvious objection to such a view is, as Hacker recognizes, that it 'merely replaces the puzzle about the semantic properties of sign-language with a mystery about the semantic properties of the language of thought' (p. 25). If we imagine a 'method of projection', somehow 'linking' name and object, which the thinker recognizes and acts on and thereby *guides* the application of the name, we are presupposing that the thinker can see in particular cases whether an entity in front of him is the relevant kind of entity to which, according to the method of projection, the name applies. At the root of our dissatisfaction with this account of the guidedness of language is the problem of concept acquisition (identified in Sect. 1.3): the understanding embodied in our use of a name is fundamentally the same kind of understanding that we take for granted in invoking the thinker's capacity to recognize relevant objects. Hence, an invocation of the latter will not explain what puzzled us about the former.

According to Hacker, Wittgenstein believed that this problem could be evaded on the grounds that 'mental acts possess intrinsic intentionality' (p. 681), though 'Wittgenstein was later to realize' that this view 'is irremediably flawed' (p. 24).

Indeed it is, as Hacker puts it, 'like being told that the Earth does not fall through space because it is supported on the back of the Great Tortoise and that it is an intrinsic property of the Great Tortoise not to fall through space!' (1992, p. 264). I will argue that the *Tractatus* can instead be read as confronting, rather than ducking, the problem set out here, and as seeing in it the need to abandon any image of the subject as the active entity that 'makes language happen'.[5]

8.3 LEARNING A FIRST LANGUAGE

The second objection I will consider to the proposal that 'language and world are internally related' is: 'If that is so, and the relation is not mediated by, for example, the Subject, how then do we *learn* language?'

Now it may well be asked, 'Where does the early Wittgenstein discuss language learning? Wouldn't he have regarded this as a matter of psychology, and irrelevant given his concerns?' I discuss language learning because it provides an intuitive way into Wittgenstein's reflection on a powerful, unreflective, philosophical vision of the meaningfulness of language and what it is to use a language with understanding. I will argue ultimately that the apparent impossibility of language learning that is to be discussed emerges only if one adopts that vision and that that vision and the understanding of language learning that rests upon it must be abandoned as confused; that vision is the early Wittgenstein's ultimate target, but its character can be made clearest by beginning with that understanding of language learning, as Wittgenstein himself does in the passage from *NB* 25 to be discussed below: 'How can I be *told how* the proposition represents? Or can this not be *said* to me at all? And if that is so can I "*know*" it?'[6]

So let us begin by considering the difference between learning a first language and learning a second language. If we leave aside some interesting subtleties, the latter can be seen as a matter of learning a collection of contingent facts about *signs*, learning that a language uses particular signs to express what is expressed in one's first language by other particular signs. But what happens when we learn a first language? It cannot be the same kind of process, because that process presupposes our mastery of a first language. Strikingly, the *Tractatus* seems to assert that there is an incoherence in the very idea of explaining a first language, of explaining not signs but symbols:

---

[5] *PG* 40 attacks such a conception, ascribing it to Frege, but not to Wittgenstein's earlier self.

[6] Sect. 14.8 will argue that the image of learning is essentially that of the coming to have something like a reason; I say 'something like a reason' because reflection on the problems that this notion involves suggests that it is both a fantasy *for* reasons—for the role that they might play in our lives—and a fantasy *of* reasons—assigning them that role requires that we operate with mythic entities that claim to be what we call 'reasons'.

The meaning of primitive signs can be explained by elucidations. Elucidations are propositions which contain the primitive signs. They can, therefore, only be understood when the meanings of these signs are already known. (3.263)[7],[8]

The meanings of the simple signs (the words) must be explained to us, if we are to understand them.

However, it is by means of propositions that we make ourselves understood. [*Mit den Saetzen aber verstaendigen wir uns.*] (4.026)

Now one construal of these passages takes them to express opposition to an atomistic conception of how we come to understand propositions by first coming to understand their component parts. But the moral of these passages may be broader, a moral that a passage from *Philosophical Remarks* articulates:

[A]ny kind of explanation of language presupposes a language already. And in a certain sense, the use of language is something that cannot be taught . . . I cannot use language to get outside language. (*PR* 54)

Indeed, something very like this thought can also be found in an early *Notebook* entry too:

How can I be *told how* the proposition represents? Or can this not be *said* to me at all? And if that is so can I '*know*' it? If it was supposed to be said to me, then this would have to be done by means of a proposition; but the proposition could only show it.

What can be said can only be said by means of a proposition, and so nothing that is necessary for the understanding of *all* propositions can be said. (*NB* 25)

All explanations of propositions terminate at some point in our simply *seeing* what a proposition shows, and that will be a matter of our *already* understanding the world in the terms in which that proposition represents it. The proposal that a proposition must simply 'show its sense' (4.022) and, with it, the world it represents, thus emerges here out of a sense of a confusion in the notion that one might be told how propositions represent.

The most obvious candidate for the role of an 'explanation' which would 'get outside language' is the giving of an ostensive definition. If we imagine learning a

---

[7] Hacker acknowledges that 3.263 is 'at first, baffling', but insists that 'the idea is a simple and straightforward one', 'though expressed with needless obscurity' (1999, p. 125). He goes on to suggest that the idea is 'much the same as Russell's account of the explanation of primitive signs' in the *Principia*: 'The primitive signs are explained by means of descriptions intended to point out to the reader what is meant; but the explanations do not constitute definitions, because they really involve the ideas they explain' (Russell and Whitehead 1927, *1). On my reading, there is nothing 'needless' about the obscurity of 3.263. Instead, it is precisely intended to bring us up short before the shocking, neither simple nor straightforward, conclusion that 'the use of language is something that cannot be taught', that we cannot be *told* 'how a proposition represents' (cf. *PR* 54 and *NB* 25, quoted below).

[8] A question I do not address here is why Wittgenstein uses '*erläutern*' of both his own propositions and the explanations we give of simple signs. I don't think the answer to this question is clear. But one possibility is that both would seem to involve bringing an audience to make a kind of leap from one 'space of sense' to another. In both cases, the audience is to be brought to see a sense in what is being said which they cannot see initially.

sign in that way, we imagine learning that some particular sign is used to refer to what my first language calls 'red', say. But if we imagined that an ostensive definition might teach someone a *symbol*, a first-language expression, as it were, we confront the problem of concept acquisition again: in order to see *what* is being pointed at, the pupil must already have a mastery of the relevant symbol, which is precisely what the 'explanation' was to 'make possible'.[9] At *PR* 54, we read:

> If I explain the meaning of a word 'A' to someone by pointing to something and saying 'This is A', then this proposition may be meant in two different ways. Either it is itself a proposition already, in which case it can only be understood once the meaning of 'A' is known, i.e. I must now leave it to chance whether he takes it as I meant or not. Or the sentence is a definition.

On neither construal does this procedure explain what A-ness is. On the first construal, we are being told that something is an A, and understanding that requires that we know already what A-ness is. On the second construal, it is a statement of fact about a sign: ' "A" is to be used of this sort of thing', where an understanding of what makes something 'this sort of thing' is again presupposed. If one is hoping to make sense of the teaching of symbols, one must unfortunately recognize that the ostensive definitions that one is tempted to imagine here will 'only be understood when the meanings of [the signs they contain] are already known' (3.263).[10]

Must we then accept something like a doctrine of innate ideas, in the light of which our inability to *acquire* a mastery of symbols would no longer imply that we do not *have* a mastery of symbols? The price that such a doctrine demands is an implausible idealism. But certainly the seeming impossibility of learning

[9] The plausibility of the objection that opens this section turns on 'words' being construed as referring to signs, rather than symbols, second-language rather than first-language expressions.

[10] Hacker has argued that it was only after writing the *Tractatus* that Wittgenstein came to realize that ostensive definitions do not 'exit from language' (cf. 1986, pp. 75–8; 1999, p. 125; Baker and Hacker 2001). My suggestion is, first, that this realization follows directly from a recognition of the 'problem of concept acquisition', and secondly, that Wittgenstein's having made this connection provides natural interpretations of 3.263, 4.026, the passages quoted from *NB* 25 and 23 (the latter quoted in Sect. 7.2), and Wittgenstein's description of language and world as 'internally related'. Most of the evidence that Hacker provides comes in the form of later criticisms of the notion that ostensive definitions 'exit from language' (e.g., *PR* 54, quoted above), with the insinuation that these ought to be read as criticizing the *Tractatus*. The only item of evidence that he provides for this insinuation is the following comment contained in Waismann's record of conversations with Wittgenstein: 'In the *Tractatus* logical analysis and ostensive definition were unclear to me. At that time I thought there was "a connexion between language and reality" ' (*VC* 209–10). There is no record of Wittgenstein's explanation of what he meant by this, if indeed he provided one, and a possible alternative reading to Hacker's starts from the fact that the remarks that immediately follow discuss 'hypotheses'. Wittgenstein distinguishes hypotheses from propositions as 'a completely different grammatical structure' (*VC* 210), and in the roughly contemporary *PR*, asserts that hypotheses have 'a different formal relation to reality from that of verification' (*PR* 285). (For further discussion, cf. Sect. 12.5.) If so, they and ostensive definitions would each provide grounds for doubting whether all legitimate proposition-like structures exemplify 'a connexion between language and reality', the emphasis of doubt falling now on 'a'.

symbols suggests a reading for the remark that Wittgenstein says 'provides a key to the question, to what extent solipsism is a truth' (5.62):

The limits of my language mean the limits of my world. (5.6)[11]

Our using the particular symbols that we use cannot itself be understood as a response to 'how the world is'. Nor can new symbols be explained to me by presenting me with entities of the type that such symbols pick out. In this way, the limits of my world—understood as the range of kinds of events that I might experience, involving the range of entities I might encounter in the range of circumstances I might encounter—coincide with the limits of the language I understand—understood as the total set of symbols of which I have mastery. Anything I might experience—anything that might happen in my world—must be articulated within my language, and no experience of mine might teach me a new symbol, might expand 'the language I understand'.

This, in turn, suggests a reading now for the proposition 'The world is *my* world' (5.62), which Wittgenstein proposes 'shows itself' in the remark that is the key to solipsism. To adapt 5.552's comment on coming to understand logic, 'the "experience" that we need to understand [a symbol] is not that such and such is the case, but that something *is*; but that is *no* experience'. In the light of the explanatory failures identified above, one might say that the world is my world, in that the space within which I may experience events coming to pass must always already be available to me; it must be so because there is no experience that could be my coming to find it.

We are led to the same place by Section 8.2's recognition of the futility of invoking the subject as an explanation of the representational capacity of language, as 'knowing *how* the proposition represents'. The 'explanation' we imagine 'works' only if we think of the subject as possessing 'intrinsic intentionality'. When we recognize that this *explanans* takes for granted a fundamentally similar capacity to that which puzzled us, the subject must be hauled down from the 'management role' to which we were tempted to assign it.[12] Instead, the subject is in the same boat as that which it pretended to manage, the words it might be thought to 'animate':

[T]hinking is a kind of language. For a thought too is, of course, a logical picture of the proposition, and therefore it just is a kind of proposition. (*NB* 82)

Consequently, to extend the gloss with which Section 8.2 began, one might also say that, like language, the subject is 'internally related' to the world it 'is

---

[11] In line with the *Tractatus*'s system of numbering its propositions (which is meant to indicate which constitute comments upon which others), *NB* 49 quoted below suggests that the reference of 'this remark' in 5.62 is 5.6, rather than 5.61, the immediately preceding remark.

[12] Cf. McGuinness 1981; Goldfarb, unpublished *a*; Winch 1987. Among the complexities I ignore here is the difference between claiming that a language of thought 'animates' language and claiming that the thinker 'animates' the language of thought.

about'. The sovereign subject that is capable of stepping back from—standing at a distance from—that world and its capacity to grasp that world vanishes: 'there is no such thing' as '[t]he thinking, presenting subject' (5.631) if that is meant to be conceivable in isolation from the world that it thinks about. Instead, the subject, one might say, is face to face with—in an ungroundable immediacy with—the world; the subject finds itself in the midst of—*belonging to*—that world. Thinker and world are internally related, the subject *constituted* by its relation to its world:

I am my world. (5.63)[13]

8.4 IS SOLIPSISM A SOLUTION TO THE PUZZLE?

The fact that our using the particular symbols that we use cannot itself be understood as a response to 'how the world is' illustrates the earlier proposal that conformity cannot be explained by my bringing my thought into con-formity with the world. The question of acquired con-formity remains unanswered: if the possibility of my thinking requires that it and the world con-form, how does the con-formity come about? What would seem to be necessary is a speculative metaphysical solution: since we know that we can think, we must conclude that this con-formity exists, and the insolubility of the problem of concept acquisition shows us that that con-formity must be prior to, not observable in, but making possible, our ordinary experiences. Prior to—and necessary for the possibility of—all that experience might reveal is a deeper kinship between thinker and world: myself, my thoughts, and their subject-matter must all be, in some sense, aspects of 'one world soul' (*NB* 49). For example, if ideas, in some sense, constitute the world, then both the world and I are informed by ideas, and our con-formity will have a basis.[14] Such a metaphysics would answer the question 'How, then, is it that thought is possible?', as it so manifestly would seem to be ('I think, therefore it is possible to think!') and our formulation of these very panic-inducing arguments would seem to require.[15] So, since Section 8.3 has suggested that Wittgenstein sees the realist's problem of concept acquisition as insoluble and has shown how such a realization naturally expresses itself in solipsistic terms, might we go one more step and ascribe to him a solipsistic metaphysics?

[13] Though I will not make the case here, I take two other important images that Wittgenstein uses—that of the eye in its visual field and the book *The World as I Found It* (5.631–5.6331)—to elaborate on this point, arguing, roughly speaking, that we cannot make sense of the subject in isolation from, or as externally related to, its perspective on the world, its intentionality.

[14] Cf. Sect. 1.3.

[15] One might suggest that solipsism is a metaphysics that *prevents* that question arising: there is no 'gap between subject and object' to be crossed. None the less, that metaphysics does provide us with an answer to the underlying question of how thought 'is possible', to which the notion of intelligibility as con-formity responds. The reading I will offer maintains that that question is confused too.

Conspicuously, however, Wittgenstein talks not of solipsism as being true but of 'the extent [to which] solipsism is a truth' (5.62), since 'what solipsism *means*, is quite correct, only it cannot be *said*, but it shows itself' (5.62). And of course, the proposal that thinker and world are 'internally related' belongs to a book whose author compares its propositions to a ladder to be climbed and then thrown away. Nevertheless, the preceding paragraph does not strike me as expressing an obviously mistaken interpretation: quite what Wittgenstein's sympathy for solipsism amounts to, and quite how it is qualified, not least by 6.54's pronouncement, are questions that run to the heart of the difficulty of reading the *Tractatus*, and if one is comfortable with the notion that that work offers a metaphysics but one which is ineffable, then it would take little further effort to develop interpretations of Wittgenstein's opaque qualifications to his admiration for solipsism that might make just as much sense as that notion.[16] All the same, I will not develop such a reading further.

8.5 AN UNSURVEYABLE CONDITION OF THOUGHT?

Another response to the puzzle that might seem to have some basis in the *Tractatus* is the view that meaning is somehow unsurveyable—its possibility ungraspable—by us. What the problem of concept acquisition demonstrates, according to this view, is that we live, as it were, in the midst of, bathed in, meaning, and can never step outside it so as to see that, or how, it is. This fact, like the fact that the world is one fit for our comprehension, is one so fundamental as to be unjudgeable.

An analogy suggests itself here with the notion that one might judge whether one is sane or not. This notion faces a familiar problem. On one natural construal, what it is to be sane is to be capable of making judgements; if so, arriving through some test or other at the conclusion that one is sane does not demonstrate that one is sane; one might equally well arrive at that conclusion as a result of carrying out the test in an insane manner. So, it seems, one cannot test or judge one's sanity, one's capacity to test or judge. But, all the same, this does not entail that there is no issue of sanity to worry over, or that we would not be insane were we to think and act in certain ways.

So, analogously, perhaps we should conclude that the intelligibility of our thought and talk stands as an unsurveyable condition on our thinking and talking as we do. That our thought and talk is intelligible is something that one cannot come to see happens to be the case; it is a condition of every thought or proposition I might entertain. It is a fact, one might say, that *shows* itself

---

[16] That I have reservations about such a reading is probably obvious: not least, let us not forget that it is *solipsism* that we are contemplating ascribing to Wittgenstein, a view which, prima facie, is crazy, whether sayable or unsayable.

in everything I say or think.[17] That fact does not entail that we would not be thinking incoherently and talking nonsensically were we to think and act in certain ways. There still are 'bounds of sense', but we cannot survey them in the manner that philosophers have supposed. 'Logic', one might say, 'is transcendental' (6.13); but this does not mean that there are no such things as logical laws that coherent thought respects; we simply aren't in a position to establish what they are, or note that they are indeed logical laws.[18]

Now can we make sense of this view? One resolute criticism is obvious: if the existence of meaning is such an ineffable fact, how come we have managed to say so much about it in the last couple of paragraphs? A proponent of the view might not be too shaken by this criticism, however. He might say that the view points to a limit on what we can comprehend, and hence cannot be expected to be explicable without contradiction or graspable without the need for an extraordinary kind of insight. As Descartes says of God, this may be a 'fact' or 'possibility' that, like a mountain, we can only 'touch [but not] put our arms around' (Descartes 1991, p. 35). And even if one did convince oneself that this view was philosophically confused, one might still argue that the early Wittgenstein held it, he being, after all, only mortal.[19]

So ought we to accept such a reading? It is, in fact, a reading with which I have had sympathy in the past, but I will not defend it here. My reason is, basically, that I think the *Tractatus* offers us an elucidation of con-formism which shows it and the reading just sketched to be confused; that elucidation questions whether we really have a sense of what it is that, according to that reading, we cannot do. Rather than the con-formity of thought and world being a matter that cannot be judged, we simply have not assigned sense to that very 'possibility', to that 'feat', nor to the corresponding 'unintelligibility' that we might take the 'failure of con-formity' to be.[20] It is not that we are incapable of talking about the issue of con-formity/non-con-formity; rather, we have not assigned sense to this 'issue'; not only are we incapable of saying, without revealing ourselves as confused, what it is that exercises us—that, after all, could be offered as a formulation of what

---

[17] Clearly, there are other philosophical and theological analogies here too, with, e.g., Anselm's adaptation of the Platonic image of a 'supreme and unapproachable light': '[W]hatsoever I see, I see through it, as the weak eye sees what it sees through the light of the sun, which in the sun itself it cannot look upon. . . . O supreme and unapproachable light! . . . Everywhere thou art, and I see thee not. In thee I move, and in thee I have my being; and I cannot come to thee. Thou art within me, and about me, and I feel thee not' (1926 [1078], ch. 16).
[18] Cf. n. 25 below for my own reading of 6.13.
[19] A further philosophical worry is, of course, that this inexpressible issue is also unthinkable; the kind of unattainable perspective imagined is one which we must attain not only in order to be able to *say* that 'meaning is' or, to take a verificationist twist, to *test* whether 'meaning is'; it is also one that we must attain if we are to contemplate its being so, as we may imagine we are doing right now.
[20] Cf. Sect. 3.5's discussion of how a god who could stand outside our ways of making sense would not know which test to perform.

the view being criticized requires—but we also have an alternative and far more prosaic explanation—in terms of sign/symbol conflation—of how we come to be so exercised.[21] Philosophy is 'full' of confusions that arise out of such conflations (3.324), and according to the reading I have set out in Chapters 5–7, that is exactly what our concern over con-formity is too. So, for example, the 'illogical thinking' into which we may fear to descend through the failure of con-formity of our thought and the world is not the violation of any 'bounds of sense', but simply the mistaking of combinations of signs without sense for combinations with sense; and this distinction between *signs* is not the kind of 'logical/illogical' distinction that a con-formist story, even an ineffable one, might be imagined to explain.

Now one might wonder whether con-formity is all there is to the 'intelligibility' of thought and talk anyway. But the question that my reading raises is: What else might this be? What does one mean when one says that 'meaning exists' or 'that', or 'how', 'meaning is', that we '*can* think' or '*can* speak meaningfully'? Even if these are 'inexpressible', one feels the need for *some* sense of the *kind* of 'fact' or 'phenomenon' that is being alluded to; what the critique of con-formity that I see in the early Wittgenstein requires is that, if this sense is to be provided, it be provided without drawing on a con-formist image of thought and talk 'fitting' the world.

What, then, of the sanity analogy? Am I committed to some analogue of the claim that there is no issue of sanity to worry over? I think not. What I am committed to is the notion that, if utterances are meaningless, then that is not a matter of their possessing 'the wrong sense'; instead they lack sense. An analogous view of insanity would be that it is the absence of thoughts rather than the thinking of 'illogical thoughts'. There is an issue of sanity to worry about, just as there is one of meaningfulness to worry about; but in both cases it is the danger of our receding into the mere mouthing of words.[22]

What I offer next is a sketch of a third view of Wittgenstein's solipsistic sympathies, one consistent with the reading I have offered of other issues in the *Tractatus* and one which brings to the fore the idea that we have not assigned sense to the demand for 'intelligibility', expressible or inexpressible.[23]

[21] This prosaic quality is worth flagging, since some critics, and indeed some advocates, of resolute readings associate such readings with 'the post-modern predilection for paradox' (Hacker 2000, p. 360) or with Zen (cf. Hacker 2000, pp. 370, 378, and 381, and forthcoming work by Rupert Read). I do, however, think that this prosaic explanation is profound; as Chs. 14–15 will argue, it is as profound as the prosaic distinction between the letter and the spirit.

[22] I won't attempt to assess here quite what the implications of this view of sanity are, or whether this is a tenable view.

[23] In McManus 2004*a* I draw on this interpretation of solipsism to explain the *Tractatus*'s striking remarks on scepticism (cf. 6.51).

8.6 SOLIPSISM, INTERNAL RELATIONS,
AND THE SIGN/SYMBOL HYBRID

If the truth in (not *of*) solipsism is the truth in (not *of*) the assertion of an internal relation, Section 4.10 suggests that the person who hears the assertion in question—'what the solipsist says'—*as* an assertion, as articulating a position on an issue, has yet to see what the person who offers this 'assertion' means: their offering that 'assertion' is meant to throw into relief a contextualizing confusion in our thought. My suggestion is that this context is the confused notion of intelligibility as con-formity, and that the truth *in* solipsism—'what solipsism means'—'shows itself' when we find ourselves unable to imagine con-formity or its absence between propositions and world without taking for granted the meaning of the propositions in question. The conclusion we should then draw is that we have not given sense to this notion of language 'working', or of the associated notions of our thinking 'making sense' or 'being possible'.

'What solipsism means', which Wittgenstein describes as something that 'shows itself', is, I suggest, what the argument of Section 3.5 shows. 'What solipsism says' emerged in that argument at the point at which the argument revealed a circularity in our thinking. What is misleading about the gloss on that argument with which Section 8.2 opened—that it demonstrates that 'language and world are internally related'—and which Section 8.3 developed—that it demonstrates that 'subject and world are internally related'—is that it presents as conclusions of that argument what are really interim conclusions, our arrival at which shows us that our thinking—which led us to those interim conclusions—is confused.

What the argument of Section 3.5 actually demonstrates is that *when* we puzzle over the con-formity of language and world, we must take for granted the meaning of the words whose use we are imagining con-forming or failing to con-form to the form of the world. *In the course of thinking through this (confused) project*, we find that we are obliged to take for granted what that project conceives of as the 'meaningfulness' of our language. But this does not imply that we, *when 'outside' that project*, must take our propositions *as* meaning*ful*, that we cannot question their con-formity to reality. That would leave in place the contextualizing 'assumption' that, I suggest, it is Wittgenstein's concern to shift: that 'intelligibility as con-formity' has a clear sense. If it does not, then we are confused when we think of 'it' as an issue that one might question (whether and how language and world con-form) or as something that must be taken for granted (as something internal to the constitution of a proposition or beyond the range of possible judgement or test). The work of the argument of Section 3.5 is to show that we have not assigned sense to this 'intelligibility', to this 'con-formity', whether it 'holds' or 'does not hold', is an 'external' or 'internal property', is 'effable' or 'ineffable', 'empirical' or 'transcendental', or indeed whether 'the subject con-forms to the world' (as the realist thinks) or 'the world con-forms to the Subject' (as an idealist, such as the solipsist, thinks).

The conclusion of the argument of Section 3.5 is that, unless we *surreptitiously* rely on the meaning of the proposition in question, we cannot fill out a story of the 'intelligibility' of a proposition as a matter of its con-formity to a possible fact. The argument could be seen as showing how (to modify 5.64) realism—which would hold the form of reality over the form of thought as a standard to which the latter must be brought to con-form—leads to solipsism if it is thought through strictly. But realism does not lead us there to leave us there. The fact that our strictly thought-through realism has turned out to rest upon a solipsism shows that something went wrong somewhere, that in some way we don't understand what we are doing. Hence the solipsism we are led to is a 'conclusion' we reach and then *abandon*, because having reached 'it' we should see that there was a move earlier in the conjuring trick (*PI* § 308) that we missed and which confused us. Our 'conclusion' is not a free-standing positive discovery; it is the discovery that a certain explanatory project fails, that it is in some way wrong-headed.[24]

For example, when thinking about the notion that thought links language and world, we found ourselves realizing that the subject we had invoked was an agency with the capacity we sought to explain. To think that that argument shows that our 'capacity to think' is something we cannot coherently question—that intelligibility as con-formity is an 'internal property' of a thought, and the possession of such thoughts an 'internal property' of a subject—is to misunderstand, and underestimate, our embarrassment. It is to over-elaborate on the fact that *we* have tied ourselves in knots. The final step is to hear these interim 'assertions' as we hear the 'assertion' that the person who crosses the line first *always* wins: namely, not as assertions at all, but as things that our being confused endowed with the air of being assertions.

Thus, to take the arguments presented as showing that we need a solipsistic metaphysics or an ineffable transcendentalism is to turn off the road too early. It is to attempt to 'account for' what we need to recognize as *perplexing* and *interim* conclusions, conclusions which only those who misunderstand them would try

---

[24] There is a certain analogy perhaps with proof by *reductio ad absurdum*. First, the conclusion we ought to draw when we understand the proof is not necessarily the conclusion which we find as the final line in the argument; instead, what we ought to take away is suspicion about the argument's premisses. Secondly, what we then discover is that we did not really understand what it was that we were saying when we articulated those premisses. Thirdly, it is just about possible that someone who offers a *reductio ad absurdum* argument might be seen as *defending* the conclusion that that argument reaches, rather than trying to force our critical attention back on to the argument's premisses; to make this mistake is to miss the fact that there is something seriously problematic about the conclusion, that it is self-contradictory. We don't quite have that in the case of the *Tractatus*, but we have the 'conclusion' that the propositions that make up the 'argument' presented are nonsensical, which, it seems to me, is not far off. (An obvious disanalogy is that reductios are normally taken to show that one of their premisses must be *false*, rather than nonsensical.)

to account for. To react in this way to our finding that we were having to take for granted 'feats' we were seeking to explain—by developing either a speculative metaphysical theory that would explain how we *can* take those feats for granted or a quasi-mystical view that says that we cannot but take them for granted—is to misunderstand that finding: it is to jump in with an answer to a question which only someone who has got the wrong end of the stick raises. Our taking those feats for granted is an embarrassment, something we do not need to 'account for'; instead, we must go in search of the earlier move in the conjuring trick that led us up what we now recognize as a blind alley.[25]

A proposal I offered is that the earlier move in our cases is a glossing over of the sign/symbol distinction.[26] Our succumbing to that confusion 'allows' us to 'imagine' a matter of fact about whether a proposition and a possible fact correspond, endowing with pseudo-content the philosophically interesting pseudo-question of whether a proposition 'works'. As a sign, there is no reason to think that the hybrid sentence/proposition 'corresponds' or 'fails to correspond' to any aspect of reality. But as a symbol, there is an already established way for the hybrid sentence/proposition to be used, and hence a possible fact to which its use ought to conform. In the confusion of a sign/symbol hybrid, these two incompatible characteristics are combined, and we generate a feat that will define for us the 'meaningfulness' of a proposition: the maintenance of a con-formity between the

---

[25] I would interpret Wittgenstein's leading us to the proposal 'Logic is transcendental' (6.13) in a similar fashion. When we say that our ways of thinking and talking are 'intelligible', 'meaningful', or 'logical', we imagine ourselves evaluating them in a way which makes sense only if those ways of thinking and talking are indeed what we think of as 'intelligible', 'meaningful', or 'logical'; but this does not show that the 'logicality' of what we say is shown in everything we say, but, rather, that we do not really understand what we mean by our ways of thinking and talking being 'logical'. If we are tempted by the interpretation sketched in Sect. 8.5, it is tempting to say that we must take our ways of thinking and talking as 'basic' or 'given'. But my reading questions whether we understand the explanatory urge that we imagine here being disappointed or being held back: rather than seeing their 'possibility', say, as unquestionable or unexaminable, we have failed to assign sense to this 'possibility'. (But why think that an expression like 'the transcendental' is meant to signal that all is not well with our thinking? What considerations might be offered that parallel those offered in connection with 'internal relations' in Sect. 4.9? All I will say here is that the notion that a proposal like 'Logic is transcendental' might conclude a search for philosophical illumination would have struck 'recovering ex-idealists' such as Russell and Moore, in particular, as absurd. (Cf. also Sect. 13.2's reflections on the proposal that '[e]thics is transcendental' (6.421) and Ch. 14's exploration of how that proposal might be 'climbed and then thrown away'.))

[26] What exactly is the analogue of this distinction in the case of thought? Wittgenstein does not make this particularly clear, but we can, I think, make a suggestion. In a famous letter to Russell, Wittgenstein confesses: 'I don't know *what* the constituents of a thought are but I know *that* it must have such constituents which correspond to the words of Language.' Such matters are 'a matter of psychology to find out' (*NB* 130). A suggestion that might be offered, though it is not without difficulty, is that thought-signs might be compared to brain states; thought-symbols might then be compared to the type of item which plays the role in thinkers that those brain states play in us. One difficulty that this obvious allusion to functionalism raises is that the roles alluded to are typically thought to be causal. As long as this interpretation of functionalism's insights is accepted, that aspect of the comparison is questionable; but there are reasons to doubt that interpretation (cf. McManus 1999, sect. 8.2).

hybrid and a possible fact. The contingency of that relation is 'provided' by its 'independent' character as a *sign*—'it is arbitrary'—and the relevance of its relation to only this particular possible fact by its 'already committed' character as a *symbol*—its identification is in itself an identification of its use.

David Pears suggests that the following strategy informs the *Tractatus*:

> The argument which [Wittgenstein] uses to establish [his metaphysic] starts from the existence of factual language. We evidently do succeed in using this language to describe the world, but how is it done? His answer is that we succeed only because there is a fixed grid of possible combinations of objects to which the structure of our language conforms. The grid must exist and connections must be made with it if language is going to work. But it clearly does work and so the metaphysical conclusions follow. (Pears 1987, p. 6)

Wittgenstein's intent, I suggest, is to point out that we have confused ourselves in thinking that we have at our disposal an understanding of what it is for language to 'work'. It seems utterly innocent to say that since we use language, language 'is possible', or to infer from the fact that I am thinking that 'I *can* think', that I have 'the capacity to think'. But are the philosophically interesting 'feats' that we (hope we) have in mind really clear to us? My hangover may lead me to say, 'I just can't think today', or the noise of machinery may lead me to say, 'Talking is impossible here'. But I would suggest that it is Wittgenstein's aim to show that 'the possibility of thought' and 'the possibility of language' that the conception of intelligibility as con-formity articulates are 'feats' that 'manifest themselves' before us only when we become confused. I may describe one string of signs as meaningful, and another as meaningless, but is the 'achievement' of the former more philosophically interesting than their having been given a use in a language, while the latter have not? My suggestion is that, according to Wittgenstein, we have failed to assign to 'language' or 'thought' a sense by reference to which we can pose the question of intelligibility as con-formity.[27]

---

[27] I want to mention briefly here the view set out by Peter Sullivan (1996) in a short but dense discussion. He too organizes his reading of the *Tractatus* around the question of whether we can acquire 'an assurance of the harmony through which thinking genuinely engages with the world' (p. 203). He argues that '[t]he insight that leads the solipsist to give voice is that the notions of world and thought are ... intrinsically tied, that the world is not something *other*, so that it would need the kind of positive philosophy aimed at establishing an *a priori* order to ensure thought's engagement with it' (p. 204). He proposes that the 'worry that reality might outrun language is silenced only by conceiving of language directly as that which embraces reality' (p. 209). Sullivan's reading is subtle and complex, but a misgiving that my discussion suggests is over whether there are clear senses behind its terms 'harmony', 'engagement', 'outrunning', and 'embracing'. My worry, as with Pears's seemingly innocent talk of 'language working', is that there isn't. Now if that were to be Sullivan's point, his view would be closer to a view of the kind I have presented here, though that is not an outcome that, I take it, he would welcome. (Sullivan (2002) sets out some of his views on 'resolute' readings.) But, in any case, it seems to me that he is driven to make claims—about 'the *transparency* or intrinsic truth-directedness of the proposition' (1996, p. 197), about language's 'transparency or intrinsic sense' (p. 212), and about 'the very notions of what it is for there to be a world ... and of what it is to think [being] intrinsically tied' (p. 203)—that evoke instead the mid-point of the dialectic of the argument set out in Sect. 3.5.

That argument attempted to show that our need to take the 'meaningfulness' of propositions for granted when we consider the 'harmony' between them and the world drives us to 'assertions' of which 'propositions possess sense intrinsically' might be another excellent example. But, crucially, the argument is that we come to these 'assertions' only as problematic, 'transitional' formulations which represent not stable views on philosophical issues but indications of confusion in our thinking.

9

Objects Revisited

For Wittgenstein, internal properties and relations emerge in contexts of mis-understanding. The thrust of asserting that there are internal relations between objects and possible facts, and between language and world, might seem to be to indicate an explanation of what makes sense. But when seen through, they illuminate the *illusory* nature of—rather than a basis for—such an explanation. Our talk of these 'internal relations' suggests that the way we talk reflects the way things are; but, viewed through the picture analogy, we see that what we have done here is glimpse in a distorted fashion the fact that we do talk as we do, and then mistakenly misconstrue what we see before us as a reason for why we talk as we do.

Chapter 8 has shown how a parallel confusion informs our thinking about thought. A certain confusion presents thinkers as 'externally related' to the world that they think about, a confusion to which Wittgenstein responds by depict-ing that relation as 'internal', but with the ultimate intent of showing that we have not ascribed sense to the 'space' within which we imagine subject and world 'apart' or indeed 'together', *related* externally *or* internally. This chapter returns to Wittgenstein's proposals about 'objects' in order to reveal how they too can be seen as reflecting our failure to ascribe sense to the notion of the thinker 'coming to', or indeed already being 'in contact with', its world.

There is, none the less, a certain bland construal that one can give to Witt-genstein's specification of 'objects', which parallels Chapter 7's bland construal of 'shared form': when we use a particular proposition, we look at the world as possessed of a certain form, but that match of form between language and world is not a basis on which that proposition might be said to 'make sense'. Similarly, we can't make sense of deep worries about the capacity of 'what we think about' to be thought about: there are no questions to be raised, in connection with the referents of the terms of the ultimate analyses of our propositions, about 'their existence', 'their composition', or 'how they can combine to form facts'. But this points not to how the world must be constituted in order for thought to be pos-sible, but to a confusion at the root of the idea of 'thought being possible'. A con-formist sees in these non-issues, which one might express as the holding of certain 'internal relations', a deep metaphysical moral about how the referents of the terms of our ultimate analyses must be; but what they should see before them are *counter*-con-formist insights.

9.1 LIMITS ON DOUBTING THE FULFILMENT
OF 'CONDITIONS OF MEANING'

Recall our kitchen table model. There is nothing in that model corresponding to
the destruction of the cars or of Frank. One can imagine another system of representation within which those events might be represented: one in which a broken
cup is a destroyed car, and a pepper-pot without its lid is a dead person; or one
in which destruction is represented by the removal of the cup or the pepper-pot
from the table. But these possible events are not represented within our original
example; they are not 'asserted', 'expressed', or 'put into words'.

But it certainly would seem to make a difference to the success of the descriptions we would give using this model if Frank did not exist. Such a description is
not simply false (presenting something as being there that wasn't), because within
the system of representation to which the proposition in question belongs, there
is no way to represent the relevant *truth*, his not being there. There might be in
another system: for example, an adapted version of the model that represented
Frank's non-existence by removing the pepper-pot from the table. But in the
model as it stands, there is no way to represent Frank's non-existence or, by the
same token, his existence. So we seem to confront here an example of a real condition on the meaningfulness of a description, a contingent fact that undermines
the capacity of that description to say something true or false. We may imagine
this condition as a fact about the 'component parts' of Frank; those parts being
arranged in a particular way is what we mean when we say that Frank exists. If they
are not so arranged—if that condition does not hold—then our model of Frank
at the crossroads can be used to say neither something true nor something false.

There is an undeniable sense in which our making statements with a determinate meaning often depends on the holding of background facts about the things
we are discussing. Our thought and talk seem to be embedded in particular contexts, and to be vulnerable to a variety of different kinds of misfire when those
contexts change. The issues here are complicated. To take just one example,
the relevant form of dependency seems to be different for 'expressions' like the
pepper-pot, which operates as a proper name, and the cups, which, depending on
the uses to which we put this model—which is to say, the particular things we
want to say using it—could pick out some car or other or instead a particular car.
Which function it performs will affect what difference it makes should it turn out
that what the cup represents does not exist.

Though the resources needed to deal seriously with these difficulties may perhaps be found in Wittgenstein's later work (for example, in the discussion of
names in the *Philosophical Investigations*),[1] they are not to be found, I think, in

---

[1] Clearly these topics also overlap with some of the central topics of twentieth-century analytic
philosophy, and are explored in the work of Russell, Strawson, Kripke, Kaplan, Donellan, Searle,
and many others. They also overlap with issues on which Sect. 16.6 touches.

his early work. There his concern seems different, focusing on the status of the 'conditions of meaningfulness' that we think we have uncovered.

Wittgenstein proposes that objects 'form the substance of the world' (2.021); on this basis, their existence cannot be denied: 'If the world had no substance ... [i]t would then be impossible to form a picture of the world (true or false)' (2.021, 2.0212). If the world's having 'substance' is what 'allows us' to make claims with meaning, then one cannot deny the existence of the 'substance of the world' without 'implying' that one's own claim is without meaning. What corresponds to this abstract case in the world of the picture analogy? Consider the following question: if the fact that Frank does not exist makes a sentence like 'Frank crossed the road' meaningless, doesn't it make the sentence 'Frank does not exist' meaningless too? In which case, what does it mean to assert that Frank does exist? This may be too quick: as indicated above, to specify the relevant condition, we may not mention Frank (though there are, I suspect, problems lying in this direction); instead, the condition concerns his 'component parts', and statements about Frank are to be understood as abbreviations of statements about those parts. But do the expressions that are meant to pick out those parts have reference? Setting aside the particular issues that arise with different kinds of referring expressions (with which, as I have indicated, the early Wittgenstein does not engage seriously), a more general point arises here: our asking questions about the 'fulfilment' of 'conditions of meaning' must, at some point, come to an end, in that those questions must themselves have meaning. We may have worries of some sort about the sense of our words, but those worries cannot 'go all the way down' without their own meaning—their identity as the worries that we take them to be—being eroded. I will return to this issue after placing it in a broader context, inspired by Chapter 8's discussion, which will also tie this issue in with (O-S).

9.2 LEARNING A FIRST LANGUAGE AND LEARNING OF THE WORLD AND ITS ORDER

Learning a second language is learning which concepts are expressed by which words; but learning a first language is a matter of learning the concepts themselves, of coming to see what they pick out in the world. Thus one learns that there are *x*s and what it is about them that makes them *x*s. But Section 8.3 revealed a sense in which this feat seems impossible: our learning anything about the world depends upon our already dividing up the world using concepts, into *x*s and non-*x*s. In this way, the issue of the existence of that about which we think and our having correctly appreciated its character is, one might say, always prejudged, though it is also something we cannot coherently doubt: only those whose thoughts have content can doubt. So, as with the 'discovery' of other 'internal properties' and 'internal relations', what we encounter here is an apparent explanatory failure of sorts: there can be no deep question about the existence of the ultimate referents of our terms or about whether we have successfully grasped how they are constituted. One might then conclude that since we can think—'We evidently do succeed in using this language to describe the world' (Pears 1987, p. 6)—these referents must 'necessarily exist' and must 'necessarily be simple'.

But is this the right response to what we have discovered? Or instead—again as previous encounters with 'internal properties' and 'internal relations' should lead us to expect—should we examine whether we really understand the explanations, the perspective, that we seek, but which we feel cannot be provided? Ought we instead to concede that we cannot make sense of the questions that we have been posing: that we cannot ultimately make sense of our learning of—latching on to—the objects of our thought, learning of—latching on to—their ordered character, or the image of a possible self-consciousness of a supposed mastery of the 'existence' and 'order' of those objects that this image of learning expresses?

Compare the manner in which we reached the conclusion that a proposition must eventually show its sense. That, I argued, is an interim conclusion which reveals that something has gone wrong with our grasp of what it is to understand a proposition: thinking that one might be told how a proposition represents is confused, in that our attempt to make good on this demand requires us eventually to postulate a proposition which simply shows its sense, a proposition which we grasp *without* that demand being met.

A parallel picture emerges of the necessary existence and simplicity of objects. Any learning we do has to be done on the basis of already treating the world as available and ordered. Ought we to conclude that therefore it is? The interpretation that I have been developing suggests instead that we should conclude that we therefore haven't really assigned sense to 'coming to grasp the world and its order'. Our arriving at the conclusion that any learning presupposes that the world is available and ordered does not show 'how things are', but that we have confused ourselves: it is an interim conclusion that is to be 'thrown away' with the confused project within which it emerges as a sign of our confusion, the 'project' of understanding how we come to grasp the world and its order. What is true in saying that objects necessarily exist and are simple is that we can make no sense of there being a question about the existence and character of the ultimate referents of our terms. But this shows that we can't make sense of the question, not that these referents having these internal properties is its answer.

On this construal, the metaphysics of objects 'accounts for' in the same way that solipsism 'accounts for'. As with solipsism, to react—to our finding that we were having to take for granted 'feats' we were seeking to explain—by developing a speculative metaphysical theory (here, the necessary existence and simplicity of objects) that would explain how we *can* take those feats for granted is to misunderstand that finding; the metaphysics of objects jumps in with an answer to a question raised only by someone who has got the wrong end of the stick. Our taking those feats for granted is an embarrassment, something we do not need to 'account for'; instead, we must go in search of the earlier moves in the conjuring trick that led us up this (now recognized) blind alley. What we have discovered is that we have assigned no sense to the 'issue' of 'whether the world is available to us or ordered'; to conclude that, therefore, it is, is to underestimate our embarrassment.

9.3 THE DEMAND FOR EXPLANATION AND A SHADOW CAST BY LANGUAGE

Having seen the problems that we face in understanding our mastery of a first language as a response to the way that the world is, the picture of the world that we have deduced presents itself as a particular mythology of the world: it is the way the world looks to those who think that our mastery of a first language rests on something like a judgement of the way that the world is. The view of the world that we have deduced 'makes sense' inasmuch as it is the way that the world *must* look if you happen to be in the grip of that particular fantasy of 'our mastery of symbols', its justification, and the 'possibility' of thought; that world is the world that the pseudo-logic of that fantasy demands.

The point of showing us this is, I suggest, to bring us to a knife-edge, where we recognize for the first time that our thoughts do not have the form 'This is how the world must be', but rather the form 'If one holds to this conception of meaning and one's relationship to it, this is how the world must be'. The correct way of understanding these conclusions, I would suggest, is as the elaboration of a perspective that we now recognize as confused, as nonsensical. Having reached these conclusions, we 'throw them away', along with the confusions whose elaboration culminated in those conclusions and which we now recognize as a commitment of ours, and as a confused commitment at that. Wittgensteinian objects are what we must ultimately 'observe' if we think that our understanding 'rests on' something like an observation of how things are; but Wittgenstein's ultimate point is to show us that we have failed to assign sense to that 'thought'.

Our failure to complete our confused explanatory project casts a shadow not only on the world, but on our mental lives too. Corresponding to the features of the world which would underpin the intelligibility of our talk is a certain perception of those features; when we cannot see how this project is to be completed, but are still in its grip, and thus believe it somehow must be—hazily believing that we know what these 'features' and 'perceptions' are—the former 'features' and the latter 'perception' must be nothings (since the project is confused) which we misunderstand as somethings (since we do not yet see that confusion). We have actually run out of anything sensible to say, and anything real to say it about, and our last, confused step is to propose that the 'features' and the 'perception' (to which we are confusedly committed) are inarticulable: we ascribe to ourselves an inarticulably basic acquaintance with something beyond description, 'colourless objects' (2.0232), without composition and without describable relation to anything outside themselves. My suggestion is that to declare that our talk ultimately rests on an immediate 'seeing' of 'colourless objects' is one step away from recognizing that the 'project' of explaining the 'possibility' of 'meaningful' talk leaves us nothing to say or think: our 'experience' of the pure and simple here is the experience of empty words.[2]

9.4 A BLAND 'BELIEF IN OBJECTS'

But, it could be objected, doesn't Wittgenstein himself believe in elementary propositions, in names and objects? Isn't he committed, at the very least, to views about the nature of language that involve those notions? He does indeed seem to be;[3] but this does not imply that he thinks that the 'objects' that emerge from our analysis of language show us '*the* joints of reality', or that the ways in which we use language are grounded in the world being 'formed' metaphysically in line with the 'form' that language takes. 'There are objects', in that language breaks reality up into units that in some sense correspond to its words; but that correspondence does not explain why language breaks up the world as it does; to think so is to hear an echo, or see the shadow, of language as if it were an object there to be perceived. Language-use may present the world as formed, but this does not mean that language-use is a response to the world's own 'form'.

Chapter 7 argued that there is a certain innocent construal that can be given to the notion that language and world share a form: having adopted a particular means of comparing states of affairs, they can then present themselves as having or lacking a matching form. But such a match cannot be seen as a *basis* on which such a means of comparison, such a method of description, is established: we have not assigned any sense to such a match or mismatch if a means of comparison is not already in place. I would suggest that a corresponding, and equally innocent, gloss can be given to the notion that our propositions divide up into

[2] Though the metaphor of 'colourless objects' doesn't encourage this thought, I would suggest that the component 'demands' that make up the 'demand' that language 'works' can be seen at work in our demand that qualia exist: entities that are, one might say, *constituted* by a single property (redness, being-middle-C, etc.), whose existence is not subject to the kind of doubt that 'ordinary samples' are, and about which we are necessarily inarticulate. But I am inclined to see here not a reason for believing in qualia—as a certain kind of phenomenalistic reading of the *Tractatus* might—but a possible way into the puzzle of how we seem forced into that belief. But I cannot make that case here.

[3] *PI* §46, e.g., certainly suggests an earlier 'belief' in 'objects', as does Wittgenstein's well-known reply to a query of Malcolm's: 'I asked Wittgenstein whether, when he wrote the *Tractatus*, he had ever decided upon anything as an *example* of a "simple object". His reply was that at that time his thought had been that he was a *logician*; and that it was not his business, as a logician, to try to decide whether this thing or that was a simple thing or a complex thing' (Malcolm 1984, p. 70). Chs. 11–12 will explain his understanding of atomic facts and elementary propositions.

names and represent facts that divide up into 'objects' with particular 'internal properties'; metaphysical substance begins to leak into such a claim when we take that division to be a *response* to having found objects of that form, endowed with those 'properties'. A proposition is a projection of a certain framework on to what it is applied to, a division of that subject-matter into 'things' that can then be 'so' or 'not so'. But adopting such a proposition cannot itself be a response to having seen that 'things are so': until a proposition has been 'adopted', the question of 'how things are' has no determinate answer.

I suggest that there is something wittingly bland about Wittgenstein's specification of 'objects'. By 'objects', Wittgenstein means, I suggest, 'what we talk about'. Note *TLP* 2.01's oddly bland gloss on 'objects':

An atomic fact is a combination of objects (entities, things).

The 'subject-matter' of elementary propositions is then 'entities', 'things that there are'; conspicuously, this is not meant to dictate, for example, that properties and relations are somehow unreal. Anscombe (1959, pp. 98–101) and Ricketts (1996, p. 72) have both claimed that it does, but at *NB* 61, Wittgenstein tells us that '[r]elations and properties, etc. are *objects*, too'.[4] This makes the above 'claim' about the composition of atomic facts bland, oddly uninformative, and uncontentious for anyone interested in traditional metaphysical questions about what 'kinds of things' there are.[5] Moreover, the 'claims' that Wittgenstein makes in ascribing to them the internal properties that he does could be heard as articulating little more than the 'claim' that what we talk about makes up states of affairs that we represent through propositions, and that it doesn't make sense for there to be *talk* of an 'issue' of whether there *is* anything to talk about or whether what we talk about is fit for talk about it.[6]

Section 9.2 has described how con-formist content leaks into these 'claims' when we imagine them as revealing characteristics of the world upon which our adoption of the propositions we use somehow rests. But substance may seem to be introduced into these claims from two other sources, through the meeting of the impossibility of two 'demands': 'determinacy of sense' and the impossibility

---

[4] Cf. also *L I* 120 (' "Objects" also include relations') and *VC* 252 ('A state of affairs, a phenomenon, is a combination of elements. But there is nothing in that combination which indicates that there is something thing-like, something property-like in it ... [Y]ou can no longer ask whether the primitive signs mean something thing-like or whether they represent properties or relations'). Ramsey discusses related issues in his 1925*b*.

[5] It is this blandness, along with a parallel 'blandness' that marks, I suggest, Wittgenstein's use of the term 'name' to denote 'constituents of propositions', that allows Wittgenstein's discussion some claim to be an elucidation of con-formism as such, rather than of a particular brand of con-formism.

[6] Wittgenstein's final, sustained, pre-*Tractatus* discussion of objects that has been preserved (from June 1915) clarifies how the 'proposals' we are tempted to make about 'objects' rest not, e.g., on having observed how they happen to be, but on, so to speak, their 'job description': '[W]e do not infer the existence of simple objects from the existence of particular simple objects, but rather know them—by description, as it were—as the end-product of analysis, by means of a process that leads to them' (*NB* 50). Cf. also *NB* 60.

of 'surprises in logic'. The latter we have already encountered, and struck Wittgenstein, I think, as just good sense (good sense rehearsed in Sect. 2.7). Among its consequences is the requirement that objects 'fit into one another like the links in a chain' (2.03), meaning '*that there isn't anything third* that connects the links but the links *themselves* make connexion with one another' (*LO* 23). Capacity so to link is an 'internal property' of objects, and there is no 'room' for a mediating 'third thing' that might explain why they are fit to form facts: such a role for 'logical forms' was one which Russell certainly entertained, the logical form of a fact such as 'Object *a* stands in relation *R* to object *b*' being part of the explanation of why a fact can be formed from two objects and a relation, but not one object and two relations.[7]

In this context, Wittgenstein's rejection of such a 'third thing' might seem like the making of a substantial claim about the composition of facts. But if 'logical substance' is an illusion, something that we come to 'believe in' through confusion, then it can only be misunderstanding that makes us believe that there is such a thing or that we would 'miss it' were there to be no such thing; indeed, Chapters 5–7 have argued that, following Wittgenstein's broader metaphilosophical hypothesis, the impression that there are substantial facts about how propositions or facts can be formed—an explanation of which we might imagine 'logical forms' contributing to—is the product of sign/symbol conflation and—in line with Section 4.10's proposal—the 'internal property' of constituents of facts ('objects') that they are fit to form facts is something of which we only 'need to learn' when confused.

What then of the 'determinacy of sense' requirement?

If a proposition tells us something . . . it must be susceptible of SHARP definition. (*NB* 61)

It is often said that Wittgenstein took over the 'determinacy of sense' as an unquestioned given,[8] a reflection of the very idea of meaning, perhaps adopted from Frege.[9] But it is a requirement over which Wittgenstein does worry. He connects it to the notion of a 'final analysis' of a proposition:

The demand for simple things *is* the demand for definiteness of sense. . . . If there is a final sense and a proposition expressing it completely, then there are also names for simple objects. (*NB* 63–4)

As a basis for embracing the 'determinacy' requirement, this leaves something to be desired, because whether there is such a 'final' or 'complete analysis' is itself

---

[7] Cf., e.g., Russell 1984 [1913].
[8] Glendinning says that the early Wittgenstein 'uncritically assumed' that 'a sentence . . . must have *a* definite sense' (1998, p. 81); Fogelin's reading of the *Tractatus* leads him to propose that '[t]here seems to be no compelling reason for adopting the doctrine of determinacy at all' (1987, p. 16).
[9] Cf., e.g., Glock 1996, p. 98: 'Wittgenstein imbibed Frege's ideal of determinacy of sense and the demand for completeness of definition.' Frege maintained that 'a concept that is not sharply defined is wrongly termed a concept' (Frege 1997 [1903], p. 139). Cf. also Ch. 2 n. 16.

something about which Wittgenstein had doubts.[10] These were assuaged by the time he wrote the *Tractatus*, but it is not clear how. In Appendix A, I will argue that the notion of a 'complete analysis' rests upon assumptions about the 'homogeneity' of language which the early Wittgenstein was unaware of making; this suggests that the author of the *Tractatus* may well have managed to convince himself that the possibility of such a 'complete analysis' is a matter of common sense; if so, so would be the 'determinacy of sense'.

There is another route, though, by which Wittgenstein comes to the 'determinacy' requirement; he sees it as a corollary of the mere good sense of the 'no logical surprises' requirement:

We might demand definiteness in this way too!: if a proposition is to make sense then the syntactical employment of each of its parts must be settled in advance.—It is, e.g., not possible *only subsequently to come upon* the fact that a proposition follows from it. But, e.g., what propositions follow from a proposition must be completely settled before that proposition can have a sense! (*NB* 64)[11]

Thus, if one follows these routes, the 'determinacy' requirement emerges either as a bland, commonsensical 'requirement' or as a corollary of the good sense that some 'explanatory needs' are illusions. In retrospect, and thanks largely to the later Wittgenstein, we tend to see it as neither. But at the time of writing the *Tractatus*, the 'determinacy' requirement would appear to have struck Wittgenstein as not really a substantial 'demand' at all.

9.5 DESCRIPTIONS MISCONSTRUED AS PRESCRIPTIONS

What the preceding discussion suggests is that, inasmuch as the early Wittgenstein does see his description of 'objects' as capturing something real, it expresses, at most, the 'requirement' that the world be 'logically bland', that certain explanatory projects cannot get off the ground because they are confused, illusory; we cannot make sense of questions of 'existence' and 'composition' about the referents of the terms of the ultimate analyses of our propositions, and there can be no 'logical substance' lurking within those propositions (or within facts) in the shape of 'mediating logical forms' or 'logical surprises' about which propositions follow from which (or which facts are 'supra-physically' incompatible with which others—a topic to which I will return in Ch. 11).

It should perhaps not be all that surprising that these 'counter-con-formist' 'requirements' invite a con-formist construal; like our response to the Straw Man, they sound like answers to the con-formist's questions, and indeed, I have argued

---

[10] Cf., e.g., *NB* 2 and 62.

[11] Cf. also *PT* 3.20102–3 and *PR* 87. This thought does have Fregean roots: '[A]s regards concepts, we have a requirement of sharp delimitation; if this were not satisfied it would be impossible to set forth logical laws about them' (1980 [1891], p. 33).

that a working through of the pseudo-logic of con-formism leads to these same requirements; but the final step is to recognize them *as* counter-con-formist. To evade that conclusion is to see that specification as a specification of how the world must be *before*, so to speak, it can be described in language, specifying certain properties which, if possessed by the world, might then make sense of our 'being able' to make sense of—describe—it. It is this same 'conclusion' that we come to when we conclude that the ultimate referents of the terms we use must be simple and necessarily existent entities. From the innocent-sounding claim that our talk and thought 'make sense', our inability to make sense of a certain kind of foundational judgement at the root of our thought and talk (through which we 'come to' the subject-matter of our thought and talk) is transformed into an apparently well-founded belief that the way we happen to think and talk is an accurate response to how the world must actually be, and an apparently well-founded belief about how the world is.

What the metaphysician's 'understanding' of 'objects' does, then, is conjure out of the fact that we use propositions with a particular sense a belief of the form, 'these are the utterances that it makes sense to use'; and our using these particular propositions is then articulated in terms of their sense corresponding to something real to which we, their users, are (somehow) sensitive. The (confused) desire to assert the necessary existence and simplicity of Wittgensteinian objects is a (confused) desire to assert that our propositions 'work'. What emerges is not merely empty flattery, in that this new kind of reason for thinking and talking as we do—'these propositions make sense'—obscures the many real reasons why we think and talk as we do. That I ignore certain aspects of what I see before me is now 'justified' by how things are before me; whatever reasons I may have or lack for only caring about what I do happen to care about are now occluded by (mythical) demands on the part of the world itself. This, I will argue later, helps to articulate how the *Tractatus* has an ethical point.

10

Method Revisited

This chapter will look back once again at Wittgenstein's methodology, picking out aspects that, I think, may be more easily understood in the light of Chapters 5–9.

10.1 ELUCIDATION AND 'THE ONLY STRICTLY CORRECT METHOD IN PHILOSOPHY'

We have seen how we can make sense of Wittgenstein's declaration that 'he who understands me finally recognizes [my propositions] as nonsensical' (6.54): to understand what is meant when Wittgenstein asserts that an internal relation holds is to learn that there is nothing to learn where the hearer had thought there was. To be told that winning and crossing the line first are 'internally related' is not to learn the answer to one's question; instead, it is to see that this 'question', and the kind of 'answer' we crave, embody a confusion. One needs to come to see an earlier confusion in one's thinking, an earlier step in the conjuring trick that one missed. Then one can hear what one thought was Wittgenstein's novel answer to one's question as instead helping to articulate why that question is a mirage. Thus Wittgenstein's book of asserted internal relations should be 'thrown away' once we have 'climbed out through, on and over' its 'propositions'. Such a book is not a book of answers: it is 'not a text-book' (*TLP* preface). Our philosophical questions about 'how names and propositions are related', or 'how names and objects are related', are not answered. What we learn is that our understanding of, and interest in, these matters were confused. Once such a book has done its work on us, it has rendered itself redundant for us.

But then why not just *tell* the confused person that his 'questions' are illusions? Why offer instead a book of asserted internal relations that he will ultimately 'throw away', after he has 'climbed up' the 'ladder' they provide? There are two reasons, one of which I will address in this section, the other in the following section. These will help us to understand what is perhaps the second most perplexing methodological remark of the *Tractatus* after 6.54. In the immediately preceding paragraph, Wittgenstein talks about what 'the right method of philosophy *would* be' (italics added), clearly intimating that this is not the method he has himself used. The 'right method' would involve demonstrating to 'someone [who] wished to say something metaphysical' 'that he had given no meaning to certain signs in his propositions':

This method would be unsatisfying to the other—he would not have the feeling that we were teaching him philosophy—but it would be the only strictly correct method. (6.53)

Wittgenstein's purpose is to show that the problems of philosophy emerge from misunderstanding. The people he must address are those who believe in the problems of philosophy, and they, *ex hypothesi*, are people who are confused. In particular, they see issues which are, in fact, illusions, and, as philosophers, these 'issues' are what interest them; these 'issues' are their distinctive business. This population, 'the philosophers', and these problems, 'the problems of philosophy', are internally related, one might say. Wittgenstein later described the metaphysician as like someone with an illness, as someone who needs a kind of treatment. The project of developing a *Begriffsschrift* is, for the early Wittgenstein, the key measure in our efforts at *preventative* medicine. I suggest that translating the propositions we use into the *Begriffsschrift* represents what 'the right method in philosophy' *would* be. In our existing notations, one can substitute for one another similar-looking signs that express different symbols, producing strings of signs that have no sense but which *look* or *sound* as if they do. This is impossible within the *Begriffsschrift*: the *Alice* books couldn't have been written in such a notation, and the philosopher would find that nothing corresponds to his propositions in that notation either.

But prevention is one thing, cure another. The world is already populated by plenty of the already infected, and it is they who discuss, and claim an understanding of, the problems of philosophy. How ought one to treat such an existing sufferer? First of all, one needs to reach him, and this requires that we enter into his (nonsensical) conversation; if one wants to talk to such a person, one needs to address his issues. Such a person might well have no interest in the *Begriffsschrift* project, because he may not feel as if that will teach him any philosophy; he may, as a matter of contingent fact, be interested in your observations about different uses of words, just as he may be interested in your observations about stamp collecting; but he won't think that this has anything to do with philosophy, with his questions, with him *as a philosopher*.[1] He is not interested in how meaning has been assigned to a variety of words; he is interested in making progress with

---

[1] Clearly, the most immediate targets of many of Wittgenstein's critical insights are Frege and Russell, and it would be absurd to describe either as lacking interest in the *Begriffsschrift*. But the crucial question that must be addressed (and which would require two separate studies of their own) is: Do these philosophers see the *Begriffsschrift* merely as a weapon against confused metaphysical claims that surface grammar may inspire, or also as an aid to better metaphysics? There are some strongly Wittgensteinian readings of Frege (cf., e.g., Weiner 1990) which suggest that he embraced the former Wittgensteinian option. The case is stronger, at least superficially, with respect to Russell: passages quoted in Sect. 2.4 suggest that he saw analysis as promising a radical elimination of philosophical problems. Nevertheless, even during the phases when he held such views, Russell undertook projects that, from a Wittgensteinian point of view, rest upon significant metaphysical commitments (such as his analyses of matter and mind in Russell 1918 [1914c] and 1921). The reason why this is not simple inconsistency on Russell's part is that opinions may differ over the difficult issue of what constitutes a metaphysical claim. That difficulty is the reason why I have tied Wittgenstein's 'critique of metaphysics' to the ideas of con-formism and logical truth (though I

the questions—which he thinks are real and pressing—of metaphysics and the philosophy of language, mind, and logic.

Recall our confused observer of races: he thinks he needs to learn something about how those who come first train, or about their diet or their tactics in the race, not something that he might learn by looking in a rule book, at the rule about how the *word* 'winner' is defined. Imagine now the outlook of a pre-Fregean philosopher who mulls over 'Nobody' and 'Something' as referring to deeply puzzling 'things', things that might be seen as the most basic subjects of thought in general. The oddity of these amorphous 'things' might lead him to say that these terms actually work by referring first and foremost to certain kinds of ideas, ideas of a specifically abstract sort. Perhaps that idea might be explained by invoking mental images, with 'Somebody', say, conjuring up in our mind a fuzzy image that is of a person but is sufficiently fuzzy as not to pick out any particular person. Now imagine how uninterested such a philosopher might be on hearing of the work of Frege: 'What possible impression could the formulation of a new notation make on my profound problems?'[2] And in one sense that reaction is an accurate assessment of the insight that Frege articulates: Frege did *not* answer the question 'To what does "Nobody" refer?' What Frege rendered explicit is what is known implicitly by the person who understands what is funny about the White King's discussion of Nobody: that 'Nobody' looks like a name, but isn't one. It doesn't work by referring to something or somebody at all. The question does not need answering; as Wittgenstein might put it, Frege's analysis *dissolves* the question. It cannot, and would not, be formulated in the *Begriffsschrift*. But it already has been in the words of the philosopher, and he wants answers; he wants to be taught philosophy. The confused enter the conversation of the *Tractatus* because it appears to (and, as Sect. 10.3 will argue, in one sense, really does) extend and develop their own.

10.2 DESCENT INTO PRIMEVAL CHAOS

So what good can Wittgenstein's joining in such confused conversations do? Why isn't he just adding to the nonsense? Here an analogy that Wittgenstein himself offered later may help. The psychoanalyst who shouts at his patient, 'Pull

have on occasion talked more generally about 'metaphysics' when I think a more general moral is worth considering). 'Does that take in all of metaphysics?', one might very well ask. A better way to proceed is to establish which questions the thinkers in question want to answer: thus, although Russell saw his causal analysis of intentionality as anti-metaphysical in doing without anything other than humble causal contingencies, it does attempt to answer a question that con-formity sets for us and which Wittgenstein works to undermine. From the latter's perspective, the question that Russell attempts to answer, about 'the relation between an expectation and its fulfilment', is confused, and trying to construe that 'relation' as an external one, as Russell does, does nothing to help us see that confusion.

[2] The same reaction is not uncommon to the way in which the *Tractatus* makes 'at once clear' how 'Russell's paradox vanishes' (3.333); I will not discuss this here.

yourself together, you lunatic!', is unlikely to meet with success. If psychoanaly-sis is to be a *cure*—and a *talking* one at that—rather than the mere issuing of a diagnosis, then the psychoanalyst has to help the patient to come to see what the psychoanalyst can see. Moreover, that needs to be done starting from where the patient stands. The starting-point is the patient's current preoccupations and fixations, the nature of which is partly to direct attention specifically away from what the psychoanalyst will suggest are the most relevant facts. The psychoanalyst needs to be able to maintain a kind of double vision: as well as his own diagnost-ic vision, he needs to be able to make his own the patient's distorted vision. He needs to be able to see how things look from that perspective, in order to begin to nudge the patient towards the point from which he will be able to see what the diagnostic perspective sees. This is the skill, the discipline, that Wittgenstein is trying to exercise. As he put it in 1948:

When you are philosophizing you have to descend into primeval chaos [*in's alte Chaos*] and feel at home there. (*CV* 74 (1948))

To help others out of nonsense, one needs to think through it, to uncover how that vulnerability 'works'. This requires a certain sympathy with the confusions in question—what might seem to some Wittgensteinians a perverse or nostalgic love of the problems of philosophy. One needs to be able to see things as the confused see them, but also to be able to escape that addled perspective.[3] To maintain that double vision is to be able to enter and then escape—which is to say, truly understand—this 'chaos'. If one loses this double vision, one may either become captured by the confusions—losing one's appreciation of how our talk here *is* mere nonsense—or lose one's appreciation of their power—losing one's grasp of how they can appear utterly real to those in their grip.

When successful, this approach demonstrates a better understanding of the philosopher's own project, as a result of understanding her unwitting borrow-ings and conflations of meanings. We reconstruct that outlook, going beyond the adherent's own understanding, but in ways that she can follow and recognize as appropriate developments of her 'commitments', which are, in fact, her unwit-ting borrowings and conflations. We follow through their pseudo-logic, asking, say, 'If one really did think that the propositions we use "make sense" because of how the "objects" that make up any possible reality are, what could and would we say about those "objects"?' Wittgenstein suggests: these objects would end up having to be *internally* related to one another, wouldn't they? And that would mean that there'd be nothing one could say about these relations, yes?[4]

---

[3] Cf. Mulhall 2001, p. 137: '[T]he influence of a fantasy is best broken not by flatly denying its reality but by accepting the terms it sets, working through them from within and hoping thereby to work beyond them. Psychoanalysis would call it transference: the analysts suffers the analysand's projection of her fantasies, but does so precisely in order to put its mechanisms and motivations in question, to work with and upon the material rather than simply reiterating it.'

[4] A more important influence on Wittgenstein in this regard than Freud himself might be Kraus, in whose work one finds 'the refutation of positions from within the very language they are expressed

The following passage from the Big Typescript[5] captures well what the *Tractatus* does:

> One of the most important tasks is to express all false thought processes so characteristically that the reader says, 'Yes, that's exactly the way I meant it'. To make a tracing of the physiognomy of every error.
>
> Indeed we can only convict someone else of a mistake if he acknowledges that this really is the expression of his feeling. // . . . if he (<u>really</u>) acknowledges this expression as the correct expression of his feeling.//
>
> For only if he acknowledges it as such, *is* it the correct expression. (Psychoanalysis.)
>
> What the other person acknowledges is the analogy I am proposing to him as the source of his thought. (Ph 165)

Such an attempt to capture the movement of the philosopher's thought, and to do so in such a way that one might come to see the analogies that drive that movement—that endow that thought with its pseudo-content—is compatible with that thought being confused and the claims that issue from it nonsensical. In articulating the argument of Section 3.5, I argued to the conclusion that we had not really understood what we were doing: we asked how it was that we arrived at our standard of sense lying out there in the world, and came to the realization that it was only by taking for granted how the words in question are used. Similarly, confronted with the person who marvels that the first across the line always wins or that the ocean is always near the shore, we would need to enter into their conversation. We would talk to them about their explanatory project and how they see it working, trying to bring them to see how their project requires them to overlook how they set it up: 'So who is the winner? And how do you tell that?' 'So where is the shore? How can I find it?' 'So which object's form determines the name's grammar? Why did you choose that one?'

Finally, this psychoanalytic analogy may also help us to see why it is quite natural for the *Tractatus* to mix nonsensical elucidations with 'sensical' observations, and, thus, why a reading that presents it so need not be guilty of an *ad hoc* cherry-picking.[6] In conversation with a patient with delusions, some of the psychoanalyst's remarks will be elaborations of the patient's delusions; but others will be very obviously and straightforwardly 'sensical'. The psychoanalyst may suggest how things would look to the patient were certain things to happen: for example, 'If A was to do x, you would say it was because A would be seeking to

---

in' (McGuinness 2002, p. 162), Kraus 'resort[ing] time and again to the technique of taking his victim "at his word", that is, of driving home his accusation and exposing threadbare intentions by the simple means of citing the accused's own words and phrases' (Engelmann, in *LPE* 124). Cf. also Janik and Toulmin 1973, ch. 3, esp. pp. 89–90.

[5] The Big Typescript is TS 213 (1933). Parts of this work have been published, some as revised versions and others in their original form, as *PG* (for an explanation of how this published text relates to the Big Typescript itself, cf. Kenny 1976). The passage quoted comes from a chapter of TS 213 not included in *PG* but which has since been published as Ph.

[6] Cf. Sect. 4.9.

bring about y, wouldn't you?' But the patient does not live on another planet, and in exploring their viewpoint on life, there is no reason why every such elucidatory remark need be expressive of delusion; some will be, and in the depths of their delusion the patient may react to these suggestions with an 'Exactly!' or with a 'So you see it too!'; but the patient will have understood what the analyst's point was in making these suggestions when he also comes to see that they were expressive of delusion. The patient may then look back over the conversation and recognize that parts—but *only parts*—of it were shaped in ways he hadn't realized at the time by certain distorting confusions, including the analyst's forays into, and elaborations on, the patient's delusions.

10.3 THERAPY, ARGUMENT, AND THE DOUBLE LIFE OF ELUCIDATIONS

In a number of respects, Wittgenstein's elucidations lead a double life. Section 5.4 discussed how they can be seen both as yet more nonsense and as valid deductions, and this section will examine further aspects of the reasoning they must embody. They must do so in order to lead the 'patient' on to 'implications' (such as (N-P) and (O-F)) that will help him see that his thinking too exemplifies the confusion that passages like 3.323–3.324 and 4.003 identify. But the plausibility of the picture of our confused reasoning that Wittgenstein presents also depends upon its character as a quasi-rational reconstruction.

I have already mentioned that the 'talking cure' is not to be identified with the pronouncement of a diagnosis. Crucial to the effectiveness of such a cure is its plausibility to the patient, inasmuch as the cure depends on successfully capturing his movement of thought. That movement has a characteristic form: what the metaphysician expects of a metaphysical conversation—of a conversation that involves him as a metaphysician—is to see reasoning about claims, the challenging of them by asking whether they are consistent with one another, etc. So, for Wittgenstein, even more so than for the psychoanalyst, his intervention in this conversation must be structured by inference, by reasoning. But this need is not merely a matter of keeping the philosopher's attention; it is by virtue of borrowing sense from elsewhere, from other particular propositions with a logic, that these pieces of nonsense appear sensical, and part of what that borrowing is is their standing in pseudo-logical relations with other nonsensical 'propositions' that borrow their sense from corresponding sources (just as Carroll's humour depends upon the conclusions that his characters draw 'following' from their premises). So Wittgenstein's reading of the philosopher's pseudo-propositions must also be a reading of the pseudo-reasoning by which the philosopher moves from one to the next. Wittgenstein's elaboration of the philosopher's confusion follows an identifiable pseudo-logic: if one succumbed to a confusion of a recognizable sort, one would find natural the lines of 'thought' he identifies, and certain 'conclusions' would emerge. What distinguishes a correct elucidation from one that misfires is that the former successfully identifies the sources of our confused borrowings and follows out their 'logic'.

This understanding of elucidation as a kind of rational/irrational reconstruction gives it a double life with a number of interesting properties.

First, if philosophical claims endow themselves with pseudo-content and pseudo-implications by drawing on other propositions with meaning and a logic, then one and the same proposition could function either as a defence of such a philosophical claim or as an elucidation of a philosophical confusion; an elucidation will 'work through' the same borrowed logics, drawing on the same 'source' propositions and their logical relations, as would a defence of a philosophical 'claim', since, if Wittgenstein is right, that is what we do *unwittingly* when we 'grasp', and 'reason' about, those 'claims' anyway. Post-'enlightenment', we do exactly the same thing, but *wittingly*. This would explain how we can be taken in and enlightened by *the very same book*.

If one dramatizes the process of understanding the work of the book as a matter of reading the book twice, then, on first reading, one talks nonsense, and does so unaware of the confusions that are shaping one's thoughts; one pseudo-understands Wittgenstein's propositions, though that does not mean that nothing happens: one unreflectively draws on certain grammars and analogies to animate these pseudo-claims and to see how the other pseudo-claims that are presented as following from them represent an elaboration of those claims that makes pseudo-sense.[7] On second reading, one talks nonsense but with understanding; one can see how confusions shaped our thoughts on first reading: one comes to see the determinate pseudo-sense one attached to Wittgenstein's 'propositions' and how one pseudo-understood it.

But on both readings, the very same analogies drive the dialectic of the book, and must be engaged with if one is to follow it. What distinguishes the second reading is our recognition of those analogies for what they are, how they captured and confused us during our first reading. One's reading has brought one to the conclusion that the same flow of argumentation that one followed on the first reading expresses a set of confusions, empowered by superficial but overlooked grammatical similarities and differences.[8] One has now acquired the requisite double vision.

Thus Wittgenstein will sometimes 'say the same things as' the confused person, but he does so without confusion, because he understands the confusion that

[7] Thus, in case it needs saying, genuine understanding provides essential sustenance for this kind of pseudo-understanding. Without an understanding of English (or, in the original, German), one cannot be sucked into these confusions—one cannot experience the illusions of sense or the (pseudo-)arguments that articulate them—and that is not the case with reading pure gibberish. But does the need for such 'understanding' demonstrate that these propositions make sense full stop after all? No, because such 'understanding' is necessary where we are dealing with what we can recognize clearly and unproblematically as nonsense—the White King's reasoning, e.g.

[8] Chs. 11–13 argue that they also derive support from certain existential needs that embracing those commitments 'serves'.

they express in the mouth of the latter. Both 'the enlightened' and the confused may say, 'Propositions and facts are internally related', but the former understands that this 'claim' can only really be understood by those with their characteristic double vision.

Secondly, while we may disagree over the kind of ultimate insight that it offers, I can share not only Hacker's opinion of the *Tractatus* as a 'great book' which presents 'philosophical insights'[9] but also his identification of some of the insights that he sees the book as offering: for example, critical insights into the confusion of making the logic of language answerable to matters of fact and of identifying the significant properties of language and world that bear on the former's making 'intelligible claims' about the latter as external properties. On my view, however, these represent a working through of the perverse logic of con-formism. If Wittgenstein's assessment of con-formism is correct, that strikes me as a very deep philosophical insight.

Finally, it would, I think, be a mistake to overstate the psychoanalytic analogy explored in Section 10.3 (or the notion that Wittgenstein is playing a kind of trick on his reader for the reader's own good[10]), and the double life of elucidations allows us also to see the *Tractatus* as presenting Wittgenstein's own honest working through of what con-formism demands, with the outcomes including the realization that it doesn't and an awareness of how it comes to appear otherwise. Since the very same sentences can articulate 'straight' philosophical deductions and elucidations of nonsense, the possibility opens up that one can set out to write the former but come to the conclusion that one has actually written the latter.[11] If this were to be what happened to Wittgenstein—perhaps with formulations first arrived at in the 'unframed' (and hence apparent 'straight') talk of, for example, the *Notebooks* surviving as 'framed' (and wittingly offered) nonsense in the *Tractatus*—then what would be left would be an accurate working through of what Wittgenstein came to see was the *pseudo*-logic of con-formism. I offer this as no more than a tentative proposal, but it is conspicuous that we have no sources for such crucial passages as 3.324, 4.003, and 6.54 earlier than the *Prototractatus*.[12] If, as seems likely, there was another notebook which followed

---

[9] Cf. Sect. 4.1.

[10] In *PPO* 131's 1931 remarks on Kierkegaard's 'reduction of the aesthetic to absurdity', Wittgenstein asserts that 'the idea that someone uses a trick to get me to do something is unpleasant'; it articulates a strategy which 'takes great courage', which Wittgenstein himself does not have and would 'take a lack of love of one's fellow human beings'. This might seem to count against any strongly 'therapeutic' understanding of the *Tractatus*; but the importance of these remarks too mustn't be overstated, since 6.53 clearly shows that Wittgenstein has *some* kind of concern with the management, so to speak, of the expectations of his readers.

[11] By analogy, one might find that an argument that one is trying to develop in support of a particular conclusion turns out to prove the opposite. Cf. also Ch. 8 n. 24.

[12] 6.53 is to be found on the fourth from last page of the last of Wittgenstein's surviving pre-Prototractarian notebooks.

those published in *NB* but which has been lost, one would expect to find there
the thinking that immediately led to those startling conclusions; but quite what
form it took is a matter about which we can only speculate.

10.4 WHAT IS 'THE LADDER' MADE OF?

I hope I have made clear now what kind of substance 'the ladder' has, and in
particular how its 'rungs' are steps in *arguments*. Propositions that elaborate nonsense can get one somewhere, and this can be done well or badly; to do it well,
to provide a construal of a nonsensical proposition as nonsensical that is compelling, one needs to show how it seemingly forms part of a network of logically
connected propositions; one must provide an understanding of the pseudo-logic
that characterizes the confusion in question. Thus the propositions that work
through that pseudo-logic, ultimately revealing that this is what it is, work on us
not, to use Sullivan's expression, 'like a blow on the head' (2003, p. 196), but by
developing an understanding.

But how 'resolute' is this understanding of elucidation? My discussion does
suggest that there is something misleading in the claim that 'entailment is a relation between sentences only in so far as they are meaningful'.[13] The White King
amuses us, we can 'get' the joke, because we can also see how his nonsense 'makes
sense'; similarly, we can 'quasi-follow' 'quasi-logical relations' within philosophical nonsense, relations that Wittgensteinian elucidations track and elaborate.[14]
My discussion also suggests that there is something misleading in saying that
'when Wittgenstein calls something nonsensical he implies that it has really and
truly got no articulable content' (Diamond 2000*b*, p. 155), as there is in Conant's emphasis on the 'recognition of the nonsensical character' of Wittgenstein's propositions as a matter of our being '*unable* to recognize the symbol in
the sign' (1998, p. 238 n. 19, and 2000, p. 194, emphasis added).[15] Similarly,
it seems to me misleading to say, as the non-resolute A. W. Moore says, that we
understand Wittgenstein 'by discovering that we cannot in the end make sense
of the book', that 'it falls apart in our hands' (2003, p. 190). Rather than being
an *unsuccessful* but thereby indicative attempt to express certain (perhaps ineffable) insights, the book (at least partially) *successfully* articulates some confusions.
What we come to see is a quite determinate structure or, perhaps better, a structure which is overdetermined in certain specific ways, as one might say that some

---

[13] Cf. Sect. 4.3.

[14] Thus I take my discussion to have shown, *pace* Witherspoon (2000), that one can talk of
'quasi-following' and 'quasi-logical relations' without being 'irresolute'.

[15] The same can be said of their claim that 'any kind of system for reading [the nonsensical
sentences of the *Tractatus*] (or in some other way extracting insights from them) would appear to
explain in what way they were meaningful' (Conant and Diamond 2004, p. 53).

of Escher's drawings are; we come to see the multiple foundations of that 'structure', the multiple sources of sense upon which it draws and which provide it with its characteristic and specific pseudo-logic.[16] One might say that our 'propositions' had 'no articulable content', but one might also say that they had *too much*, confused hybrids of several particular senses.

In this respect, Moore is right to say that 'where illusions of sense are concerned, there are always relevant concepts', reflection on which 'is required to recognize the illusions as illusions' (2003, p. 187) and it is misleading to say that the 'only "insight" [that the *Tractatus*] imparts . . . is one about the reader himself' (Conant 1991a, p. 157). In 1931, Wittgenstein described language as 'an immense network of easily accessible wrong turnings' which 'sets everyone the same traps':

[H]ence we see one person after another walking down the same paths and we know in advance the point at which they will branch off, at which they will walk straight on without noticing the turnings, etc., etc. (*CV* 25)

It is indeed Wittgenstein's view that when we talk of a sentence as nonsensical, we are talking about a tendency on the part of certain readers to take it as saying something when it doesn't, and that is what is right in Conant's 'individualistic' emphasis. But the early Wittgenstein traces this tendency to the reader's use of particular signs in particular systems of representation.[17] Just as Carroll's humour cannot be translated into some languages, neither can the speakers of certain languages succumb to some of the confusions that Wittgenstein targets (his dream of a *Begriffsschrift* being a language into which none can be so translated). That I make use of a particular language is clearly not a peculiarity of me as an individual; and thus the insight that the *Tractatus* imparts can be about us as speakers of particular languages, identifying some of 'the same traps' that language 'sets everyone' by tracing the confusing influence on our thinking of particular, multiple sources of items of pseudo-sense to which we speakers of that language are vulnerable.

[16] A misleading characterization that one sometimes encounters of what a resolute reading would require proposes that such a reading implies that we ought not to 'take what Wittgenstein says in the *Tractatus* seriously', that there is something philosophically frivolous in a work that 'merely' shows that we were talking nonsense all along. One might believe that if one believed that the only way of saying something philosophically serious is to say something that helps us to improve philosophical theories of the nature of language, thought, or world; but someone who thinks that the demand for such philosophical theories is confused doesn't believe that. Similarly, one might think that elucidations of nonsense, which I have argued can be understood as themselves nonsensical, cannot themselves have philosophical importance; I have argued that this is not the case, in that those elucidations can help us come to see that the nonsense elucidated is indeed nonsense; that is a philosophically important outcome if the elucidated nonsense plays an important part in our philosophical thinking, as I have argued it does.

[17] This is compatible, however, with these illusions also being vehicles for significant existential and spiritual purposes, as Chs. 13–15 will argue.

But fundamentally what I offer is in the spirit of 'resolution'.[18] By broadening our 'diet' of examples (*PI* § 593), Sections 4.3–4.5 exhibited senses that can be ascribed to notions to which the resolute need to ascribe some kind of sense if they are to have a plausible story to tell about how Wittgenstein's 'ladder' can be 'climbed' in the way that it surely is: namely, by engaging our capacity to reason. This account makes clear what kind of substance the ladder can have, how its 'rungs' can be steps in what are recognizably *arguments* (and thus why they work on us not 'like a blow on the head' but by developing an understanding), and how 'ascending' such 'rungs' can actually get us somewhere.

[18] Indeed, my proposals could be seen as showing how a suggestion that Conant makes in two of his early papers on the *Tractatus* (cf. 1991*b*, pp. 346–7, and 1993, pp. 218–19) can be given substance. I do not see this suggestion or my proposals as incompatible with his later talk of 'going through the motions of "inferring" (apparent) conclusions from (apparent) "premises" ' or, for that matter, with Diamond's suggestion that reading the *Tractatus* calls on 'a kind of imaginative activity': 'an exercise of the capacity to enter into the taking of nonsense for sense, of the capacity to share imaginatively the inclination to think that one is thinking something in it' (2000*b*, pp. 157–8). My proposals might be used to give concrete form to an account of these very activities, and of how they might get one somewhere.

11

The General Form of the Proposition

There is another force that shapes Wittgenstein's discussion of the proposition which I have yet to explain. So far I have presented the influence upon that discussion of his elaboration of con-formism and the ways in which the picture analogy and reflection on the learning of a first language modulate radically how we look at the conclusions that that elaboration yields. But on to that outlook Wittgenstein imposes another set of demands, dictated in part by the way in which he believes we must understand another apparent source of (impossibly) substantial logical truths.

11.1 INTRODUCTION

Presented alongside the internal properties and relations outlined in Sections 3.1–3.3, Wittgenstein makes a further set of claims about the structure of propositions. He claims that there is a set of propositions (which he calls 'elementary propositions') which are logically independent of each other, that there is another set of propositions (which he calls 'complex propositions') which are made up of elementary propositions linked together by truth-functional connectives like 'v' and '&', and that

(GFP) Every proposition is an elementary proposition or a (possibly very complex) complex proposition.

I use (GFP) as the term for this third claim, because Wittgenstein insists that it captures 'the general form of the proposition' (6).

Corresponding to these claims about propositions are a further set of claims about the nature of reality. He claims that 'atomic facts', which elementary propositions represent, are logically independent of each other, and that

(GFW) 'The world is the totality of existent atomic facts.' (2.04)

I use (GFW)—'general form of the world'—as the term for this final claim because Wittgenstein insists that to give the GFP is 'to give the essence of all description [and] therefore the essence of the world' (5.471–5.4711).

The GFP poses a significant problem for interpreters of the *Tractatus*. First, what basis does this proposal have? There are some recognizable arguments offered in the *Tractatus* for why we should endorse the internal properties and relations identified in Chapter 3, arguments set out in that chapter. But the basis of the above additional requirements is much less clear. Secondly, the GFP seems to pose a particular problem for those who, like me, doubt whether the *Tractatus* should be viewed as intended to defend a metaphysical theory. By, in some sense, asserting that the GFP is the GFP, and that there is thus a GFW, Wittgenstein appears to be making substantial claims about the nature of language and of any reality that we might come to describe.

But, thirdly, the very character of these requirements is unclear. On one level, the GFP seems to impose corresponding and substantial demands on the 'composition' of the world. But Wittgenstein also states that '[t]here is no order of things *a priori*' (5.634), and gives us the following strikingly bland gloss upon the GFP:

The general form of proposition is: Such and such is the case. (4.5)

That remark comes at the end of a set of reflections in which Wittgenstein claims that the existence of a GFP is proved 'by the fact that there cannot be a proposition whose form could not have been foreseen (*i.e.* constructed)'. His reason for thinking that there must be *some* general form is logic's 'anticipation' of all possibilities, the impossibility of the 'accidental', of the 'surprising', in logic (2.012, 6.1251):

The fact that it is possible to erect the general form of proposition means nothing but: every possible form of proposition must be FORESEEABLE.

And *that* means: We can never come upon a form of proposition of which we could say: it could not have been foreseen that there was such a thing as this.

For that would mean that we had had a new experience, and that it took that to make this form of proposition possible. (*NB* 89)

In the *Tractatus*, Wittgenstein observes:

Only that which we ourselves construct can we foresee. (5.556)[1]

So, rather than imposing a significant demand on the character of reality, this line of thought suggests that the GFP serves to show that the 'form' of reality is something 'we ourselves construct'. I will argue that if all propositions could be understood within the strictures that the GFP embodies, then the reason why 'there can *never* be surprises' in logic and why 'every possible form of proposition [is] FORESEEABLE' would be one and the same: namely, that the 'truths' that logic embodies are actually empty.

I know of no account of why Wittgenstein should have embraced the GFP and the requirements it embodies that does not ascribe them to him ultimately as themselves prejudices, naïveties, or uncritically accepted legacies from earlier philosophers or as derived from other views of his with similarly unappealing

---

[1] Cf. *VC* 62: 'The rules of syntax are not about anything; they are laid down by us. *We can stipulate only something that we ourselves do.*'

pedigrees. An extreme example is Cook, who sees an unquestioned empiricism behind these proposals. He claims that Wittgenstein 'took it for granted that all philosophical disputes about logical form are to be decided always in favour of empiricism', the philosophical theory that Wittgenstein failed to recognize as such 'because it never occurred to him to challenge the empiricist's notion of "experience"' (1994, p. 52). But even more restrained commentators such as Fogelin and Stern have suggested that Wittgenstein took for granted the requirements that the GFP embodies, their resting on no more than his 'vaunting confidence [in] the *truth* of his thoughts' (Fogelin 1987, p. 92):

Wittgenstein took it for granted that the true form of all logical relations between propositions is truth-functional. (Stern 1995, p. 65)

Recently, Conant and Diamond have embraced the notion that the GFP embodies substantial metaphysical commitments, though ones which are 'not of a sort that early Wittgenstein, at the time of writing the *Tractatus*, would have taken to be metaphysical'. They quote (2004, p. 96) with approval the following proposal of Kuusela's (subsequently published in his 2005):

[A]lthough there is a theory of propositions, it is not recognized as one. Rather, it is as if we had caught a glimpse of something: as if we were directly perceiving the essence of propositions. (Kuusela 2005, p. 103)

I think that this is true, as far as it goes. But in order to understand how Wittgenstein could have succumbed to this confusion, could have been so ready to imagine that what he had grasped in the GFP was an unproblematic and unproblematically general insight, we must see how the commitments that it embodies resonate with the book's central commitments. Explaining how is the task of the present chapter. That Wittgenstein was none the less confused on this count is one of his earliest realizations on his 'return' to philosophy in the late 1920s; in the process whereby the later Wittgenstein emerges, he abandons first the claims that the GFP embodies, and observing how he does so is a useful aid in understanding these claims and the basis that they had seemed, to the early Wittgenstein, to have.

11.2 THE DOUBLE SIGNIFICANCE OF ELEMENTARY PROPOSITIONS

There are at least two forces at work in Wittgenstein's conception of 'elementary propositions'. Wittgenstein points us in their direction in his conversations with members of the Vienna Circle in January 1930:

I used to have two conceptions of an elementary proposition, one of which seems correct to me, while I was completely wrong in holding the other. My first assumption was this:

that in analysing propositions we must eventually reach propositions that are immediate connections of objects without any help from logical constants, for 'not', 'and', 'or', and 'if' do not connect objects. And I still adhere to that. Secondly I had the idea that elementary propositions must be independent of one another. A complete description of the world would be a product of elementary propositions, as it were ... In holding this I was wrong ... (*VC* 73–4)

That it was when he wrote the *Tractatus* that Wittgenstein 'used' to see elementary propositions as possessed of this double significance is clear: there he describes them as 'consist[ing] of names in immediate combination' (4.221), and states that 'a sign of an elementary proposition' is that 'no elementary proposition can contradict it' (4.211).

One way of looking at the need that the GFP tries to satisfy is to think of the sources of the impression that there are substantial logical truths as arising either *within* propositions or *between* propositions. The 'immediate combination' requirement addresses the former, and arises out of Wittgenstein's reflections on con-formism set out in Chapter 3 and modulated through the picture analogy. Theories of Types seem to present explanations of why certain propositions cannot be formed, and to do so on the grounds that the 'sub-propositional' elements that these propositions would combine cannot be combined: for example, a proposition might combine a referring expression and a predicate, but not two predicates. One way of understanding part of the contribution of the picture analogy was as showing how these apparent restrictions do not embody an 'accidental' or 'impossibly real' logic. Objects stand in immediate connection with one another in atomic facts, because objects are constituted by the ways in which they can combine with one another: their 'connection' must be immediate, in that there is no such thing as their being 'glued together' by 'anything third' (*LO* 23). But as Chapter 7 explained, the significance of this is to undermine the notion that there might be some body of substantial logical truths that explain how elementary propositions or atomic facts are made up. These truths would identify and characterize that which binds objects together; but there is no such glue, in that 'how objects can combine' is another way of *identifying* the objects one is considering.

These thoughts, the significance of which is only fully made clear by the picture analogy, seem to me well-founded, and they continue to inform Wittgenstein's later work. However, the second requirement that Wittgenstein imposes on elementary propositions, the 'independence' requirement, emerges out of an unsustainable attempt to understand logical inference without postulating substantial logical truths.

The second place in which substantial logical truths may seem to be revealed is *between* propositions, in the validity and invalidity of inferences that can be made from one proposition to another. In the Big Typescript, Wittgenstein comments retrospectively:

I believed, when I wrote the *Tractatus* (and also/later still), that fa = fa & not-fb would only be possible if fa was the logical product of another proposition and not-fb—so fa = p & not-fb—and was of the opinion that fa (e.g. a colour proposition) could be analysed as such a product. (TS 213, 474–5 (1933))

The commitment that Wittgenstein spells out here is to contradiction being the only real form of logical incompatibility. The reason that *fa* is incompatible with *fb* is that *fa* is a complex proposition which can be understood as a logical product of ¬*fb* and another proposition; hence *fa* is incompatible with *fb* because (*p* & ¬*fb*) > ¬*fb*. Roughly speaking, the reason why one can deduce *q* from *p* is that in saying *p*, one has already said *q*, because *q* is 'contained within' *p*. At the level of analysis at which the nature of the logical incompatibilities between propositions is rendered intelligible, any sign of any other species of logical incompatibility other than flat contradiction will have vanished. At that ultimate level, propositions will turn out to be made up of combinations of component propositions that are logically independent of one another or are straightforward negations of one another: *p* and ¬*p*.[2] In other words, every proposition must either itself be what Wittgenstein calls an 'elementary proposition' or be a complex proposition made up of combinations of elementary propositions.

This raises many questions, of which I will mention here two. First, why does Wittgenstein think that contradiction is the only real form of logical incompatibility? Secondly, what is the significance of complex propositions being truth-functional combinations of elementary propositions? The answer in both cases depends on Wittgenstein's conviction that '[i]n logic nothing is accidental' (2.012). The rest of this chapter will be devoted to explaining how this conviction is expressed in this second, 'independence' requirement of Wittgenstein's GFP.

11.3 LOGICAL LAWS, INTERNAL RELATIONS, AND INFERENCE AS 'UNPACKING'

If one combines in certain ways certain propositions, propositions which themselves make a claim about how the world happens to be, what one is left with is not more complex propositions that themselves make a claim about how the world happens to be. For example, if we combine 'it is raining' and 'it is not raining' to give 'it is raining and it is not raining', we have combined two propositions which make a claim about how the world happens to be to yield a more complex proposition that itself does not. A corresponding body of logical truths now seems to loom, truths that state which combinations of propositions can be combined to yield a description of how things might be and which cannot be so

---

[2] We touch here on the significance that Wittgenstein attaches to the Sheffer stroke, though I will not comment on that here.

combined. This is one way of understanding what the rules of logical inference are. The formula

$$(p \,\&\, (p \to q)) \to q)$$

dictates that one cannot combine, using &, the following propositions

$$p$$
$$(p \to q)$$
$$\neg q$$

to produce a description of how things might be. But why not? A natural response is that what the proposition that combines those propositions in this way represents is logically impossible. But what does that mean? Here we run into the problems discussed in Section 2.7.

Without entering into a consideration of particular philosophies of logic, we can say straightaway that, for Wittgenstein, that a particular combination of propositions embodies a contradiction, and that a particular proposition entails another, cannot be *external* properties of those propositions. Psychologism, for example, violates this requirement, in that certain combinations of propositions are unthinkable only because of how we thinkers happen to be constituted; were we differently constituted, those combinations might not be unthinkable; hence, if the logically impossible were the unthinkable, logic would be 'accidental'. If we are to avoid an accidental logic, logical relations between propositions must then be internal (5.131). It cannot be a mere matter of fact that p happens to imply q; this cannot be something that one discovers—perhaps to one's surprise—happens to be the case. Instead, a grasp of p or of q must tell one of this relation straightaway, so to speak. So what are these internal relations?

In line with my broader hypothesis about the significance of internal relations for Wittgenstein, I will argue that these internal relations emerge only as a result of a misapprehension on our part, inspired, once again, by a sign/symbol confusion. To believe in logical relations between propositions that stand in need of some sort of grounding is to fail to see how the propositions in question figure within each other's very constitution. When we believe we glimpse distinct propositions between which external 'logical relations' hold, we have identified unwittingly the propositions with the genuinely externally related signs that express them. Which combinations of signs express logically impossible 'claims' in a particular language is a matter of contingent—'accidental'—fact. The philosopher's question about symbols is confused, and arises partly out of a confused reflection on this intelligible but philosophically uninteresting question about signs.

Wittgenstein's GFP is an attempt to provide an account of propositions which accommodates the obvious fact that certain propositions can be deduced from others, while rejecting a substantial logic. Since complex propositions are truth-functional combinations of elementary propositions, the truth or falsity of complex propositions is dependent on the truth or falsity of the elementary propositions of which they are made up. In some cases, it will be impossible for a proposition to be false if certain other propositions are true, and vice versa. If two complex propositions are constructed from the same set of elementary propositions, what makes one of those complex propositions true or false will also determine whether the other is true or false. If, for instance, the complex proposition, p & q, is made true by its component elementary propositions, p and q, then the complex proposition, $p \lor q$, will be true also. Wittgenstein argues that what we understand by 'logical entailment' is the holding of dependencies of which the previous example is a very simple case. According to this view, when complex proposition p entails complex proposition q, it is because (i) in asserting p, one asserts that certain combinations of elementary propositions must be variously true or false; (ii) q is made up of an overlapping set of elementary propositions; and (iii) the combinations of true and false elementary propositions that make p true also make q true. If q follows from p, it will be because 'the truth-grounds of q are contained in those of p' (5.121). One might say that logical relations are 'internal', in that the deduced proposition is, in a sense, *part of* the proposition from which it is deduced. But once again what is crucial about these 'internal relations' is that the impression that we are dealing with *relations* between distinct things is misleading; to recognize these 'internal relations' is a step towards recognizing that they 'emerge' only in a context characterized by misunderstanding.

11.4 TRUTH-FUNCTIONS AND TRUTH-TABLES

But what of the connectives which bind the elementary propositions together to form complex propositions? Do they not make some kind of contribution to the truth or falsity of the propositions in which they are included? If so, if we are to grasp these propositions, mustn't we grasp what expressions like '&' and '∨' refer to, whatever that might be? And won't it be a consequence of what or how these referents are that certain propositions logically entail others? Russell thought so, and at one point proposed that our understanding of the logical constants rests upon an acquaintance with 'logical objects' that they name.[3]

But, according to Wittgenstein, the line of thought that the previous paragraph sketches is confused, turning on another kind of sign/symbol conflation. In the *Tractatus*, he proclaims as his *Grundgedanke*, his fundamental thought, that there are no such logical objects to which logical constant expressions might be thought to refer (4.0312): as early as 1912, Wittgenstein declared that 'there are NO *logical* constants' (*NB* 120). To succumb, as Russell seems to have done, to

---

[3] Cf., e.g., Russell 1984 [1913], p. 97–101. For discussion, cf. Hacker 1986, pp. 35–7.

the illusion that there are, is to fail to appreciate the different ways in which similar signs may be used in expressing very different symbols. In asking what it is to which '&' refers, we implicitly assimilate the way that '&' 'works' to that in which terms like 'chair' and 'Frank' 'work': just as to understand what 'chair' means, we need to understand what kind of thing a chair is, so too to understand '&', we need to understand what kind of thing & is.

That p & q entails q but $p \lor q$ doesn't shows that there is undoubtedly a sense in which the connectives 'make a difference'. But of what kind? Wittgenstein argues that, once we have arrived at the fully analysed version of complex propositions, the contribution made by a truth-functional connective can be revealed to be akin to that of a syntactic device. The belief that an entity to which '&', for example, refers being the way it is, rather than some other way, affects the truth or falsity of the 'substance' of what we say, is an illusion.[4] Following in the Fregean/Russellian tradition of eliminating problematic entities by re-expressing the propositions that seemingly refer to them in ways that show that such references are inessential, Wittgenstein, through the definition of the truth-functional connectives in truth-tables, sought to 'eliminate' the supposed entities to which these connectives refer. For '&', the table is:

p	q	$p \& q$
T	T	T
T	F	F
F	T	F
F	F	F

For '$\lor$', it is:

p	q	$p \lor q$
T	T	T
T	F	T
F	T	T
F	F	F

The philosophical virtue of this mode of representation is that reference to the problematic entities to which we might believe truth-functional connectives refer vanishes when complex sentences in which those connectives occur are presented in this way:

It is clear that to the complex of the signs 'F' and 'T' no object (or complex of objects) corresponds; any more than to horizontal and vertical lines or to brackets. There are no 'logical objects'. (4.441)

Since 'something analogous holds ... for all signs that express the same as the schemata of "T" and "F"' (4.441), Wittgenstein uses his truth-tables to show

---

[4] As early as 1913, Wittgenstein claimed that '[m]olecular propositions contain nothing beyond what is contained in their atoms': 'they add no material information above that contained in their atoms' (*NB* 98).

that to understand the truth-functional connectives, we do not need to have acquaintance with 'logical objects' of some sort. Wittgenstein elaborated upon this in later lectures. G. E. Moore reports that

[Wittgenstein] gave his truth-table notation for '$p \lor q$' and '$p \,\&\, q$', and said that the 'criterion' for the statement that the former follows from the latter was that 'to every T in the latter there corresponds a T in the former.' He said that, in saying this, he had stated 'a rule of inference', but that this rule was only 'a rule of grammar' and 'treated only of the symbolism'. (M 295)

Which propositions are true and which logical relations hold between certain propositions depend on 'what "&" means'; but to understand this dependency is a matter of knowing 'only "a rule of grammar"', something that 'treat[s] only of the symbolism', and not, *pace* Russell, a matter of knowing of some logical object to which '&' refers, some logical fact to which our use of '&' responds. '&' could have been defined differently, with a different final line of 'T's and 'F's in the corresponding truth-table above; but this would simply be to give the mere sign '&' a different use.

Thus, according to Wittgenstein, rather than requiring acquaintance with some peculiar kind of object, '&', like all 'the so-called logical constants', belongs to that class of expressions which 'can be understood simply by a study of their occurrence in symbolism' (*L I* 116).[5]

11.5 TAUTOLOGIES AND CONTRADICTIONS

On this basis, an account can now be given of logical propositions that explains their necessity without endowing them with 'substance', which, as 6.111 insists, would show that we had gone astray. In essence, this account turns on the notion that once we have adopted a particular set of truth-functional connectives, there will be complex propositions which have 'truth-grounds' that 'cancel one another out' (4.462), making either complex propositions that are always true or ones that are always false. Wittgenstein labels the former 'tautologies' and the latter 'contradictions' (4.46); together, he claims, they make up what we understand by logical propositions.

While explaining their necessity, this account could be said to be deflationary, in that which propositions are logical propositions depends not on how the world is, but on which syntactic devices we adopt in constructing complex propositions. For example, from

$$(p \,\&\, (p \to q)) \to q$$

---

[5] Regarding the other logical constants, Wittgenstein attacks the supposed indispensability of the identity sign ('=') in 5.53–5.5352, and his analysis of the quantifiers is discussed in Ch. 12.

one can conclude that

$$(p \& (p \to q)) \& \neg q$$

is an impossible situation. Moreover, it is not impossible because that combination of states of affairs that the combination of propositions represents is physically impossible. But to understand this supra-physical impossibility, we do not need to speculate about laws of what is thinkable or metaphysically possible; rather, it is the arbitrary rules that we adopt for the use of certain signs in our language that throw up these supposedly 'super-natural' truths:

1	4	1	3	2	5	2
(p	&	(p	→	q))	→	q
T	T	T	T	T	T	T
T	F	T	F	F	T	F
F	F	F	T	T	T	T
F	F	F	T	F	T	F

Working through this table, we first assign the full range of possible values to the *p*s and *q*s—the (1) and (2) columns. Then we see what values these assign to the combinations of *p*s and *q*s of which the principle as a whole is made up—line 3 (for $(p \to q)$), then line 4 (for $(p \& (p \to q))$), and finally line 5 (for the whole thing). It turns out that the principle as a whole always turns out to be true—line 5—and it does so simply because of how we have defined the truth-functional connectives. Truth-table analysis also shows us that we can see why (p & $(p \to q)$) & ¬q is never the case, simply by understanding the arbitrary rules that we adopt for the use of the logical constant expressions it includes:

1	4	1	3	2	5	2
(p	&	(p	→	q))	&	¬q
T	T	T	T	T	F	F
T	F	T	F	F	F	T
F	F	F	T	T	F	F
F	F	F	T	F	F	T

Line 5 is all Fs. The rules we have assigned to &, →, and ¬ doom this combination to self-contradiction.

Although it is in a different sense than that used in connection with 'the illogical', tautologies and contradictions could be seen as further cases of 'dead space' within our systems of representation. Wittgenstein marks the difference with the terms, '*unsinnig*' and '*sinnlos*'. 'Illogical combinations' are '*unsinnig*' ('nonsensical' (4.4611)), as no meaning has been assigned to the combination of signs in question. Tautologies and contradictions, on the other hand, are *sinnlos* ('senseless' (4.461)), as 'the conditions of agreement with the world [of the propositions combined] cancel one another' (4.462); thus, why a particular proposition is tautologous depends on the meaning of the propositions it combines.[6] The crucial point, from the point of view of an assault on substantial laws of logic, is that an understanding of impossibilities such as

$$(p\&(p \rightarrow q))\&\neg q$$

does not rest on an understanding of some sort of logical object or logical super-truth. Rather, it rests on an understanding of how certain syntactic devices are used; such impossibilities themselves 'can be understood simply by a study of [the] occurrence [of those devices] in symbolism' (*L I* 116); correspondingly, it is 'the characteristic mark' of 'logical truths' that 'one can recognize that they are true from the symbol alone':

[A]nd this fact contains in itself the whole philosophy of logic. (6.113)

11.6 NEGATION AND THE PICTURE ANALOGY

Our discussion so far still leaves unanswered the question of why Wittgenstein should want to maintain that all logical incompatibility is a matter of contradiction and hence that all propositions are, or are complexes made up of, elementary propositions. What I should say at once is that I do not think it's clear why. But a plausible story can be told.

The topic of negation in the *Tractatus* is a complex one. What I will concentrate on is the perspective that the picture analogy offers on negation, a perspective which, roughly speaking, suggests that negation is internally related to assertion: that, once one has assertion, one gets denial 'for free'. Wittgenstein maintains that knowledge of what it would be to deny a particular proposition is already 'contained' in knowledge of what it would be to assert it: 'the possibility of denial is already prejudged in affirmation' (5.44).[7] There are two different morals on that topic that one might draw from our working through of that analogy, two morals that point in rather different directions.

The first and perhaps most natural is one which Wittgenstein does not explore, but which can be seen at work in the undoing of the GFP in his transitional work. According to this moral, when one says that Frank is at the crossroads, one has thereby said that he is not further down the street, entering the town-hall, etc.,

---

[6] I gloss over here an issue that has played a large role in shaping the 'resolute' literature: the question of whether that which is *unsinnig* is so by virtue of the meaning of the words it combines (cf., e.g., Conant 2000; Hacker 2003). Other issues that the *unsinnig/sinnlos* distinction raises are addressed in Kremer 2002.

[7] Sect. 4.9 explains my reservations about Hacker's claim that the 'bipolarity principle' is fundamental to the *Tractatus*. What I would add here is that, from my perspective, Wittgenstein's concern in this territory is not with discerning the form that any 'legitimate proposition' must take, but rather with puzzles about how an assertion relates to its negation; and one might assert that when an assertion *can* be negated, an understanding of its negation is 'prejudged' in an understanding of its assertion, without asserting that it must be possible to negate any genuine assertion.

etc. That is to say, a positive proposition excludes a host of other possibilities, and implies a set of negative propositions. So one might represent the fact that Frank is not at the crossroads through a disjunction of the 'propositions' in our kitchen table model that represent him as being in other positions that he could be in (setting aside, for the sake of argument, the possibility that he is not anywhere in the scene presented, a possibility that would raise the difficulties discussed in Ch. 12's examination of generality). Now if it is natural to think of this disjunction as doing the job of negating the proposition in question, it is because one recognizes that these different propositions are logically related to one another: these propositions constitute a *system*, in that only one can be asserted at a time and to assert one is to deny the others.[8]

It is, however, a second moral that one might take from the picture analogy that influences Wittgenstein's early thinking. According to this moral, making a negative statement is done drawing on what is, in a sense, the very same proposition that one draws on in making the corresponding positive statement. In the *Notebooks*, Wittgenstein observes:

That two people are not fighting can be represented by representing them as not fighting and also representing them as fighting and saying that the picture shows how things are *not*. (*NB* 23)

Let us consider how one might articulate within our kitchen table model what we say in English when we say 'Frank is not at the crossroads', and in doing so, let us try to imagine what Wittgenstein means when he says the following:

[T]he sign '¬' corresponds to nothing in reality.
That negation occurs in a proposition, is no characteristic of its sense ($\neg\neg p = p$).
The propositions 'p' and '$\neg p$' have opposite senses, but to them corresponds one and the same reality. (4.0621)

A natural suggestion would be that one uses the same 'proposition' with some kind of index attached to indicate what we would indicate in English by 'It's not like this'. So one places the pepper-pot where the four folded napkins meet and, say, places the salt-cellar somewhere on the table. Now one thing that thinking through the analogy makes it natural to say is that the salt-cellar does not itself represent anything: the difference that negation makes is not to place another entity at the scene of the accident, as placing a cup there would. (It makes no difference, for example, where on the table one puts the salt-cellar, but it does make a difference where one places the pepper-pot, the cups, the napkins, etc.) So one might say that 'the sign "¬" corresponds to nothing in reality'. Similarly, it seems natural to say that placing the salt-cellar by the pepper-pot does not specify 'another way in which things could be'. By placing a cup next to the pepper-pot,

[8] Cf. *L II* 105–6. Reasons why Wittgenstein might have wanted to avoid commitment to such systems is discussed in Sects. 11.7–11.8.

one says that rather than Frank being on his own at the crossroads, a car could also be here or here or here. The negated proposition, on the other hand, does not evoke another particular way in which things might be arranged; rather, it evokes the same way in which things might be arranged as the proposition it negates, though it then declares that things are not *like that*. Hence one might say that '[t]he propositions "*p*" and "¬*p*" have opposite senses, but to them corresponds one and the same reality':

If a picture represents what-is-not-the-case . . . this only happens through it representing *that* which *is* not the case. For the picture says, as it were: '*This* is how it is *not*', and to the question 'How is it not?' just the positive proposition is the answer. (*NB* 25)

Now one might well want to dispute some of the glosses given above to the different 'contribution' that negation makes. So is it that our negating salt-cellar does not represent *anything*, or is it that it does not represent anything *in the way* that the pepper-pot represents Frank and the cups represent cars? Similarly, is it that placing the salt-cellar by the pepper-pot does *not* specify another way in which things could be, or is it that it does not do so *in the way* that placing a cup next to the pepper-pot does? Given that there are philosophers (such as, at one point, Russell) who do want to understand logical constant expressions such as '¬' as naming in very much the same way as 'regular names' do, the picture analogy gives us a sense of why one might think that the glosses that I initially gave might be less misleading than the alternatives just considered.

It is this second moral, bolstered by other arguments,[9] that encourages the early Wittgenstein's belief that his truth-table analyses can show that every logical constant expression 'corresponds to nothing in reality'. If our grasp of affirmation, of truth, brings with it a grasp of denial, of falsity, and if the moral of the truth-table analysis is correct—that an understanding of the other logical constants requires nothing more of substance than an understanding of the difference between the truth and falsity of the propositions that these constants combine—then one's grasp of the logical inferences in which a set of propositions can figure requires no more than a grasp of those propositions. The 'addition' of negation and the other logical constants to our understanding adds nothing of substance.

11.7 ISLANDS OF SENSE

The previous section shows the rewards that reducing all logical incompatibility to contradiction would bring. But what made Wittgenstein think that he could reasonably claim those rewards without having actually demonstrated—as he hadn't—that all logical incompatibility can indeed be reduced to contradiction?

---

[9] Cf., e.g., 5.44–5.441.

Why should Wittgenstein maintain that all logical incompatibility really is a matter of contradiction, and hence that all propositions really are elementary propositions or complexes made up of truth-functionally combined elementary propositions? What bolstered this mere possibility, in Wittgenstein's eyes, into something to which he was committed was the case? Again, I do not think it's clear why. But again, a plausible story can be told.

One tempting way of looking at this problem would be to say that Wittgenstein was simply swept away by the apparent power of the understanding of inference that 'unpacking' plus the truth-functional analyses of the logical constants offers. It is a way of understanding *some* inferences in such a way that they no longer threaten us with a substantial logic; the temptation to believe that it can be applied to *all* inferences arises naturally if one also believes that there cannot be a substantial logic. Wittgenstein's GFP now becomes an expression of the belief that all inferences can be handled in this way: *any* inference could then be understood as a matter of overlap between the elementary propositions that are truth-functionally combined in the premiss and the conclusion.

That a temptation of this sort grabbed Wittgenstein seems to fit the evidence that we have. In particular, it seems to account for his reaction when it becomes apparent to him that the GFP story faces problems: what happens is that he changes his story. He considers the possibility that propositions form *systems*, within which are patterns of inference that are peculiar to those systems but 'between which' the old analysis of inference stands: 'in cases where propositions are independent everything remains valid—the whole theory of inference and so forth' (*VC* 74). He also considers the possibility that awkward logical relations such as colour exclusion (discussed in Sect. 12.1) and those between generalities and their instances (discussed in Sects. 12.2–12.5) might have to be understood as 'elementary': he considers 'elementary propositions' whose analysis involves numbers and the possibility of generality being a characteristic of elementary propositions themselves, rather than of their truth-functional combination.[10] Nevertheless, he quickly realizes that, through such radical alterations, 'the concept of an "elementary proposition" . . . loses all of its earlier significance' (*PR* 111).

The important point here is that, when faced with problems for the GFP, Wittgenstein abandons it, pursuing what we can now see are his core concerns in other ways. This suggests that, when we puzzle over what good reason Wittgenstein can have had for embracing the GFP, we should not discount the possibility that there were no profoundly powerful reasons. His subsequent reaction to problems with the GFP would seem to support that conclusion: if it doesn't work, it doesn't work, and we have to find another way to get to where we want to go.

But still, why should the author of the *Tractatus* have been so convinced of the sufficiency of his GFP? The next section will sketch two considerations that may

---

[10] Cf. *PR* 108 and 115; *VC* 39–40; M 298.

have transformed the reduction of logical incompatibility to contradiction from a rewarding, and hence understandably appealing, possibility into something Wittgenstein believed must be so. To lead us to those considerations, let us note an argument which we have already identified, which at least points us in the direction in which a commitment to elementary propositions lies. The argument set out in Section 3.2 showed that there is no such thing as grasping a name prior to grasping the propositions it may figure in; it cannot merely turn out that a name happens to be capable of figuring in a particular proposition. If so, if a name is to have a determinate identity, the set of propositions that it figures in must already constitute a delimitable set. A pressure is established here on how we must understand our language to be made up: to offer a visual image, we see the land mass, Language, the many different things we might say, breaking up into a collection of distinct islands. As Section 9.4 made clear, Wittgenstein takes it to be a corollary of the requirement that there be no such thing as a 'logical surprise' that '[i]t is ... not possible *only subsequently to come upon* the fact that a proposition follows from [another]' (*NB* 64). Since a proposition's logical relations determine its very identity, logical relations cannot then be allowed to extend out from one collection of logically interrelated propositions (from one island) to others (to other islands)—this is what makes them *islands*—if that means that one's grasp of a name does not bring with it simultaneously, as it were, a grasp of all the logical relations that hold between the propositions in which it might figure. For names to have a determinate use, webs of logical relations must withdraw into these logically independent 'islands', confined within sets of propositions whose members are logically independent of members of other sets (that, again, is what makes them *islands*).

But Wittgenstein's position in the *Tractatus* is not that language is made up of logically independent *sets* of propositions. He goes further, and depicts each 'island' as a single proposition (or, more precisely, a single proposition and its negation). Logical analysis will reveal, he maintains, that the 'substance' of what we say will turn out to be constituted by our asserting and denying elementary propositions. Why go this extra step, from the idea of 'islands' (which might admit logically independent sets or systems of propositions as islands) to the insistence that those islands are elementary propositions? It is in this respect that the argument identified in the preceding paragraph only points us in the direction of a commitment to elementary propositions, rather than explaining why such a commitment is actually necessary.[11]

Another immediate objection to our 'island' story is that there appear to be rules of logical inference that hold sway across language as a whole; they govern anything that we might say, not just things that fall within particular 'regions'

---

[11] The story told in this section up to this point overlaps, to some degree, that told in Part II of Diamond 1991, ch. 6; from here on they diverge.

of language. To echo Frege, these rules seem to 'transcend all particulars' (1967 [1879], p. 5).

$$(p \,\&\, (p \to q)) \to q$$

is unlike, for example, the laws of biology, in that it holds not only of plants and animals but of anything and everything. There seems to be nothing obviously wrong about inferring from:

> If we are the hollow men, then industry tends to be located near to a source of raw material

and

> We are the hollow men

to

> Industry tends to be located near to a source of raw material.

Here we seem to find logical relations between propositions that one would not imagine belong to the same logical 'island'. Indeed, it seems to be possible to conjure up inferences of this sort, drawing on just about any kind of proposition one likes; for example, there seems to be nothing obviously wrong about inferring from:

> If murder is wrong, then $2 + 2 = 4$

and

> Murder is wrong

to

> $2 + 2 = 4$.[12]

Such inferences seem to reveal, then, a countervailing pressure, pushing the islands of sense back together to fuse once again into a single land mass.

11.8 RULES OF INFERENCE, UNIVOCAL AND 'HETERODOX'

We can now bring out two particular considerations that favour the *Tractatus*'s GFP and its assimilation of logical incompatibility to contradiction. First, the GFP allows a univocal understanding of the logical constants. &, v, and > seem to figure, so to speak, in all 'regions' of our reasoning; but if language is made up of islands of sense that are systems of propositions, then the reason why $(p \,\&\, q)$ implies p 'on' one island need have nothing to do with the reason why $(p \,\&\, q)$ implies p 'on' another island, or with why $(p \,\&\, q)$ implies p when p and q belong to different islands. If instead, the logical constants are univocal, then there must

---

[12] I set aside here particular worries arising out of how the *Tractatus* presents mathematical and ethical propositions.

be one account that applies across all of these territories. The natural response now is to believe that the inter-island account can be extended to take in intra-island inferences. But, in doing so, this extension would, of course, show that the latter inferences were only *apparently* intra-island, and our islands would then shrink to individual, logically independent propositions. The truth-table analyses capture the use of '&' and 'v' only when the propositions they join are logically independent, but not otherwise; if that understanding of the constants is to penetrate the inferential practices of all of the islands of Language—to rule over all the inferences carried out on those islands—then there can be no patterns of inference peculiar to those islands; hence those islands cannot be systems of propositions after all. If this consideration did hold sway with Wittgenstein, what we would expect to see when the GFP runs into problems is his contemplating the possibility that the logical constants are not univocal after all. And that is what one finds:

> The generality notation of our ordinary language grasps the logical form even more superficially than I earlier believed. ... There are as many different 'alls' as there are different 'ones'.
>
> So it is no use using the word 'all' for clarification unless we know its grammar in this particular case. (*PG* 269)

Similarly, rather than there being some one thing called 'negation', Wittgenstein comes to explore the notion that there is a 'family of negations' (*L II* 101). Belief in a univocal 'not' and a univocal 'all' turns out to be another confused prejudice resting on sign/symbol conflation, on a faith—questionable once recognized as such—in surface grammar, in the '*notation* of our ordinary language', as revealing how our words work.

But why should the possibility of a univocal account of the logical constants be so important? That question needs careful treatment, and to help I will look at the second consideration that may seem to favour the *Tractatus*'s GFP over the alternatives that Wittgenstein contemplates in the early stages of his 'transition'.

The notion of *systems* of propositions is one of the first 'patches' that 'the transitional Wittgenstein' attempts to apply to his early thinking. He attempts, for example, to solve the problem of colour-exclusion by suggesting that the propositions that exclude each other form part of a system of propositions which are compared with reality *en masse*, rather than individually: they are laid against reality collectively, in such a way as to prevent any more than one of these propositions being true at any one time and in any one place, and this, it is suggested, explains the non-empirical exclusion relation.[13] To adopt this view is, in effect, to embrace the conception of language as made up of 'islands', which means that ways must now be found of getting round the problems to which that conception gives rise. For example, if we trace back the relations of exclusion

---

[13] Cf., e.g., RLF 168–71; *VC* 63, 76, and 89.

and implication that hold between propositions to characteristics of propositional systems, we are then confronted with the question of why these systems are
as they are. What determines the way we presently handle colour judgements?
Don't the rules, which our use of colour terms embodies, reflect something one
might call 'the way colours actually relate to each other'? Tracing non-logical,
metaphysical necessities back to characteristics of propositional systems will not
save us from a substantial logic if these characteristics are themselves determined
by some kind of fact: *these* would then be the (impossible) facts of logic. Schlick
articulates an epistemological ramification of this problem as follows:

How do I know that such-and-such rules of syntax are valid? How do I know that red and
blue cannot be in one place simultaneously? Have we not in this case a kind of empirical
knowledge? ... [H]ow do I know that precisely these rules are valid and no others? Can I
not be wrong? (*VC* 76–7)

If our islands of sense are sets of propositions, a description of the incompatibilities and entailments that hold between the propositions of each set (and make
them into systems) would seem to capture accidental—unanticipatable—logical
truths. Given Wittgenstein's understanding of logic, the presupposition that
there is something to be answerable to here, some kind of subsistent logical fact to
which our talk may or may not conform, cannot make sense.

There is something to this worry; it would also seem to arise out of the loss, to
use Hacker's expression (2001*a*, p. 28), of 'topic-neutral' logical constants, and
to receive further support from a remark in RLF made in response to the colour
exclusion problem:

[W]e can only arrive at a correct analysis by, what might be called, the logical investigation of the phenomena themselves, *i.e.*, in a certain sense *a posteriori*, and not by
conjecturing about *a priori* possibilities. ... [I]t would be surprising if the actual phenomena had nothing more to teach us about their structure. (RLF 163–4)

But we should be careful how we proceed here. Does the need to investigate 'the
phenomena themselves' signal an embracing of a realism about logical relations?
According to my interpretation, this would run counter to one of the fundamental thoughts of the early Wittgenstein. Though I cannot argue the point
here, these remarks in RLF give a misleading impression of the broader character of Wittgenstein's transitional thinking: what Wittgenstein does come to
appreciate is the need to look carefully at the functioning of the different parts
of our language, not because we must read substantial truths of logic off 'the
phenomena themselves', but because the impression that there are such truths
cannot be done away with in one go, in the manner imagined by the architect
of the GFP. Wittgenstein's problem is that there is nothing *obviously* awry with
Schlick's questions, questions which, if we were to take them as legitimate and
attempt to answer them, could surely be answered by identifying (impossible)
logic-determining facts of the kind that Wittgenstein wishes to avoid. But this

does not mean that there are such facts. Instead, the job of exposing what is confused about Schlick's questions must be handled in a more nuanced way, one which involves careful scrutiny of the disparate linguistic tools we use. So I suggest that Wittgenstein's desire to avoid 'elementary' systems of propositions and 'non-topic-neutral' logical constants is fundamentally the desire to make a quick fix—the GFP—work. Wittgenstein was thus tempted into a kind of 'dogmatism' that he later recognized and regretted:

In my book . . . I saw something from far away and . . . wanted to elicit from it as much as possible. (*VC* 184)

11.9 DOES THE GFP EMBODY A METAPHYSICAL MORAL?

Finally, I come to the question that seems to be so awkward for a resolute reading of the *Tractatus*, of which my own is an example: doesn't the GFP being the GFP commit us to a view on the metaphysical character of the world? Doesn't the claim that this is how propositions are imply something about how the world they describe must be? By drawing on the preceding discussion and that of objects developed in Chapters 6, 7, and 9, I will argue that this was not the view of the early Wittgenstein (even if he was to later realize that his earlier view did embody some confusions).

In Chapter 9, I argued that there is a blandness to the specification of 'objects' that Wittgenstein offers us, which only con-formist misunderstanding turns into the basis of an account of sense. Nevertheless, I indicated there how what was later to strike Wittgenstein as a metaphysical demand insinuates itself into that specification in the form of the demand for 'determinacy of sense'. The early Wittgenstein's understanding of this demand seems to alternate between seeing it as a truism about meaning and as a corollary of the absurdity of the idea of a substantial logic. What I suggest is that the GFP struck Wittgenstein as a bland requirement, but that it too was informed by a 'demand' which he was only later to recognize as such: the requirement that 'logical constants' be 'topic-neutral'. Combined once again with the good sense of avoiding 'logical substance', this 'requirement' leads one to the GFP.

One might get the impression that the internal properties and relations that Wittgenstein deduces impose a certain general form on atomic facts. But he also proposes that the form of elementary propositions that represent atomic facts is 'unanticipatable'.[14] I have suggested that the 'internal properties' of objects point to what I called in Chapter 9 the 'logical blandness' of the world: each atomic fact has its own endogenous ways of 'combining objects', and no exogenous doctrine of objects or of how atomic facts must be constructed can penetrate within;

---

[14] Cf. the discussion in the 5.55s.

similarly, there is what one might call a kind of 'logical anarchism' in the fact that each elementary proposition has its own endogenous ways of 'combining names', and no exogenous doctrine of names or of how elementary propositions must be constructed can penetrate within: one cannot prescribe to a name how it *ought* to combine in order to form propositions, because the identity of a name is indeterminate until how it combines to form propositions is settled, just as each object is a 'law unto itself', in that its identity is determined by the 'laws of combination' it 'follows'. The form of elementary propositions and the atomic facts that they represent is thus 'unanticipatable': there can be no body of truths about how the elements of such propositions and such facts can be combined to form such propositions and such facts, because the identity of those elements is indeterminate as long as the ways in which they combine to form propositions and facts is yet to be established.

But in addition to the 'immediate connection' requirement, Wittgenstein also imposes on his understanding of propositions the 'independence' requirement. I have argued that Wittgenstein's GFP is an attempt to explain how logical inference can be understood without recourse to an absurdly 'substantial' logic. Just as the 'immediate connection' requirement works against the impossible 'third thing' of a logical form that would mediate within facts between objects or within propositions between names, the 'independence' requirement works against the impossible 'third thing' of a logical constant object that would mediate between propositions or between facts. Just as the former 'third thing' would—impossibly—explain why certain names can form propositions that say something about how the world is, the latter 'third thing' would—impossibly—explain why certain propositions can be combined to form complex propositions that say something about how the world is.

Now how could this outcome seem bland? First, the picture of propositions that emerges is produced in order to show that the world is 'logically bland'; our ultimate analyses reveal atomic facts that are logically independent of each other: the 'logical landscape' between such facts is featureless and imposes no demands on the complex propositions that combine elementary propositions. We can anticipate the form of all propositions, such that, for example, we can anticipate all their logical relations, because the only unanticipatable realm is that of elementary propositions—propositions that do not stand in (problematic, potentially unanticipatable) logical relations with one another—and the logical relations that we do encounter emerge only as a result of our constructing complex propositions by adopting certain 'non-representing' logical constants: these constants 'can be understood simply by a study of their occurrence in symbolism' (*L I* 116), as can the logical relationships that they 'introduce'. If the most basic facts were instead sometimes, somehow, logically incompatible with one another, then propositions that combined representations of such incompatible basic facts would articulate not mere 'physical impossibilities' but 'ontological impossibilities': 'sensible talk' might then be seen as not incorporating such propositions and thereby as responding to a demand made by the form of the world on our language. But by saying that the most basic facts are logically independent, Wittgenstein does not introduce another kind of demand made by the world, because the upshot is that one can combine representations of such facts however the (merely) conventional rules of one's symbolism will allow.

But, secondly, Sections 11.7–11.8 have shown how the GFP accommodates what at the time of the *Tractatus* struck Wittgenstein as the bland requirement that logical constants be 'topic-neutral'. What basis, one might ask, does this requirement have? Wittgenstein's later conclusion is 'Not much', and, at the time of the *Tractatus*, it represented a non-issue for Wittgenstein; but if so, so would any demand that it might impose on an account of the composition of propositions, just like that other 'bland requirement' that insinuates itself into Wittgenstein's account of 'objects', the requirement that 'sense be determinate'. In both cases, in his 'claims' about the internal constitution of elementary propositions and that of complex propositions, what lends those claims substance is something which only the later Wittgenstein recognized as a substantial (and problematic) metaphysical demand.

I will end this section by considering two objections to my reading. First, doesn't the GFP still require that the world take a certain form? Mustn't every proposition turn out to represent a *mosaic*, so to speak, of atomic facts? My answer is yes, but my suggestion is that the early Wittgenstein would have heard this 'claim' as he heard the 'claim' that every proposition imposes a certain form on the world (discussed in Ch. 7) and the 'claim' that '[a]n atomic fact is a combination of objects' (discussed in Ch. 9). Wittgenstein's 'claims' about the composition of both elementary propositions and complex propositions invite us to see the world 'behind them' through a certain frame. But what is important about the world revealed is that it is a logically bland one, one that does not impose logical demands 'of its own', determining either how the objects revealed can be combined or how the atomic facts revealed can be combined.

Secondly, doesn't Wittgenstein talk about the world having a 'logic' (6.22)? Indeed, he does. But that logic is shown by tautologies (6.22),[15] which themselves articulate the structure of the complex propositions that we use and show how that structure prevents certain combinations of those propositions from forming descriptions of how things might or might not be. Our use of elementary propositions gives us descriptions of the world, but ones which are logically independent of one another; what allows the world to 'take on a logic'—to present itself as made up in such a way that certain combinations of certain states of affairs are logically impossible—is our descriptions of those states of affairs being complex propositions with certain kinds of overlapping 'truth-grounds'. These conventionally adopted complex descriptions allow the *impression* that there are

---

[15] Wittgenstein also states that mathematics shows that form 'in equations', but I will not address that topic here.

logical incompatibilities beyond mere contradiction, beyond the incompatibility of p and $\neg p$. Using complex propositions allows the world to present itself as possessed of an 'essence', in that there are ways in which the world cannot be. The GFP, by showing how we can build up complex propositions out of elementary propositions, explains how our descriptions of the world can stand in logical tension with each other, and thus how the world presents itself as possessed of 'an essence', with certain 'logical incompatibilities' written into how it may present itself to be; but the GFP does this without implying that this frame, this 'scaffold', arises out of the world's possession of necessary, metaphysical features. Rather, it results from conventionally adopted modes of description. What creates the impression of a foreseeable logical order to the world is convention: '[o]nly that which we ourselves construct can we foresee' (5.556).

I do not wish to pretend that the account of the GFP that I have offered is watertight. The argument it informs is sketched only schematically, but this is not least because it involves our imagining how descriptions that must ultimately be resolved into elementary propositions might work when we have no examples of elementary propositions[16] and reasons (provided by 'the transitional Wittgenstein') to think that the very idea of such a proposition may make no sense. What I think my account does do is offer a plausible story about how the different demands that are made on the GFP tie together. My account explains its significance—why Wittgenstein believed it must really *be* the GFP—but also its blandness—the form in question is 'Such and such is the case', and allows us to anticipate every form of proposition by insisting that there is nothing to anticipate. I have explained the burdensome analytical demands that the GFP imposes—which, in his transitional work, Wittgenstein realizes embody an unsustainable 'dogmatism' on the part of his earlier self—but also—in line with the resolute interpretation that I have offered—its apparent lack of metaphysical import. According to my reading, to give the GFP, which is 'to give the essence of all description', is to give 'the essence of the world' (5.471–5.4711), in that it shows us what the latter 'essence' comes to.

---

[16] Compare Wittgenstein's remark quoted in Ch. 9 n. 3.

12

Problem Cases for the General Form

12.1 THE COLOUR-EXCLUSION PROBLEM

According to Wittgenstein, complex propositions are just abbreviated statements of how things stand with some set of elementary propositions, and their formation requires no more than certain syntactical innovations. Drawing on this notion of a complex proposition, Wittgenstein presents an understanding of logical deduction that does not commit us to a substantial logic: when such deductions are valid, this is because the deduced proposition, in a sense, 'overlaps' the propositions from which it is deduced. This might not be obvious; but Wittgenstein believed that an appropriate analysis of the propositions would reveal that it was so. This chapter will review cases that do not obviously fit the GFP and will explain how Wittgenstein thought they could be accommodated, as well as indicate how he responded when he came to accept that this project could not be made to work.

The best-known problem case for Wittgenstein is the 'colour-exclusion problem'; this problem is the focus of the paper, 'Some Remarks on Logical Form', one of the first public signs that he had returned to philosophy at the end of the 1920s. The 'problem' in question is that of understanding the relationship between colour propositions which appear to exclude one another without being direct denials of one another. For instance, 'Object *a* is blue all over at time *t*' excludes 'Object *a* is red all over at time *t*'. That red excludes blue, that green excludes orange, etc. do not seem to be empirical claims: 'these remarks do not express an experience but are in some sense tautologies' (RLF 167). The accommodation of these relations within the framework that the *Tractatus*'s GFP imposes requires that these propositions be either logically independent of each other or truth-functionally related to each other. Assuming that exclusion relations between colour propositions are not empirical (that they are 'conceptual' or 'logical' in some sense), the relation is clearly not one of logical independence; so it must then be truth-functional, and, as an understanding of exclusion, the obvious truth-functional relation is contradiction. Thus the *Tractatus* claims that '[t]he statement that a point in the visual field has two different colours at the same time is a contradiction' (6.3751). Wittgenstein's comments from the 'Big Typescript' pp. 474–5 quoted in Section 11.2, in which he explained the

Tractatus's general approach to logical incompatibility, precede an explanation of how he thought that approach would apply to colour exclusion:

Then when I wanted to perform such an analysis of a colour-statement, it came to light //, it became clear //, what it was that I had imagined the analysis to be like. I believed I could understand colour statements as a logical product r & s & t . . . , the factors of which specified the ingredients (if there were several) of which colours (colour, not pigment) consist.

Wittgenstein later came to doubt the adequacy of this analytic manœuvre. This concession is more important than may at first appear, because this same manœuvre was to expose as illusory other apparent cases of logical but non-truth-functional relations holding between propositions—most notably, those involving general propositions.

12.2 GENERALITY

There are two ways of looking at the problem that general propositions pose for Wittgenstein. First, as with colour propositions, general propositions seem to involve some kind of non-truth-functional inference, a form of inference incompatible with the *Tractatus*'s account.[1] Secondly, the quantifiers are another pair of logical constants whose character threatens to provide an impossible explanation of logical inference—in their cases, the peculiar logic of generality and instance. If 'there are no logical constants', their apparent reality needs to be dispelled.

Although the *Tractatus*'s perspective on generality is notoriously difficult to fathom,[2] Wittgenstein's success in divorcing the truth-functional connectives from any reference to logical objects naturally suggests an analysis of general propositions as logical products or logical sums of their instances.[3] Thus 'All philosophers are wise' would be analysed as 'Socrates is wise and Plato is wise and . . .'. Among the virtues of such an analysis is its making clear how an instance follows from this generalization and how the negation of one of the instances contradicts the generalization. The 'unpacking' story spelt out in Section 11.3 can be applied here too:

---

[1] RLF 167 makes remarks in connection with colour exclusion that are strikingly similar to those discussed below regarding the need for 'supplementary propositions' in analysing general propositions as logical sums/products. *Pace* Klagge and Nordmann (Introduction to RLF in *PO* 28) and, before them, von Wright (1954, p. 13), 'generality and infinity in mathematics' and the colour-exclusion problem were not at all, for Wittgenstein, 'entirely different topic[s]'.

[2] Cf. the discussions in Anscombe 1959, ch. 11; Fogelin 1987, ch. 5; Ostrow 2002, ch. 3.

[3] Although Wittgenstein occasionally appears to be ascribing just this view of generality to Frege and Russell (cf. 5.521), his later comments on the *Tractatus* show that this was indeed his own view (cf. also *VC* 39; M 297; *L II* 5–6; *PG* 268, quoted below). I will discuss below several collateral commitments of Wittgenstein's that deal with objections that this analysis would otherwise confront.

The possibility of inferring completely general propositions from material propositions—the fact that the former are capable of standing in *meaningful* internal relations with the latter—shows that the completely general propositions are logical constructions from situations. (*NB* 16)

Moreover, an analysis of general propositions as logical products or logical sums would rely on no more than the truth-functional connectives which truth-table analysis has already shown can be understood without postulating logical objects as referents. In doing so, this analysis would deal with both the problematic aspects identified in the preceding paragraph.

Now some general statements are immediately likely candidates for an analysis along these lines. Statements of the form 'the primary colours are x' can be analysed as:

Blue is x & Green is x & Red is x & Yellow is x.

It is a condition of understanding the general statement that one recognizes that once the product of the four conjuncts presented has been asserted, there is nothing more to say. But, crucially, such an analysis presupposes that the general proposition in question corresponds to some predetermined totality of its instances, and many general statements do not seem to meet this requirement. Moreover, that a particular group constitutes a totality in the relevant way may not be at all apparent. In discussing the analysis of 'All men in this room are wearing trousers' as a logical product of its instances (that is, as 'Schlick is wearing trousers and Waismann is . . . '), Wittgenstein asserts that '[e]very complete enumeration must end with the words "and nothing else" ' (*VC* 38). But how is this exclusion to be expressed? Our candidate exclusion clause ('and there is no one/nothing else') runs into the same difficulty as the initial logical product: namely, the need to say 'and that covers everything'.[4] So this 'solution' faces the problem it was to solve.

G. E. Moore reported that Wittgenstein claimed to have been aware of the problems associated with this kind of supplementary clause at the time of writing the *Tractatus* (M 297). Why, then, did it not worry him? The notes from *VC* 38 quoted above continue as follows:

There is a conception here according to which one says: 'Mr Carnap is not in this room, Mr . . . , etc.' And the proposition one might expect here, namely 'these are all things,' this proposition does not exist. (*VC* 38)

What does Wittgenstein mean by saying that the proposition which indicates the 'bounds' of our generalization 'does not exist'? It is reminiscent of the *Tractatus*'s proposal that what a proposition such as Russell's Axiom of Infinity (which asserts that there are an infinite number of individual entities)[5] 'is meant to say would be expressed in language by the fact that there is an infinite number of names with

---

[4] Ramsey discusses this problem in 1927, pp. 50–1.
[5] Cf., e.g., Russell 1993 [1919], ch. 13.

different meanings' (5.535).[6] If so, in the case of a general truth about objects, there would be no need for, and indeed there could not be, the kind of supplementary proposition that we seek, because our conjunction's being about all objects would be something not said but, in some sense, *shown*.

Though what this claim comes to is not clear, Wittgenstein's later criticisms of the *Tractatus* allow us to see that it is an instance of a wider claim. Supplementary propositions are unnecessary, not only when dealing with the class of objects but also whenever '[t]he class in question . . . [is] determined not by a proposition but by our "dictionary" ', when it is 'defined by grammar' (M 297). For example, if we consider the class 'the primary colours', red, green, blue, and yellow 'are not the extension of a concept: they alone are the concept' (M 297; *PR* 138). If a general statement regarding the primary colours were analysed as a statement about red, green, blue, and yellow, it would make no sense to say at the end 'and there are no other primary colours' because an understanding of 'primary colour' presupposes a knowledge that once one has stated that red is x, green is x, blue is x, and yellow is x, one has said that the primary colours are x. '[I]f I say "And there is no other" it must also make sense to say "There is another" ' (*L I* 15), and here, Wittgenstein suggests, it doesn't. Thus, as would be the case with general propositions regarding objects, general propositions regarding primary colours *can* be analysed as logical sums and products, because the exhaustiveness of the conjunction or disjunction *shows* itself.[7]

The class of properties of which *being an object* and *being a primary colour* are instances, for which Wittgenstein reserves the term 'forms' (*VC* 44), and for which the problem of supplementary propositions would not arise, seem key to Wittgenstein's approach to generality:

Every variable is the sign for a formal concept.

For every variable expression represents a constant form that all its values possess, and this can be regarded as a formal property of those values. (4.1271)

Every time we hold some part of a proposition constant and make claims about the propositions which share that part—that is to say, every time we make claims about the different values of a 'propositional variable' (3.313)—we are generalizing over the instances of a formal concept. 'Whenever [a formal concept word] is used . . . as a proper concept-word' (such as when we try to say 'these are all the primary colours'), 'nonsensical pseudo-propositions are the result' (4.1272), and hence, none of our general propositions can require a completing, supplementary proposition. If every variable corresponds to a form, we cannot state that a particular product or sum includes all the instances of our variable: there is no such proposition. A form is 'defined by grammar', and our 'dictionary' will

---

[6] Cf. also 4.1272.

[7] Obviously this exhaustiveness is *not* apparent as our colour statements are ordinarily expressed. But expressed in 'a sign-language . . . governed by *logical* grammar—by logical syntax' (3.325), this exhaustiveness would be manifest.

show whether our proposition covers all its instances. Later remarks support this understanding of the relationship between 'forms' and generality:

My view about general propositions was that (x).øx is a logical sum and that though its terms aren't enumerated *here*, they are capable of being enumerated (from the dictionary and the grammar of language).
    For if they can't be enumerated we don't have a logical sum. (*PG* 268)

If one constructs a logical product of all the elementary propositions that have as one of their constituents an element which has a particular form, one would have constructed a proposition which generalizes over that form, a proposition which says 'All *x*s are *y*'. Thus one can generalize over those subgroups of objects that share a particular form without needing an impossible supplementary clause. In such cases, it would be *apparent* that there is no difference between a statement about all the instances of a form and a statement which just happens to concatenate claims about all those instances. Hearing a description of these two statements might make one think that they are different. But when stated in the *Begriffsschrift*, it would be apparent that there is no such difference. The difference which thereby vanishes was unreal all along. If we have a statement about red, green, blue, and yellow, we already have a statement about 'all the primary colours'.

12.3 WHERE DO OUR MODELS 'END'?

But how is this story of forms supposed to work?[8] It is not clear; but I will argue that issues that arose in three earlier sections give us some sense of how it might be understood. Recall first the argument presented in Section 8.3 for the impossibility of learning a first language. An example was ostensive definition, which seems to work as an explanation of a symbol only if we ascribe to the pupil the capacity to recognize the ostended object as an instance of the concept to be explained—in other words, if the pupil *already has* a mastery of the symbol that was to be explained. The explanation itself needs to be expressed within a system of representation, when what we hoped to be explaining are the very symbols that such a system of representation involves.[9]
    Consider now how that realization might bear on a particular kind of explanation that one might imagine could be given for an aspect of our kitchen table

---

    [8] A full account of the resources available to Wittgenstein in the *Tractatus*'s efforts to understand generality would also need to examine Wittgenstein's notion of an 'operation'. Sounding a note familiar from the above discussion, 'operations' are also meant, it seems, to group propositions together by their 'forms', without thereby implying that this delimitation rests on a truth of some sort. Operations are central in the *Tractatus*'s difficult exposition of its philosophy of mathematics, and at *NB* 89–90, Wittgenstein suggests that they are crucial to our understanding of the gesture, 'and so on'.
    [9] As Sect. 14.8 discusses, learning a first language obviously isn't impossible; my concern here is to expose a certain confusion that we may succumb to when thinking about that learning process.

model. The model was being used to explain a car accident: cups represented cars, a pepper-pot a person, and folded napkins were roads. An equally essential 'sign' within the model was the relevant part of the kitchen table itself, representing the space within which the roads, the cars, etc. were to be found. Suppose now that at the other end of the table was a tea-pot and the morning paper, and on a nearby work-surface, a toaster and a loaf of bread. Suppose that in using the model, I pick up one of the cups and remove it to the other end of the table, meaning to indicate a situation where the car it represents has left the scene of the action. Now suppose someone asks, 'Are you sure that that car really was there?' My first reaction will probably be 'Where?' When the person points to the cup standing next to the tea-pot, he shows that he has failed to understand that the cup has ceased to represent the car, and that that part of the table is not part of the model. The range of spatial locations that the model represents is limited, in that at some point along the table the model *ends*. But how would one explain this to someone?

To make the problem more apparent, let us step back again from the 'commentary', which, for the sake of simplicity, I have been using, and change to another way of representing our model. (That is, after all, what the commentary has been doing.) Let us imagine another model whose purpose is to show what the original model represents. Imagine a model of the kitchen table made up of letters written on a page of a notebook: a 'C' represents a cup, 'PP' represents the pepper-pot, elongated 'N's represent the napkins, and so on. We may now imagine explaining the kitchen table model by going outside, pointing at features of our notebook picture and then pointing at the relevant items in the outside world that are represented by the items in the kitchen table model that the features of the notebook picture represent. In this way, one might offer an explanation of our original model. (Why someone might want to explain it in this way is another matter; to make it a little less implausible, suppose that our mother won't let us take her fine china outside.)

But we also need to explain what doesn't represent in our original model. Suppose we have other marks on the page: a 'TP' representing the tea-pot, a 'MP', the morning paper, and a 'T' the toaster. Now we point at these, and instead of pointing to something, we just shake our heads. But our original problem looms again here: what if, on the opposite page of the notebook, there are other marks, perhaps a shopping list. The teacher has neither pointed to anything nor shaken his head in connection with these. What might they say about the kitchen table model? Might they represent the toaster and the loaf of bread on the nearby work-surface, and might those represent something or other within the kitchen table model? So the pupil needs to know that these signs on the opposite page don't represent anything: the pupil needs to recognize where the second-order model 'ends'.

But how is this to be conveyed? Consider also other pages in the same notebook: what is said about the original model by the teacher leaving these blank?

And what about pages in other notebooks in the room? What of other notebooks in the house? In the country? In principle, they could play a role in our second-order model. But, in fact, they don't. How might one explain this without using another model to represent the second-order model, and without the limits of that third-order model being equally in need of explanation? Otherwise that third-order model must take in . . . everything, indicating, for example, that no symbolic role is played in our second-order model by the *Mona Lisa*, the Great Pyramid, and the contents of the cubic metre of space which, at the present moment, is exactly half-way between the earth and the planet Neptune.

(They could, after all, though they don't. There are familiar enough ways in which we try to make such matters clear: we clear the kitchen table of everything but the items that represent; we use a kitchen table instead of the kitchen floor, because of the more obvious boundary that the former's edges provide; similarly, we wouldn't set out our second-order model on a piece of paper that already had other letters marked on it. But none of these 'natural' limitations are 'logical' limitations; it might be hard to understand our second-order model if it is set out on a piece of paper that has already been written on; but, in principle, the model could still be understood and used.)

But the problem here is not merely one of not being able to delimit the variables that one is currently using, as opposed to those one is describing. Not being able to delimit the former also calls into question our descriptions of the latter. We want to know, for example, whether the represent*ing* space of our first-order model 'starts up again', so to speak, on the work-surface where the toaster is to be found, whether it 'continues' in the room next door, etc. We want to know whether the represent*ed* space of our first-order model 'starts up again' in a nearby town. It certainly could, in that such a model is possible. Our second-order model might be thought able to represent these limits. But when is the latter's delimiting description *complete*? When does its own modelling *end*?[10] Without knowing this, it remains unclear how we are to determine whether the representing and represented 'ranges' of the first-order model might not 'start up again' in the further, indeterminate reaches of what the second-order model represents. Yet any description of the limits of that second-order model, by a third-order model, will face the same problem.

Our problem is that the second-order model needs to be more 'expansive' than the first-order model: to explain that model, the second-order model needs to represent what it represents *and more*, in order to say what the first-order model does *not* represent. But if we want to draw a limit to the range of significance of our model, it seems that we must at some point use a model whose own

---

[10] This also now suggests a parallel aspect to the impossibility of stating how many objects there are. Any such proposition would need to say that these objects exist and there are no others, and would need a way of referring to these non-existent others in order to say that they do not exist. But such a proposition would thus need to use more names than there are. One would need more than *n* names to state that there are *n* objects; but if there are *n* objects, there can only be *n* names.

range of significance remains to be drawn: to draw on Wittgenstein's notion of 'logical multiplicity', the 'multiplicity' of the variables that a system of representation uses 'cannot be represented', since '[o]ne cannot get outside it in the representation' (4.041). We confront another aspect of the problem identified in the passage from *NB* 25 quoted in Section 8.3: 'How can I be *told how* [a model] represents? . . . [T]his would have to be done by means of a [model], but [a model] could only show it.' There is no way of describing the 'extent' of a variable, because that could be done only by drawing on a more 'expansive' variable whose own 'extent' would then simply have to (somehow) 'show itself'.

12.4 HOW VARIABLES 'SHOW'

So we have a sense now of why one might say that the expanse of the variables we use must at some point *show* itself. The issue we are trying to settle cannot be resolved through some kind of description of the variable, as the issue arises again in connection with the description. I have argued that Wittgenstein's invocation of 'showing' ought to be understood, first, as articulating certain explanatory impossibilities and then, secondly, as drawing our attention to how the explanatory project being pursued itself arises out of confusion on our part. How might that story run here?

Wittgenstein states that '[e]very variable is the sign of a formal concept' (4.1271); he also states that '[w]henever [a formal concept word] is used . . . as a proper concept-word' (such as when we try to say 'these are all the primary colours'), 'nonsensical pseudo-propositions are the result' (4.1272). The impossibility of giving a delimiting description of a variable has shown us why this is so, since attempts to ascribe properties to formal concepts are attempts to describe variables. Similarly, attempts to state that a particular entity falls under a particular formal concept must also fail, since such an attempt is an attempt to state what the values of a variable are. Thus Wittgenstein describes the issue of whether an entity falls under a formal concept as another something that shows itself (4.126).

I turn now to the third of our earlier discussions that sheds light on how the *Tractatus* may have understood generality. In Chapter 6's discussion of our sense that we 'know logical distinctions', we saw that our attempts to articulate that knowledge use equally problematic logical distinctions; the frames of reference that we crave as a context within which to articulate the *ontological* distinctions between purple and winter, and between middle-C and mummification, simply don't seem to be 'there', in that, when we are asked, in response to answers like 'One's a colour and the other is a season' and 'One's a note and the other's a burial practice', what the differences between a colour and a season, and between a note and a burial practice, are, we have nothing more to say. Are these differences, then, differences that, somehow, *show*? What is that supposed to mean?

In Chapter 6 I sketched an explanation of how Wittgenstein thinks we should 'handle' logical distinctions: they are essentially the product of unwitting word-play, of expressions being 'allowed'—by surface-grammatical similarities—to wander from the contexts in which they have sense into others where they do not. (This reflects Wittgenstein's understanding of 'the illogical' (explained in Sect. 5.2) as 'grammatical monsters', as pseudo-sentences that simply have not had a sense assigned to them, though they look like sentences that have.) As a result, 'logical distinctions' are, in a sense, not represented at all in Wittgenstein's ideal notation; rather, the forms of confusion in which we seem to treat the members of different 'logical categories' as different kinds of thing are prevented from arising. (English notation, as the last sentence shows, does not attain that ideal.) In that notation, signs that represent days of the week simply will not fit into the 'slots' either side of 'darker than'; nor will signs that represent geometrical shapes or musical notes.

If failure to understand variables and the logic of generality were to constitute another way of 'misunderstanding logical distinctions', they would be forms of word-play encouraged by a misleading notation. This would explain why, for Wittgenstein, 'there is no proposition' that 'closes' a generalization: supposed 'further instances' are actually cases of sets of signs to which no sense has been assigned. One prevents their 'deduction' not through a description of the range of a 'variable'—which, for the reasons given above, is a non-starter in any case—but by the 'mechanical expedient' of a notation with 'slots' only for genuine instances, where what makes an 'instance' 'genuine' is simply its being a combinations of signs to which sense has been assigned. What determines the range of such instances is 'the dictionary and the grammar of language'.

So, for example, in the kitchen table model, we would see someone who says, 'Ah, but what if this had happened?' while putting bread in the toaster as either very confused about how the model works or perhaps as making a joke about the model. Such a joke would be a form of 'word'-play, a kind of pun. In the model as we use it, there is nothing that that combination of 'signs' says; and if we wished to represent the scene 10 minutes prior to the accident—when 'nothing was happening'—we would not need to stop the person who is about to put toast into the toaster because that, in the model as we use it, does not represent anything happening. To think that it does is to misunderstand the signs in question. To prevent that misunderstanding, what we need is not a delimitation of what corresponds here to the variable in 'nothing was happening'—which is a non-starter—but instead a notation that does not tempt us to construct these pseudo-propositions.

It is characteristic of a philosophical problem that its victim does not see that what he needs to grasp is an explanation of a *sign*; that would not give him 'the feeling that we were teaching him philosophy' (6.53); instead, what he craves we have no clear grasp of: namely, an explanation of the *symbol*, here of 'the formal concept' in question. According to the reading I have developed, Wittgenstein sees the failure of understanding as requiring a 'mechanical' solution; this is not an explanation that will convey 'the necessary understanding', but an elimination of the temptation to misunderstand, the temptation to believe that the difficulty one is experiencing is to be dealt with in anything like the way in which, through our misunderstanding, we believe. 'Failures to understand logical and ontological sameness and difference' show themselves inasmuch as an appropriate symbolism will show them up for what they are: grammatical monsters.

This is a radical 'solution' to the problem of how we are to handle generality, in that it gives no answer to the question of what makes something an instance of a generalization. Instead, it trusts in notational reform to prevent anyone misunderstanding what another person includes when they group together a set of propositions in a general proposition. Will this solution work? Since the notational reform in question has never been carried out, one cannot say; but I have my doubts. For example, it isn't clear that the way in which this solution presents generalization is the only way in which it actually works: it is not clear that we only generalize using what we could credibly see as 'formal concepts'. It appears that we use generalizations that turn on 'genuine concepts' too, and then the question of a closing proposition returns.[11]

The problem that we are attempting to duck is essentially the problem with which Wittgenstein wrestles in his later writings on rule-following. The discussion of what it would be to delimit a variable helps, I think, to show why in those later writings also there is no 'straight solution' to the problem. Such an explanation of why something is an instance of a generalization (an explanation of the sort that the radical 'solution' does not give) would be an explanation of why that something falls under a concept; but our using such an explanation to guide our application of that concept would itself presuppose our capacity to decide when something falls under a concept; any identification of a feature that instances of a concept share, and by reference to which we hope to guide our application of that concept, would itself have to be picked out by a concept; thus, if there is a general problem with ensuring that our subsumption of instances under concepts is ordered, is genuinely rule-governed, the proposed solution would run into the same problem. To echo *NB* 25, it seems that our pursuit of an explanation of how a concept subsumes its instances must end with the application of concepts which simply show us their instances and show us that that is what they are.

---

[11] An issue I do not address here is how this account might be extended to take in the *Tractatus*'s remarks on mathematics. Generally speaking, I have concentrated here on explaining how this account fits with the broader story I am telling about the *Tractatus*, perhaps at the expense of showing how it is rooted in the text; I have already indicated that the textual evidence we have is problematic, but some does indeed point in the direction I have sketched, such as 3.317's insistence that 'the determination of the values of [a] propositional variable' is a description (of those instantiating propositions) to which '*only* this is essential': '*that it is only a description of symbols and asserts nothing about what is symbolized*'.

As I have interpreted the *Tractatus*, Wittgenstein's invocations of 'showing' pick out cases where we are attempting to answer questions we do not understand. Perhaps a different interpretation of 'showing' might yield something more like a straight solution to the problem in question. But it is not clear to me right now what that solution would be.[12] The negative result that our discussion gives seems sound to me: a certain kind of self-consciousness about the use of concepts makes no sense. The problem is one which leaves its mark on the work of Frege and Russell and is similar to one which a Theory of Types faces. Such a theory tries to delimit the range subsumed by a particular variable, and the problem that Wittgenstein identifies for such a theory arises out of the fact that the delimiting theory must itself use concepts that include the range in question and more.

Now Wittgenstein insisted that we must do away with all Theories of Types and, in some sense, replace them with a symbolism. In Section 6.4, I questioned one construal of how such a symbolism might be thought to show the distinctions that such a theory attempts to say, and have explored another possible construal of how the symbolism might 'replace' the Theory; this construal, encouraged by my reading of the picture analogy, takes quite literally the notion that 'illogical combinations' are a matter of confused word-play. What the radical 'solution' sketched here does is treat the problem of delimiting variables, that makes us seek the mirage of self-consciousness described, as unreal. Though this particular 'solution' may fail, I remain inclined, as I think the later Wittgenstein was also, to try to find some way of seeing through the problem, of revealing an account of how we come to pose it which convinces us that we do so as a result of our being confused.

12.5 HYPOTHESES

I will end this chapter by noting briefly how Wittgenstein intended to handle general propositions that cannot be understood as conjunctions or disjunctions of a finite number of elementary propositions. Unlike general propositions such

---

[12] A certain natural, though crude, understanding of how generality 'works'—which 5.501 just might suggest—is not an option, at least for those who embrace an 'austere' conception of nonsense (cf. Sect. 4.2). That paragraph offers three different ways in which the values of a variable can be determined: 'direct enumeration' (i.e., sheer listing), the giving of a formal law, and the 'giving [of] a function fx, whose values for all values of x are the propositions to be described'. Wittgenstein tells us very little about how we are to understand 'formal laws', and I won't address that second option here (though Sect. 12.5 touches on what may be a related issue). What I want to point to here is that, on the 'austere' conception of nonsense, the third option cannot be taken a certain way: we cannot be imagined to be removing a name from a proposition, to produce a propositional variable, into which we then attempt to 'insert' other names in order to determine whether the resultant proposition is a value of this propositional variable; according to such a picture, and assuming that we are not operating purely on the level of signs, 'the resultant proposition' would express, if it is a value of that variable, 'a possible possibility', and if it isn't a value, 'an impossible possibility', 'a sense that is senseless'. By invoking the latter notion, such an explanation of generality is unavailable to the austere.

as 'Nobody was in the street', which make claims concerning more or less strictly delimited areas, what Wittgenstein was to call 'hypotheses', such as 'All men are mortal' and 'Arsenic is poisonous', make claims about a domain of indefinite extent: namely, all past, present, and future men and samples of arsenic. But Wittgenstein maintains that we must have gone astray if, to understand such propositions as logical sums or logical products, we must invoke infinite totalities, because 'an infinite totality ... is nonsense' (*L I* 15). If the instances of our generalization 'can't be enumerated, we don't have a logical sum' (*PG* 268, quoted in Sect. 12.2). This is not simply a claim about whether we can *know* a generalization to be true or false. The logical sum or product was to tell us what a generalization *says*, *which* generalization it is. Analyses of propositions as finite sums or products might be acceptable. But when we claim that to grasp a particular generalization is to grasp an indefinitely extended sum or product, we are claiming to have given an explanation of the problematic sense of generalizations but one the statement of which we could never complete. Prima facie, since it cannot be 'completely settled' which propositions follow from hypotheses (*PT* 3.20103), in that we cannot finitely state what they say, hypotheses represent a counter-example to the claim that '[b]efore a proposition can have a sense it must be completely settled what propositions follow from it' (*PT* 3.20103), and cannot be subsumed by the *Tractatus*'s account of inference.

As a result, Wittgenstein tries to give an account of hypotheses which frees us from the need to see them as propositions after all. Instead, '[a]n hypothesis is a law for forming propositions' (*PR* 285). The passage from *PG* 268 continues as follows:

[I]f [the 'terms' of a general proposition] can't be enumerated we don't have a logical sum.
(A rule, perhaps, for the construction of logical sums.)

In comments on his claim that 'outside logic everything is accidental' (6.3), Wittgenstein attacks the impression that natural laws harbour a non-logical necessity. He claims, for example, that '[m]echanics is an attempt to construct according to a single plan all the *true* propositions that we need for the description of the world' (6.343). Thus the laws of mechanics, which would also appear to hold of an indefinitely extended domain, are not themselves true propositions, but 'rules for the construction of logical sums'. Such laws are 'about the net' we use to describe reality 'and not about what the net describes' (6.35).[13]

Despite the efforts explained in this chapter, Wittgenstein comes to accept that the GFP is not the GFP. His response to that realization in his transitional work is not, as a 'metaphysical' reading of the GFP would lead us to expect, a

---

[13] The *Tractatus*'s treatment of the concept of 'natural law' is made more vivid in those early transitional writings of Wittgenstein's (such as *PR*, ch. 22) that have been labelled 'verificationist', though I would argue that this label is misleading.

working out of a new metaphysical outlook. Instead, as Sections 11.7–11.8 and Appendix A explain, what one finds is the rejection of his earlier 'dogmatism'[14] and the exploration of new ways of analysing propositions. That exploration is governed by the attempt to show that 'syntax is empty', is not 'about anything', that 'symbolism' is 'self-sufficient', and 'grammar' 'arbitrary' or 'autonomous'; these formulations are reinterpretations of his earlier claims that logical propositions cannot be 'substantial' (6.111): if meaning were read off some kind of independent fact, that is to say, if 'grammar' were not 'autonomous', there would be a substantial logic after all. But as a means of demonstrating that this is indeed a confusion, the GFP came to strike Wittgenstein as an overly general, ineffectual, and indeed confused quick-fix.

[14] Cf. Sect. 11.8.

13

Ethics and 'the Inexpressible'

The topic on which Wittgenstein's comments in the *Tractatus* have been seen as most perplexing of all is arguably ethics. As a result, it is not untypical for commentators to discount this topic altogether, and to do so despite recorded remarks of Wittgenstein's that insist on its importance for his work: famously, Wittgenstein wrote to Ludwig von Ficker that 'the point of [the *Tractatus*] is ethical'.[1]

Wittgenstein's early remarks on ethics are few and opaque. Help can be had by considering not only the *Tractatus* and the wartime notebooks, but also his 1929 'Lecture on Ethics' (LE), where he appears to be articulating a fundamentally similar outlook, and other remarks from that period (some of which have been published in *CV* and *VC*). In LE, Wittgenstein specifies two ways in which, faced with the request that we justify our actions, that request can be met: we can try to show that the act has 'relative' or 'absolute value'. When we ascribe to an act 'relative value', we indicate that the act is good because it satisfies 'a certain predetermined purpose' (LE 38). One might still ask of such an act whether the purpose it serves is valuable, and if one justifies that purpose by indicating that serving it serves a further end, we might still ask of this further end whether it is to be valued. 'Relative value', argues Wittgenstein, does not 'present any difficult or deep problems' (LE 38): 'Every statement of relative value is a mere statement of fact' (LE 39) by virtue of not addressing the question of whether the predetermined purposes that it invokes ought to be taken seriously, ought to be acted on. Ethics concerns the good, not in this 'trivial or relative sense' (LE 38), but in the 'absolute sense'. But what is that? Here Wittgenstein's remarks take a mysterious turn. He insists that 'no description that I can think of would do to describe what I mean by absolute value' (LE 44); such a description 'does not and never will touch the essence of the matter' (*VC* 69):

I would reject every significant description that anybody could possibly suggest, *ab initio*, on the grounds of its significance. (LE 44)

'Ethics', the *Tractatus* declares, 'is transcendental' and 'cannot be expressed' (6.421). But why think that? The argument in the text (6.41) is, roughly, that anything that might be asserted must also be capable of being denied, and

---

[1] Quoted in Sect. 1.1.

as such is unfit to declare that something or other is of value, since such a declaration is meant to articulate what we *must* do. I think we would do well, none the less, to look beyond this argument, since, as with propositions that express a priori synthetic necessities or propositions that assert the holding of internal relations, the conclusion above seems, on the face of it, a good reason for believing that the conception of the sayable in play is mistaken, or is inapplicable to these kinds of truths.[2] Has Wittgenstein, like some stereotypical positivistically minded philosopher, constructed a theory about the nature of representation, and then gone on to draw the counter-intuitive but comforting conclusion that ethics—an area about which such a stereotype feels, by turns, uncomfortable and dismissive—is not a subject for serious thought? My suspicion is, instead, that Wittgenstein is motivated by an ethical concern that is significant in its own right, and that his view of ethics is not merely a ramification of another theory that he happens to hold. I will argue that Wittgenstein's thinking expresses a different kind of response, one which is recognizably of a piece with his other concerns, and which gives sense to his proposal that 'the point' of the *Tractatus* 'is ethical'.

On the face of it, the resolute reader is in a tricky position when it comes to Wittgenstein's remarks on ethics. The most obvious option when interpreting a philosopher's remarks on ethics is not available to the resolute reader: namely, interpreting them as setting out a moral philosophy, a 'position on ethics' from the same stable as natural law conceptions, emotivism, projectivism, etc., etc. Diamond captures this predicament in early 'confessional' parts of her paper 'Ethics, Imagination and the Method of Wittgenstein's *Tractatus*', where she describes articulations of what is at stake in Wittgenstein's remarks on ethics to which she is drawn, but which draw on phrases from the text which her 'resolution' suggests must be 'simply nonsense'. She concludes:

[I]t would appear to be confused of me to think that I can talk nonsense and be giving the content of a kind of ethical position. For is that not what I keep trying to do? Do I not keep trying to give the content of his ethical views? If we must keep silent about that about which we cannot talk, and if I really take that seriously, what can I be doing in making so much noise? (Diamond 2000*b*, p. 155)

My reading avoids this problem[3] by arguing that, ultimately, Wittgenstein's point is metaphilosophical, a point not so much about the nature of the ethical as about the nature of the philosophical.[4]

---

2 Cf. Sect. 4.9.

3 Diamond offers her own complex response to this problem, one which doesn't appeal to me, partly because it seems to construe Wittgenstein's 'ethical concerns' as only just recognizably ethical, but primarily because I just don't think I understand it.

4 In addition to Diamond's, other important attempts to read Wittgenstein's ethical remarks within the strictures of 'resolution' are Kremer 2001; Friedlander 2001, ch. 9; Ostrow 2002, pp. 128–35; Conant 2005; Mulhall, forthcoming. In what follows, I touch on several themes

I will argue that a certain natural sense can be ascribed to the notion that 'ethics is inexpressible' if we reflect on what we know to have been perhaps Wittgenstein's central ethical or spiritual concern: a concern with what he calls 'decency'. The concern points us to notions of 'conscience' and 'good will' as necessary background 'capacities' without which our ethical talk lacks substance, and which cannot themselves be 'condensed' into principles that might be followed. But these insights must be handled with care; Chapter 12 will explain how a full appreciation of what 'conscience' and 'good will' denote reveals a distortion embodied in our first recognition of these 'phenomena'. Like Wittgenstein's 'deduction' of internal relations, these discoveries, once made, are to be 'thrown away'. As Wittgenstein's 'ladder' metaphor suggests, though the philosopher needs to recognize what she interprets as these profound forms of 'inexpressible knowledge', what this 'discovery' ultimately point us to is a confusion in the outlook from which that interpretation is derived. If we can shed that outlook, we will shed, at the same time, our initial understanding of what is at stake in our talk of 'conscience' and 'good will'; the 'ladder' will thus be 'thrown away'.

In line with my broader interpretative principles, the root confusion that we must unearth turns out once again to be a sign/symbol conflation, a certain fantasy of, and for, principle or doctrine as something that might capture within itself the essence of the good life. The reason why Wittgenstein does not here make a 'positive philosophical claim' in pointing to this 'limitation' on principle or doctrine is that it is only the philosopher who ever harboured such fantasies. In this way, Wittgenstein's demand is not so much that we rethink the nature of the good life, but that we recognize a fantasy in how *philosophy* approaches it. When Wittgenstein claims that his early work delimits the ethical 'from within',[5] one might ask: from within what? On first encounter, our understanding of conscience suggests that the answer is something like 'the proposition', that we learn what the ethical is when we recognize limitations on what propositions can do. On my reading, this is a transitional step, and a proper appreciation of the ethical challenge that concerns Wittgenstein comes by working our way out from within *philosophy*: we confront once again the ordinary difficulties of the ethical life by coming to see philosophy's fantasy of that life as a fantasy.

The evidence upon which any commentator can draw in trying to make sense of Wittgenstein's comments on ethics is sparse. These comments are few and far between; this is one of the reasons why they are so puzzling—they seem to come out of nowhere—and are so easy for commentators to disregard. As a result of this insubstantial basis, any reading of Wittgenstein's remarks on ethics will be speculative; and anyone unwilling to entertain such a reading will simply have to suspend judgement on what these remarks mean. My own reading is certainly

explored by Kremer, and in Ch. 14 n. 28 I explain how I see the similarities and differences between my reading and his.

[5] Cf. Sect. 1.1.

speculative; but, in its defence, it presents Wittgenstein's concerns as continuous with his more general philosophical and ethical concerns (for which, by contrast, much evidence is available), and helps illuminate these more general concerns (as Wittgenstein's own comments on the ethical 'point' of the *Tractatus* would seem to demand).

13.1 DECENCY AND PHILOSOPHY

Monk has proposed that

[Wittgenstein's] life might be said to have been dominated by an ethical struggle—the struggle to be *anständig* (decent), which for him, meant, above all, overcoming the temptation presented by his pride and vanity to be dishonest. (1990, p. 278)

Similarly, McGuinness claims that

[Wittgenstein sought] to engage his friends and disciples in a moral enterprise character-ized above all by the effort to see clearly and to be completely honest with oneself and others. (2002, p. 6)[6]

I will argue that Wittgenstein's concern with this struggle expresses itself in a struggle with—on a construal which we have independent grounds to believe Wittgenstein embraced—philosophy itself. A letter to Engelmann from 1918 illustrates this connection:

It is true there is a difference between myself now and as I was when we met in Olmütz. And, as far as I know, the difference is that I am now *slightly* more decent [*anständiger*]. By this I only mean that I am slightly clearer in my own mind about my lack of decency [*meine Unanständigkeit*]. If you tell me now that I have no faith, you are *perfectly right*, only I did not have it before either. It is plain, isn't it, that when a man wants, as it were, to invent a machine for becoming decent [*anständig*], such a man has no faith. But what am I to do? *I am clear about one thing:* I am far too bad to be able to theorize [*spintisieren*] about myself; in fact I shall either remain a swine or else I shall improve, and that's that! Only let's cut out the transcendental twaddle [*Geschwätz*] when the whole thing is as plain as a sock on the jaw. (*LPE* 11)[7]

In a 1929 remark to Schlick, Wittgenstein calls for

an end to all the claptrap [*Geschwätz*] about ethics—whether intuitive knowledge exists, whether values exist, whether the good is definable. (*VC* 68)

---

    6 Similarly, von Wright, when asked if there were 'any special personal qualities' of Wittgenstein's that had made an impression on him, singles out 'a vast intellectual capacity, moral qualities and demands for unconditional veracity and candour' (1994, p. 165).
    7 I examine just what Wittgenstein might mean here by 'faith' in Sect. 15.6. Other uses of '*anständig*' and '*Anständigkeit*' in Wittgenstein's early diaries and personal reflections can be found at *GT* 19, 22, 28, 40, 41, 48; MS 107, 88, 129 (both 1929); MS 109, 212 (1930) (published at *CV* 11 and quoted below).

This follows on immediately from the following striking statement:

[R]unning up against the limits of language is *ethics*.

This same sense that the good life poses a challenge with respect to which language leaves us in the lurch emerges in some remarks from 1930. Having commented on the 'great temptation to want to make the spirit explicit' (*CV* 11), the next day, Wittgenstein observes:

When you bump against the limits of your own decency [*Anständigkeit*] it is as though a whirlpool of thoughts is generated, (&) an endless regress: you may *say* what you like, it gets you no further. (*CV* 11)

But what does Wittgenstein mean by 'decency'? The passage just quoted can be found in MS 109, and immediately follows the following sentences which end what has been published as the foreword to *PR*:

[T]he book is written in good will, and in so far as it is not so written, but out of vanity, etc., the author would wish to see it condemned. He cannot free it of these impurities further than he himself is free of them.

In what follows I will explore these connections with 'good will' and 'vanity', as well as with the notion of 'conscience'.

In doing so, it may seem here that I am, to use Diamond's words, 'trying to give the content of [Wittgenstein's] ethical views'. But, as we will see, the 'view' to which Wittgenstein's 'view' on 'decency' stands opposed is a philosophical fantasy, Wittgenstein's own 'view' being a truism that only the philosopher in us overlooks or misunderstands. I will argue that Wittgenstein's ethical concern is the flip side of a metaphilosophical concern, that Wittgenstein's concern with *Anständigkeit* is simultaneously a concern with philosophy's *Geschwätz*. Put extremely succinctly, philosophy can be compared to that confused pursuit of a 'machine for becoming decent'.

13.2 LOGIC AND ETHICS: AN INITIAL PARALLEL

Our best hope of tying the *Tractatus*'s discussion of ethics into the body of the book must lie in the parallel that Wittgenstein suggests between the ethical and the logical:

Ethics does not treat of the world. Ethics must be a condition of the world, like logic. (*NB* 77)

The logic of our propositions 'cannot be represented' (4.0312), and 'ethics cannot be expressed' (6.421); instead, both are 'transcendental'. Wittgenstein declares indeed that

What is ethical cannot be taught. (*VC* 117)

Is there any reason to think that 'the logical' is unteachable too?

I suggest that there is, and that it was revealed in Section 8.3's discussion of the apparent impossibility of teaching or learning symbols. This I compared to the process of teaching or learning a first language. Roughly speaking, learning a second language can be seen as a matter of learning a collection of contingent facts about *signs*, learning that 'x' refers to *x*s; but this presupposes a capacity to distinguish *x*s from non-*x*s, and it is that capacity that corresponds to mastery of a first language, to a mastery of symbols. On the sentential level, the second-language learner learns that this sentence is used to represent that fact; but learning a first language cannot be the same kind of feat; mastery of a first language corresponds to the capacity to discriminate facts upon which, according to our sketch, second-language learning draws.

An initial parallel with the problem of conveying ethical insight is clear if we consider a 1931 remark from *CV*:

Nothing we do can be defended absolutely and finally. But only by reference to something else that is not questioned. I.e. no reason can be given why you should act (or should have acted) *like this*, except that by doing so you bring about such and such a situation, which again has to be an aim you *accept*. (*CV* 23)

Inasmuch as such reasons cannot bring it about that one ultimately accepts this final aim, it seems impossible to teach someone how they should act; such a reason seems confined to explaining a matter of 'relative value', the mere fact that an act is a means to attaining an end which one may or may not then value. In the *Tractatus*, Wittgenstein proposes that 'When a general ethical law of the form "Thou shalt ..." is set up, the first thought is: Suppose I do not do it?' In other words, what difference will it make? What seems untouched by the presentation of such a law or the kind of 'reasons' envisaged in *CV* 23 is my underlying inclination to care or not care, to value or not value.[8] As Wittgenstein puts in the following 1929 remark, 'You cannot lead people to what is good; you can only lead them to some place or other', which they may or may not then see as a valuable place to reach; since such 'leading' can reveal only the mundane facts of relative value, 'the good', one might say, 'lies outside the space of facts' (*CV* 5 (1929)).

The parallel with the logical case is clear. Efforts to tell someone how a proposition represents must be made 'by means of a proposition' (*NB* 25)—'it is by means of propositions that we explain ourselves' (4.026). But such explanations can only move one on, so to speak, to a proposition one already understands, just

---

[8] In conversations with members of the Vienna Circle, Wittgenstein comments on the Euthyphro problem: is it that 'the good is good because it is what God wants', or is it that 'God wants the good because it is good' (*VC* 115)? He declares the first to be the more profound, '[f]or it cuts off the way to an explanation "why" it is good'. The second interpretation 'is the shallow, rationalist one, which proceeds "as if" you could give reasons for what is good' (*VC* 115). Cf. also LE 39 and Rhees 1970, p. 96: ' "You ought to want to behave better." "What if I don't?" What more could I tell you?'

as justifications of actions can only move one on to an aim one already accepts. What we crave and miss here is an explanation that will 'exit' the language one has already mastered and an explanation which will 'exit' one's already established view of what is valuable.

This negative insight—which Kremer has emphasized too[9]—must, I think, be part of the story. But I want to press on. Where, in particular, is the connection to *decency*? What place does a seeming obsession with honesty with oneself have here? And even if one cannot convince another person that the aims one values are ethically valuable, what's stopping one from *expressing* the view that they are?

13.3 AN INTUITION THAT THE ETHICAL IS 'INEXPRESSIBLE'

So let us start again, as it were, and consider why one might be inclined to say that, in ethics, 'you may *say* what you like, it gets you no further'. A familiar thought is that what reveals one's ethical commitments is not what one says but what one does. *Three Men in a Boat* gives us a light-hearted example:

I lived with a man once who . . . would loll on the sofa and watch me doing things by the hour together, following me round the room with his eyes, wherever I went. He said it did him real good to look on at me messing about. He said it made him feel that life was not an idle dream to be gaped at and yawned through, but a noble task, full of duty and stern work. He said he often wondered now how he could have gone on before he met me, never having anybody to look at while they worked. (Jerome 1994 [1889], p. 36)

What does such a character lack? A concept we naturally reach for here is conscience, a concept that Wittgenstein discusses—if obscurely—in *NB*, and uses in his personal diaries of the period.[10] In both contexts, 'conscience' plays the role of some kind of intimation that we are acting rightly or wrongly, an intimation that Wittgenstein does not look to *principle* to provide:

When my conscience upsets my equilibrium, then I am not in agreement with Something. But what is this? Is it the world?
    Certainly it is correct to say: Conscience is the voice of God.
    For example: it makes me unhappy to think that I have offended such and such a man. Is that my conscience?
    Can one say "Act according to your conscience whatever it may be"? (*NB* 75)

---

[9] Cf. Ch. 14 n. 28.
[10] Cf. *NB* 81 and *GT* 58. Cf. also *LPE* 49; MS 107, 115, 133, 242 (1929–30); and later (1937) diary entries such as *PPO* 175 (1937) and 157–63 (1937), the latter being an extended discussion of conscience discussed below in Ch. 14.

So what is conscience? Conscience is a concept discussed most thoroughly in philosophy in the medieval period, where (in a variety of ways) *synderesis*, understood as insight into the general and fundamental principles of right action, is seen as requiring augmentation by *conscientia*, understood as the faculty of applying ethical principles in deliberation.[11] One might describe conscience as the means by which our knowledge of right and wrong is applied, the glue between what we *believe* is right and our *treating* it as right.[12]

The dominant metaphor used in the Christian tradition to articulate the notion of conscience is that of an 'inner voice'. It is an *inner* voice because it must be a 'natural gift'; it cannot be taught, in that the only person who could benefit from guidance in the application of a principle is someone who is already of good conscience, someone who can already apply the *guidance* appropriately. Hence, the reason why conscience is only *metaphorically* a *voice* is because a (fantasized) conscience—inner *or* outer—that *did* say something would still leave us facing 'the problem of conscience': how to apply what that (impossible) conscience said to us.

Thus already at large in the philosophical tradition, if not frequently discussed these days, is a concept, that of conscience, that articulates a limitation on 'what can be said'. The justification of acts must ultimately terminate in principles that have weight with us, the outcomes that they endorse striking us as valuable without that impact on us being mediated by yet another principle. At some point, demands for further reasons must cease, and there one must find reasons that one not *merely* accepts—a passive acceptance whereby we merely cease causing a fuss—but rather that one actively accepts by getting off one's behind and acting in the manner those reasons require. Bringing about that kind of relation to reasons cannot itself be something we look to reasons to do.

13.4 CAN WE USE CONSCIENCE AS A KEY TO WITTGENSTEIN'S ETHICAL CONCERNS?

So might the supposed unavoidable silence at the foundation of our ethical responsiveness, the silence hazily set forth in the preceding section, stand behind Wittgenstein's remarks on ethics? Certainly it suggests an interpretation of the parallel that Wittgenstein sees between ethics and logic, an interpretation that the following section will spell out. Here I want to explain how it also suggests readings of some of Wittgenstein's other ethical proposals (though in all four cases, we will come to think again about these readings).

---

[11] Different notions of 'conscience' have, of course, figured in the history of philosophy: e.g., Kant's discussion of conscience characteristically treats it as an ability applied *retrospectively* (cf. O'Neill 2002).

[12] For useful discussions, cf. Potts 1980 and 1982.

First, for Wittgenstein, declaring that ethics 'cannot be expressed' (6.421) associates ethics with the mystical: 'There is indeed the inexpressible. This *shows* itself; it is the mystical' (6.522). In the notebook formulation of 6.52, Wittgenstein talks of the 'urge towards the mystical' as emerging at the moment where 'there are no questions any more' (*NB* 51). The notion of conscience provides a relatively concrete sense of why there is nothing more to say when we confront deep moments of ethical responsibility. If your conscience—understood as the capacity to 'apply' what you say—fails you, then 'you may *say* what you like, it gets you no further'. For the same reason, the crucial ethical lessons of life cannot be passed on as a set of rules or claims to knowledge; the only person who might benefit from 'ethical instruction' is a person disposed to do so, the person of good will, something which therefore cannot be brought about through such instruction.

Secondly, if the person of good conscience is the person who lives her life in a way in which she knows it should be led, but good conscience is not itself something that can be brought about through instruction, through the passing on of some item of knowledge, then might not this be 'the reason why men to whom, after long doubting, the sense of life became clear, could not then say wherein this sense consisted?' (6.521). Coming to live as one knows one should is not an issue about which one might come to say, 'Now I know the solution, and it is . . .'; to understand the issue is to recognize that one must no longer chase any such 'solution' and that, as long as one does, one is trying to solve a mythical 'problem of life'. As one might put it, 'The solution of the problem of life is seen in the vanishing of the problem' (6.521).[13]

Thirdly, the notion of conscience provides a sense for why '[o]f the will as the subject of the ethical we cannot speak' (6.423). If we construe the difference between good will and ill will as one of conscience, as one which turns on different ways of applying principles, then that someone's acts fit a particular principle will not demonstrate that they are of good will unless we ourselves, the describers of those acts, are of good will; and that we are cannot itself be something we establish by holding our acts up against principle, since if we are of ill will, we may well still conclude that the principle fits, since as lacking good will, our applications of principle are misleading. The futility of 'making the spirit explicit' lies in the fact that if I am not of good will, monitoring my thoughts and acts cannot reveal that fact, as the ill-willed misdescribe what they see; moreover, anything that anyone might say to me to draw attention to my ill will I will interpret in an ill-willed fashion.

We see here that conscience is a concept that points in two directions. First, it points towards the world, as a capacity to apply our beliefs to the world; but secondly, it also points towards the self, as a matter of being true to oneself: to

---

[13] Sect. 15.6 returns to these remarks.

have a conscience that fails us is to not truly believe what we think—and might, for example, say—we believe. It is to be incapable of saying something and meaning it, even to oneself; what I offer as my reasons—even to myself—may not be my reasons, in that they may not inform the way I live. This failure to bring the way one lives into line with what one says is a failure to respond *to* what one says, a failure to take responsibility *for* what one says; it is also a failure of integrity, of one's capacity to speak for oneself, one's words no more than the par-roting of the words of others, of what is expected or the opinion of the day. If this were indeed Wittgenstein's concern, it would give sense to remarks he makes in conversations with the members of the Vienna Circle about LE:

At the end of my lecture on ethics I spoke in the first person: I think that this is some-thing very essential. Here there is nothing to be stated any more; all I can do is to step forth as an individual and speak in the first person. (*VC* 117)

When the 'what one says' for which one fails to take responsibility is said to one-self, we also encounter a failure of self-knowledge, one that cannot be remedied by adducing more facts, more doctrine, more guidance or rules, because the self-deceiving will misinterpret such further facts or guidance. Consider the following exchange from *Pilgrim's Progress*:

Ignorance. But my heart and life agree together, and therefore my hope is well grounded.
Christian. Who told thee that thy heart and life agrees together?
Ignorance. My heart tells me so.

(Bunyan 1965 [1678], p. 185)

Offering more 'heartfelt' words provides no proof of one's sincerity if the worry is that one ultimately doesn't 'mean it in one's heart of hearts'.

From this perspective, the limitations of an image of self-knowledge as a matter of looking inwards to see what one says to oneself are vivid. Even if one could root through 'the contents of one's mind' to see which 'opinions' belong to that collection, what difference would such discoveries make? What we need to know is whether they are *meant*, just as we might ask of our 'public' utterances. All that the pursuit of self-knowledge, understood in the way envisaged, can find are 'inner sentences', as externally linked to 'what we really think' as 'outer sentences' are: to adapt one of Wittgenstein's later remarks (*PI* p. 217), even if God could look into our minds, he would not be able to tell whether we mean what we inwardly say.[14]

Finally, and perhaps most importantly, the notion of conscience set out here has a clear echo in the idea of decency: one may profess ethical commitments

---

[14] Though I will not explore this idea here, what needs to be appreciated is, I think, similar to what one sees when one recognizes the superficiality of the epistemological gloss of the argument of Sect. 3.5. Sect. 14.8 will explore further how the philosopher's 'inner sentences' (like the metaphor of 'the inner voice of conscience' when taken literally) mythologize the target of the pursuit of self-knowledge, directing our attention away from what that pursuit really requires.

with gusto and with frequency, but unless one has a certain basic decency, the commitments described will make no impression on one's life. To echo *CV* 11 (quoted in Sect. 11.5), '[w]hen you bump against the limits of your own decency', the opinions one expresses swirl as in a 'whirlpool', 'endlessly regressing' in that they make no difference to what you actually do. Such a person, one might say, may have ethical commitments, but lacks the decency that would allow those commitments to make him a good person; he 'may *say* what [he] like[s], it gets [him] no further'.

13.5 LOGIC AND ETHICS: 'CONSCIENCE' AND 'JUDGEMENT'

The notion that 'the ethical' and 'the logical' parallel one another can be developed by seeing how the problem of teaching a first language can be viewed as a problem of 'application' too, and as throwing up the need for a power analogous to conscience. Roughly speaking, a second-language learner comes to understand that a particular term denotes the kind of thing that a particular expression in his first language denotes. But our mastery of language cannot be a matter of mastery of such rules 'all the way down'. We seem to run into the need for a capacity which, following Kant, we might call 'judgement':

If understanding in general is to be viewed as the faculty of rules, judgment will be the faculty of subsuming under rules; that is, of distinguishing whether something does or does not stand under a given rule ... If [we] sought to give general instructions how we are to subsume under these rules, that is, to distinguish whether something does or does not come under them, that could only be by means of another rule. This in turn, for the very reason that it is a rule, again demands guidance from judgment. And thus it appears that, though understanding is capable of being instructed, and of being equipped with rules, judgment is a peculiar talent which can be practised only, and cannot be taught. (Kant 1961 [1781/1787], A133/B172)

Like the 'inner voice' of conscience, this 'talent' 'must belong to the learner himself', must be 'a natural gift'; it is a brand of 'mother-wit' the absence of which 'no school can make good' (Kant 1961 [1781/1787], A133–4/B172–3).

These passages might be compared with that from *NB* 25 discussed in Sections 8.3 and 12.4: if we imagine being '*told*' how [a] proposition represents', then, since 'this would have to be done by means of a proposition', there must come a point at which a proposition simply '*shows*' how it represents, something which we must simply *see*. The second-language learner who learns that this particular sentence is used to represent that particular fact draws upon the ability to discriminate facts that mastery of a first language brings; in that ability, we seem to confront, as McGuinness puts it, 'an inexplicable human capacity':

There could be no process by which people were taught to apprehend a fact, since all instruction takes place through the presentation of facts to the pupil. Likewise there can be no true explanation of our ability to apprehend a fact: we must regard it simply as an inexplicable human capacity ... The considerations thus vaguely indicated seem, or seemed to Wittgenstein to suggest that in our ability to apprehend a fact we have a sort of *a priori* knowledge, which there is no way of expressing. (McGuinness 2002, p. 80)

In both the 'logical' and the 'ethical' cases, we seem to run into a basic responsiveness to the world with which our envisaged explanations cannot provide us. Beyond knowing that being an *x* is a matter of being a *y*, we must at some point *see* that what stands before us is indeed a *y*; similarly, beyond knowing that action *y* is immoral, we must at some point be moved to *do* something about a case of *y* that stands before us. The 'logical' pupil must at some point *see*—his experience must actually be informed, shaped, by concepts—as the 'ethical' pupil must at some point *act*—his life must actually be informed, shaped, by principle.

So does the need for this unteachable, basic responsiveness demonstrate that logic ultimately cannot be 'represented'? By analogy, is this conscience 'an a priori knowledge, which there is no way of expressing'? And does this reveal ethics—what makes a good person good and a bad person bad—to be 'inexpressible'? If so, doesn't the need to accept such ineffables precisely undermine a resolute reading? Isn't that just the kind of thing resolute readings are meant to avoid?

13.6 ETHICS AND 'THE LADDER'

Well, so much the worse for a resolute reading, one might say. I suggested earlier that our analysis of the *Tractatus* on subjectivity could perhaps have ended with Section 8.3. What would then have emerged as crucial would have been the problem of what I have subsequently called 'judgement' and a (oddly expressed) species of solipsism. This view would draw on a seemingly clear and interesting interpretation of the say/show distinction, point in quite a clear way to a fundamental need for judgement as an overlooked power to apply our concepts, and reveal solipsism as a not unreasonable view of our relation to reality, given the necessity that we possess that power (as my 'capacity to think' seems to reveal).

But that analysis did not, of course, end there, and I will argue that our understanding of Wittgenstein's outlook on ethics ought not to stop here either.[15] As with solipsism and the other internal properties and internal relations to which Wittgenstein leads us, there are two depths at which the 'discovery' of judgement and conscience might be said to make sense. The *Tractatus* could be said to demonstrate correctly that the pseudo-logic of certain background confusions demands that there be such powers playing such roles; but the ultimate point of this demonstration is to help us see these confusions as such.

---

[15] Though it doesn't do justice to the complexities of his view, one way of understanding how my view differs from Kremer's might be as differing over this point. Cf. Ch. 14 n. 28.

We must 'see through' these deductions, as indicative not of (unusual) answers to our questions, but of confusions that 'present' us with these pseudo-questions and pseudo-answers.

Our discussion of judgement and conscience might seem to be revealing the importance of action over thought, practice over theory, seeing over saying, with the former of each pair needing to be reinstated alongside our appreciation of the latter of each pair. But a more radical moral that can be drawn questions our understanding of these distinctions. I will argue, for example, that, according to Wittgenstein, the philosopher's 'preoccupation' with saying needs not to be supplemented but to be undone. This will lead us to an important inflection of the conclusions reached so far, suggesting that the root problem that the philosopher faces is not a failure to recognize that ethics is inexpressible or that mastery of concepts is unteachable. Rather, the philosopher is in the grip of confused fantasies of 'expression' and 'teaching'. The 'problems of application' presented above are problems for someone in the grip of these fantasies, and the 'revelation' of these pseudo-problems represents 'rungs' on a 'ladder' to be 'thrown away'. In line with my treatment of internal relations, I will argue that the 'revelation' of the need for judgement and conscience constitutes news for the confused, and not a stable stopping-point; these 'revelations' point to a confused movement of thought that has swept us along, a fantasized demand for explanation and a corresponding 'how it is' that would provide the substance of that explanation; but in doing so, these 'revelations' also cast doubt on our understanding of the terms in which they are themselves articulated. The next chapter will put in place the ideas that we need to allow us to see how these 'revelations' should themselves be rethought, 'climbed', and then 'thrown away'.

14

Ethics and 'the Ladder'

This chapter will argue that the proposal that 'ethics is inexpressible' ought to be 'climbed' and then 'thrown away', following a parallel course to that followed with the other 'inexpressibles' that we have explored, internal properties and internal relations.

Section 4.10 proposed that grasping an 'internal relation' is seeing that we have been confused. Recall our observer who wondered over the remarkable 'fact' that 'the first across the line *always* wins'; then one day he understood what was meant by the worried-looking individual who had tried to draw him away from the track with the words 'Winning and crossing the line are *internally related*!' The observer's question—the question that he sought to answer through long hours standing by the track studying training methods and nutrition—was not *answered*; instead, he came to see that his question was expressive of a misunderstanding. It remains the case 'that the first across the line *always* wins', but he hears that 'claim' differently: he had believed that his problem was the elusive problem of winning, but now he sees that his problem really was a problem with *him*. To assert *with understanding* the holding of an internal relation is to recognize the confusion of the question to which those in the grip of that confusion hear that same assertion as an answer. To understand Wittgenstein's making of these assertions is to see how we have confused ourselves, how certain confused demands have taken hold of us, endowing us with puzzles in need of solutions: 'Why does the first person across the line always win?'

It is within the 'space' that our confused demands bring into pseudo-existence that such inexpressible internal relations emerge; and the same is true, I will argue, of the 'discovery' of the need for judgement and conscience. They present us with 'inexpressibles' and 'unteachables' that ought, ultimately, to make us aware of particular confusions oriented around the words 'teaching' and 'expression'. These 'relations' and these 'needs' ought not, then, to be seen as revealing 'the way things are'. Instead, they indicate misunderstandings, providing news for the confused. The philosopher does need to recognize what *he* will see as the 'inexpressible'. But ultimately what he needs to recognize is how, in interpreting it as 'the inexpressible', his interpretation of what he has come to recognize is informed by a confusion.

In moving from confusion to understanding here, there will be an instant in which we balance on a knife-edge, tottering between seeing before us an extraordinary discovery about races, ethics, etc., and seeing that 'extraordinary discovery' as a discovery about ourselves, about a confusion in our thinking. So, for example, our 'recognition of conscience' totters: on one side lies an extraordinary discovery about ethics and, on the other, the recognition of a fantasy that has set before us a task calling itself 'being ethically serious'. One 'climbs' the 'ladder' thinking through one's philosophical questions with their (mythically construed) subject-matter; using the 'ladder', we reach the point of balance; then to 'throw away the ladder' is to recognize where 'our problem' lies: not in the 'subject-matter', but in ourselves. That problem will turn out to fit Wittgenstein's general diagnosis of philosophical problems: namely, as rooted in sign/symbol confusions. The 'inexpressibility of ethics' is not a final conclusion to be embraced, but something which points us to this confusion, and which, having done so—having been 'climbed'—ought to be 'thrown away'.

14.1 A SKETCH OF AN INITIAL CASE FOR 'THROWING AWAY' 'THE INEXPRESSIBLE'

To raise some initial doubts, I want to note some features of some of the textual evidence offered in Section 13.1, features that our discussion so far does not illuminate. To begin, however, let us consider the following passage from a January 1937 diary entry:

To have an ideal is alright. But how difficult not to want to playact one's ideal. Instead to see it at that distance from oneself at which it is! (*PPO* 163)

Such an achievement is itself a crucial ethical achievement, requiring one 'to become *good*', to have 'the strength to clearly and without ambiguity acknowledge the deficit on the balance sheet' (*PPO* 163).

And that means: to become modest: not in a few words which one says once but in life. (*PPO* 163)

The 'modesty' described here certainly seems to have some similarities with the 'conscience' or 'decency' examined in the preceding chapter, it being what allows an ideal to inform one's actions, to figure not merely as words one says, but in one's life.[1] But it is conspicuous that Wittgenstein begins by insisting that '[t]o have an ideal is alright'; what his remarks on 'modesty' and 'the strength to ... acknowledge the deficit on the balance sheet' seem to be doing is setting out a condition that must be met if 'having an ideal' is to be 'alright', rather than

---

[1] The passage discussed follows a reflection on how a 'document' like the Bible could be expected to ' "attach" me to any belief in the doctrines which it contains'. Wittgenstein declares: 'Not the letter, only conscience can command me—to believe in resurrection, judgment etc. ... Believing begins with *belief*. One must begin with belief, from words no belief follows. Enough' (*PPO* 157–9). But, as the following note explains, he goes on to give this claim a twist.

something 'playacted'. But if so, talk about 'ideals', though it must meet some conditions, is not meaningless in itself; in this sense, ethics is 'expressible'.[2]

Is this an example of the later Wittgenstein rejecting his earlier views? I think not. First, in the letter to Engelmann quoted in Section 13.1, Wittgenstein declares not that 'theorizing'[3] is impossible in matters where decency is at stake, but instead

I am clear about one thing: I am far too bad to be able to theorize about myself. (*LPE* 11)

Similarly, the remark from *CV* 11 also quoted in Section 13.1 does not say that, in matters where decency is at stake, 'what you may *say*' 'gets you no further': that is only one's fate '*[w]hen* you bump against the limits of your own decency' (italics added). If so, 'what one may say'—'theorizing'—is not ruled out here; rather, a condition is set out that must be met if that is to 'get you further': if one has decency—if one is 'good enough'—then it may.

The person who makes these complaints seems not to be insisting that 'ethics is inexpressible', but instead to be pointing out a condition on the 'expression' of ethical matters that is overlooked by a certain tendency to *fixate* on 'theorizing' and on 'what one says'. Compare the following remarks of Wittgenstein's on what it is to speak the truth of oneself:

One can write the truth about oneself in the greatest variety of spirits. With decency and indecency [*Im anständigsten und unanständigsten.*] And according to which it is, it is either very desirable or very wrong to have written that truth. Indeed, there are, among all the honest autobiographies one could write, all levels, from the highest to the lowest. I, for example, cannot write my biography at a higher level than I am. And by the mere fact of writing it, I do not *necessarily* raise myself. I *can* even make myself dirtier (*schmutziger*) than I already was. (MS 108, 46–7 (1929/30))

To echo the passage from MS 109 quoted in Section 13.1, one cannot free what one writes of the 'impurities' of ill will and vanity further than one is oneself free of them: if it is not written with 'decency', it may serve to make one 'dirtier', deepening one's unclarity about oneself and one's life.[4]

What I will suggest is that the 'great temptation to want to make the spirit explicit' (*CV* 11) leads to a distorted understanding of living well ethically,

[2] At *PPO* 159, Wittgenstein goes on to wonder, 'But aren't there various ways of being interested in ink and paper? Am I not interested in ink and paper when I read a letter attentively?' As ink strokes, 'no belief follows', but that is 'the letter' explicitly denied its life and hence rendered obviously irrelevant to 'belief'; and there are other ways of 'being interested in' words. It is the day after these reflections on the *life* of 'the letter' that Wittgenstein turns to the above reflections on the life of 'ideals'.

[3] The word translated here is '*spintisieren*', which could also be rendered as 'ruminating', or even 'musing'.

[4] Cf. *PPO* 125 (1931) ('the *vain person* cannot confess') and *CV* 41 (1939–40) ('One *cannot* speak the truth;—if one has not yet conquered oneself. One *cannot* speak it—but not, because one is still not clever enough. The truth can be spoken only by someone who is already *at home* in it; not by someone who still lives in untruthfulness, & does no more than reach out towards it from within untruthfulness.').

one which overlooks the fact that what one might say about ethical matters 'gets you further' only if it is said in the right spirit, with 'decency' or 'modesty'; that itself is a moral achievement, a way of 'becom[ing] *good*' that such a 'temptation' leads us to overlook. Such an attitude towards 'ideals' is one which someone like Aristotle might applaud, and it is one to which, I will argue, any sober reflection on 'ideals' ought to lead; the principle reason why our reflection often doesn't lead there is, to invoke the spirit of Aristotle again, a confused philosophical demand that we bring to our reflection on ethics. Indeed, I will argue that Wittgenstein's ultimate point in declaring 'ethics' to be 'inexpressible' is not to change our ordinary thinking on ethical matters—in which, at least prima facie, we often express ethical opinions—but instead to draw our attention to a confused philosophical notion of 'expression'. The 'moral' of 'ethics is inexpressible' is a metaphilosophical one, which, once learnt, frees us of a fantasy that calls itself 'expression', in terms of which that very 'assertion' is articulated. That assertion is to be 'climbed' and then 'thrown away'.

In addition to accommodating the aspects noted above of the passages quoted in Section 13.1, this interpretation is also consistent with my broader approach to the *Tractatus* and leaves Wittgenstein with a view that is simply more plausible than one that straightforwardly declares ethics to be 'inexpressible'; that claim just seems false. We express ourselves all the time about ethical matters; what we may not do much of—and I think this is Wittgenstein's underlying ethical concern—is express ourselves on those matters in the right spirit; our lives are riddled with 'idle' ethical talk, mere signs passing themselves off as symbols.

14.2 ANOTHER KANTIAN PARALLEL: A CRAVING FOR REASONS AND THE REJECTION OF RESPONSIBILITY

> I told him that Goldsmith had said to me a few days before, 'As I take my shoes from the shoemaker, and my coat from the tailor, so I take my religion from the priest.' I regretted this loose way of talking. Johnson [replied]: 'Sir, he knows nothing; he has made up his mind about nothing.'
>
> (Boswell 1980 [1791], p. 511)

Our inability to meet the philosophical demand that conceptual and ethical understanding be expressed through explanations that take something like the form of a reason may seem to reveal the need for inexpressible knowledge in the form of judgement and conscience. But my suggestion is that ultimately we do not understand this demand that we feel we cannot meet, and judgement and conscience, invoked to deal with this inability, will turn out to represent rungs on a 'ladder' to be 'thrown away': like the 'inexpressible' internal properties and relations of 'Wittgenstein's metaphysics', they bring us to realize that we do not understand the problems for which they would provide a solutions. This will open up a new perspective on the notions on which we have drawn in our claims about 'the inexpressible' and the 'unteachable'. And this, in turn, will offer a reinterpretation of 'the need for judgement' and for 'conscience'.

I will begin this process of re-evaluation by arguing that we must re-examine the philosophical pursuit of ethical reasons: that pursuit is not so much destined to be frustrated—as the need for the ineffable knowledge that is conscience may seem to show—as confused. To see this is to undo our sense that there is 'something that we cannot do' here, a Wittgensteinian theme that Diamond, in particular, has emphasized.[5] My suggestion is that even if—*per impossibile*—we could uncover foundational ethical reasons, we wouldn't want them; in other words—and crucially—we don't actually understand what it is that we want. Moreover, we can see this when we recognize that this confused pursuit is a recognizably *unethical* pursuit. Section 13.4 suggested that conscience is a concept that points in two directions: towards the world, as a capacity to apply our beliefs to the world, and towards the self, as a matter of being true to oneself. This section will argue that we must press on further in this second direction.

Between ethical principle or doctrine and the ethical life lies a gulf populated by rationalization, hypocrisy, and self-deception, and believing that a body of such doctrine might capture the character of such a life is an attempt to deny that this gulf and its denizens exist. From this perspective, the pursuit of ethical doctrine, understood as the demand for finally and foundationally 'principled' action, appears not merely philosophically confused; it also has an ethical, or perhaps spiritual, meaning. We may not have previously seen the 'phenomena' in question in this light, but we already know what it is to adhere to that demand; it is to succumb to certain species of immorality, if not in- or sub-humanity. That demand is not an admirable philosophical ideal but a refusal to be a moral agent, someone who takes responsibility for their actions; it is to desire to be *told* what to do, to have responsibility for what happens taken on by someone—or something— else.

That there may be something awry with the notion of an 'ethical fact' is a claim familiar in moral philosophy, expressed, for example, in Hume's criticism of efforts to derive an 'ought' from an 'is' (Hume 1978 [1740], p. 469), G. E. Moore's 'Naturalistic Fallacy' (1903), and Mackie's 'Argument from Queerness' (1977, pp. 38–42). But more fundamental is the ethical or spiritual worry that Kant captures in his conception of 'immaturity':

Laziness and cowardice are the reasons why so great a proportion of men, long after nature has released them from alien guidance ... nonetheless gladly remain in lifelong immaturity. ... It is so easy to be immature! If I have a book to serve as my understanding, a pastor to serve as my conscience, a physician to determine my diet for me, and so

---

[5] Cf., e.g., Diamond 1991, p. 195, and 2001, p. 137, and *PI* §374.

on, I need not exert myself at all. I need not think, if only I can pay; others will readily undertake the irksome work for me. (Kant 1996 [1784], p. 573)

If our maturity is a matter of renouncing the notion of an ethical expert who would tell us how we should act, then we must also renounce the notion of an 'ethical fact' which would make Nature or God that ethical expert.[6]

This confused notion of 'ethical fact' hides an uncomfortable truth about responsibility. The ethical expert can tell me to take certain facts seriously and act on those. But I must still decide whether to take the ethical expert seriously. And the same will be true of any ethical principle that one might cite; to revisit 6.422, 'When a general ethical law of the form "Thou shalt . . ." is set up, the first thought is: Suppose I do not do it?'[7] If this question can always be asked, would that show that ethical judgements are groundless? An alternative interpretation of this predicament is that responsibility for my actions ultimately lies with *me*. One way of characterizing what makes something *my* decision, one for which *I* am responsible, is that it exists in a space where I know there is room for argument, where I know that my reasons might be questioned. This is not to act without reasons. Rather, it is a willingness to adopt reasons as my own; to let a rule have weight with me by guiding my actions, without having yet another explanation to hand of why I interpreted the reason in the way that I did. It may always be possible to argue over the application of ethical principles, but from the perspective developed here, the refusal to act until such arguments are settled is not an exemplary instance of responsible action but a rejection of the conditions under which responsible conduct happens.

From this perspective, the moral philosopher's pursuit of ethical doctrine appears to be a repeated *deferral* of responsibility, a refusal to be willing to be the person who will be held to account for what is done, to be the person whose reasons critics of the action will scrutinize. Such a refusal is a refusal to take decisions, an insistence that one will only 'decide' when the decision is taken out of one's hands by the force of the better argument. We find here the distinction between justification and rationalization, where defending my decision merges with showing that it was not my decision but a consequence of relevant rules, where showing I was not irresponsible merges with a refusal to take on responsibility. A supposed model of rational action here serves a will to deny

---

[6] We touch here on another central concept in Kant's charactization of what is problematic in certain kinds of moral realism: viz., 'heteronomy'. Although I draw on Kant at a number of points here, in particular in articulating Wittgenstein's critique of ethical theory, a full exploration of the similarities and differences between the Wittgensteinian perspective and Kant's moral philosophy is beyond the scope of this book.

[7] Though I will not pursue the matter here, 6.422's apparent anti-consequentialism and its obscure remarks about 'reward' and 'punishment' might, I think, be best understood by exploring the (arguably not much less obscure) discussion of happiness that runs though *NB* 73–9 (with 6.422's first formulation at *NB* 78).

that one must eventually speak for oneself; one must take responsibility on one-self rather than acting on orders, acting out the will of a higher authority. So beyond the 'logical' limitation that 'judgement' and 'conscience'—understood as capacities to apply doctrine—seem to reveal is the ethical point that the search for a well-founded ethical doctrine, one that would legitimize my acts in the way that uncovering the fact that p legitimizes my belief that p, expresses a dream of anonymity, of a freedom from responsibility. Through his evasion of the chal-lenge of assuming responsibility, of acting with conscience, the philosopher's project could be seen as the confused and morally poisonous one of trying to build 'a machine for becoming decent'.[8]

14.3 DISSOLVING OUR 'PROBLEMS OF APPLICATION'

Faithful. Well, I see that saying and doing are two things, and hereafter I shall better observe this distinction.
Christian. They are two things indeed, and are as diverse as the soul and the body; for as the body without the soul is but a dead carcass; so, saying, if it be alone, is but a dead carcass also.

(Bunyan 1965 [1678], p. 115)

So what, then, of conscience understood as that '*a priori* [ethical] knowledge, which there is no way of expressing', and the problem of applying principles that I earlier presented it as solving? Chapter 13 may have served to remind us of the following, surely at least partial, truth: the beliefs that one genuinely holds are revealed not by what one says but by how one lives. In this spirit, one might assert that the reason why what I say cannot reveal my true ethical con-victions—they are thus, in this way, inexpressible—is because we would need to know whether I *mean* what I say, and that is something I show through what I do, through the life I live. The time for talking, for saying—even, one might say, for believing!—is over, and now it is down to a question of my judgement, my

---

[8] Parallel concerns over the nature of the religious are well known, though, once again, not under the descriptions offered so far. There are recognizable species of 'impiety' or 'godlessness' that require precisely that we turn God into an object and his wishes into instructions that we might cite in absolving ourselves of culpability. That philosophical demand does indeed seem to render invisible an analogue of the problems of judgement and of conscience that one might call the problem of worship or of love. The demand interprets our relation to God not as one of love, say, but as perhaps one of obedience based on one of knowledge; the root problem becomes an epistemological or metaphysical problem: 'How can we know such a being?'; 'How can there be such a being?' By analogy with the ethical case, I would suggest that the root problem is that even if we could determine that God existed, we would still struggle to explain why that should matter in the way that it matters to believers of anything other than a prudential sort. A question of which the metaphysical question could be seen as a confused interpretation (as the problem of conscience is misleadingly expressed by worries over the metaphysics of ethical facts) is 'How can there be a being that makes this kind of difference?'

conscience, my showing my 'true view' by what I go on to *do*. In this way, the problems of judgement and conscience identified in Chapter 13 offer a natural sense to a distinction between saying and showing: the real meaning of my commitments—which I may attempt to articulate verbally—is shown in how I act.[9]

But do we have a clear sense here of what it is that is said and what is shown? One might argue that what I say about my ethical commitments precisely *does* capture them *when I mean what I say*. Moreover, isn't saying something a kind of acting? Might it not be other things that I *say* that show whether I mean what I say?[10] And, in any case, why say that what our actions show 'cannot be expressed'? Why not say that this is precisely how it is indeed expressed? If 'the inexpressible' is shown—is *expressed* through what one does—why call it 'the inexpressible'?

These questions ought to make us wonder whether this particular saying/showing distinction really 'works': to be specific, whether we can demarcate in a *general* way, cutting through all human life's manifestations, 'what we say' as opposed to 'what our actions show'. But this, I will argue, is Wittgenstein's deeper intention: to show that our notion of 'saying' is confused. This confusion gets us into a mess that the need for such 'showing' signals. Like the 'recognition' of internal relations, to recognize the 'need' for judgement and conscience is to be on the point of seeing that the explanatory project one is in the midst of is confused.

I suggest that the emergence of conscience—of 'a sort of *a priori* [ethical] knowledge, which there is no way of expressing'—is *a step on the way* to recognizing the *philosopher's* confused aspiration, a way in which the confusion can be made to reveal itself. That the need for an inexpressible power arises when we cannot understand the exercise of a particular capacity as resting on the grasping of a reason—a doctrine, something that might be said—ought ultimately to direct our attention back to our understanding of, and ambitions for, such a 'reason', for that which we do deem 'expressible'; running into the need for *conscientia* ought ultimately to make us re-examine what we understand by *synderesis*. And this, of course, will bring a reassessment of *conscientia* too, and it is here that we will come to recognize its character as a 'rung' of a 'ladder' to be 'climbed' and 'thrown away'.[11] To see how, let us consider how the 'problem' that *conscientia* solves is not quite what it seems.

---

[9] The say/show distinction that I elaborate here captures only one part of what is at stake when the *Tractatus* invokes that distinction. As Sects. 15.1–15.3 make clear, the distinction set out above is part of what is 'thrown away'.

[10] It is interesting that in the line from the diary entry presented above, 'to become modest: not in a few words which one says once but in life' (*PPO* 163), the word 'once' was an afterthought. Might the correction be that such words being said often enough or—better—at the right times and places would *be* one's being 'modest in life'?

[11] Conant has sometimes suggested that the notion of ineffable truth is precisely Wittgenstein's target in the *Tractatus* (as opposed to being a notion that it endorses, as 'irresolute' views would suggest) (cf., e.g., 2000, p. 178). But embracing such a notion is, the criticism then comes, 'not a disease of which anyone had ever needed to be cured' (Hacker 2000, p. 370). In opposition to

In certain contexts, using concepts including those of lying, self-deception, and weakness of the will, we may talk of believing something but not acting in line with that belief, of 'failing to apply what we believe'. But can we sensibly distinguish in a quite general way between a principle or belief and its application? It is easy to think that we can imagine the kinds of particular 'misapplication' mentioned worsening, and that these 'imagined situations' would sensibly be described as 'cases of greater and greater breakdown in our capacity to apply our beliefs'. But though one certainly may say that someone 'says something is wrong though he still does it', one also sometimes comes to say that 'he can't really mean it when he says this act is wrong or he wouldn't do it': there comes a point at which one will ask why we still ascribe those particular beliefs to the person, and a further point at which we will ask why we ascribe *beliefs* to this (seeming) person at all.

A certain, crude construal of our talk of *synderesis* and *conscientia* suggests the possibility that a general breakdown in *conscientia* might leave us stranded with our *synderesis*, our knowledge of prinicples, unable to bring those principles to bear on the world. But a certain minimal *conscientia* is necessary before we can ascribe *synderesis*. In order to think of someone as guided by principle, we need to see their acts as, at least partially, *successfully* guided by principle; their lives must manifest a sufficient degree of appropriate order; if we are to imagine someone *trying* to follow a particular rule, rather than another or none at all, we must see that rule as having *some* sort of anchor in that person's thinking and behaviour. The same kind of anchor is also necessary if we are to see someone as prejudiced, hypocritical, or self-deluded: such forms of inconsistency have a consistency in word and action of their own. Without such consistency, without such an anchor, we will be confronted with babbling, or perhaps the following of altogether different rules.

This collapse would affect not only our verbal acts. We cannot see the movements of our imagined 'man without conscience' as actions, because we cannot see them as governed by reasons. Only if one can distinguish kinds of events can the occurrence of, or the desire to produce, such an event provide a reason why one acts as one does; without that 'ur-discipline' of calling a spade a spade, actions are replaced by 'grey, colourless movements', just as utterances are replaced by noise. We misdescribe the 'problem' that this 'individual' experiences—heaping confusion on confusion—if we present it as one of misapplication; it has become instead one of dissolution. If we strip away *conscientia*, what is left in place of *synderesis* is a propensity to produce certain dead signs, marks on paper and waves in the air. These are not 'unapplied claims'; they are not *claims* at all. Rather than 'things that we said', they are 'words that we uttered', 'noises that we made'—in Bunyan's words, 'the dead carcass' of language.

this, Conant has argued that there are indeed sufferers: Frege, e.g. (Conant 2000). But on my interpretation, though 'the ineffable' is indeed to be 'thrown away', that is done only once we recognize a deeper confusion about 'the effable'.

14.4 'THE INTERNAL RELATION BETWEEN BELIEF AND ITS APPLICATION'

One might then say that it is only against a background in which sayings are generally successfully 'applied' that we can make sense of problems of application; when we imagine a *general* 'problem of application', one in which the majority of our sayings are 'misapplied', what we are really envisaging is a situation in which that background has collapsed. One might now be tempted to gloss these conclusions as revealing that *real* belief is '*applied* belief', that 'belief' and 'its application' are 'internally related'. This 'realization' would suggest once again that we cannot make sense of the subject in isolation from its world, a 'realization' we have already heard in 'the internal relation of depicting' and the solipsistic 'I am my world'. But, as I have argued throughout, running into an 'internal relation' should prompt us to question the terms in which we have found ourselves thinking.

Our ultimate realization is not that all forms of representation must be applied in order to have content; rather, it is that we were operating with a distorted picture in the first place, *within* which one might come in time to a suspicion of the form, 'All representations must be applied in order to have content'. The problems of judgement and conscience understood as 'problems of application' belong to—and, if not thought through, will help perpetuate—that picture.

One would perpetuate the picture, for example, by taking the discussion above to have provided something like a transcendental deduction of the fact that most of our beliefs are applied successfully. That discussion did not provide any reason to think that a breakdown in our capacity to represent the world, our capacity to have thoughts, is inconceivable. What it showed was that such a breakdown is not a matter of a breakdown in *application*. The predicament that we fear when we seek the kind of transcendental argument envisaged is one of the thinker locked up inside himself, his thoughts having lost traction on the world outside him. That is indeed a fantasy, but not because our 'powers of application' are generally faultless. We are right to fear 'a breakdown', but this real possibility is misdescribed through the image of applying one's thoughts and, in a sense, is made more palatable by that misdescription. What we ought to fear is not some kind of confinement 'within ourselves', but, as I put it towards the end of the last section, dissolution: the leaking away of all content from the supposed vehicles of our thought, leaving those vehicles mere signs.[12]

[12] In the diary passage quoted at the beginning of Sect. 14.1, Wittgenstein echoes this sense that what—at best—corresponds to failure in the supposedly cognitive task of making sure that one's actions are in line with one's ideals is a descent into emptiness; not the containment of our ideals behind a failure of application, but the vanishing of a moral agent. That passage continues: 'Yes, is this even possible—or would one either have to become good or go mad over it? Wouldn't this tension, if it were fully grasped either open the person to everything or destroy him' (*PPO* 163).

In line with my broader treatment of the 'discovery' of 'internal relations', the philosopher's problem is not a mistake in the sense of holding a false view of something; rather, it is that he doesn't ultimately understand the explanatory demands that he feels must somehow be met. A confusion creates an illusion of a demand for explanation and a corresponding 'how it is'. Here, whatever it is in connection with which our envisaged 'problem of application' arises, *it isn't belief*, despite the fact that it is the form of the illusion to suggest that it is; the illusion raises pseudo-problems which, *ex hypothesi*, are not real problems for our understanding of belief. What allows the illusion to insinuate that they are is that the illusion draws upon our understanding of belief in constructing its mirage. Its pseudo-problems take the language of 'belief' and 'application' as its vehicle. By projecting an alien 'grammar' on to the language of 'belief', we manufacture an ersatz belief, an illusory 'problem of application' for that ersatz, and a correlate ersatz conscience to solve it.

14.5 CONSCIENCE AS A SUPPLEMENT TO A SIGN/SYMBOL CONFUSION

So how did we come by our 'problem'? I will argue that we did so in the way that the early Wittgenstein suggests we generate 'the most fundamental confusions' of which 'the whole of philosophy is full' (3.324), by conflating sign and symbol.

In seeing that it makes no sense to ascribe *synderesis* to someone without *conscientia*, we see that there can be no '*general* problem of application' that *conscientia* (or judgement) solves, no *general* issue of how our *synderesis* can go on to find application. In attempting to formulate the 'general problem', we want to imagine, say, two people who hold the same principle—have the same *synderesis*—but differ in that one 'can apply it correctly' while the other 'cannot'. But '[i]n order to recognize the symbol in the sign we must consider the significant use' (3.326); without that use in view, all we have is a mark on a piece of paper or a sound-wave in the air; thus all we are actually entitled to say about these people is that, in the face of the question 'What do you believe?', they produce the same string of marks on paper or sound-waves in the air; such entities do not embody any kind of 'semantic' demand that one might imagine competent 'capacities to apply' respect, and thus there is no 'problem of application' for these so-called principles; such entities can be 'applied' however one wants: such mere signs are 'arbitrary'. Given how the two people use these strings of signs—the place that they have, the difference that they make, in their lives—'where then would be what was common in the symbolisation?' (3.322). The supposedly 'as-yet-unapplied ethical doctrine' which might yet be applied successfully or not is also a string of marks or sound-waves, which thus raises no 'problem of application': such 'claims' are 'the dead carcass' of language.[13]

---

[13] For corresponding reasons, it would be wrong to say 'Oh, so it's all about application!' One may wonder, when someone says 'I love you', whether she means it, and reflect on how she behaves.

Thus, 'victims of a general problem of application' are illusions in our thinking; this expression is a mere combination of words which, as individual words, have happy, useful lives, but upon which our confusion has fed. In *some* contexts, we can draw our 'believing it'/'applying it' distinction. But that does not imply that this distinction can be meaningfully drawn in *any* context, or that there is a 'general problem of application' which something we might call 'conscience' overcomes.

My suggestion is that, to raise the 'problem of application', we need to equivocate over what we take the 'principles' in question to be: we must simultaneously and confusedly think of these 'principles' as signs, as 'dead' sentences, and as symbols, as signs-in-use, as meaningful. As the former, they are contingently connected to their use (in any particular language); but, as the latter, they are 'internally related' to their use; one has not identified something as a symbol if one does not know how it is used. The confused fantasy of 'application' and 'misapplication' arises when we hear the former contingency and the latter necessity but fail to see that they concern two different things: 'it' (the sign) can be used in all sorts of ways that would not be in line with 'its' (the sign-in-use) meaning. What power, the 'problem' forces us to ask, allows us to keep them in line?[14]

14.6 CON-FORMISM AND 'THE INDEPENDENT LIFE OF SENTENCES'

There is a parallel here with the anti-con-formist argument set out in Section 3.5. There we asked: for what reason do we come to worry over the match between this particular 'piece' of language and this particular 'piece' of world? The cause (we can't dignify it as a reason) is the fact that we already think and talk this particular way, that we use this concept and do not use these others, or temporarily overlook the fact that we do. So we return to that which we imagined ourselves grounding, drawing upon it in the construction of our pseudo-demand. The recipe is: first, select an aspect of the world we talk about from among the many aspects that we actually or possibly could talk about; second, forget this act

But this is not to investigate, as it were, something *other than* what she said. What one is trying to ascertain is whether *what she said* is true. The question that one wants to answer is: does she love me?

[14] Throughout the present and preceding chapter, the reader may have been harbouring the objection that Wittgenstein takes issue not with ethical principles, but with ethical talk in a much less focused way. There may be something to this objection. I have allowed myself to introduce this focus because I think it helps us see what might be at stake in Wittgenstein's less focused concern—e.g., in his concern with decency. But it may well be that a more general worry about saying what one means, about the relationship between 'the spirit' and 'the word', is closer to Wittgenstein's. Reconceiving what I offer (in these two chapters) in those more general terms would, I think, be possible, and the present section would perhaps be the best starting-point; but such a reinterpretation would still be something more easily performed after my more focused version has been considered.

of selection; third, and finally, ask yourself the unanswerable question of why our talk *ought* to match this particular aspect of the world ('It does, after all!'—well, yes, *this* bit does!). We want a reason, an explanation, when the object of that explanation is a confusion. Does the incoherence of this vision of a tracking make our application of concepts arbitrary, ungrounded? No, it shows that we don't understand the grounding that we think we must provide. Con-formity presents a pseudo-demand that we 'grasp' only by allowing ourselves to slip into confusion.

Similarly, faced with the general 'problem of application', we invoke something we call 'conscience' or 'judgement', imagining it as belonging to the family of 'powers' that includes insight, cognition, recognition, awareness, and know-ledge, and endowing its possessor with an understanding of how a belief ought to be applied. But in the mouth of 'the victim of the general problem of applic-ation', these 'beliefs' are mere 'signs', ink strokes, sound-waves in the air. The power that such a person lacks is not that of judgement conceived of as a capa-city to apply these signs correctly (or incorrectly!). For that to make sense, the signs would need a sense, and it is precisely this that they lack in the mouth of this individual. It is only when we think of these signs as used—perhaps as used in the ways that *we* use them—that a 'right' or 'wrong application' looms; lingering at the back of our mind, it is these uses that provide the imagined 'man without conscience' with standards which we can declare his 'powers of applica-tion' incapable of tracking.[15]

There is also a parallel with Section 5.2's explanation of how we generate questions about the possible forms that propositions can take by unwittingly assigning to their parts 'independent lives', a confusion I labelled there 'the inde-pendent life of names'. These 'independent lives' are actually their temporarily forgotten lives *in* propositions; we unwittingly think of them as *symbols*. We con-sider some bizarre combinations, and we ask whether they express 'an intelligible thought'—'this table penholders the book', for example (*NB* 103)—with, at the *back* of our minds, an understanding of how these signs are used in form-ing sentences; we conclude that they don't, and that therefore there must be some explanation which would contribute to an explanation of 'how propositions can be constructed'. We succumb to this confusion when dealing with familiar words, words behind which an established usage lurks.

Another way in which this illusion can arise is through deceptive, 'surface' sim-ilarities between signs that actually have quite different uses. When confronted with a noun, it may be natural to assimilate the word to something like a referring expression. This generates an image of 'how the word represents' by virtue of its character as a noun: it represents in the way that 'that kind of word' represents. So we now have a standard before our mind, by reference to which the 'application'

---

[15] The need for these standards to linger in the background is analogous to that for the 'reason' discussed in Ch. 3 n. 14.

of that word might be evaluated. The confusion at work here is that, where the division of language into 'parts of speech' is more than a merely superficial exercise, it arises out of similarities in the use of words. So for our labelling of a word as a noun to do more than merely remark on a surface similarity between signs, it must depend on an already established appreciation of how the word is used.

This confusion again arises out of a failure to keep the sign/symbol distinction in focus. We feel that the part of speech tells us something about how the word ought to be applied, when in fact its classification as a particular part of speech turns on how the word *is* applied. We allow ourselves to treat 'part of speech' as an expression that applies to signs *and* symbols. By focusing on its application to signs, to items of 'surface grammar', we open up a gap between the arbitrary sign and 'how it represents'; by focusing on its application to symbols, to items of 'depth grammar', we establish the immediate relevance of a particular 'how it represents'. By merging these two well-understood ways of thinking and talking, we arrive at the confused 'question' of whether 'it' (the sign) is being used in line with 'its' (the symbol's) meaning.[16]

Part of the power of Wittgenstein's picture analogy is to break familiar sign/symbol connections: now, when confronted with 'illogical combinations', what we see is not 'Seven is darker than your hat', but a napkin on a cup; whether that says something is an issue we quite naturally see as settled by information about how these signs happen to be being used, how they are used to say something by contributing to the formation of sentences. There is no tendency with these unfamiliar systems to allow the individual signs to 'absorb' those roles into themselves, and thereby 'make possible' matters of fact about 'how propositions can be constructed'.

I suggest that we generate the philosopher's question about the 'application of beliefs' in the same way. We unwittingly assign to sentences 'independent lives', lives which are actually the temporarily forgotten ways in which they are in fact used, thought, '*applied*'. Familiar sentences absorb into themselves the meaning that they have by virtue of being used by us to say things. Having absorbed that meaning, the pseudo-question of whether one is using them 'in line with their meaning' looms. There is a sensible question in the neighbourhood of these 'thoughts': namely, whether we have grasped the proposition that a particular propositional sign expresses in a particular language. One could use such a propositional sign incorrectly in the sense that one uses it not in line with its meaning in a particular language; but the philosophically interesting pseudo-question is constructed by confusedly treating the sentence simultaneously as a sign and as a

---

[16] A certain innocent talk of 'logical types' might emerge here too; but it would still be misleading to imagine that 'knowledge of' or 'seeing' an expression's 'logical type' might tell one how one ought to go on to use that expression; the reason it is misleading is that how the expression ought to be used is what determines its 'logical type'.

symbol. Just as magical thinking sees power over a person in possession of their name, so the 'independent life of sentences' is a fantastical entombing within them of the manner in which they are used. By failing to recognize that this is what we have done, we can come to think of 'the way in which a sentence is used'—'the way in which it is applied'—as contingently related to 'the sentence's meaning'.[17]

14.7 THE 'REVELATION' OF 'THE INEXPRESSIBLE' AS A MOVE WITHIN A CONFUSION

The 'problems of judgement' and 'conscience' that we have identified—these 'problems of application'—are problems *for* those who succumb to a fantasy of 'belief', and to related fantasies articulated in terms of 'saying', 'theory', or 'doctrine'. We encounter these 'problems' in the course of an effort to resolve the capacity to think and to live a good life into the having of certain 'beliefs'—or rather, into the fantasized 'having' of certain fantasized 'beliefs'. The 'problem' that 'reveals' the inexpressible and unteachable powers of 'judgement' and 'conscience' arises when we fail to make sense of aspirations that we have for an illusion, a sign/symbol conflation upon which we have drawn in assigning what we now see are confused senses to 'expressible' and 'teachable'. Our notion of what is expressible is that which is capturable within the, so to speak, 'enchanted' sentences that our sign/symbol confusion conjures up; the supplements that they 'need' are what we think of as—in contrast—'unteachable' and 'inexpressible'. The 'inexpressible' powers of 'judgement' and 'conscience' belong to a story told from within that misunderstanding, and, as the 'ladder' metaphor suggests, in shaking off that misunderstanding, these concepts will also lose the significance that, in the grip of that misunderstanding, we took them to have.

Crucially, then, the capacities of judgement and conscience are themselves articulated in terms of the notions upon which their 'discovery' should cast doubt. Our fantasies about 'expression' and about 'the inexpressible' are two sides of the same coin, in that encountering something that *resists* capture in such a 'reason' or 'saying' is taken to be an encounter with something that cannot be 'expressed'; our finding ourselves forced to postulate these 'inexpressible' and 'unteachable' capacities does *not* reveal the limits of the 'expressible' or the 'teachable', the limits of 'reason' or the 'sayable', but throws into relief hitherto unrecognized, confused fantasies *for*—and *of*—'expression', 'teaching', 'reasons', and 'saying': discovering the 'inexpressible' and 'unteachable' ought to make us turn around, so to speak, and examine how we have understood 'expression' and 'teaching'.

---

[17] Clearly there are other ways in which one might try to open up such a gap (one might, e.g., point to ironic remarks as illustrating ways of using utterances to 'say one thing but mean another'), but I will not address those here.

In doing so, we will also be forced to reconsider what that 'discovery' is: the 'uncovering' of judgement and conscience are 'rungs' on a 'ladder' that is to be 'thrown away'. For example, such aspirations would distinguish the good person from the bad by reference to something entombed in a sentence-like formula that the good person 'knows' and the bad person doesn't—the 'knowing' in question understood as some kind of holding within, a literal internalization.[18] If we now 'throw away' the fantasies that have hijacked our talk and thought about 'teaching', 'expression', etc., we will also 'throw away' the proposals whose formulation they informed. We are on the point of rejecting a fantasy of 'teaching' *along with* the 'claims' that it led us to make about what might be '*un*-teachable', and a myth calling itself 'expression' *along with* the 'claims' that it led us to make about what might be '*in*-expressible'.[19]

14.8 'THROWING AWAY' 'THE INEXPRESSIBLE' AND 'THE UNTEACHABLE'

From the perspective presented, the philosopher *creates* the conditions in which her 'issues' emerge; she does so not through an obsession with belief, with doctrine, or with what is said, but by succumbing to a confusion that happens to take 'belief', 'doctrine', and 'what is said' and the logic of that talk as the vehicle for its fantasy. By repressing what she may later reacknowledge as the need for 'application', she conjures up a vision of 'rationality' or 'morality' as the possession of the right set of 'beliefs' or 'doctrines'. I have used scare-quotes for these because the philosopher's claims on behalf of 'belief', 'doctrine', 'theory', etc. systematically misconstrue these 'phenomena' too. Her fantasies *for* 'theory', for example, require fantasies *of* theory. It is through such misconstruals that she splits the 'theoretical' from what she will then come to call 'application' or 'what one shows'. The philosopher's underlying problem is not, then, an obsession with doctrine at the expense of action or other modes of thought. Instead, what she is 'getting wrong' is something she is not even aware of addressing. The root confusion is a fetishizing not of doctrine, but of the assertoric sentence, conjuring up a vision of human action that draws on the language of 'doctrine' and 'practice' in articulating its nonsense.

So where does this leave us? We can now hear differently the proposals that 'ethics cannot be expressed' (6.421) or 'taught' (*VC* 117), since we have learnt not that these concepts are inapplicable to ethics, but how certain fantasies of 'expression' and 'teaching' have gripped us. So let us ask again: can ethics be taught? The philosopher's answer to this question—positive or negative—turns

---

[18] Cf. Sect. 13.4's discussion of 'inner sentences'.
[19] A. W. Moore 2003, sect. 2, emphasizes the variety of standards that may be invoked in declaring something 'expressible' or 'inexpressible'. I take Wittgenstein to be making us aware of a pseudo-standard which shapes our thinking, but which goes unnoticed.

on a distinction we no longer trust, and the wisest response would seem to be: it depends on what counts as 'teaching'. Consider, for example, an Aristotelian inculcation of good habits of judgement and action. Is the inculcation of such habits 'teaching'? Let us think about what the process in question looks like. It conspicuously involves drawing comparisons, offering analogies, and requesting imaginative exploration; it significantly involves a lot of *talk*, peppered with words like 'so' and 'if . . . then'. It may not look like 'the communication of theory' or of 'doctrine'; but do we still have enough of the philosopher's faith to refuse, on that account, to call it 'teaching' or to accommodate it as, at best, a mysterious 'conveying' of an 'inexpressible power'? It certainly does not look or sound like a thoughtless or inarticulate process.[20] My sense is that if one were to have asked the author of the *Tractatus*, 'Might one not teach ethics in this way?', his answer would be 'Yes'.

A similar rehabilitation might be provided for the 'teaching of a first language' or 'of how to use concepts or symbols (as opposed to mere signs)'. We have seen such teaching come to appear impossible, but the notion of 'teaching' upon which this impression draws is precisely the philosopher's. Once our confidence that we understand a notion is weakened, we may open up to a broader conception of what 'teaching' and 'learning' is. What the real teaching of a first language looks like is the process whereby we initiate children into adult life. We do not teach the child about relations between words and types of objects, because they have no understanding of either end of any such relationship. Instead, we show them things and involve the child with them, talking about the things as we do so, talking about how they are, and what is happening to them, acting out stories with them on which we commentate, all the time in the terms that the child is to master.

Described in this way, this kind of explanation may hardly sound like explanation at all, and the superficial lesson of 'the problem of judgement' and Section 8.3 is that this cannot be real teaching or learning. But the deeper lesson is: Why not call it teaching and learning after all? It is difficult to make descriptions such as 'the teaching of a doctrine' or 'the learning of a fact' stick to these processes as anything

---

[20] A prima facie problem for the view I offer here is the fact that Wittgenstein makes claims about the inexpressibility and unteachability of ethics not only inside the contextualizing 'frame' of 6.54's 'self-denunciation', but also *outside* that frame (cf. the various quotations from *VC*, *CV*, and *LE*). The first thing to say on this is that, like the 'cherry-picking' that is supposedly such a problem for resolute readings (cf. Sect. 4.9), this is a problem for *any* reading of these remarks, and so not a problem peculiar to my view or other resolute views. But, more constructively, I would tentatively suggest that these remarks of Wittgenstein need to be seen in relation to the audience that he is addressing. The 'second difficulty' that he invokes in introducing LE is 'that probably many of you come to this lecture of mine with slightly wrong expectations' (LE 37). At a stage in the conversation in which ethical problems immediately present themselves to that audience as demanding a theoretical response, Wittgenstein will want to show that they must confront what will strike *them* as the inexpressibility and unteachability of ethics. But the conversation will hopefully move on to the stage at which those claims can be re-evaluated in the light of a new awareness on the part of that audience of their preconceptions about what it is to 'express' and 'teach'.

more than forced, unilluminating metaphors. But to adapt a later remark, perhaps '[t]his is what "learning" and "teaching" are like here' (*PI* p. 227). The philosopher's claim to know better now sounds forced and unilluminating, turning on distinctions by which we now see her as having been bewitched. With 'real teaching' understood as some kind of passing on of 'sayings', we are forced to see the teaching of a first language as a *mysterious* 'showing': reasons why such showing might succeed or fail remain something about which we are utterly inarticulate. But that notion of 'saying' has revealed itself to be confused, and to have its roots in the illusions of con-formity. Consequently, we ought to re-examine what is 'shown'. Then, instead of forcing ourselves to see such teaching as performed with mystical gestures and inarticulate intimations, we may once again be able to see such teaching as performed with intelligence, patience, art, care, or skill; and my sense is that if one were to have asked the author of the *Tractatus*, 'Might one not represent for someone the logic of our language in this way?', his answer would be 'Yes'.

One might well be sceptical about whether the more constructive-sounding thoughts offered here about the learning of symbols can be seen as emerging from the *Tractatus* itself; but they follow naturally from the negative point which that work establishes: the con-formist confusion provides not only an image of what it is for a proposition to 'make sense'—con-formity of proposition and possible fact—but also an image of what coming to master a proposition is—a process of grasping that con-formity—and we need to dispense with both.[21]

We may also now re-evaluate the 'inexplicable human capacity to apprehend facts' that McGuinness suggests Wittgenstein believed he had revealed. Our 'capacity' to apprehend facts is indeed 'inexplicable'—it must constitute 'a sort of *a priori* knowledge'—*if* one thinks that 'all instruction', that 'learning from experience', 'takes place through the presentation of facts to the pupil' (McGuinness 2002, p. 80, quoted in Sect. 13.5). To believe this is to be destined to run into trouble which judgement, conscience, or another kind of 'inexplicable capacity' will be needed to 'resolve'. But these 'unteachables' emerge only relative to a particular notion of 'teaching'; these forms of '*a priori* knowledge' emerge only relative to a particular notion of 'learning from experience'. Wittgenstein asks us whether these notions that shape our thinking are what we think they are.[22]

Similarly, Section 13.4 might seem to have presented a Wittgensteinian case for seeing self-knowledge as another 'unteachable' species of 'vision'; but as was

---

[21] That, of course, is more easily said than done; the sources of inspiration for those confusions are greater in number and in diversity than the *Tractatus* supposed, and a proper exploration of these sources is perhaps what the later rule-following considerations provide.

[22] It is for similar reasons that I am suspicious of seeing Wittgenstein as depicting our understanding of symbols as a *practical* form of knowledge, as a form of 'know-how' or as a mode of 'seeing'. If we have not assigned a clear sense to the notions of 'the theoretical' and 'knowing-that' with which these alternatives are taken to contrast, then they, like judgement and conscience, will be confused too (though they might well usefully articulate 'transitional steps', 'rungs' of a 'ladder' to be 'climbed' and then 'thrown away').

suggested there, the target is really a particular philosophical myth that steals for itself the title 'self-knowledge': effectively, the recognition of inner sentences that the philosopher identifies with beliefs. Among the benefits of this picture is its distracting us from what it is really like to wonder whether one is lying to oneself. That process requires one to think about one's life, one's dealings with others, and one's own past and future; it may require—odd as it sounds to articulate such mundane facts—that we *talk to others*, willingly tell them things we have not told them before, and risk humiliation and alteration of the way we live in ways we cannot predict, control, or undo; it may require us to revise what we think we are and have been, what we think our friends and family are and have been, what we have done and what we can do. Faced with this process, it is no wonder that the philosopher's 'pursuit of self-knowledge', a rooting around for quasi-sentences in the contents of an inner container called 'the mind', appeals. (We might prefer to believe in this task even if, paradoxically, it turns out that we cannot make sense of how it can be performed; the philosopher will still have managed to substitute a settled, universal impossibility for indefinitely determinable, avoidable, personal failures.[23])

14.9 ENCHANTED WORDS AND 'LIVING WORDS'

So is ethics, then, inexpressible? I will re-examine this proposal by reflecting on a discussion to be found in Engelmann's memoir published in *LPE*. When evidence is sought that Wittgenstein 'really did believe in the inexpressible', commentators often turn to the letters exchanged, and conversations had, between Wittgenstein and Engelmann. But I want to suggest that pervading the final chapter of his memoir, a chapter entitled 'Wordless Faith', is the kind of dialectical tension that I have suggested characterizes Wittgenstein's reflections on the ethical as 'inexpressible', an attraction to, and repulsion from, that formulation.

Engelmann claims that '[w]hat Wittgenstein's life and work shows is the possibility of a new *spiritual attitude*', which if 'adopted by other individuals of the right stature will be the source from which new forms of society will spring, forms that need no verbal communication, because they will be lived and thus made manifest'. He goes on:

In the future, ideals will not be communicated by attempts to describe them, which inevitably distort, but by the models of an appropriate conduct of life.

And such exemplary lives will be of incomparable value educationally; no doctrine conveyed in words can be a substitute for them. For even if such communication should succeed to the extent of enabling those who have already grasped its point through personal experience to apply it and realise it in their own lives, the fact remains—of which

---

[23] This observation and the comments above on self-knowledge might be compared to Stanley Cavell's comments on knowing other minds (cf., e.g., 1979, part 4).

historical instances abound—that any doctrine uttered in words is the source of its own misconstruction by worshippers, disciples, and supporters. It is they who have so far without exception robbed all doctrines laid down in words of their effect, and who always threaten to turn the blessing into a curse. (*LPE* 135–6)

This passage embodies what seems to me a poor argument for believing that we must embrace a 'wordless faith' (*LPE* 133). That 'a doctrine uttered in words' *can* be 'misconstrued' does not show that it *cannot* be passed on successfully through words; such words may not provide an infallible guarantee that those who hear them will grasp the doctrine, but it seems to me that only someone who believed in 'enchanted' words would expect that.

Engelmann seems to recognize this earlier in the same passage:

'[I]deals' themselves, insofar as they are meant seriously as something to be translated into reality, cannot be communicated in words. They are of the spirit, and can be indestructibly demonstrated only by making them real. What still needs to be said after that by way of showing, explaining, teaching can be done in relatively few words. Only in this way can 'the word' be restored to the value, the weight, that belongs to it by right. (*LPE* 133)

Engelmann insists that the 'necessary talking . . . can and should be a realization of the spirit and not a cheap substitute', not 'empty phrases', 'verbiage and clichés' (*LPE* 133). But to condemn phrases in general for the sins of 'empty phrases' would be unjust; the lesson that a recognition of such potential emptiness should teach us is that we must ensure that the 'phrases' we use are 'full', not that we should abandon 'phrases' altogether for some 'wordless faith'.

Who, one must ask, would react in the latter way? By reference to whose ambitions for 'phrases' would a recognition of the possibility of their 'misconstruction'—and of their inability to convey to us how their message ought to be 'applied and realized in our lives'—indicate that we may as well be done with 'phrases' altogether? Again, it seems to me, it is those who believe in enchanted words whose ambition suffers, a confused philosophical idolatry that believes that something akin to mere, dead words might capture the good life. If so, the conclusion we should reach, and one to which Engelmann himself is driven in his inconsistent text, is not, so to speak, the puritanical one, that we must dispense with words, but the counter-reformatory one, that we must 'restore' to 'the word' 'the value, the weight, that belongs to it by right' (*LPE* 133): we are 'estrang[ed] from the *devalued*, not the living word' (*LPE* 133).

Engelmann, it seems to me, is confused, but in an illuminating way; despite his call for a 'wordless faith', he also ends up holding out the possibility of 'a cliché-free propaganda', in which 'the word' can 'regain its power to move the world' and 'is prized again as the treasure it is, instead of being treated as a shoeshine rag' (*LPE* 134). Now to accept such a possibility does not in any way imply that, when passing on an ethical education, a 'doctrine uttered in words' 'can be a substitute for' 'the models of an appropriate conduct of life'. Rather, 'passing on ideals' is a business that involves presenting examples, comparisons, and analogies, imaginative exploration, and the telling of stories: in other words, among other things, a lot of talk. My suggestion is that Wittgenstein is trying to help us let our attention return to what this 'business' really looks like. His claim that 'ethics is inexpressible' forms part of a 'ladder' to be 'climbed' and then 'discarded', leading us out of the sway of enchanted words and their fantasies for—and of—principle to a recognition of what *living* words' and 'living principles' look like.

My sense is that Wittgenstein is acutely aware of a demand that any speaker who would express such words and such principles must meet, a demand that a certain philosophical outlook acts as if it can manage without. That outlook fantasizes that the good man might be distinguished by the opinions, theories, or principles that he holds; if that is one's outlook, what one needs to see is that these could never do this job; in this sense, one might say that the difference between the good and the bad cannot be expressed, and one might find here something like Engelmann's outlook. But I have argued that Wittgenstein's is a step on from there: a proper recognition of spirit, conscience, decency, good will, etc. reveals a demand on ethical talk, not its futility.

14.10 RECOGNITION OF CONSCIENCE IS A METAPHILOSOPHICAL INSIGHT

So where does this leave our earlier proposals about conscience, decency, and honesty with oneself? In one sense, they still stand, but they have been inflected or modulated, one might say—and this is what allows this reading to claim to be 'resolute'—from philosophical claims into metaphilosophical claims. To understand this modulation will be to understand my proposal in the introduction to Chapter 13 that when Wittgenstein talks of delimiting the ethical 'from within', he means from within *philosophy*: we confront once again the ordinary difficulties of the ethical life by coming to see philosophy's fantasies of that life as fantasies.

Those fantasies obscure the dependence of that life on good will, on the decency and diligence of people. But this 'modesty' or 'realism' needs to be applied to all of the concepts by which we might become enchanted. Wittgenstein does not specifically have it in for 'principle', 'truth', or the 'sayable' as concepts used to characterize or articulate our ethical lives, and we need to give *proper* place to the role of conscience in our ethical reflections too; we need to do so soberly, without construing conscience as an inarticulate thunderbolt that delivers to us 'the right answer' in a blinding flash impenetrable to any kind of reflection, a construal that is the flip side of the philosopher's fantasy of enchanted words. Again one might ask: who would have thought otherwise? The answer, it seems to me, is precisely the philosopher.

There remains a sense in which a recognition of the philosopher's fantasy of, and for, principle *does* point us to judgement, to conscience, or perhaps one ought to say something like 'what we call in our ordinary, non-philosophical talk "judgement" and "conscience"', to distinguish those notions from—and thus help us evade—philosophical fantasies that bear those very same names. When we recognize the need to think about what it is to understand and adopt a principle, 'judgement' and 'conscience' are indeed names for what we need to recognize; but our founding fantasy is not yet done with us if we accommodate these further capacities by declaring them opaque, non-rational gifts, *sui generis*, inarticulate species of vision, of peculiar and inexpressible insight. Embracing this exoticism is *another* way of avoiding the real, messy business of discerning what responsible and rational action is.[24] In that business we confront a 'mundane ineffable' which keeps us awake at night, divides friends and families, and is the site of the making or breaking of individual lives. The extramundane, intoxicating ineffable, before which the philosopher sinks to his knees in an accepting helplessness, is a fantastical, comforting caricature of what real 'crises of conscience' involve.[25]

Wittgenstein does not deny us the right to use any particular concept: what he wants to free us from is a kind of misunderstanding of those concepts, our being dazzled by,[26] or our fetishizing, particular uses of those concepts. 'Throwing away' the 'ladder' liberates the full range of concepts that we actually use in our ordinary thinking about questions of rationality and responsibility—concepts like 'principle', 'judgement', 'conscience', 'justification', 'integrity', 'deliberation', 'decency', and 'soul searching'.[27] Whether one ought to call this an 'insight' is unclear, since, in a sense, it 'leaves everything as it is', as the later Wittgenstein puts it (*PI* § 124). But it might be considered such for one descending from the philosopher's heights. Once embraced, however, it takes on the air of a truism: crucially, *who would ever have thought differently?* We are left with homespun 'demands' such as 'Go ahead and seek principles that help articulate what we think is right and wrong, but do so soberly, without believing that they might

---

[24] I take myself here to be making a parallel point to Conant's when he proposes that 'the dream of a scientific philosophy and the refuge of mysticism are two different responses to one and the same impulse' (1989, p. 277 n. 23), a proposal that he makes in elaborating another—I think ultimately Cavellian—claim that I would also endorse: 'Nothing is more human according to the vision of ourselves that [the *Tractatus* urges] upon us than the inclination to evade the weary and messy details of the task of attempting to make progress in the problems of life by substituting for them the problems of philosophy. Philosophy can instil a fantasy of progress in which the tasks of life appear only to require the application of a purely intellectual form of effort.'

[25] Sect. 15.4 explores these issues further.

[26] This turn of phrase was suggested to me by T. P. Uschanov.

[27] If my claim here is true, then the early Wittgenstein, like the later Wittgenstein, rejects, as Stone puts it, 'the idea that any words (including "sign", "representation", "intention", "meaning", etc.) are, in themselves, lost to metaphysics, that any words, just as such, "belong" to metaphysics' (2000, p. 209). The words I would add to Stone's parenthetical list would include 'ethical truths' and 'representations of logic'.

one day spare us the trouble of thinking'. But who ever *did* think that one might
entomb responsibility in a sentence, in a string of ink marks on paper? The only
people who ever did were philosophers, *and even they had to be confused to think
it.* It is they who conjure up issues by reflecting on 'words' in a way that confusedly and unwittingly slips back and forth between reflections on signs and on
symbols. It is they who enchant and are enchanted by words, by words—*mere
words*—with a seeming life of their own.

14.11 FURTHER IMPLICATIONS, AND A NARROW CONCEPTION OF ETHICS

I have suggested that the early Wittgenstein sees in philosophy a fantasy of rationality and responsibility understood as something that can be captured in a set
of sayings; but this is also a fantasy of saying, rather than a fixation on saying. Recognizing the capacities that we express when we adopt reasons—when
we mean what we say—shows that reasons understood in isolation from those
capacities do not hold the key to an appreciation of the rational, even to a proper understanding of reasons. These fantasies *for* reason are fantasies *of* reason,
fantasies *for* saying that are fantasies *of* saying. In line with the remarks discussed
in Section 14.1, the reading I have offered suggests, then, that Wittgenstein is not
opposed to ethical 'saying' or 'theorizing' as such; this leaves open the possibility
of serious ethical talk and argument '*within* the limits of one's decency', among
those who *are* 'good enough' to theorize.

So, for example, rather than forcing us to see ethics as a matter of inarticulable mystical insight or unreasonable will, the *Tractatus* can be seen as freeing us
to see once again what deliberation on ethical questions actually looks like. The
philosopher may not deign to call it the 'trading of ethical philosophical theories';
but do we have confidence in denying the trading of analogies, extrapolated cases,
and the exploration of different parties' perspectives the label of 'deliberation', of
'thinking', of 'expressing' and 'defending views'? What we have been reminded
of, by identifying and seeing beyond the philosopher's need for a quasi-mystical,
ineffable conscience is that ethical deliberation has to be done in the right spirit:
as Aristotle might have put it, one must deliberate and talk as the good man does.
Without a certain underlying decency, one's reasoning will be empty or ill-willed,
and fathoming whether it is or not is, of course, another matter for ethical deliberation, soul searching, and careful listening to one's conscience—concepts all of
which we may need in order to express what moral agents do. But the fact that, in
this sense, 'reasons come to an end' does not imply that 'reasoning' has no place
in our effort to do the right thing either.[28]

---

[28] I came across Kremer's 2001 paper regrettably late in the composition of these chapters on
ethics, and there are some obvious parallels. For example, my emphasis on the notion of 'conscience'

This rehabilitation of the terms that the philosopher fetishizes may also leave room for 'ethical truths' of a de-fantasized or de-fetishized form ('To have an ideal is alright'), ones which will not spare us what Kant calls 'the irksome work' of thinking for ourselves, a job for which we require conscience or good will; distinguishing whether one is, in following such a truth, merely paying lip-service, or whether someone is 'a terrorist' rather than 'a soldier', 'a person of principle' rather than 'a fanatic', etc., may sometimes be accomplished by citing another ethical truth or principle; but we must not seek, to use a phrase of McGuinness's, 'a happy formulation as a substitute for thought' (2002, p. 7); one might always be forced back into a 'judgement call', a test that those of 'bad conscience' fail.

Similarly, once we have recognized the confused picture calling itself 'the teaching of ethical beliefs', we may wish to reassert that the teaching described in Section 14.8 is 'the teaching of ethical beliefs'. One might say that the process

corresponds in some important respects to his notion of 'faith'. There are, however, also illuminating differences some of which I will mention here. (1) According to Kremer, Wittgenstein 'show[s] us how to abandon the search for self-justification, and so the search for ethical principles by which to rule our lives' (2001, p. 58). From my perspective, such a reaction is a 'rung' on the 'ladder' to be 'thrown away', a reaction one experiences during the course of the *Tractatus*'s 'therapy', not at its end. We may well feel inclined to abandon those searches when we recognize how, operating under an appealing philosophical confusion about principle, those principles cannot do for us what we think they can; but the ultimate realization is that this confusion is playing a role in our thinking. Our despair over principles is 'transitional', in that this despair ought to lead us to re-examine these 'principles' which now disappoint us. This view also has the appeal of being more plausible: I am not at all convinced that we really can make sense of abandoning the demand that people sometimes provide reasons why they act as they do. (A fair adjudication of this dispute would have to take into account other remarks that Kremer makes on p. 58; but I am afraid that I don't know quite what to make of these.) (2) Kremer draws on a certain regress argument to demonstrate that our 'felt need to justify ourselves, our thoughts, deeds and words' (p. 51) will inevitably be frustrated on the grounds that what we seek here as a reason is something like a proposition, but such a thing 'is just the sort of thing that can itself be brought into question' (p. 52). Sullivan has attacked this argument, claiming that the latter premiss only seems true if one embraces a particular substantial philosophical commitment about the nature of propositions; such an undertaking is one that Sullivan takes Kremer to be unwilling to accept—Kremer seems to see that premiss as an uncontentious truth about 'propositions in the ordinary sense'—and unable to accept—insisting, as Kremer does, that Wittgenstein (at least *wittingly*) provides 'no theory of meaning, sense and nonsense' (pp. 52, 42, quoted in Sullivan 2002, p. 68). I think that the regress argument I have offered does not face this criticism: the propositions it addresses are indeed odd creatures, but realizing this is the ultimate point of the argument. When confronted with 'the problem of application' that propositions seem to raise, any other proposition will seem to face the same problem, that of bridging the gap between proposition and world, as it were. One might imagine a Sullivanesque question here: 'Who says? And on what understanding of "proposition"?' On my understanding of the argument, these turn out to be good questions, because the ultimate point is to help us see how the 'propositions' in question are confused sign/symbol hybrids; only on the basis of a particular philosophical confusion do these 'entities' and that 'problem' loom. (3) I do not think that Wittgenstein wishes to promote the kinds of virtue that Kremer does; Sects. 15.4–15.7 discuss the kind of 'virtue' that I believe he sees endangered by philosophy, a virtue which is orthogonal to the kinds that Kremer emphasizes: someone who is, in Kremer's sense, thoroughly evil could still be a paragon of the 'virtue' that I will emphasize. (4) Less easy to pin down, but perhaps illuminating, is the difference between Kremer and myself over just what the questionable craving or ideal is that marks philosophers: my sense is that, for Kremer's Wittgenstein, that craving is the crazy hubris of wanting to become God; whereas for my Wittgenstein, it is something more like a craving not to exist at all.

described is '*really* what it is to teach ethical beliefs' or 'what it is to teach *real* ethical beliefs'.

So does the early Wittgenstein explore any of these 'rehabilitative' possibilities in any depth? No, he doesn't; and the 'return to the everyday' that I have sketched may seem too indebted to borrowings from the later Wittgenstein. I think, however, that the early Wittgenstein's 'throwing away of the ladder' leaves these possibilities open. What worries him most is a naïve and pernicious philosophical tendency to avoid the real difficulties of the moral life, and its most powerful expression—and thus that which he is indeed most concerned to combat—is a fantasy of 'saying' and of what 'sayings' can do for us. This focus may also be encouraged by a real narrowness in Wittgenstein's thinking about how we are likely to hide from the moral life. Engelmann reports that a favourite quotation of Wittgenstein's was the following from Wilhelm Busch's *Eduards Traum*:

[J]oking apart, my friends, only a man who has a heart can feel and say truly, indeed from the heart, that he is good for nothing. That done, things will sort themselves out. (Quoted in *LPE* 116)

In seeing the most pressing moral problems as concerning one's relationship with oneself, with what one can 'feel and say truly' with one's own words,[29] and in believing that once those problems are dealt with 'things will sort themselves out', Wittgenstein seems untroubled by the notion that profound moral problems might stem from different principles to which people are committed.[30] Something like the view that the early Wittgenstein here seems to express may seem more plausible in particular historical eras[31]—though not perhaps in our own, when the damaging influences of ideologies are vivid—and might conceivably be defended philosophically—though it has to be admitted that he himself doesn't provide any such defence; but, according to my reading, that he doesn't is what one would expect, because the view in question isn't his. Pressing for a recognition of the 'positive possibilities' of 'moral reasoning' is not near the top of his list of priorities. But we must not, to use a phrase of Engelmann's, 'plung[e] from one nonsense into an opposite kind' (*LPE* 89).

---

[29] Such a thought might express itself in the words 'running up against the limits of language [simply] is *ethics*' (cf. *VC* 68), meaning that ethical problems are always a matter of striving to be able to say (sometimes perhaps only to oneself) what one means.

[30] Something like this kind of thought might also be behind the story from Engelmann that Michael Nedo reports: 'When, in the 'twenties, Russell wanted to establish, or join, a "World Organization for Peace and Freedom" or something similar, Wittgenstein rebuked him so severely, that Russell said to him: "Well, I suppose *you* would rather establish a World Organization for War and Slavery", to which Wittgenstein passionately assented: "Yes, rather that, rather that!"' (quoted in Monk 1990, p. 211).

[31] It is a familiar theme in existentialist literature and philosophy, and is not alien to Wittgenstein's immediate influences: e.g., according to Janik and Toulmin, '[t]he distinguishing characteristic of all that is moral and artistic, for Kraus, is *integrity*' (1973, p. 81).

15

Conclusion

This last chapter of the book examines the fate of the four 'keys' to Wittgenstein's early work identified in Section 1.1: 'the point' of the book, its 'whole meaning', its author's 'fundamental thought', and his 'main contention'.

15.1 SAYING AND SHOWING

Though Wittgenstein told Russell that the say/show distinction embodied his 'main contention' (*CL* 124), I have addressed that distinction only briefly so far; nevertheless, it has represented an important sub-current in my discussion, and here I want to make clear how. The present section will sketch an abstract description of what I believe is going on when Wittgenstein talks of 'showing'; the following two sections will clarify how that abstract description can be seen to fit the different cases of 'showing' that we have examined. In doing so, those sections act as a summary of sorts of what has gone before.

There are many different 'things' that Wittgenstein says show: the holding of internal properties and relations shows itself (4.122) (from which it would follow that (O-F), (O-E), (O-S), (N-P), (N-E), and (N-S) show themselves, as do (O-N) and (F-P)); propositions show their sense (4.022), what they say (4.461); logical propositions show that they say nothing (4.461); propositions show the logical form of reality [*die logische Form der Wirklichkeit*] (4.121); logical propositions show the logic of the world [*die Logik der Welt*] (6.22); that something falls under a formal concept shows itself (4.126); that one proposition follows from another shows itself (4.1211; *NB* 44), as does what solipsism means (5.62) and the mystical (6.522).[1]

One can see, I suggest, six sides to cases of showing:

(a) *Internal relations*   These relations that are not what they seem emerge in the course of the exploration of explanatory projects, and to understand the significance of asserting that an internal relation holds, we must move through three steps (b–d). (For brevity's sake, my comments here mention only internal relations, but they are meant to apply to internal properties too, as will be apparent in the following section.)

---

[1] This is not a comprehensive list. So, e.g., operations show themselves in variables (5.24), and mathematics shows the logic of the world in equations (6.22). My reading has concentrated on those listed in the main text.

(b) *A question seemingly answered*   An internal relation is discovered where one would expect to find the explanatory project completed, as the matter of fact that explains why what we want to explain is so.

(c) *An explanatory impossibility*   The second stage is one at which we see the emergence of the internal relation as showing that the explanatory project cannot be performed, as showing that there are certain givens into which we cannot penetrate further, certain things that must simply be *seen*. There is, to this extent, always a truth to the holding of internal relations in their revelation of how certain cravings for explanation cannot be fulfilled.

(d) *The explanatory project revealed as confused*   The third stage is one at which we see the emergence of the internal relation as pointing to an incoherence in the explanatory project that we are pursuing. What sounds initially like an answer to one's question (b), then sounds like a denial that the question can be answered (c), and is finally understood when we hear it as a comment on the question itself, indicating that the question is confused (d). In the step from (c) to (d), we balance on a knife-edge, on one side an insight into the 'subject-matter' of our explanatory project, and on the other an insight into ourselves, into *our* role in the *creation* of the 'issue' at hand. We come to see the impossibility of certain explanations as illuminating a confusion in the explanations sought. We have in actual fact got ourselves into a mess and, from *within* that mess, what one needs to know emerges as an internal relation. From within that confusion, the confusion manifests itself through the emergence of an internal relation. But that this relation holds is not a self-standing conclusion or view in its own right, in that we come to recognize that this relation and the project which is its home emerge out of confusion on our part.

(e) *Posing the question presupposes its 'answer'*   Crucially, in all but an important few of the internal relations that Wittgenstein uncovers,[2] the way in which our explanation grinds to a halt is in a recognition that our posing of our question and our sense of what an answer would be like actually take for granted the 'feat' we thought we were trying to explain.

(f) *A sign/symbol confusion*   Each of the cases to be reviewed in the next section involve confusions that can be diagnosed as arising out of a sign/symbol confusion, the type of confusion of which Wittgenstein declared 'the whole of philosophy is full' (3.324).

15.2 SHOWING IN ACTION

This section will briefly summarize some of our earlier discussions with an eye to giving substance to the abstract structure identified in the previous section.

---

[2] Cf. the discussion of inferential relations and 'the logic of the world' in the next section.

(I consider (f) separately, simply to avoid repetition; I discuss 'the mystical' in Sect. 15.4.)

(N-P)

If we are trying to determine how names can be combined to form propositions, with an eye to understanding why, for example, 'My coat is darker than your hat' is a 'logical combination', whereas 'Seven is darker than your hat' is an 'illogical combination', it may sound like an answer to be told of internal relations that hold between names and propositions: how these relations are will determine which propositions can be formed and which ones cannot, which combinations of names are logically possible and which are logically impossible. That these relations must be internal, Wittgenstein demonstrates on the basis that otherwise logic would be 'accidental'.

Thinking through the picture analogy shows up a truth in the internal relation in question: one indeed cannot identify a name without identifying the propositions in which it figures. But this apparent confirmation of the relation's 'existence' also points to the impossibility of understanding 'how names can be combined to form propositions' if that is construed as anything other than the philosophically uninteresting issue of which combinations of signs, as a matter of contingent fact, have sense assigned to them in particular languages, and which do not. The entities which our question concerns are names considered as symbols, and what (N-P) shows is that these come into view, and hence our question can be asked, only once we have an understanding of how they figure in propositions. In other words, we see that our 'question' is confused when we see that posing it presupposes its 'answer'. The assertion 'Names and propositions are internally related', which at first sounds like an identification of what determines how names can be combined to form propositions, actually indicates why there is no such thing as an explanation of how names can be combined to form propositions. To see why is to see that we did not understand our question.

(O-F)

The fate of (O-F) follows a parallel path. If we are trying to determine how objects can be combined to form facts, with an eye to understanding why, for example, my coat being darker than your hat is a metaphysical possibility, while seven being darker than your hat is a metaphysical impossibility, it may sound like an answer to be told of internal relations that hold between objects and facts: how these relations are will determine which facts can be formed and which ones cannot, which combinations of objects are metaphysically possible and which are metaphysically impossible. That these relations must be internal is demonstrated in the opening pages of the *Tractatus*: if there were external relations between objects and possible facts, then which combinations of objects are metaphysically possible would be a contingent matter of fact; the relations in question must therefore be internal.

Thinking through the picture analogy shows up a truth in the internal relation in question. One may think that one can identify an object quite independently of its combinatorial possibilities, through, for example, ostension: 'The object in question is that!' Successful uptake of such ostension depends upon our placing *that* in the correct space of possibilities: is *that* darker than your hat, faster than a Ford, or stronger than brass? Put another way, which object a name picks out is indeterminate until the range of facts in which it may figure has been settled. But this apparent confirmation of the internal relation's 'existence' brings us to balance on a knife-edge: are we looking at an answer to our question, one which explains how objects can be combined to form facts, or a demonstration that we did not understand our question? The entities which our question concerns come into view only once we have an understanding of how they may figure in facts; in other words, the issue we wished to come to understand by seeing how objects are constituted must actually be resolved before we have any objects before us to contemplate. Our 'question'—how can objects be combined to form facts?—is confused, because posing it presupposes its 'answer'.

(O-N)

The internal relation of depicting sounds like the basis of an explanation of how propositions can represent reality: to take (O-N), if names and objects share combinatorial possibilities, then the range of possible placings of the entity being used to represent parallels the range of possible placings of the entity to be represented.

But having seen through (N-P) and (O-F), we are now in a position to see through (O-N) and (F-P). The isomorphism envisaged does not reveal how the two may be set in comparison with one another, because identifying the isomorphism *presupposes* that they can be set in comparison with one another. Instead, to recognize that the two are internally related is to recognize that they are themselves the *product* of a method of comparison, that we are already contemplating them within a single framework that such a method provides. Only our already being able to place a name and an object using such a framework gives sense to efforts to see whether they 'agree' or not; only relative to a method of comparison does their 'agreeing' or 'disagreeing' have a determinate sense. Our notion of understanding the possibility of the name standing in a comparable space to that of the object is then confused, because what we think makes that possible is a matter which itself presupposes that they can be placed in comparison with each other. That two entities agree cannot be the basis of the possibility of comparing the two: our envisaged answer to the question that puzzles us requires that we not be troubled by the question.

Propositions show their sense, what they say

That propositions show their sense emerged as the conclusion of a reflection at *NB* 25 on whether one might be told 'how a proposition represents'. The conclusion was that, since such explanations come in the form of other propositions, any such chain of explanations must ultimately terminate in a proposition that shows its sense. This may sound like the revelation of a matter of fact that provides an explanation (we come to master propositions by virtue of their showing their sense); but what this articulates first and foremost is our inability to make good on understanding how we come to grasp propositions on the basis of something one might be told: we come to the conclusion that at some point a proposition must simply show what we imagined we had to be told. Our vision of explanation requires the emergence of a proposition that is internally related to the state of affairs that it represents.

But this is not a self-standing conclusion; rather, it is a conclusion that one reaches in attempting to execute this explanatory project, and reaching it ought to indicate to us that something has gone wrong with the project; what our coming to this conclusion indicates is that the way we have envisaged the explanation of how a proposition represents actually requires that at some point no such explanation will be necessary; if we believe that a proposition provides the explanation we seek, then we must think that at some point a proposition simply shows its sense. We balance, then, on a knife-edge: are we looking at an answer to our question, one which explains how we do come to grasp a proposition, or a demonstration that we did not understand our question? To see it as the latter is to see it as elucidating the question by showing that we have no clear understanding of what an answer would even look like: our envisaged answer requires that we not be troubled by the question.

What solipsism means

The claim that Wittgenstein says 'provides a key to the question, to what extent solipsism is a truth' (5.62) is '*The limits of my language* mean the limits of my world' (5.6); what shows itself in that claim is that 'the world is *my* world' (5.62). I have argued that reflection on learning a first language can lead us to these conclusions by revealing that such a feat is impossible if we imagine it as a matter of learning something about how the world is: any explanation that we might be offered must already be articulated in terms we understand. Any such chain of explanations must terminate in an explanation which just 'shows its sense', in perhaps an ostensive definition which I can simply see illustrates the concept, *x*. But to do that requires that I already understand what *x*s are. This is what I have called 'the problem of concept acquisition'.

To find ourselves led to the need for this ultimate facility with the ways of the world may seem to show that I and the world must somehow be kin. Is Wittgenstein endorsing this solipsistic conclusion? I think not. The conclusion that we have come to and which we might articulate by asserting an internal relation—that of subject and world—is not a self-standing conclusion; rather, it is a conclusion that one reaches in attempting to execute an explanatory project, and reaching it ought to indicate to us that something has gone wrong with that project. What our coming to this conclusion indicates is that the way we have envisaged the explanation of how a proposition represents actually requires that at some point no such explanation will be necessary; if we believe that we learn of the world's order from the world, then we must help ourselves to the availability of the world and our capacity to understand its order. The truth in solipsism is that a realist story of subject and world coming into con-formity actually requires that we take their con-formity for granted. So the 'internal relatedness of subject and world' brings us to balance again on a knife-edge: on the one side, an explanation of how thought and world happen to con-form; on the other, a recognition that this conclusion is an embarrassment for us, a sign that something has gone wrong in our pursuing our explanatory project. On the latter construal, that realism leads to solipsism makes solipsism not a conclusion to be endorsed but an interim conclusion to be reached, recognized as a demonstration of our confusion, and then abandoned along with the project that led us to this conclusion.

(O-S) and (O-E)

As Chapter 3 showed, elucidating the very idea of the ultimate referents of our terms yields certain conclusions, among which are (O-E) and (O-S): these referents are necessarily simple, and necessarily exist, because if there were facts about their composition or about their existing, they would not be the ultimate referents of our terms. But these internal properties, in their 'truth' and in their 'falsity', also emerge from our reflection on the learning of a first language inspired by the *NB* 25 argument. Since anything we might learn about the world is mediated by the use of concepts, the question of whether those concepts pick out anything real and really ordered (do they each pick out a type?) cannot go 'all the way down'.

The explanatory project in hand, that of understanding how we come to grasp the world and its order, cannot, it seems, be completed. One might express this by saying that, ultimately, it makes no sense to question whether the terms we use pick out something real and track order in the world, since any doubt we might have has content only if the terms in which it is expressed pick out something real and track order in the world. But it would be a mistake, I have argued, to take away from that realization the seemingly self-standing conclusion that the ultimate referents of our terms must possess, as internal properties, necessary existence and simplicity. This is not a self-standing conclusion, but a conclusion that one reaches in attempting to execute an explanatory project which our having arrived at that conclusion ought to indicate to us is confused. Our coming to this conclusion indicates that the way we have envisaged our coming to grasp the world and its order actually requires that at some point no such explanation will be necessary; anything we might learn is mediated through concepts, and thus questions about the existence and order of that which concepts pick out cannot go all the way down. When we 'discover' these internal properties, we come to balance on a knife-edge: are we looking at an answer to our question, one which explains how we do come to grasp the world and its order (that is, there are objects about which questions of existence and order cannot be asked), or a demonstration that we did not understand our question? To see it as the latter is to see it as elucidating the question by showing that we have no clear understanding of what an answer would even look like: our envisaged answer (our learning (in some way) of the world and its order) requires that we not be troubled by the question.

That one proposition follows from another shows itself (4.1211)

If inferential relations were external relations, logic would be made up of an impossibly substantial body of facts. Hence, Wittgenstein concludes that inferential relations must be internal.

These internal relations may now sound as if they hold the key to our evaluation of which inferences are valid. But actually they indicate that, where inferences are valid, we cannot identify the propositions prior to identifying their inferential relations, in which case we cannot assess or explain inferential relations, because we cannot identify the relata before we have seen whether such a relation holds. Wittgenstein's conception of inference as unpacking and the analytic commitments embodied in the GFP attempt to make good on this thought that inferential relations are not real relations after all. A proper grasp of the propositions in question would reveal that their truth-grounds overlap, and thus, in a sense, we are not dealing with separate propositions at all between which a relation might hold. When p implies q, the impression that there is a step to be justified arises out of an unclarity about the character of the two propositions. Thus the explanatory project that we were engaged in (coming to understand the basis of valid inferences) arises out of a misunderstanding; clarity about propositions between which inferential 'steps' are valid would reveal that there is no step to be taken, and hence no inferential relations to be grounded or explained. The perspective from which we think that there is something to say about inferential relations is one from which one does not see clearly what is so 'related'.

A neat story would find an analogue here too for the treatment of (e) that the cases discussed above all illustrate. But unfortunately, the continuity breaks down here. There is an undeniable difference between the way in which Wittgenstein handles the earlier internal relations and the way in which he handles inferential relations and those other internal relations that he deals with on the basis of his treatment of inferential relations. The case for thinking that these relations are not real relations depends not on anything quite like a demonstration that, in posing our question, we presuppose its answer. Rather, it depends on a more constructive piece of philosophy, embodied in a fateful set of analytic commitments which it is anything but obvious can be met. An a priori set of non-trivial claims about the construction of propositions 'account for' the relations in question; and our ignorance of the truth of those claims (which, with hindsight, Wittgenstein recognized as claims and as false) is, one might say, a better reason for our mistakenly coming to believe in these internal relations than are the reasons why we come to believe in the others, the latter 'reasons' being simply confusions.

From some perspectives, these discontinuities seem minor. One could argue, for example, that it is not the ordinary person in the street who is ignorant of the truth of these claims; rather, it is only philosophers who, in the grip of their sign/symbol confusions, come to believe in inferential relations as relations; only they need to learn of the GFP, because only they see the mirage that the GFP would dispel. But I think it would be misleading and confusing to deny the discontinuities flagged above. I hope to have shown why Wittgenstein saw these different kinds of case as alike; but I do not think that they ultimately are alike.

Logical propositions show the logic of the world (6.22)

That certain combinations of propositions cannot be combined to yield a description of how things might be in any possible world might be said to show that the world has a logic; that it provides a standard by which our descriptions can be evaluated, not only as true or false, but also as articulating logical possibilities rather than logical impossibilities. To mirror the argument offered above, we know that if these relations of incompatibility were external relations, logic would be made up of an impossibly substantial body of facts. Hence, we know that, for Wittgenstein, 'the logic of the world' must be a body of internal relations.

So will an identification of these relations reveal the metaphysical form of the world, revealing which states of affairs cannot coexist? Not according to the reading I have given. Instead, they indicate that, where states of affairs are 'logically incompatible', it is because they are constructed out of overlapping sets of atomic facts. Again, an explanatory project grinds to a halt and, if this story were right, would be shown to be misconceived: we cannot fathom such incompatibility relations, because we are not dealing with separate states of affairs at all between which relations might hold. The explanatory project of coming to understand why a logical incompatibility relation holds between two states of affairs is confused, because clarity about what those states of affairs are would show us that there is no such relation. Logical propositions show which propositions follow from one another and show the logic of the world, in that they show how the states of affairs that propositions pick out may overlap. The perspective from which we think that these incompatibility relations have substance is one from which we do not see clearly what is so 'related'. The world's 'logic' reflects not necessary, metaphysical features that it might be thought to possess but our use of conventionally adopted complex propositions with overlapping 'truth-grounds'.

The explanation we seek for what gives these relations of incompatibility sub-stance is misconceived, because they do not have substance.

Regarding (e), as with inferential relations, there is, I feel, a discontinuity between the present case and the majority of the internal properties and relations that Wittgenstein discusses. He dispels the logic of the world at least partly by resorting, perhaps unwittingly, to a piece of constructive philosophical work that brings with it non-trivial commitments about how propositions can be analysed.

15.3 SIGNS, SYMBOLS, SAYING, AND SHOWING

As I argued in Section 3.5, a sign/symbol confusion can be seen behind the con-formist story. No one thinks that one might discover rules for the use of signs, since 'the sign is arbitrary' (3.22). But also, no one thinks that one might dis-cover rules for the use of symbols, since when considered as symbols, we take for granted how the words in question ought to be used; that cannot be seen as a matter to be determined. Rather, the illusion of con-formity, of a determination of how words must be used to describe the world, arises when we treat words simultaneously as signs and as symbols.

This confusion can be seen as operating on large and small scales in genera-ting the confusions which, when elucidated, yield internal properties and internal relations. On a small scale, deceptive, 'surface' similarities between signs that actually have quite different uses can combine to lend apparent substance to con-formism. For example, we may find ourselves treating nouns like 'truth-function', 'concept', and 'meaning' as if they were referring expressions. Doing so, we generate an image of 'how the word ought to work' which is 'externally related' to how it is actually used: it represents in 'the way that that kind of word' represents, and a standard by which its actual use might be evaluated seems to loom. What we overlook, of course, is, that if the division of language into 'parts of speech' is to tell us anything about these 'parts' as symbols rather than as mere signs, that division must arise out of similarities in the use of words: the external relation we thought we had identified thus vanishes.

This confusion manifests itself in connection with many of the internal rela-tions discussed in this book, and clarity about sign and symbol is a way to see through the confusion surrounding them. So with (N-P), we would eliminate the temptation to ask how names *ought* to be combined to form propositions by constructing notations in which, for example, expressions that correspond to 'being darker than' and 'being lighter than' do not even look like expressions that are applied to entities other than those to which we also ascribe expressions that correspond to 'red', 'blue', etc. That 'red', 'blue', 'table', 'chair', 'top-C', and 'middle-C' are all nouns may prompt us to think of that to which they refer as all being 'kinds of object'; similarly, that 'being darker than', 'being more expen-sive than', and 'being higher than' are all relational expressions may prompt us to think of that which they pick out as all being 'kinds of relation'. Such moves of thought are harmless until we start wondering why it is that a shade of red can be darker than another, but not darker than top-C. What is it, we wonder, about these different objects that makes that eventuality impossible, and a confused need for an ontology of colours, sounds, and furniture looms.[3]

Clarity over sign and symbol is also what lets us see through the internal relations that are inferential relations and the logical scaffold of the world. Analysis will reveal that inferentially linked propositions are not the separate entities that they appear to be; neither are logically incompatible states of affairs, despite their representation using propositional signs that are indeed externally linked. Similarly, the 'logical objects' to which truth-functions 'refer' are dispelled when we consider other notations that express what we express through '&', 'v', '>', etc.; truth-tables, for example, show that the logical constants 'can be understood simply by a study of their occurrence in symbolism' (*L I* 116). We can do away with an ontology of 'logical objects', acquaintance with which we may previously have been tempted to see as what 'understanding the logical constants' amounts to.

On a larger scale, the manner in which the picture analogy itself works might be compared with the *modus operandi* of this 'notational' solution: both undermine philosophical illusions by 'disenchanting' words. By asking us to think about models that are 'made up of spatial objects (such as tables, chairs, books) instead of written signs' (3.1431), Wittgenstein breaks up the familiar sign/symbol associations upon which our philosophical confusions feed: the 'expressions' used no longer carry their meanings outside the uses in which they represent in the particular systems of representation in which they figure, and the temptation to see confusing illusions of meaning in non-representing combinations—in 'illogical combinations'—is dissipated. Then it becomes obvious to us that the question with which 'logical impossibilities' such as 'Seven is darker than your hat'—next to which sentences with sense (like 'My coat is darker than your hat') look like 'logical possibilities' that 'respect' the internal relations between objects and possible facts—ought to be met is not, 'Might that be true?' (followed by 'How do you know?'), but 'What does that represent?'

Again on a large scale, I have argued that a certain fantasy that depicts itself as our ordinary understanding of reasons, principles, and doctrine, but which is more accurately the notion of assertoric sentences that somehow contain their own meaning, lies behind our sense of the limitations on what we may learn or

---

[3] The roles played by sign/symbol confusion in the confusion surrounding (O-F) parallel those involved in (N-P). For example, as ostended, one can combine an object in an indeterminate number of different ways with other objects to form facts, in that what the object is remains indeterminate. What gives the impression that there is a matter of fact to be established is our having at the back of our minds a particular determinate object with a particular space of possibilities; then one finds ways in which *that* 'can be' combined to form facts; but this identifies—delimits—the object rather than limiting it. To conjure up the issue of how 'the object' can be combined with others, our thinking about 'the object' must alternate between thought about a particular determinate object and a sheer *that*.

be taught about ethics and symbols more generally. This lies behind the truth in solipsism, the 'need' for propositions to show their sense, and, as I will argue next, at least part of what Wittgenstein means by 'the mystical'. For example, the crucial fantasy that underpins the model of ethical seriousness that Chapters 13 and 14 question is a vision of enchanted words, the fantasy that the difference between good and evil people might be understood on the basis of the presence 'within them' of different 'principles' or 'doctrines', a fantasy that itself requires fantasies of principle and doctrine.

15.4 THE MYSTICAL, A MUNDANE INEFFABLE, AND A HIGHER-ORDER CONSCIENCE

Let us look now at 'the mystical', which the *Tractatus* states 'shows itself' (6.522). Quite what Wittgenstein understands by 'the mystical' is unclear. My sense is that there is nothing of the mystic in Wittgenstein, if that is taken to mean a belief in ethical or spiritual insights revealed in a wordless, mysterious, perhaps even supernatural way. In this, Engelmann concurs:

Above all, [Wittgenstein] was never a mystic in the sense of occupying his mind with mystic-gnostic fantasies. Nothing was further from his mind than the attempt to paint a picture of a world beyond . . . about which we cannot speak. (*LPE* 79)

But what are we then to make of 'the mystical' that 'shows itself' if not a 'bluish haze surrounding things' (a dismissal by Wittgenstein that Engelmann reports (*LPE* 98))? My suggestion is that Wittgenstein's focus is a mismatch between the difficulties of ordinary life and the resources and mind-set of philosophy. (We must 'cut out the transcendental twaddle [*Geschwätz*] when the whole thing is as plain as a sock on the jaw' (*LPE* 11).) The mundane ethical demands of ordinary life, of being straight with other people and with oneself, are obscured by the demand that we make ourselves receptive to mystical insight; such a notion encourages us to look in the wrong place for what is difficult about 'doing the right thing'. But a step towards recognizing that ordinary life that we already know, recognizing it having been in the grip of philosophical fantasy, is a confrontation with what that fantasy can understand only as 'the mystical'.

According to the book's numbering system, 6.522 is a comment on 6.52, which discusses the 'disappearance' of 'the problems of life'. 'The mystical' is also addressed in 6.44:

Not *how* the world is, is the mystical, but *that* it is.

In LE, Wittgenstein picks out '*wonder at the existence of the world*' as one of his 'ethical experiences *par excellence*' (LE 41), and the *Tractatus*'s numbering system presents *TLP* 6.44 as a comment on 6.4:

All propositions are of equal value.

Thus, considered together with Section 13.4's proposed gloss on 6.52, it would appear that understanding Wittgenstein's remarks on the ethical may help us understand his remarks on the mystical. The story I have told about Wittgenstein's treatment of the ethical certainly can be seen as following a similar path to that which we have followed in connection with Sections 15.1–15.3s' other cases of 'showing'.

Since the significance of a principle can be questioned, justifying an act must terminate in a principle that we see as having weight, as consequential. But how does this come about? At some point, it seems, sheer conscience must make us act on a principle for which we seek no further justification. Thus an inexpressible conscience here seems to provide an answer to the problem we were trying to solve. Or does it? I have suggested that it too can be seen as bringing us to balance on a knife-edge: is the need for conscience an explanation of how we can live in an ethically serious way, or a comment on how we have conceived of ethical seriousness, as the pursuit of principles to cite in support of our actions? If we conceive of ethical seriousness in this way, we see that it can work only if we also help ourselves to an inarticulable 'seeing', conscience. Does this then show how our acts are ethically serious? Or does it show that in our pursuit of principle, we have no clear understanding of what ethical seriousness requires, since that pursuit requires at some point that we not be troubled by the question that it pushes forward as crucial. I have argued that the 'discovery' of conscience as a kind of impenetrable vision is not a self-standing conclusion, a discovery of how things are; instead, it represents an interim conclusion that forces us to look back at the project that has led us here, to recognize the way in which we have conceived of ethical principle, and ultimately recognize the roots of that project and that conception in sign/symbol conflation. Having done this, we also come to reflect on what loomed as the necessary supplement of principle understood in that way, the inexpressible knowledge of conscience.

The root confusion that we must unearth is a moral and spiritual immaturity or pathology, under the guise of a project of finding the 'real justification' for our acts, which presents as *the* crucial ethical question, 'What doctrine will you cite should the rectitude of your acts be questioned?' As an unconditional, uncritical demand, this is the demand of the *mere* bureaucrat who wants to know which set of protocols governed a decision, which set of recognized defences were envisaged as applying when the act was performed. The response is: 'Tell them it falls under rule *x*', with the insinuated conclusion being 'So I *had to* do that'. This philosophical outlook refuses to hear 'Tell them *I* made the decision' as a serious response on the part of someone trying to 'do the right thing'. But in doing so, that outlook threatens us with an endless deferral of responsibility, responsibility lost in 'mechanisms' of 'accountability', 'taken care of' by 'a machine for becoming decent'. This represents a fantasy of what serious ethical thinking is, which citing the need for conscience begins to expose.

The image of conscience that first breaks open the philosophical fantasy of the 'sayings' that capture the living of a well-lived life is one which presents conscience as an unteachable, inexpressible, *sui generis* vision. But Chapter 14 suggested that this exotic image of conscience is another expression of the philosophical fantasy that fetishes saying. While still in the grip of that fantasy, the mismatch between it and the difficulty of leading and teaching the ordinary moral life can only be interpreted as revealing 'the inexpressible': the ordinary need for judgement in ethical matters—the need to demonstrate a capacity that cannot be captured in, and taught through the passing on of, yet more principles—appears to be the requirement that, if we are not to take an arbitrary leap, we experience some kind of mystical, inexpressible insight into 'what to do': 'What else can it be?' asks the philosopher in the grip of his fantasy of 'expression'.[4] In this way, from this philosophical perspective, the capacity to live an ordinary ethical life seems a mystical feat.[5]

But this, I would suggest, is another way of failing to face the challenge of doing the right thing. Having found that the challenge cannot be dealt with within the initially favoured fantasy of 'saying', and inspired now by this exotic image of conscience, we throw up our hands in despair and declare that what the challenge represents is simply a matter of conscience: one either sees or one doesn't. 'Conscience' is indeed a name for what a person must possess and exercise if he is to think seriously about doing the right thing. But the exotic gift of an inexpressible conscience—an impenetrable seeing—is another way of covering over the real difficulties of conscience, the real ways in which this 'faculty' is exercised: reflecting on one's past, trying to think how situations look from other people's perspectives, talking to others about what they think and about how they feel, etc. And is such insight unteachable? Is there nothing one can do to help someone come to be able to exercise this kind of judgement carefully and decisively? It certainly will not resolve itself into a set of 'sayings' that would render a well-exercised conscience redundant, because the person without conscience would misapply these. Indeed, there may well be no guaranteed way of imparting this capacity. But to conclude that, therefore, it cannot be imparted may be another expression of the philosophical fantasy of 'saying'—who ever *did* believe such 'teachings' exist?—and perhaps another case of a hysterical philosophical preference for impossibilities in the face of the difficult and the questionable.[6]

---

[4] I make no comment here on which philosophers have indeed been in the grip of this fantasy, except to say that there is a case for thinking that Aristotle wasn't.

[5] Wittgenstein expresses something like this anxiety when he ends *PO* 163's reflections on the problem of not 'playacting' one's 'ideals' by asking (surely wistfully): 'Is it a way out here to cast oneself into the arms of grace?' Conscience may be interpreted as offering a similar 'way out' in the face of the 'inability' of ideals to command us, as it were, all by themselves: if 'you must now follow your conscience in what it tells you', 'I can be reproached for my unbelief only insofar as . . . my conscience commands the belief' (*PO* 157–9). But the sense that this too is a kind of ethical evasion can be heard in Wittgenstein's early notebooks: 'Can one say "Act according to your conscience whatever it may be"?' (*NB* 75).

[6] Cf. Sect. 14.8.

We now have some sense of why the very point of the *Tractatus* might be 'ethical'. Wittgenstein demanded that we 'put an end to all the claptrap about ethics—whether intuitive knowledge exists, whether values exist, whether the good is definable' (*VC* 68–9). What such 'claptrap' does is not merely confuse us; it also distracts us from—indeed, suggests the unreality of—the real challenge of the ethical life. Fantasies of both saying and the inexpressible can then provide a vehicle for the will to refuse responsibility, fantasies of moral seriousness that blind us to, render us inarticulate about, and perhaps ill-prepared for, the actual challenge of moral seriousness. Philosophy here represents a form of moral danger: the filling of one's life with what sound like justifications but aren't, and the refusal to give justifications when they can and ought to be given. There may be situations in which problems connected with conscience render 'if you don't see my point, there's no point in talking further' the only sensible thing to say; but such a remark could also be a way of avoiding a legitimate ethical demand that we explain ourselves; deciding which situation is which is a task for moral deliberation, and a difficult task: identifying not when one's claims have become false, but when one's claims have become empty; identifying not when one's acts are unjustified, but when a request for justification is itself legitimate. The challenge we face is identifying when the time for talking is over, and when the time to explain oneself has begun: identifying when to talk is to bluff, and when refusing to talk is to bluff.[7]

This suggests a reading for the second key to the *Tractatus*, to Wittgenstein's strange concluding injunction: 'Whereof one cannot speak, thereof one must be silent'. This is, as I think is often overlooked, a very odd remark: rephrased in slightly more contemporary, idiomatic English, it tells us that we mustn't talk about what we cannot talk about. What is odd about this is that, just as 'must' normally implies 'can', so normally does 'must not'; but not here. This 'undisobeyable' injunction would make a sense of sorts, however, if it were the case that we sometimes fail to recognize when our talk is empty babbling.[8] What the preface of the *Tractatus* labels as a summing up of the book's 'whole meaning' now represents a call for vigilance, for talk where talk makes sense and silence where it doesn't. The 'throwing away' of the 'ladder' described in Chapter 14 calls into question a literal identification of 'saying' with talk and 'showing' with silent action; but it leaves in place the demand that we allow to moral seriousness its diverse modes of expression. This demand is one recognized 'from within' philosophy's confusions, because to fail to meet it is to succumb to fantasies of moral seriousness, allowing our minds to be filled with fetishized formulae and empty slogans in an aping of just such seriousness, in both the demand that the

---

[7] Cf. Ch. 14 n. 28's discussion of Kremer's notion of 'abandon[ing] the search for self-justification, and so the search for ethical principles by which to rule our lives' (2001, p. 58).

[8] Sect. 8.6 points to how 'I think' does not always imply 'I can think'; but the broader point is that if we are guided only by surface grammar, we have no guarantee that the inferences we draw will make sense.

role of conscience be eliminated through the perfection of our principles and in the insistence that debate over real issues of principle belongs in the domain of an inarticulate conscience. What is demanded of us is, as it were, a higher-order conscience, through the exercise of which we resist fantasies of principle and of conscience, resist the temptation to flee in any direction from the mundane conditions of the effort to do the right thing. In a sense, we encounter here an ineffable, but not the exotic ineffable before which the philosopher sinks into an ultimately calming despair. Instead it is a mundane ineffable before which we must 'modestly' carry on; not so much a discovery, as the recollection that words do not possess magical powers, that they will not live our lives for us. This ineffable is, one might say, common sense for all but the philosopher; this form of conscience is 'delimited from within', in that it is delimited specifically by reference to the philosopher's confusion. The only people who need to be *told* about this form of conscience are the philosophers in us anyway; only their thinking expresses a confused commitment to its elimination.

15.5 THE ANIMISM OF LOGICAL TRUTH

I am afraid that we're not rid of God because we still believe in grammar.

(Nietzsche 1997 [1888], p. 21)

But how, then, might 'logical truth' be seen as playing a part in some such ethico-philosophical failure? Why might it matter from an ethical point of view that, as the third key demands, 'the *logic* of the facts cannot be represented'? Here is a suggestion: logical truth represents an animistic fantasy that sustains a dream of anonymity, of freedom from responsibility. In acting, we may choose which of our beliefs to act on. But is the range of beliefs itself a given? If so, by whom or by what? When we imagine a pupil reading a concept off a sample that we give in an ostensive definition, we imagine that sample as dictating how it ought to be described. This is a vision of the world having a language of its own, being shot through with its own 'natural' meanings. Similarly, the metaphysician of simples misconstrues the ways we speak so as to conjure up reasons why we speak as we do. Thereby, he fills our mouths and our heads with empty reasons; he redescribes our having nothing to say as if it was a perception of simplicity, and a delimitation of what we do say as if it reflected a limit on what one *can* say.

The *Tractatus* exposes as confused the notion that there are facts of the matter about which of our propositions make sense. Understood fully, this is the revelation not of an impossibility but of an illusion, an illusion of a dimension in which we thought our talk could be evaluated and found good. But these standards of evaluation that we confusedly believe we glimpse in this dimension are no more than a misconstrual of how we do as a matter of fact talk. Such a fantasy serves, then, to distract us from the real reasons why we talk as we do, from other senses in which talking as we do 'makes sense': such reasons are the myriad reasons why we choose to attend to what we choose to attend. The notion that we, and the way we live, might play a part in our using the particular descriptions that we use is, in these ways, obscured. Any responsibility that we might have for the range of beliefs from which we choose is thus resisted: we have simply described what is there before our eyes. But, as Chapter 7 emphasized, every object that comes before our eyes—every 'that'—is, in a sense, an indefinite number of different objects; this is no challenge to the truth of our descriptions of objects; but it does challenge the notion that objects themselves dictate which of their aspects are worth describing, which ought to be considered before acting.[9] That animistic fantasy allows us to ignore the role that our living certain lives plays in the descriptions we happen to use and act on; we can embrace a fantasy of being the anonymous observer who simply describes the world as the world dictates it should be described, and then acts on the basis of those descriptions.

This confusion 'finds' reasons where there are none. It redescribes what we actually do as if it were what we ought to do. In doing so, it saturates our lives with illusions of reasons—what we self-deceivingly take to be reasons—and thus distances us from the real reasons—if we have any—why we talk and live as we do. To be dissociated in this way from those real reasons is to fail to be honest with oneself, to take responsibility for what one says and does, and to say what one means.

What the philosopher in the grip of this animistic fantasy is seeking is 'natural meaning', '*the* meaning' of the objects that he encounters in the world which will tell him which aspects of those objects to take seriously. What that philosopher needs to recognize first of all is that there are no such meanings; the person who, in this way, seeks value *in* the world needs to be told that 'there is no value in it' (6.41). We find there, of course, all sorts of reasons for acting: doing what is required of me by justice, by benevolence, by my vocation, what is required of me

---

[9] A parallel can be drawn with a certain understanding of 'ethical facts', if we bear in mind Kant's criticism of the idea of an ethical expert. When we seek ethical and logical facts, we ask of 'the world' questions about how we ought to respond to that world. When we seek logical facts, we imagine the world instructing us in how to describe the world; what we must do in order to endow this 'project' with a semblance of sense is help ourselves to categories using which we will articulate what the world tells us; but this is to prejudge the precise issue that the 'project' was to decide: which categories to use in describing the world. When we seek ethical facts, we imagine the world instructing us on which aspect of the world to take most seriously, to make the basis of our acting; what we must do in order to endow this 'project' with a semblance of sense is select categories using which we will articulate what the world has to tell us; but this is again to prejudge the issue that the 'project' was to decide: we have settled on the aspect of the world that those categories articulate as most deserving of our attention. In both cases, the choice we are to make cannot be settled by the uncovering of a fact, because in pursuing any particular fact the decision must already have been made: the mode of description that is to guide our response to the world has already been chosen. Our attempt to find a standard 'in the world' founders, because of our need to have adopted such an authority in order to address the world.

as an employee, as a parent, as a child, as a husband, etc., etc. But to justify one's acts by presenting them as responses to one of these demands leaves unanswered the question that Kant asks of us: why did we take that demand seriously? This act may be what is required of one as an employee, that act as a husband; but these are matters of 'relative value', mere facts that leave the question of absolute value—of what one actually ought now to do, of which reason one will make one's own—untouched: '[t]he facts all belong to the task and not to its perform-ance' (6.4321).

15.6 LIFE AS A WHOLE

Ultimately these issues raise the question of identity, and that of the possibility of locating responsibility for acts. The challenge that we face is, as Heidegger would have put it, that of *accomplishing* a self.[10] To do so we must pull ourselves out of the stupefaction that arises from a life spent trading pseudo-reasons, explaining our actions by reference to goals that, deep down, are empty for us. To live that way is to live like Aristotle's 'akratic man', who 'may *say* he has knowledge' but whose moral knowledge has yet to be 'worked into the living structure of the mind'. Such people are 'like actors—mouthpieces for the sentiments of other people' (*Nicomachean Ethics* 1147ᵃ 19–24).

To have sentiments of one's own—not in the sense of having unusual or idio-syncratic sentiments, but in the way in which an actor does not—may be a more acute challenge in certain places and times: in modern Western societies, most people's working life is spent, in some way or other, *representing* organiza-tions and their associated ethos, explaining their actions by reference to what is required of those who hold the offices they happen to hold. But the challenge is also timeless: it has no doubt always been possible to duck responsibility by invoking what one must do as a parent, a friend, or an ally. And, of course, these structures of value are real enough; the demand that we act merely as ourselves, on our own behalf, is also liable to interpretation in fanciful or immature ways, in what Johnson called 'perversity of integrity' (Boswell 1980 [1791], p. 596 n. 1), and may itself represent a way of avoiding one's responsibilities.[11] But we may still recognize as real and important a willingness to bear an identity of one's own:

[10] As is well known, Wittgenstein remarked to Schlick: 'To be sure, I can imagine what Heidegger means by being and anxiety' (*VC* 68). I will not explore here the profound and illuminating parallels that I would suggest can be drawn between Wittgenstein's thought and Heidegger's. Someone familiar with both will no doubt recognize some in the present and preceding sections, not least in the envisaged experience of a 'valueless' world, an experience which is avoided by our 'falling into the world' and confronted by finding a way of treating the world as a whole, the latter response being also marked by a certain silence, a willingness to cease searching for yet more exculpatory reasons, and instead to manifest something called 'conscience'.

[11] Cf. Heidegger 1962, p. 164: 'We take pleasure and enjoy ourselves as *they* take pleasure; we read, see, and judge about literature and art as *they* see and judge; likewise we shrink back from the "great mass" as *they* shrink back.'

to deal with people straight, to hold and express honest opinions, to understand how one is living and to acknowledge the reasons why one lives as one lives, to spend one's life acting with a good conscience.

To be capable of living that way is, one might say, to be capable of living one's life as a whole, a notion to which Wittgenstein is drawn in what may otherwise seem some of his most opaque ethical remarks. Certain courses of action make sense because of offices one holds: they are the expression of one's duty and one's authority as a fireman, as a teacher, as a club secretary, etc. If one ceases to hold those offices, then those courses of action are no longer called for or permissible, as the case may be. Principles of one's own, however, motivate irrespective of the context in which one finds oneself; there is no point at which their relevance lapses. The challenge, then, of possessing principles of one's own — commitments which, when one states them, one means — is that of being capable of living one's life as a whole, as opposed to a set of overlapping, loosely associated contexts through which a certain human being happens to wander, picking up and dropping reasons for acting as she moves from one to the next. Principles of one's own penetrate into every context within which one lives; that there be such principles is a demand that Wittgenstein made on himself, expressing what Engelmann calls 'an ethical totalitarianism in all questions, a single-minded and painful preservation of the purity of the uncompromising demands of ethics' (*LPE* 109).

The decent person has made her life whole, in that she possesses principles that hold sway over her life as a whole; that life is informed, without compromise, by *a* (potentially complex) framework of principles. In this sense, living one's life as a whole is living it as possessed of *an* overarching sense, *a* meaning; whereas those of bad conscience fail to make of their lives a whole, and live instead many fragmented lives. Such lives display a kind of meaninglessness or unintelligibility: not that of non-con-formity, but the austere nonsense of empty, *mere* signs, of mere movements rather than actions The significance of the acts that make up those lives is indeterminate, because, among other things, the consequences of those actions are indeterminate: it is unclear whether an undertaking made in context *a* extends to context *b*, whether a principle cited in context *c* will influence the person's conduct in context *d*, etc.[12]

We have here a recognizably ethical concern that one might articulate using just the terms that Wittgenstein uses in some of his most opaque remarks. By taking in her life as a whole, the person of good will 'change[s] the limits of the world' (6.43), in that she treats it as a delimited whole, fit to bear *a* meaning; with the difference between good and ill will, then, '[t]he world must, so to speak, wax or wane as a whole. As if by accession or loss of meaning' (*NB* 73; cf. also

---

[12] I set aside here complications such as the possibility of genuine 'conversion experiences' in which someone comes to realize that his life hitherto has been meaningless and then adopts and retains a new set of commitments.

TLP 6.43). Since '[t]he contemplation of the world *sub specie aeterni* is its contemplation as a limited whole' (6.45), then 'the good life is the world seen *sub specie aeternitatis*' (*NB* 83). The latter remark from *NB* 83 is prefaced there by the following:

The work of art is the object seen *sub specie aeternitatis*.

Wittgenstein goes on to specify what the alternative perspective is:

The usual way of looking at things sees objects as it were from the midst of them (*aus ihrer Mitte*), the view *sub specie aeternitatis* from outside.
    In such a way that they have the whole world as background. (*NB* 83)[13]

The person of bad conscience lives 'in the midst of things', in that he is pushed and pulled by the fluctuating demands of the immediate life around him; he loses himself in those demands, letting them, rather than principles he has made his own, dictate how he acts. In MS 107, we read:

The bad person needs the feeling of pressure, only the good person can also live free from all pressure. And woe, when the pressure is taken away from the bad person (for example, myself), then he will sense immediately that something is not right. For he knows that perfect inner freedom could only arise from a perfectly pure conscience. (p. 159 (1929))

Living 'in the midst of things', the bad person surrenders his own judgement to matters of mere 'relative value' that cannot bear that burden:

It would be as if one saw a pair of scales in equilibrium, whose pans are not equally weighted. Then one must say, these scales are not well-adjusted, but are stuck.

    We also have a sense now of why

If by eternity is understood not endless temporal duration but timelessness, then he lives eternally who lives in the present. (6.4311)

Someone who lives his life as a whole lives a life informed by a set of principles that have a 'timeless' bearing on that life, in that those principles bear irrespective of the contexts, the particular times and places, in which he happens to find himself; only such a person, I have suggested, takes responsibility for his acts, rather than treating them as empty movements from which their

---

[13] These and many other ethical remarks by the early Wittgenstein clearly have a Schopenhauerian air, and my reading explores different understandings of the Schopenhauerian notion that 'abstract dogmas are without influence on virtue', virtue resting not upon an 'abstract knowledge communicable through words' (1969 [1844], p. 368) (cf. also §§ 53 and 66 *passim*). My principal doubt about a more thoroughgoing Schopenhauerian reading of the early Wittgenstein (cf., e.g., Glock 1999) is whether anything like Schopenhauer's metaphysics can be found in the early Wittgenstein. For what it's worth, it seems to me, rather, that Wittgenstein hears something true in a lot of Schopenhauerian formulations, is unsure quite what that truth is, but suspects that it isn't what Schopenhauer himself took it to be (cf. *CV* 41 (1939–40): 'Where real depth starts, [Schopenhauer's] finishes'). I think Janaway strikes a useful note: 'It is as if [Wittgenstein] possesses Schopenhauerian vocabulary, but is unclear really what he wants to do with it' (1989, p. 321).

'author' might dissociate himself later; hence, only someone who lives eternally—'timelessly'—expresses himself, commits himself, in his acts: only such a
person can be said to be here in his acts in the present.

To live a life possessed of an overarching sense, *a* meaning, is to possess what
I suggest Wittgenstein means by 'faith', when he confesses to Engelmann that he
has none (*LPE* 11). The term suggests a belief in God but, in *NB*, we read:

> [G]ood and evil are somehow connected with the meaning of the world.
> The meaning of life, i.e. the meaning of the world, we can call God . . .
> To believe in God means to understand the question about the meaning of life.
> To believe in God means to see that the facts of the world are not the end of the
> matter.
> To believe in God means to see that life has a meaning. (*NB* 73–4)

Such 'faith' is a sense that there is something that one can be doing with one's life
that is worthwhile, that one's life has a meaning to which one ought to be true;
in this way, faith poses the challenge of decency, that of ensuring that our acts are
indeed governed by the things that really matter to us, rather than dreaming our
lives away in meaningless pursuits.

One might wonder whether the challenge articulated here is one which a resolute Wittgenstein can pose: in setting out this demand that we live life 'as a whole'
and 'eternally', haven't I 'giv[en] the content of [Wittgenstein's] ethical views'
(Diamond 2000*b*, p. 155, quoted in the introduction to Ch. 13)? But, let us ask,
who needs to be told that to apply principles that are really one's own, one must
apply them throughout one's life as a whole, not just where and when one sees
fit? This, I suggest, is another *elucidatory* 'proposal', something which one might
need to 'learn' only if one was already confused. For instance, if one is unwittingly in the grip of the philosophical picture that compares a principle of one's
own with a sentence that one harbours 'deep within', then one might be struck by
the fact that we can imagine such a 'harbouring' accompanied by a falling away
of one's behaviour from the standard envisaged; but all that this shows is that this
'harbouring' and the 'principle harboured' are fantasies that conjure up possible
'situations' to which no sense has been assigned, such as that in which 'someone
really possesses a principle of her own but soon comes to ignore it'. What such a
person needs to be told is that principles of one's own are 'internally related' to
their being applied throughout one's life as a whole. In this way, the 'demands'
set out above do not serve to express an 'ethic', but instead to pull us back from
fantasies that obscure the ordinary, ethical life. Just as one might say that crossing
the line first *is* what it is to win a race, so one might say that there is no other 'way'
of 'being ethical' other than the 'ethical totalitarian' 'way'.

Who succumbs to such confusions? Philosophy does not explicitly disagree, so
to speak, with the 'demands' that one live life 'timelessly' and 'as a whole'; but it
does obscure them, in presenting itself as a heightened mode of moral seriousness
and, therefore, its own modes of thinking as relevant ways of meeting the ethical

challenges that we face. In particular, a further theory leaves the 'challenge' discussed untouched, leaving one with precisely the challenge of living a life in which theories are 'brought to bear on one's life as a whole'; correspondingly, the need for an inexpressible insight calling itself 'conscience' draws attention away from what the real 'challenge' of 'living life as a whole' looks like: it substitutes an exotic, obscure, and fantastical challenge for mundane, horribly familiar ones. Inasmuch as these two options—'the theoretical' and 'the inexpressible'—are all that the philosopher offers us,[14] his 'higher moral seriousness' is a fantasy of moral seriousness. But there may be a yet richer irony to Wittgenstein's 'ethical demands' here. It is characteristic of the philosopher simply to claim for himself the perspective from which one contemplates life 'timelessly' and 'as a whole'; but the preceding discussion suggests instead that attaining such a viewpoint is actually a moral or spiritual *achievement*, a matter of '*being* good'.

I will end this section by looking at another obvious worry that the preceding discussion raises: what if I find that there are no principles that I can appropriate in the way envisaged? What if I cannot take any consideration that seriously? That would be to be unclear about whether anything 'matters' in an absolute sense, whether there is something that my life as a whole ought to mean. To lack such a sense is to wonder whether what one does amounts to anything, means anything; it is to be constantly in danger of turning on the life that one is leading and despairing of it as empty. That such a worry afflicted Wittgenstein is shown not only in his explicit remarks to Engelmann but in the life he led.

What one can do about such a predicament is a question I won't address; but, again, seeing how philosophy is ill-suited to help helps identify just what the predicament is. I suggested earlier that the philosopher might be compared to the man who 'wants, as it were, to invent a machine for becoming decent'; Wittgenstein tells Engelmann that '[i]t is plain . . . that such a man has no faith' (*LPE* 11). Such a person is trying to find something that will compel him to do what matters, a 'machine for becoming decent'; the predicament of such a person is that he does not himself already feel drawn by anything that matters: such a person lacks 'faith'. The goal is not to be told what to do, because to experience one's life as possessed of a meaning of its own is to feel no need to be told what to do. But such a 'telling' is all that philosophy has to offer: either a 'machine' that will tell one what to do or the corresponding, comforting despair of an inarticulable, impenetrable, mystic 'seeing', an answer certainly—something that tells one what to do—but an answer—a telling—which cannot be put into words. All that the philosopher sees around him are problems that such a 'telling' might solve; thus, there is nothing for the philosopher to do here:

---

[14] Is the philosophical tradition as impoverished as it is here presented? I strongly suspect not; but what I present here is what I think Wittgenstein himself thought. Though I won't make the case here, I think that there are recognizably philosophical thinkers who do recognize the kind of challenges described, Aristotle, again, being the most obvious example.

[O]ne could say that the man is fulfilling the purpose of existence who no longer needs to have any purpose except to live. That is to say, who is content.

The solution of the problem of life is seen in the vanishing of this problem. (*NB* 73–4)

15.7 A FEAR OF LIFE

The highest expression of all morality is, Be!
Let a man so act that his *whole* individuality resides in every moment.[15]

[S]uicide is, so to speak, the elementary sin.

(*NB* 91)

Virtually all of us at some point acquiesce in situations in, or particular strands of, life in which we feel we are doing no more than doing what we are told, merely acting out a role and performing acts that mean nothing to us. This willingness to be absorbed into situations in which we see events as insignificant, meaningless, and hence, in a sense, unreal, renders our actions therein also insignificant, meaningless, and unreal: a derealization accompanies a depersonalization. Such acting is not in itself a form of insanity; but what if we came to relate in this way to the most important areas of life? Could we see this as expressive of a desire to relinquish identity? Such a desire would not be a desire to be thus-and-so or a desire to be not thus-and-so; it would be a desire to be neither thus-and-so nor not thus-and-so. Apologies in advance but . . . 'To be or not to be?'—that is the question.

Now it is not clear that this 'desire' makes sense. One can imagine an argument to the effect that all desiring is, on some level, a desiring for how things will be with *me*, so that desiring to lose one's identity is an incoherent notion. To *whom*, one might ask, ought one to ascribe the desire in the event of its being fulfilled? But does that make such a desire impossible? Or perhaps a mad kind of desire? It may be a confused desire; but then, according to the argument presented in this book, much of philosophy is a confused enterprise. If we believe that people are capable of committing themselves to, and participating in, a confused enterprise, then we believe that they can possess a confused desire. The pseudo-logic of the pseudo-tasks of the philosopher is that it serves the pseudo-objective of not existing determinately.

So how ought we to characterize this pattern of human life? It seems to be something like a fear of speaking for oneself, a craving for reasons in pursuit of a craving for anonymity, a craving to be acting under orders, a desire to dissolve a problem of *being* into yet another problem of *responding*, a desire to sleep or to die, the wish that my life not be happening to *me now*:

[W]hat men mean when they say that '*the world is there*' is something I have at heart. (*VC* 118)

---

[15] A later aphorism of Weininger's, quoted in McGuinness 1988, p. 41.

APPENDIX A

The Later Wittgenstein

A.1 SO WHY IS THERE A LATER WITTGENSTEIN?

My reading rules out one familiar kind of answer to the above question: many interpreters of the *Tractatus* take it to have advocated a kind of con-formism which Wittgenstein later recognized as mistaken. Does this mean that I have no answer to the above question? No, just not *that* answer. A proper answer to this question would require a book of its own; all I will offer here is a sketch of a couple of the themes that run through Wittgenstein's transitional writings and indicate how they relate to the *Tractatus* as I have presented it.

One of the main reasons why I came to have doubts initially about the notion that the *Tractatus* offers us an explanation of the possibility of meaning that rests on some kind of ineffable metaphysics was my reading Wittgenstein's transitional works and failing to find there the kind of critical revisions that his having advocated such a view earlier would lead one to expect. One does not find there the working out of a new metaphysical outlook, criticism of the idea of an *ineffable* metaphysics, or any substantial indication that the criticisms of con-formism that one does find there are criticisms directed at his earlier self. But the later Wittgenstein is repeatedly and explicitly critical of his earlier self for having succumbed to a misleading, homogenizing conception of language. In this Appendix, I will comment briefly on how this realization comes about, and the difference it makes to Wittgenstein's conception of philosophical problems and of how they ought to be addressed.

A.2 IRREDEEMABLE PROMISSORY NOTES

Most accounts of Wittgenstein's transition start with his worries over the 'colour-exclusion problem',[1] and that seems as good a starting-point as any. Sections 11.7–11.8 and 12.1 have already made clear the broader issue that this problem illustrates: that of understanding logical incompatibility in truth-functional terms, which is to say, ultimately as contradiction. Chapters 11–12 have explained why Wittgenstein came to believe that such an understanding must be possible, and how this led him to expect apparent cases

---

[1] Cf., e.g., Kenny 1973, ch. 6, and Hacker 1986, ch. 5.

of non-truth-functional logical incompatibility to be revealed as merely apparent. On his return to philosophy, Wittgenstein is forced to try to show that those expectations can indeed be fulfilled. When they cannot, he is forced to explore various 'patches', such as that touched on in Section 11.8. But next I will discuss two further developments with longer-term effects.

First, Wittgenstein is forced to scrutinize particular cases of apparent truth-functional logical incompatibility. In doing so, his attention focuses on how that impression arises out of the conflation of particular kinds of proposition: for example, propositions about the 'time of memory' and the 'time of physics' (*VC* 53), about 'finite' and 'infinite classes' (*VC* 70), about pictures and memories (*VC* 48), about time and motion (*L I* 60–1), about rational and irrational numbers (*PR*, chs. 17 and 18), about physical space and 'visual space' (*PR*, ch. 21), and about 'observational' propositions and hypotheses (*PR*, ch. 22).[2]

It remains Wittgenstein's view that such conflations create the impression of substantial logical necessities which we may then come to believe must be grounded in the metaphysical character of the entities concerned. Wittgenstein continues to try to show that there are no such necessities, and that any such apparent grounding is an illusion. Instead, echoing the *Tractatus*'s proposals that '[t]heories which make a proposition of logic appear substantial are always false' (6.111) and '[t]he propositions of logic ... say nothing' (6.11), Wittgenstein insists that '[t]he rules of syntax are not about anything' (*VC* 62), 'cannot be justified' (*VC* 126), are 'arbitrary' (*VC* 103), and later, that 'grammar' is 'arbitrary' (*PG* 184).[3] These general claims can be seen as giving an initial orientation to Wittgenstein's transitional reflections on meaning, mind, and mathematics; but behind these general claims is careful scrutiny of particular sets of propositions whose 'surface grammar' bears similarities that tempt us into seeing 'logical possibilities' and 'logical impossibilities'.

[2] Though I will not make the argument here, the latter two issues are what I take to be at stake in reflections that have led commentators to ascribe to the transitional Wittgenstein some substantial metaphysical commitments under the rubrics 'Wittgenstein's phenomenology' and 'Wittgenstein's verificationism'.

[3] That the latter are indeed echoes of the former is suggested, e.g., by the way in which the following passage from *PG* 246 runs these themes together seamlessly—which is to say, not at all in the fashion that commentators who ascribe to the early Wittgenstein some kind of realist con-formism would lead one to expect:

If I were to say 'whether *p* follows from *q* must result from *p* and *q* alone': it would have to mean this: that *p* follows from *q* is a stipulation that determines the sense of *p* and *q*, not some extra truth that can be asserted about the sense of both of them. Hence one can indeed give rules of inference, but in doing so one is giving for the use of the written signs rules which determine their as yet undetermined sense; and that means simply that the rules must be laid down arbitrarily, i.e. are not to be read off from reality like a description. For when I say that the rules are arbitrary, I mean that they are not determined by reality in the way the description of reality is. And that means: it is nonsense to say that they agree with reality, e.g. that the rules for the words 'blue' and 'red' agree with the facts about those colours etc.

Secondly, Wittgenstein comes to lose faith in the general approach to logic-al incompatibility that he had adopted. As I indicated in Section 11.8, a crucial consequence of this failure was his loss of faith in a 'topic-neutral' account of the logical constants; instead, he came to believe that '[t]here are as many different "alls" as there are different "ones"' (*PG* 269), and that there is a 'family of nega-tions' (*L II* 101). But if 'topic-neutral' talk about 'negation' lacks substance, this also casts doubt on 'topic-neutral' talk of *assertion* or any of the other core notions using which one might talk about 'what language, in general, does'.

A.3 FAMILY RESEMBLANCE

Wittgenstein came to see such talk as illustrating a wider tendency that informs our philosophical thinking: to presume that when we correctly apply a term to different items, those items must exemplify some common, underlying essence. Instead, many concepts are what he came to call 'family resemblance' concepts: G. E. Moore reports the following remarks by Wittgenstein about his favourite example, 'game':

[T]he reason why we call so many different activities 'games' need not be that there is anything common to them all, but only that there is 'a gradual transition' from one use to another, although there may be nothing in common between the two ends. (M 313)

Viewed schematically, although *a* and *c* may have no characteristics in common, it may make sense to call them both '*x*' because *a* and *b* share certain character-istics and so do *b* and *c*. Philosophical problems can arise when we assume that because they both 'are *x*', questions which it makes sense to ask of *a* must also make sense when asked of *c*, or when, on failing to find the similarity that we mis-takenly assume unites all *x*s, we take that similarity to be something hidden: we create a mystery called 'the true nature of *x*-hood'.

The following example illustrates the first kind of confusion. Calling π a 'number' makes sense, in that certain manipulations that can be performed on rational numbers, for example, can also be performed on π (*PR* 236, 239–40); but when we learn that 'π doesn't correspond to a point on the number line' (*PR* 239), we will come to think of our knowledge of π as compromised or incomplete if we assume that expression as a finite decimal is something to be expected of all things we call 'numbers'.

The following example illustrates the second kind of confusion. Instead of tak-ing 'understanding' to pick out a collection of 'more or less interrelated processes' (*PG* 74), we may take it as 'the name of a single process accompanying reading or hearing', comparing it to 'a particular *process* like translation from one language into another'; but then we see that 'what we would perhaps naively suggest as the hallmark of such a process is not present in every case or even in the majority of cases':

And our next step is to conclude that the essence of the process is something difficult to grasp that still awaits discovery. For we say: since I use the word 'understand' in all these cases, there must be some one thing which happens in every case and which is the essence of understanding (expecting, wishing etc.). Otherwise, why should I call them all by the same name? (*PG* 74–5)

As Section 11.2 explained, the author of the *Tractatus* thought that, for proposition p to be logically incompatible with proposition q, p must be a logical product of q and another proposition: thus, despite appearances, 'a logical product is hidden in [the] proposition' (*PG* 210). Only thus could he come to believe that they too would fit his GFP, and that the general dissolution of substantial 'laws of inference' that this seemed to make possible would be made good. 'At the root of all this', Wittgenstein later concluded, 'there was a false and idealized picture of the use of language' (*PG* 211). In his readiness to see a quite general structure 'hidden' in our propositions, 'lying *beneath* the surface' (*Z* §444), that their diverse uses and modes of expression suggest, Wittgenstein failed to see that what ties what we call 'propositions' together is not 'some one fibre [that] runs through' all but 'the overlapping of many fibres' (*PI* §67).

A.4 'LANGUAGE' AS A FAMILY RESEMBLANCE CONCEPT

General categories such as 'negation' and 'generality', when thought of as spanning language's landscape, become, for Wittgenstein, a disguise for the forcing of many different kinds of grammar into a mould derived from particular grammars. Instead, to understand what 'generality' or 'negation' is, one must examine individual cases, and these categories cannot provide an *independent* handle on 'what propositions, in general, do'. This is true of many other general concepts that we use in describing propositions; in lectures of 1934, Wittgenstein comments on our efforts to define 'the general idea of a proposition':

Most definitions of a proposition given in logic books, as what is true or false, or as the expression of a thought are futile. For we do not understand the terms of the definition. (*L II* 77)

To take the first suggestion, Wittgenstein argues that to understand what truth is is to understand what the proposition (whose truth one is contemplating) says, and thus 'truth' is as heterogeneous as the propositions which (in their different ways) affirm or deny truths and falsehoods.[4] To take the second, the definitions that we may offer for 'thought' itself ought not to disguise its own heterogeneity:

---

[4] Cf., e.g., *L II* 12; *PG* 123–4, 161–2; *RFM* 117.

We may say 'Thinking is operating with symbols'. But 'thinking' is a fluid concept, and what 'operating with symbols' is must be looked at separately in each individual case. (*PG* 106)

The same goes for concepts like 'sense' and 'language': 'Sense' is 'correlative to "proposition"', 'alter[ing] its meaning as we go from proposition to proposition' (M 273, 274), and declaring that 'a proposition belongs to a language' simply means that 'it is units of languages that I call "propositions"' (*PG* 170). As with 'generality' and 'negation', the basic building-blocks from which we may have hoped to construct a picture of 'what propositions, in general, do' prove unfit. Instead, Wittgenstein concludes that '[t]here are many things . . . which we may or may not call propositions; and not only one game can be called language' (*L II* 12).[5]

The 'transitional Wittgenstein' returns, again and again, to the question, 'Do we have a general concept of a proposition?'[6] What becomes his considered answer is that we do, but that it possesses no more unity than a concept like 'game'. 'Propositions do not all have something in common, but are a family of things having overlapping likenesses' (*L II* 67). In the light of this realization, Wittgenstein sees his early analogy between propositions and pictures as itself liable to create philosophical confusion:

To say that a proposition is a picture gives prominence to certain features of the grammar of the word 'proposition'.

Thinking is quite comparable to the drawing of pictures.

But one can also say that what looks like an analogue of a proposition is actually a particular case of our general concept. (*PG* 163–4)

There are undoubtedly respects in which a proposition can be compared with a picture, and thus the one be seen as an analogue of the other. But this does not entail that propositions and pictures are instances of a more general concept. '[U]nder the illusion' that we must uncover '*one* comprehensive essence', we look at 'a special clearly intuitive case' and conclude, '*That* shows how things are in every case; this case is the exemplar of *all* cases':

The tendency to generalize the case seems to have a strict justification in logic: . . . 'If *one* proposition is a picture, then any proposition must be a picture, for they must all be of the same nature.' (*Z* §444)[7]

By thinking only of certain varieties of proposition, the claim that all propositions 'picture' can become compelling. '[I]t is as if we had now seen something

---

[5] This is a recurrent theme in the first half of Part I of *PI* (cf. e.g., *PI* §§10–11, 22, 24, 92, 304), with critical comments accompanied by clear allusions (cf. e.g., *PI* §§65 and 108) and, on two occasions, explicit reference (*PI* §§23 and 114) to Wittgenstein's earlier views.

[6] Cf. *PG* 112–14, 120–5; M 261, 263, 273; *L II* 11, 12–13, and 20.

[7] Cf. also *RPP I* 38: 'The basic evil of Russell's logic, as also of mine in the *Tractatus*, is that what a proposition is is illustrated by a few commonplace examples, and then pre-supposed as understood in full generality.'

lying *beneath* the surface' (*Z* §444).[8] In the *Investigations*, Wittgenstein's inter-locutor complains:

> You talk about all sorts of language-games, but have nowhere said what the essence of a language-game, and hence of language, is: what is common to all these activities, and what makes them into language or parts of language. So you let yourself off the very part of the investigation that once gave you yourself the most headache, the part about the *general form of propositions* and of language. (*PI* §65)

Wittgenstein's reply is that 'this is true':

> Instead of producing something common to all that we call language, I am saying that these phenomena have no one thing in common which makes us use the same word for all,—but that they are *related* to one another in many different ways. And it is because of this relationship, or these relationships, that we call them all 'language'. (*PI* §65)

The consequences of Wittgenstein's acceptance that there is no one thing to which we refer when we use the term 'proposition' are wide-ranging and funda-mental. In the next five sections, I will briefly comment on how that acceptance affects Wittgenstein's understanding of philosophical problems and of his own philosophical work.

A.5 ABANDONING THE IDEA OF A PROPOSITION'S 'COMPLETE ANALYSIS'

Starting in around 1932, Wittgenstein began to criticize his earlier view of philo-sophical analysis as having rested upon 'a wrong idea of logical analysis', one according to which 'logical analysis is taken as being like chemical analysis' (*L II* 11):

> My notion in the *Tractatus Logico-Philosophicus* was wrong ... because I too thought that logical analysis had to bring to light what was hidden (as chemical and physical analysis does). (*PG* 210)

It would be easy to misinterpret this development. It may encourage us to force upon the *Tractatus* the alien objective of constructing a philosophical under-standing of propositions which would claim to outstrip our 'ordinary under-standing'. But, according to my 'mechanical' interpretation of the contribution of a *Begriffsschrift*, expressing propositions using such a notation simply serves to eliminate the temptation, to which only the philosophers in us succumb, to be misled by 'surface-grammatical' similarities between propositions, similarities between signs, in a way which leads us to 'glimpse', and then puzzle over, the nature and basis of, 'logical impossibilities'.

---

[8] Kuusela (2005) makes similar use of these passages in a suggestive analysis of Wittgenstein's development with which I have a lot of sympathy.

So what is the thinking behind Wittgenstein's new criticisms of the *Tractatus*'s conception of analysis? As Section A.2 mentioned, in the years after 1929, when Wittgenstein reflects on propositions which seem to conjure up substantial logical and metaphysical necessities, he focuses increasingly on the practical objective of identifying how we have confused different types of proposition. This shift of focus does not in itself cast doubt on the idea that there is something called 'a proposition's complete analysis'. In a later (1936) manuscript,[9] Wittgenstein summarizes his earlier view:

Formerly, I myself spoke of a 'complete analysis', and I used to believe that philosophy had to give a definitive dissection of propositions so as to set out all their connections and remove all possibilities of misunderstanding. (*PG* 211)

The particular confusions that Wittgenstein notes could be thought of as occurring because of our lacking this 'complete analysis', and what Wittgenstein does in examining how particular pairs of proposition-types become confused is to point us in the direction of that analysis. If the noting of differences between propositions eliminates philosophical problems, and if this is what is called 'noting logical differences', a 'complete logical analysis' would have been achieved when one had an expression of one's proposition which made it impossible to confuse it with any other proposition-type. Such an expression would 'lay bare the source of all misunderstandings' (*PG* 211).[10]

The transitional Wittgenstein's more 'pragmatic' analytic approach to the dissolution of apparently substantial philosophical necessities sought to identify differences between particular sets of propositions, rather than their 'complete analyses'; the viability of that approach and the apparent *irrelevance* to it of the fabled 'complete analyses' must have raised the suspicion that those 'analyses' were 'wheels turning idly'. Wittgenstein's insight into the structure of our concepts of 'language' and 'proposition' must then have confirmed those suspicions: the realization that the 'set of all propositions' was a confused notion reveals that there is no such thing as '*the* complete analysis': if 'it is more or less arbitrary what we call a "proposition"' (M 261), then what one takes to be 'all propositions' is 'more or less arbitrary' too; and if a 'complete analysis' is the expression of a proposition in signs that make clear how it differs from 'all other propositions', it is 'senseless to talk of a "final" analysis' (M 296).

In the *Investigations*, Wittgenstein suggests that constructing new expressions for propositions might prevent philosophical problems arising through 'certain analogies between the forms of expression in different regions in language':

---

[9] Published as Appendix 4B of *PG*.

[10] Cf. 4.5's description of the GFP as 'a description of the propositions of *any* sign-language *whatsoever* in such a way that every possible sense can be expressed by a symbol satisfying the description'.

Some of them can be removed by substituting one form of expression for another, this may be called an 'analysis' of our forms of expression, for the process is sometimes like one of taking a thing apart. (*PI* §90)

But he continues:

But now it may come to look as if there were something like a final analysis of our forms of language, and so a *single* completely resolved form of every expression. That is, as if our usual forms of expression were, essentially, unanalysed; as if there were something hidden in them that had to be brought to light. (*PI* §91)[11]

The illusion of such a 'final analysis', '[s]omething that lies within ... which an analysis digs out' (*PI* §92), 'finds expression in questions as to the *essence* of language, of propositions, of thought' (*PI* §92), and his insights into the *heterogeneity* of these super-categories confirm the suspicion that such an analysis, which we pursue 'as if this were the real goal of our investigation' (*PI* §91), is a red herring. Instead, we must address the relatively mundane problem of 'surface-grammatical' similarities leading us, without our realizing, to think of one set of propositions in terms appropriate to others.

'Surface' grammar can cause us to make mistakes, and some instances of that grammar are more misleading than others. But this does not imply that there is an ideal form of surface grammar which does not have such effects, or that pointing out such mistakes is a step on the road to this ideal form. Captured enemy soldiers may lie to us about the location of their secret weapon, and some of these soldiers may send us off on elaborate wild-goose chases. For that reason alone, it makes sense to say that the latter are misleading us more than the rest. But this does not mean that there *is* a secret weapon. If there isn't, our investigation is suffering from a kind of carelessness or over-simplification, rather than ignorance; or we might instead say that the ignorance about which we worry is not the ignorance we should be worried about. Our wasted efforts arise because of what our prisoners (our surface grammar) say; but we misunderstand how we are being misled if we think that what we really need to find is the prisoner who *will* tell us where the secret weapon is.

A.6 THE FATE OF THE IDEA OF 'THE ARBITRARINESS OF GRAMMAR'

This section will indicate how the loss of a sense of 'what propositions, in general, do' affects Wittgenstein's early transitional notions that 'syntax is empty'

---

[11] Cf. *VC* 45, 48: 'We need not invent a new language or construct a new symbolism, but our everyday language already is *the* language, provided we get rid of the obscurities that lie hidden in it. ... Our language is in order, once we have understood its syntax and recognized the wheels that turn idly.'

and 'grammar is arbitrary', descendants of the *Tractatus*'s proposal that logical propositions 'say nothing' and its elucidation of the confusion of con-formism.[12]

Since 'using propositions' is now seen as denoting a variety of activities, the 'activity' which unites them, 'making sense', is seen as no more homogeneous than the 'activity' which unites our uses of different tools.[13] One might come to think that questions are kinds of statements, because one can rephrase them using expressions like 'I wonder whether . . .' ; but once we recognize their differences, this assertion may sound like saying that a hammer is 'a kind of screw-driver'. In lectures, Wittgenstein restates his rejection of a general concept of 'proposition', insists instead that 'our way of talking about propositions is always in terms of specific examples', and reaches again for his comparison with games:

The words 'nonsense' and 'sense' get their meaning only in particular cases and may vary from case to case. We can still talk of *sense* without giving a clear meaning to 'sense', just as we talk of winning or losing without the meaning of our terms being absolutely clear. (*L II* 20–1)

'[T]he expression "makes sense" is useful just as "game" is useful, although, like "game", it "alters its meaning as we go from proposition to proposition"' (*M 274*).

But if there is no general feat of 'saying' which all language-use instantiates, what point can one make by asserting that 'logical propositions *say nothing*'? If there is no one kind of thing that we mean when we talk of 'propositions', the way in which one kind of proposition 'says' may have nothing in common with the way in which another kind of proposition 'says'; each kind of proposition 'says nothing' when inappropriate senses of 'saying' are applied, and these local-ized notions are of no use to someone who wishes to make a general claim that 'logical propositions say nothing'. The thoughts set out in Section A.4 prompt Wittgenstein to wonder 'whether if we disregard . . . sounding like a sentence we still have a general concept of proposition' (*PG* 122); if we were to take such a criterion—'sounding like a sentence'—as a criterion of what it is to say, then 'logical propositions' would *not* count as 'saying nothing'; but what other, non-arbitrary criterion do we have?

The concept of 'syntax' is itself transformed by these developments. Wittgenstein concludes that because 'proposition' is not a 'sharply bounded' concept, '"sense" is vague [and] so must be "grammar", "grammatical rule" and "syntax"' (*M 273–4*). To revert to the tool analogy, 'syntax', 'the rules for using propositions', may denote as heterogeneous a collection as 'the rules for using tools'. We can, nevertheless, still use the term 'syntax', because *in many settings* what we are talking about will be obvious (compare the rules for using

---

[12] I will discuss the impact of these developments on the latter in Sect. A.10.
[13] One of the first appearances of the tool analogy is *PG* 67. One of the first appearances of the related 'train cabin' analogy is *PR* 58.

a hammer, the rules for using pliers, etc.). But what of the context in which we wish to assert the general, philosophically minded claim that 'syntax is empty'? In some cases, it seems impossible to understand what that general claim would mean. Like the claim 'Language is essentially a form of picturing', it may be clear in some cases: for example, one may argue that the meaning of terms we use in describing a room are not dictated by what we happen to find in rooms, and, in this sense, the syntax of such terms could be said to be empty. But is the syntax of 'Hello' empty? What kind of 'saying' might we mistakenly think *it* performs? What kind of facts are threatening to dictate *that* kind of syntax? The general claim that 'grammar is arbitrary' suffers from what would appear, from the later Wittgenstein's point of view, to be a characteristic defect of general claims about 'language': the kind of claim they embody is clear in connection with certain ranges of linguistic phenomena, but not in connection with others. It is not that these claims are false; rather, it is unclear what they, in their generality, mean.

This realization transforms the kind of claim one can make when one says that a particular proposition 'says nothing' or is 'empty'. If there is no general, non-arbitrarily delimited phenomenon of 'saying' or 'having content', then to say that a particular proposition 'says nothing' or is 'empty', one must have a particular kind of 'saying' or 'having content' in mind.[14] But that kind of charge is now indistinguishable from that which we make when we declare that a proposition is nonsense: we are saying that it does not belong to the system to which it appears to belong (does not have the meaning that it might appear to have). What may be true in saying that 'syntax is empty' is that *this* proposition (which is a member of the family of propositions we call 'syntactic rules') does not belong to *this* other particular system of propositions (a member of the family of 'fact-stating' systems of propositions) to which we have taken it—perhaps because of its 'surface grammar'—to belong. (In this way, the early Wittgensteinian distinction between being described as being *sinnlos* and being charged with being *unsinnig* vanishes.)

This change has a subtle impact on Wittgenstein's philosophizing. Although he argued on a priori grounds that 'syntax' had to be 'empty', most of his transitional efforts were devoted to dealing with particular cases in which we mistake particular kinds of syntax for particular kinds of fact, and thereby conjure up the impression that syntax has 'substance' of some sort: so, for example, we may superimpose propositions from Euclidean geometry on propositions from visual geometry and derive a priori laws about the behaviour of visual phenomena, these 'laws' 'dictating' the syntax of our talk about visual phenomena. Analyses which expose how we come to 'glimpse' these 'laws' are *not* jeopardized by

---

[14] It is noticeable that Wittgenstein starts to feel the need to provide glosses on what he has in mind when he uses the expression 'grammar is arbitrary': cf., e.g., *PG* 184–8; *Z*§331; and the last two sentences of the passage from *PG* 246 quoted in n. 3 above.

Wittgenstein's rejection of his earlier monistic outlook. But the general project to which these analyses might be thought to be contributing, by undermining particular 'counter-examples' to a general claim about 'grammar', is an illusion.[15]

The notion that, when philosophizing, we fail to acknowledge 'the arbitrariness of grammar', now appears as a misleadingly homogenizing way of characterizing a highly heterogeneous class of errors which result when we inappropriately compare different types of proposition. Recognizing this mistake, Wittgenstein comes to think of the problems that he addresses in the way in which he had, in fact, come to *treat* them, returning to them their own peculiar identities. Instead of 'failures to acknowledge the arbitrariness of grammar', they are now thought of as the confusions that arise when, for example, we take psychological phenomena to dictate the meaning of people's utterances, take irrational numbers to have all the characteristics of the reals, etc., etc.

An intuition which the concept of 'the arbitrariness of grammar' *does* capture, however, is that a significant proportion of the inappropriate comparisons which create philosophical confusion are cases of our confusing propositions which express facts in one system with propositions which express rules of grammar in another. But this description should be interpreted in line with Wittgenstein's suggestion (quoted in Sect. 16.4) for understanding a claim like 'Thinking is operating with symbols': if 'grammar' is given its 'meaning only in particular cases', and 'truths' are as heterogeneous as the propositions used to assert them, cases in which we take a 'grammatical statement' to be 'asserting a truth' may be bound together by nothing but superficial similarities. 'Grammar', 'truth', and, consequently, 'confusing a grammatical proposition with an assertion of truth' are no longer the 'sharply bounded concepts' they once were. We can still use these concepts; but we must recognize that they are 'fluid', and that what they denote 'must be looked at separately in each individual case'.

It is my suggestion that Wittgenstein comes to realize that his general theme of 'the arbitrariness of grammar' was useful *and* misleading in focusing attention on certain analogies which hold between philosophical problems (much as his earlier conception of 'proposition' had enlightened and confused our thinking on the multitude of different forms of language), but that he ultimately decides that the costs outweigh the benefits. The only reference to 'the arbitrariness of grammar' that survives into the *Philosophical Investigations* occurs in the following cautious and seemingly self-conscious passage:

---

[15] That claim had come to stand as an explanation of how philosophical propositions are confused, an unacknowledged quasi-fact (about 'grammar') which we might not appreciate: we fall into the grip of a philosophical problem when we confuse certain propositions and end up suggesting that 'grammar' is not 'arbitrary'. But the rethink I have described ties that charge *immediately* to the former confusion, the 'one-time' *'cause'* of our mistaken 'opinion' about grammar. Now to think grammar non-arbitrary *is* to confuse certain propositions.

The rules of grammar may be called 'arbitrary', if that is to mean that the *aim* of the grammar is nothing but that of the language. (*PI* §497)[16]

Similarly, in response to the notion that 'surely' 'what grammar permits' 'is arbitrary', he writes:

Is it arbitrary?—It is not every sentence-like formation that we know how to do something with, not every technique has an application in our life. (*PI* §520)

I have already indicated how a recognition of the heterogeneity of language might affect one's attitude towards the notion that 'grammar is arbitrary'—for example, *with respect to what* is the grammar of 'Hello' arbitrary?—but another aspect of that recognition may underlie *PI* §520's caution. Recognition of the heterogeneity of language is a recognition that, in using different linguistic tools, one does different things and pursues different interests. I will quote just part of *PI* §23's famous list:

Giving orders, and obeying them—
    Describing the appearance of an object, or giving its measurements—
    Constructing an object from a description (a drawing)—...
    Making up a story; and reading it—
    Play-acting—
    Singing catches—
    Guessing riddles—
    Making a joke; telling it—
    Solving a problem in practical arithmetic—...
    Asking, thanking, cursing, greeting, praying.

In contemplating the diversity of linguistic tools, one comes to recognize the diversity of the lives within which they are used, and becomes aware 'that the *speaking* of language is part of an activity, or of a form of life' (*PI* §23), that '[l]anguage . . . relates to a way of living' (*RFM* 335).

Now *with respect to the living of these lives*, the grammar of the particular languages we speak is *not* 'arbitrary', in that speaking these languages is part of what it is to live those lives; thus to imagine dispensing with those languages is to imagine dispensing with those activities: 'Asking, thanking, cursing, greeting, praying'. Also the activities within which our language-use is embedded are, in turn, embedded within our broader 'natural history';[17] as a result, if we were to imagine 'certain very general facts of nature' to be different, 'then even concepts which are different from the ones we're used to no longer seem unnatural

---

[16] This reaction is comparable to *PI* 's lukewarm reaction to a proposal using which Wittgenstein had earlier contested the notion that 'grammatical rules for a word had to follow from its ostensive definition' (*PG* 60), a confusion which we must shake off in order to see that '[g]rammar is not accountable to any reality' (*PG* 184). That proposal is that a sample 'is itself a symbol' (*L I* 45), '*is* part of language' (*L I* 102), and *PI*'s reaction is: 'Well, it is as you please. . . . It is most natural, and causes least confusion, to reckon the samples among the instruments of the language' (*PI* §16).

[17] Cf. *PI* §§25, 415, and p. 230.

to us' (*LW* I 209). None of this implies that the grammar of our language can 'be justified by describing what is represented' (*PR* 55); but it does mean that the declaration 'grammar is arbitrary' may mislead us as well as enlighten us.[18, 19]

Thus, with the disintegration of the 'super-concept' 'proposition', Wittgenstein's early, neat metaphilosophical picture is stripped of the notions that gave it content: 'the arbitrariness of grammar' thesis and its Tractarian forebear 'captured the features of the physiognomy, as it were', perceiving our heterogeneous confusions 'from far away and in a very indefinite manner' (*VC* 184).

A.7 'PHILOSOPHY' AS A FAMILY RESEMBLANCE CONCEPT

The next three sections clarify how the collapse of Wittgenstein's unified conception of language affects his conception not only of philosophy, but also of what metaphilosophical reflection can be. Wittgenstein comes to view 'philosophical problems' as a 'family resemblance' concept whose instances are a variety of different confusions bound together by certain characteristic causes, but about which one cannot generalize in terms that will be both unqualified and richly contentful.

The early Wittgenstein had been captivated by a general diagnostic story according to which philosophical problems arise when we come to see 'syntax' as 'substantial' and a *Begriffsschrift*, which we currently lack, would eliminate that danger. Crucially, the collapse of this general diagnosis does *not* herald an attempt to construct a new *unified* vision, to replace that which had been abandoned. Like the 'definitions of a proposition given in logic books, as what is true or false, or as the expression of a thought' (*L II* 77), the definition of 'philosophy' that the *Tractatus* offered fails because 'we do not understand the terms of the definition' ('syntax', 'sense', 'saying', etc.). Having realized that 'we cannot achieve any greater generality in philosophy than in what we say in life and in science' (*PG* 121), and that 'if the words "language", "experience", and "world", have a use, it must be as humble a one as that of the words, "table", "lamp" [or] "door"' (*PI* §97), Wittgenstein distances himself

---

[18] Moore reports that, though Wittgenstein had 'often asserted without qualification that all "rules of grammar" are arbitrary', by the time of his 1932–3 lectures, he had come to say 'that the sense in which all are arbitrary was a "peculiar" one' (M 298).

[19] The recognition that 'the *speaking* of language is part of an activity, or of a form of life' (*PI* §23) is an important element in a set of well-known, roughly concurrent, and mutually supportive developments in Wittgenstein's thought; e.g., it is tied up with a more profound 'contextualism' about meaning than the author of the *Tractatus* ever envisaged (cf., e.g., BB 137, 145, 147; *PI* §§177 and 349) and with a critique of the notion that meaning must be exact (cf., e.g., TS 213, 253 (1933); *PG* 77; and *PI* §81) and must be governed by fixed rules (cf., e.g., TS 213, 254 (1933); *PG* 61–3; *PI* §§80 and 83); Wittgenstein's associated interest in 'natural history' may also lead us ultimately to OC's notion of 'hinge propositions'. But here is not the place to explore these topics.

from the kind of general framework that would be necessary if one were to attempt to replace his earlier general vision and answer the question 'What is philosophy?' in anything like the way a philosopher would want that question answered. Instead, Wittgenstein comes to treat 'philosophy' itself as another 'family resemblance' concept:

[P]hilosophy isn't anything except philosophical problems, the particular individual worries that we call 'philosophical problems'. (*PG* 193)

What unity philosophical problems now have is their arising because of similar misapprehensions and similar superficialities: their 'common element extends as far as the common element in different regions of language' (*PG* 193). The *Tractatus*'s articulation of what 'philosophical problems' have in common with each other now appears misguided, much as did his understanding of 'propositions', 'language', 'understanding', etc. 'Philosophy' is just one more word around which philosophical confusions arise:

One might think: if philosophy speaks of the use of the word 'philosophy' there must be a second-order philosophy. But it is not so: it is, rather, like the case of orthography, which deals with the word 'orthography' among others without then being second-order. (*PI* §121)

Orthography 'deals with the word "orthography" among others without then being second-order', and in the same way philosophy (or, at least, philosophy the way Wittgenstein does it) deals with 'philosophy' without becoming second-order, without constructing the kind of metaphilosophy that might stand to what we call 'philosophical problems' as an account of 'the nature of the proposition' stands to our many uses of the term 'proposition'.

A.8 METAPHILOSOPHICAL BREADTH AND ILLUSIONS OF UNKNOWN DEPTHS

By being over-interpretative, Wittgenstein's earlier metaphilosophy had distorted the nature of philosophical confusion and the task of the philosopher. Illustrating the pattern described in Section A.3, over-generalization about 'philosophy' creates an illusion of depth, the illusion that there is something 'to' 'philosophical problems' beyond the 'surface' similarities that lead us to apply that label as we do. That illusion also presents philosophical misunderstanding as too *reasonable*, in that it arises because there *is* something hidden and difficult to grasp: there is a single kind of measure which we do not yet deploy for dealing with such forms of misunderstanding—namely, the 'complete analysis' of propositions—and a deeper unifying truth of sorts that we fail to appreciate—'the arbitrariness of grammar'. This directs attention *away* from *our* tendencies to misconceive and over-simplify that actually cause philosophical confusion.

For example, language was presented as harbouring secrets, and thus, rather than '[w]ork on philosophy [being] ... work on oneself' (Ph 161), work on philosophy was work on language. By 1933, Wittgenstein was keen to dissociate his understanding of 'philosophy' from such themes. Moore's lecture notes report that:

[Wittgenstein] did discuss at very great length ... certain very general questions about language; but he said, more than once, that he did not discuss these questions because he thought that language was the subject-matter of philosophy. He did not think it was. He discussed it only because he thought that particular philosophical errors or 'troubles in our thought' were due to false analogies suggested by our actual use of expressions. (M 257)

'Philosophical problems' are bound up with language only in that certain linguistic structures are among the *typical causes* of the kinds of confusion typical of those problems. The general project of constructing a *Begriffsschrift* which would lack any of the flaws that an 'ordinary language' might possess is now rejected. Moore continues:

[Wittgenstein] emphasised that it was only necessary for him to discuss those points about language, which, as he thought, led to these particular errors or 'troubles'. (M 257)

In Wittgenstein's later work, philosophical problems are still thought of as 'puzzles arising from the use of language'. But this causal link is the basic reason why words like ' "[g]rammar", "proposition" [and] "meaning" ... figure more often than other words' (*L II* 31). In the later work, there is nothing corresponding to the earlier metaphilosophical vision which bound 'philosophical problems' to concepts of 'syntax', 'a hidden analysis', and a 'general form of the proposition'. To adapt words from *PG* 116, if philosophy really was concerned with those concepts, then 'there would be such a thing as metaphilosophy. (But there is not. We might so present all that we have to say that this would appear as a leading principle.)'

Remarks at *PG* 115 bring together, first, the way in which a monistic conception of language underpinned Wittgenstein's project of exposing 'complete analyses'; secondly, the way in which that project gave him a sense of 'what philosophy, in general is'; and thirdly, the way in which his reconceptualization of what was valuable in that project led to a reconceptualization of philosophy. The possibility that 'the general concept of language dissolves' prompts Wittgenstein to ask, 'doesn't philosophy dissolve as well?' He replies:

No, for the task of philosophy is not to create a new, ideal language, but to clarify the use of our language, the existing language. Its aim is to remove particular misunderstandings; not to produce a real understanding for the first time. (*PG* 115)[20]

[20] This passage represents the acceptance and development of a possibility which Wittgenstein contemplated as early as 1914: 'Does ... a complete analysis exist? *And if not*: then what is the task of philosophy?!!?' (*NB* 2).

Exposing these confusions is a task which remains, even though 'there isn't a philosophical grammar and ordinary English grammar' (*L II* 31):

> We might feel that a complete logical analysis would give the complete grammar of a word. But there is no such thing as a completed grammar. ... Logical analysis is an antidote. Its importance is to stop the muddle someone makes on reflecting on words. (*L II* 21)

Wittgenstein's rejection of his earlier metaphilosophy brought with it a renewed insistence that the difficulty that we face when in the grip of philosophical confusion is not some kind of ignorance, but our *misunderstanding*, our being subject to an illusion of ignorance, a captivation by certain pseudo-questions for which, unsurprisingly, we lack answers. The pursuit of the 'complete analysis' of propositions *encouraged* this confusion by creating the 'expectation of new, deep//unheard of//information' (Ph 12). It is true that *something* is being misunderstood in *some* sense when we are in the grip of philosophical confusion. But we eliminate these problems by reminding ourselves of the mundane facts of how different propositions are used, what makes sense in connection with each, how one explains and masters each, etc.:

> In my earlier book the solution of the problem was presented in a manner insufficiently down to earth. There is too much of an impression that discoveries are necessary for the solution of our problems, and things have been insufficiently brought to the form of grammatical truisms in ordinary language. It all appears too much like discoveries. (MS 109, 212 (1930))[21]

> [T]he solution of all philosophical difficulties ... if they are correct, must be homemade and ordinary. (Ph 8)

A.9 DEMONSTRATING A METHOD

The later Wittgenstein does have a particular outlook on philosophical problems, but we must be careful about what that amounts to. Unquestionably, Wittgenstein does generalize about 'philosophical problems', but those generalizations fall into three roughly distinguishable groups: the qualified, the bland, and the allusive. The qualified include the following: 'in philosophy we often *compare* the use of words with ... ' (*PI* §81); '[w]hen we are doing philosophy it can sometimes look like ... ' (*PI* §592); '[o]ne who philosophizes often makes ... '(*Z* §450); and '[t]his kind of mistake recurs again and again in philosophy ... ' (*BB* 6). Even the apparently sweeping 'this is a characteristic situation to find ourselves in when thinking about philosophical problems' is an introduction to '[t]here are many problems which arise in this way ... ' (*BB* 160). The

---

[21] This translation is Baker and Hacker's (1984, p. 239).

bland include the following: 'While thinking philosophically we see problems in places where there are none' (*PG* 47). 'Philosophizing is: rejecting false arguments' (Ph 6). 'Philosophy, by clarifying, stops us asking illegitimate questions' (*L I* 111).[22]

Members of the first and second group are often overlooked: the first group don't tell us anything about that in which we, as philosophers, are interested: namely, the 'nature', or 'essence', of philosophy; and the second may seem not to say anything substantial. The third group, the allusive, promise to meet both of these philosophical needs of ours:

Philosophy is a battle against the bewitchment of our intelligence by means of language. (*PI* §109)

A philosophical problem has the form: 'I don't know my way about'. (*PI* §123)

The worries that we have about the third group is that, if pressed, they are liable to reveal themselves as bland, and if not pressed, we worry that we don't understand what they mean.

This pattern of unqualified abstraction and qualified concretion characterizes Wittgenstein's positive metaphilosophical proposals. His writings often offer advice of the form: 'It will often prove useful in philosophy to say to ourselves ...' (*PI* §15); but when he finally does give us something unqualified, we don't know quite what he means, such as when he calls for 'perspicuous representations' that produce 'just that understanding which consists in "seeing connexions"' (*PI* §122).

But when asked questions about 'philosophy as such', such generalizations are all one can expect if philosophy is a 'family resemblance' concept: 'we can only give a rough answer if we are to speak about philosophy in such general terms' (*BB* 44). If philosophical problems have as little unity as Wittgenstein suggests, their elimination may be a similarly disparate affair, and there need be no *substantive* and *general* principles of the sort that we philosophers might demand of a 'philosophical methodology'. When '*the* ailment' fragments, '*the* treatment' for the ailment follows suit: 'philosophy isn't anything except ... the particular individual worries that we call "philosophical problems"' (*PG* 193), and, consequently, '[t]here is not *a* philosophical method, though there are indeed methods, like different therapies' (*PI* §133). *We philosophers* think that Wittgenstein's generalizations about the domain of 'philosophy' should be specific and still all-embracing, because *we* believe that domain to be fundamentally homogeneous; we think we glimpse 'something lying *beneath* the surface'. But instead, Wittgenstein's metaphilosophical remarks are perhaps maxims or tips, no more useful than that, but also no less.

---

[22] Compare also Wittgenstein's characterization of the problems he examines as 'troubles in our thought' (M 257), questions 'of a special kind' (Ph 7), 'mysterious difficulties' (Ph 15).

Section 133 of the *Investigations*, which originates in the Big Typescript, is regarded as one of Wittgenstein's most enigmatic later passages. In the light of my reading, it becomes intelligible:

The real discovery is the one that makes me capable of stopping doing philosophy when I want to.

The one that gives philosophy peace, so that it is no longer //being// tormented by questions which bring *itself* in question. (Ph 19)

In these sentences, which conclude what is often thought of as the metaphilosophical 'chapter' of the *Investigations*, Wittgenstein renounces the attempt to formulate a final and exact account of the nature of philosophy.[23] The 'real discovery' is the discovery which would allow me to stop searching for the *essence* of philosophy; it is the discovery which ends philosophy's self-questioning, terminates the effort to state, once and for all, what *philosophy itself* must be. Wittgenstein continues:

Instead, we now demonstrate a method by examples; and one can break off the series of examples //and the series of examples can be broken off//. But more correctly, one should say: Problems are solved (uneasiness //difficulties// eliminated), not a *single* problem.

It is to this passage that Wittgenstein appends in the *Investigations* the sentence:

There is not *a* philosophical method, though there are indeed methods, like different therapies.

Wittgenstein's 'Instead' contrasts the demonstration of his philosophical method by way of examples with the 'real philosophical discovery' and with the philosophical questioning of philosophy. But can such things contrast? In what respect could they be seen as rivals? Wittgenstein's 'series of examples [that] can be broken off' is a clear allusion to the issue of definition and, in this case, to the issue of the definition of 'philosophy' (to the 'questions which bring [philosophy] *itself* in question'). If there is no one thing that philosophy is—that is to say, if '[t]here is not *a* philosophical method' and philosophy is not constituted by 'a *single* problem'—then a definition of 'philosophy' will naturally take the form of a set of examples. One may feel that a request for a definition could never be satisfied by a set of examples; but such prejudices about what concepts are, and what it is to grasp a concept, are among Wittgenstein's principal targets in his later work: '[e]xamples are decent signs' (*PG* 273), despite the philosophical demand for definition by reference to a shared characteristic. A series of examples can serve to define a family resemblance concept, and this, I have argued, is how Wittgenstein comes to conceive of 'philosophy'.

---

[23] In McManus 1995 I defend the reading of *PI* §133 offered here within the context of the *Investigations*, and in doing so, make clear the connection between it and the material that follows it in what otherwise appears to be the 'next chapter': that material addresses the disintegration of the concept of a 'proposition'.

There is, I think, a wistful quality about Wittgenstein's remarks on 'the real discovery', but it stems not from this 'discovery' being one that he seeks but cannot attain. Rather, the problem that he faces is a peculiarity of 'the real discovery': Wittgenstein's opponents cannot see that he has achieved that discovery. To them, a finite list of examples could never suffice to define any concept, and they are not about to accept this in the case which is closest to home. Thus 'the real discovery' is almost a ruse, in that it is nothing but the recognition of something which, according to Wittgenstein, stares us in the face. Wittgenstein's 'demonstration' is an alternative to 'the questions', because 'philosophy' cannot be defined in the manner implied by questions which ask what 'the essence of philosophy' is. But the 'demonstration' also contrasts with 'the real discovery', because the approach to this problem of definition which seeks 'the real discovery' is the approach most likely to fail to recognize the solution to its problem. The 'real discovery' is the one which allows us to stop looking for the kind of final, all-embracing solution that talk of a 'real discovery' brings to mind; it would allow us to stop seeing Wittgenstein's pronouncements as ill-expressed attempts to answer the question of 'the essence of philosophy'. As Z§314 puts it,

Here we come up against a remarkable and characteristic phenomenon in philosophical investigation: the difficulty—I might say—is not that of finding the solution but rather that of recognising as the solution something that looks as if it were only a preliminary to it.

This difficulty bedevils talk of 'what philosophy is': Wittgenstein's 'demonstrat[ion of] a method, by examples' and his seemingly merely 'allusive' or 'insubstantial' metaphilosophical remarks are taken by those he most needs to reach as inarticulate intimations of a hidden, general, and substantial principle that defines 'what philosophy is', 'something lying *beneath* the surface'.

Wittgenstein's reorientation of what his own thought does is radical and difficult to appreciate. It is made more so by his continuing to use terms like 'grammar' and 'philosophy' after they have been stripped of their status as super-concepts. But that they have been so 'demoted' shows itself just as much in his philosophical 'practice' as in his explicit metaphilosophical remarks. His practice is to focus on particular problems, occasionally flagging commonalities that some happen to share, but without working toward the kind of broad conclusions toward which philosophical writing is assumed to work, conclusions that articulate themselves in super-concepts. How we are to handle philosophical problems is exhibited in the same way: Wittgenstein's method is explained through examples and the few broad indications that he feels he can give of how we might extrapolate from those examples.

One could say that learning these techniques is learning the answer to the question 'What is philosophy?' But as long as we are still tormented by that question, and by a craving to convert our knowledge of Wittgenstein's 'answer' from a mastery of a loose group of techniques into the grasp of a principle which picks out *the* defining characteristics of philosophical problems, we are still in the grip of philosophical confusion. Wittgenstein's 'real discovery', his true later radicalism, lies not in grand claims in response to this question, but in his restraint from involvement in such debates. This, of course, stands in contrast to the author of the *Tractatus*, who claims that its 'definitive' and 'unassailable' truths provide 'on all essential points, the final solution' to the problems of philosophy (*TLP* preface). Wittgenstein's earlier metaphilosophical vision itself rests on forms of philosophical confusion, and his later criticism of that vision illustrates his later criticism of philosophical problems. His early ambition belongs to a metaphilosophical vision articulated in terms that Wittgenstein came to see as loci of philosophical confusion, a vision of Philosophy-capital-P articulated in terms of Analysis-capital-A and the Arbitrariness-capital-A of Grammar-capital-G, all of which are underpinned by a vision of Language-capital-L.

A.10 SO WHY IS THE *TRACTATUS* STILL WORTH READING?

If the *Tractatus* is compromised by the confusions discussed in this Appendix, why is it still worth reading? In answering this question, I will also address a charge sometimes made against resolute readings of the *Tractatus*: that of making the philosophical world less interesting. Some critics see such readings as assimilating the early Wittgenstein to the later Wittgenstein, and since we 'already have' the latter, we seem to have lost one of the great, novel outlooks in philosophy's history. The early Wittgenstein is digested into the later one, and erased from history is the advocate of an ineffable metaphysics and a picture theory of representation.

While it is true that some important elements of the outlook that is thought to be distinctive to, and novel in, the later Wittgenstein can be found, according to my own reading, in the early Wittgenstein—for example, the notion that we do not need to formulate substantial philosophical theories of mind, language, or world—there are at least three misunderstandings expressed in the previous paragraph. First, resolute readers do not simply assimilate the early Wittgenstein to the later because they believe that the former made a host of mistakes that the latter identified and attacked. As it stands, though, this response leaves us with another version of the previous paragraph's complaint, a version to which I will return: All we get from the early Wittgenstein that is not also provided by the later Wittgenstein is a set of mistakes.

Secondly, is it true that we 'already have' the later Wittgenstein? Advocates of resolute readings of the *Tractatus* are advancing novel views of the later work too;[24] thus, if there were a resolute reader who wanted to assimilate the early to

[24] Cf., e.g., Conant 1998 and 2004; Diamond 1989 and 2001; Floyd 1991, 1996, 2000; Goldfarb 1983 and 1997*b*.

the later Wittgenstein, she would have to deal with the fact that other resolute readers are changing our understanding of the later work, rendering it, as it were, a moving target, and one which moves in response to developments in resolute understandings of the early work.

Thirdly, the resolute approach only renders the history of philosophy less interesting if the only thing that *could* be interesting about him is his advocacy of an ineffable metaphysics and a picture theory of representation. But the responsibility now lies with the resolute to explain what *else* there might be going on in the *Tractatus* that is of philosophical value and that—to respond to the adapted complaint that emerged from my response to the first misunderstanding mentioned—is not distinguished from a contribution of the later Wittgenstein solely by being a mistake the later didn't make. In this concluding section of this Appendix, I will explain one way in which I see a value in the early Wittgenstein's work that the later work lacks.

Many of the critical insights that this Appendix discusses ought perhaps to have been anticipated by the author of the *Tractatus*: to fail to recognize 'family resemblance' concepts is to display a faith in 'surface grammar' as a guide to our intent in using our words, a presumption that where we have the same sign, we have the same symbol. As Wittgenstein is reported to have himself said, he had been wrong to think that 'proposition' was a 'sharply bounded' concept, and had been ' "misled" by the expression "sense" ' (M 273). That sign/symbol conflations play an important role in the genesis of philosophical problems is a view that the later Wittgenstein retains:

[W]hat confuses us is the uniform appearance of words when we hear them spoken or meet them in script and print. For their *application* is not presented to us so clearly. Especially when we are doing philosophy! (*PI* §11)[25]

But gone now is the claim that these are the confusions of which philosophy 'is full' (3.324). Similarly, we also read in *PI* §§251 and 295 of how philosophical confusions arise out of the conflation of empirical and grammatical propositions, though the latter are no longer presented as 'saying nothing'.[26] But the later Wittgenstein's sense of how and why we succumb to philosophical confusion is richer; this Appendix, for example, has highlighted our 'contempt for the particular' and our 'craving for generality' (*BB* 18) (though, as I have indicated, this craving too is supported by sign/symbol confusion).

As well as being in that way myopic, the *Tractatus* is bedevilled by a variety of other philosophical confusions, only some of which I have examined here. But

---

[25] Cf. also *PI* §§12, 90, 111, 422, 520, and 664.

[26] One might also suggest that the question raised in the argument of Sect. 3.5—'What makes one even think that these propositions ought to conform to those possible facts?'—could naturally be extended to ask, 'What makes one even think that in uttering these propositions one is attempting to describe a possible fact, as opposed to giving an order, singing catches, asking, thanking, cursing, greeting, or praying?'

the narrow vision of philosophy that it presents is, I think, of abiding value, though it must be handled with care. According to that vision, philosophy is a confused exploration of 'intelligibility' and its supposed 'basis', a confusion made possible by sign/symbol conflation; Wittgenstein tries to expose this confusion as such through a self-conscious working through of that idea of 'intelligibility' and our interest in it, and the use of notational 'strategies' designed to break up those sign/symbol conflations.

Much of this vision is compatible with the outlook of the later Wittgenstein; but the *Tractatus* presents that vision more vividly, and thinks it through in a more systematic way, a fact that, for different reasons, is to be both applauded and regretted. As a genuinely powerful and potentially illuminating picture, it constitutes a danger, in that it has the capacity to captivate us, as it did the early Wittgenstein: it tells us one side of the story as if it were the whole story, revealing—'as if we had now seen something lying *beneath* the surface'—'what philosophy, in general, is'. But it recounts what it does recount in a way that throws into relief a particular aspect of what is confused about confused philosophical thinking.

To evaluate the early Wittgenstein's 'elucidation' of con-formity (and also the kind of a priori argument set out in Sect. 3.5), a useful model is the evaluation sketched in Section A.6 of its near relative, the proposal that 'grammar is arbitrary'. That elucidation provides a frame through which we might look at philosophical problems; sometimes it may illuminate them, sometimes it may make them more obscure. It offers, as an object of comparison, a vision of philosophy. From the later Wittgenstein's perspective, that early vision was put forward with a wild and confused ambition. But that early vision may still be useful if we recognize it as a tool to be used with judgement, with thought, and not, to use McGuinness's phrase once again, as 'a substitute for thought' (2002, p. 7).[27]

Used appropriately, used 'modestly' one might even say, that vision can still illuminate. So, for example, the anatomizing of how 'issues' like (N–P), (O–F), (O–N), and (O–E) emerge in response to real pressures within the confused pseudo-logic of con-formism and ultimately out of sign/symbol confusions is not to be found in the later work. I think there is something true and illuminating in these anatomies, and reading the later Wittgenstein will not provide one with them. Wittgenstein moves away from his early general picture with good reason; but I suspect that, if we too rapidly do the same, the illumination that this admittedly partial and potentially misleading picture does provide may be lost.

---

[27] Something similar ought to be said of the ethical picture which emerges in Chs. 14–15, that there is something illuminating but also potentially misleading in its talk of '*the* ethical life', '*the* challenge of acting on one's own behalf', '*the* demand that one bear an identity', etc. But rather than pepper that discussion with what I recognize would be some important qualifications, I will offer it as it stands, and remind any reader who might be tempted to think by reference to it that doing so will require her to use her judgement.

List of Abbreviations Used for Particular 'Theses' of the *Tractatus*

(F-P)   Facts are internally related to the propositions that represent them.

(GFP)   Every proposition is an elementary proposition or a (possibly very complex) complex proposition.

(GFW) The world is the totality of existent atomic facts.

(N-E)   Names allow us to speak *of* objects, not to say *what* or *that* they are.

(N-P)   A name's identity is internally related to the propositions in which it can occur.

(N-S)   Names are simple.

(O-E)   Objects are indestructible.

(O-F)   An object's identity is internally related to the possible facts in which it can occur.

(O-N)   Objects are internally related to the names that name them.

(O-S)   Objects are simple.

References

ANSCOMBE, G. E. M. (1959), *An Introduction to Wittgenstein's* Tractatus, London: Hutchinson.

ANSELM, St (1926 [1078]), *Proslogion*, trans. S. N. Deane, Chicago: Open Court.

ARISTOTLE (1955), *Ethics*, trans. J. Thompson, Harmondsworth: Penguin Books.

BAKER, G. P., and HACKER, P. M. S. (1984), *An Analytical Commentary on Wittgenstein's* Philosophical Investigations, vol. 1, Oxford: Blackwell.

——— (2001), 'Wittgenstein and the Vienna Circle: The Exaltation and Deposition of Ostensive Definition', revised form, in Hacker (2001*b*).

BALDWIN, T. (1990), *G. E. Moore*, London: Routledge.

BEANEY, M. (1996), *Frege: Making Sense*, London: Duckworth.

——— (1997) (ed.), *The Frege Reader*, Oxford: Blackwell.

BLACK, M. (1964), *A Companion to Wittgenstein's* Tractatus, New York: Harper & Row.

BOSWELL, J. (1980 [1791]), *Life of Johnson*, Oxford: Oxford University Press.

BRADLEY, F. H. (1897), *Appearance & Reality*, London: George Allen & Unwin.

——— (1914), *Essays on Truth and Reality*, Oxford: Clarendon Press.

BUNYAN, J. (1965 [1678]), *The Pilgrim's Progress*, Harmondsworth: Penguin Books.

CARROLL, L. (1992 [1865]), 'Alice's Adventures in Wonderland', in *Alice in Wonderland*, Ware: Wordsworth.

——— (1992 [1872]), 'Through the Looking Glass', in *Alice in Wonderland*, Ware: Wordsworth.

CAVELL, S. (1976), *Must We Mean What We Say?*, Cambridge: Cambridge University Press.

——— (1979), *The Claim of Reason*, Oxford: Oxford University Press.

CHILD, W. (2001), 'Pears's Wittgenstein: Rule-Following, Platonism, and Naturalism', in D. Charles and W. Child (eds.), *Wittgensteinian Themes*, Oxford: Clarendon Press.

CONANT, J. (1989), 'Must We Show What We Cannot Say?', in R. Fleming and M. Payne (eds.), *The Senses of Stanley Cavell*, Lewisburg, Pa.: Bucknell University Press.

——— (1991*a*), 'The Search for Logically Alien Thought: Descartes, Kant, Frege and the *Tractatus*', in *The Philosophy of Hilary Putnam, Philosophical Topics* 20: 115–80.

——— (1991*b*), 'Throwing Away the Top of the Ladder', *Yale Review* 79: 328–64.

——— (1993), 'Kierkegaard, Wittgenstein and Nonsense', in T. Cohen, P. Guyer, and H. Putnam (eds.), *Pursuits of Reason*, Lubbock, Tex.: Texas Tech University Press.

——— (1998), 'Wittgenstein on Meaning and Use', *Philosophical Investigations* 21: 222–50.

——— (2000), 'Elucidation and Nonsense in Frege and the Early Wittgenstein', in Crary and Read (2000).

——— (2001), 'Two Conceptions of *Die Überwindung der Metaphysik*: Carnap and Early Wittgenstein', in McCarthy and Stidd (2001).

——— (2002), 'The Method of the *Tractatus*', in Reck (2002).

——— (2004), 'Varieties of Scepticism', in McManus (2004*b*).

—— (2005), 'What "Ethics" in the *Tractatus* is *Not*', in D. Z. Phillips (ed.), *Religion and Wittgenstein's Legacy*, London: Ashgate.

——and DIAMOND, C. (2004), 'On Reading the *Tractatus* Resolutely: Reply to Meredith Williams and Peter Sullivan', in Kölbel and Weiss (2004).

COOK, J. (1994), *Wittgenstein's Metaphysics*, Cambridge: Cambridge University Press.

CRARY, A., and READ, R. (2000) (eds.), *The New Wittgenstein*, London: Routledge.

CURRIE, G. (1982), *Frege*, Brighton: Harvester.

DESCARTES, R. (1991), *The Philosophical Writings of Descartes*, trans. J. Cottingham, R. Stoothof, and D. Murdoch, vol. 3, Cambridge: Cambridge University Press.

DIAMOND, C. (1989), 'Rules: Looking in the Right Place', in D. Z. Phillips and P. Winch (eds.), *Wittgenstein: Attention to Particulars*, New York: St Martin's Press.

—— (1991), *The Realistic Spirit*, Cambridge, Mass.: MIT Press.

—— (2000*a*), 'Does Bismarck have a Beetle in his Box? The Private Language Argument in the *Tractatus*', in Crary and Read (2000).

—— (2000*b*), 'Ethics, Imagination and the Method of Wittgenstein's *Tractatus*', in Crary and Read (2000).

—— (2001), 'How Long is the Standard Meter in Paris?', in McCarthy and Stidd (2001).

DUMMETT, M. (1973), *Frege: Philosophy of Language*, London: Duckworth.

—— (1991), *Frege: Philosophy of Mathematics*, Cambridge, Mass.: Harvard University Press.

FLOYD, J. (1991), 'Wittgenstein on 2, 2, 2 . . .: On the Opening of *Remarks on the Foundations of Mathematics*', *Synthese* 87: 143–80.

—— (1996), 'On Saying What You Really Want to Say: Wittgenstein, Gödel and the Trisection of the Angle', in J. Hintikka (ed.), *From Dedekind to Gödel*, Dordrecht: Kluwer Academic.

—— (1998), 'The Uncaptive Eye: Solipsism in Wittgenstein's *Tractatus*', in L. Rouner (ed.), *Loneliness*, Notre Dame, Ind.: University of Notre Dame Press.

—— (2000), 'Wittgenstein, Mathematics and Philosophy', in Crary and Read (2000).

—— (2002), 'Number and Ascriptions of Number in Wittgenstein's *Tractatus*', in Reck (2002).

FOGELIN, R. J. (1987), *Wittgenstein*, London: Routledge & Kegan Paul.

FREGE, G. (1967 [1879]), '*Begriffsschrift*, a Formula Language, Modelled upon that of Arithmetic, for Pure Thought', trans. S. Bauer-Mengelberg, in *From Frege to Gödel: A Source Book in Mathematical Logic, 1879–1931*, ed. J. van Heijenoort, Cambridge, Mass.: Harvard University Press.

—— (1972 [1882]), 'On the Scientific Justification of a Conceptual Notation [*Begriffschrift*]', in *Conceptual Notation and Related Articles*, trans. and ed. T. W. Bynum, Oxford: Oxford University Press.

—— (1953 [1884]), *The Foundations of Arithmetic*, trans. J. L. Austin, Oxford: Blackwell.

—— (1971 [1885]), 'On Formal Theories of Arithmetic', trans. E.-H. W. Kluge, in Frege (1971).

—— (1980 [1891]), 'Function and Concept', trans. P. T. Geach, in *Translations from the Philosophical Writings of Gottlob Frege*, ed. P. T. Geach and M. Black, Oxford: Blackwell.

FREGE, G. (1997 [1892]), 'On Concept and Object', trans. P. T. Geach, in Beaney (1997).

——(1997 [1893]), '*Grundgesetze der Arithmetik*, Volume I: Selections', trans. M. Beaney, in Beaney (1997).

——(1997 [1897]), 'Logic', trans. P. Long and R. White, in G. Frege, *Posthumous Writings*, ed. H. Hermes, F. Kambartel, and F. Kaulbach, Oxford: Blackwell.

——(1997 [1903]), '*Grundgesetze der Arithmetik*, Volume II: Selections', trans. M. Beaney, in Beaney (1997).

——(1980 [1904]), 'What is a Function?', trans. P. T. Geach, in *Translations from the Philosophical Writings of Gottlob Frege*, ed. P. T. Geach and M. Black, Oxford: Blackwell.

——(1979 [1915]), 'My Basic Logical Insights', trans. P. Long and R. White, in G. Frege, *Posthumous Writings*, ed. H. Hermes, F. Kambartel, and F. Kaulbach, Oxford: Blackwell.

——(1997 [1919]), 'Thought', trans. P. T. Geach and R. H. Stoothoff, in Beaney (1997).

——(1971), *On the Foundations of Geometry and Formal Theories of Arithmetic*, trans. E.-H. W. Kluge, New Haven: Yale University Press.

FRIEDLANDER, E. (2001), *Signs of Sense*, Cambridge, Mass.: Harvard University Press.

GLENDINNING, S. (1998), *On Being with Others: Heidegger—Derrida—Wittgenstein*, London: Routledge.

GLOCK, H.-J. (1996), *A Wittgenstein Dictionary*, Oxford: Blackwell.

——(1999), 'Schopenhauer and Wittgenstein: Language as Representation and Will', in Janaway (1999).

GOLDFARB, W. (1983), 'I Want You to Bring Me a Slab: Remarks on the Opening Sections of the *Philosophical Investigations*', *Synthese* 56: 265–82.

——(1997*a*), 'Metaphysics and Nonsense: On Cora Diamond's *The Realistic Spirit*', *Journal of Philosophical Research* 22: 57–73.

——(1997*b*), 'Wittgenstein on Fixity of Meaning', in W. W. Tait (ed.), *Early Analytic Philosophy*, Chicago: Open Court.

——(unpublished, *a*), 'Names, Objects, and Realism in the *Tractatus*', unpublished manuscript.

——(unpublished, *b*), '*Das Überwinden*: Anti-Metaphysical Readings of the *Tractatus*', unpublished manuscript.

GRAY, G. (2004), 'For All the Saints: Catherine Dei Ricci', *Fortean Times* 181: 22.

HACKER, P. M. S. (1986) *Insight and Illusion*, rev. edn., Oxford: Clarendon Press.

——(1990), *Wittgenstein—Meaning and Mind: Volume Three of an Analytic Commentary on the* Philosophical Investigations, Oxford: Blackwell.

——(1992), 'Malcolm and Searle on "Intrinsic Mental States"', *Philosophical Investigations* 15: 245–75.

——(1996*a*), *Wittgenstein—Mind and Will: Volume Four of an Analytic Commentary on the* Philosophical Investigations, Oxford: Blackwell.

——(1996*b*), *Wittgenstein's Place in Twentieth-Century Analytic Philosophy*, Oxford: Blackwell.

——(1999), 'Naming, Thinking and Meaning in the *Tractatus*', *Philosophical Investigations* 22: 119–35; repr. with a postscript in Hacker (2001*b*).

—— (2000), 'Was He Trying to Whistle It?', in Crary and Read (2000).

—— (2001*a*), 'When the Whistling Had to Stop', in D. Charles and W. Child (eds.), *Wittgensteinian Themes*, Oxford: Clarendon Press.

—— (2001*b*), *Wittgenstein: Connections and Controversies*, Oxford: Clarendon Press.

—— (2003), 'Wittgenstein, Carnap and the New American Wittgensteinians', *Philosophical Quarterly* 53: 1–23.

HEAL, J. (1998), 'Wittgenstein, Ludwig Josef Johann (1889–1951)', in E. Craig (ed.), *Routledge Encyclopedia of Philosophy*, version 1.0, London: Routledge.

HEIDEGGER, M. (1962), *Being and Time*, trans. J. Macquarrie and E. Robinson, Oxford: Blackwell.

HUME, D. (1978 [1740]), *A Treatise of Human Nature*, ed. P. H. Nidditch, Oxford: Clarendon Press.

HYLTON, P. (1990), *Russell, Idealism and the Emergence of Analytic Philosophy*, Cambridge: Cambridge University Press.

ISHIGURO, H. (1969), 'Use and Reference of Names', in P. Winch (ed.), *Studies in the Philosophy of Wittgenstein*, London: Routledge & Kegan Paul.

JANAWAY, C. (1989), *Self and World in Schopenhauer's Philosophy*, Oxford: Oxford University Press.

—— (1999) (ed.), *The Cambridge Companion to Schopenhauer*, Cambridge: Cambridge University Press.

JANIK, A., and TOULMIN, S. (1973), *Wittgenstein's Vienna*, New York: Simon & Schuster.

JEROME, J. K. (1994 [1889]), *Three Men in a Boat*, Harmondsworth: Penguin Books.

KANT, I. (1961 [1781/1787]), *Critique of Pure Reason*, trans. N. Kemp Smith, London: Macmillan.

—— (1996 [1784]), 'An Answer to the Question: "What is Enlightenment?"', trans. T. Humphrey, in D. Wootton (ed.), *Modern Political Thought: Readings from Machiavelli to Nietzsche*, Indianapolis: Hackett.

KENNY, A. (1973), *Wittgenstein*, Harmondsworth: Penguin Books.

—— (1976), 'From the Big Typescript to the *Philosophical Grammar*', *Acta Philosophica Fennica* 28: 41–53.

—— (1995), *Frege*, Harmondsworth: Penguin Books.

KÖLBEL, M., and WEISS, B. (2004) (eds.), *Wittgenstein's Lasting Significance*, London: Routledge.

KREMER, M. (2001), 'The Purpose of Tractarian Nonsense', *Nous* 35: 39–73.

—— (2002), 'Mathematics and Meaning in the *Tractatus*', *Philosophical Investigations* 25: 272–303.

—— (2004), 'To What Extent is Solipsism a Truth?', in B. Stocker and G. Guzey (eds.), *Post-Analytic Tractatus*, London: Ashgate.

KUUSELA, O. (2005), 'From Metaphysics and Philosophical Theses to Grammar: Wittgenstein's Turn', *Philosophical Investigations* 28: 95–133.

MACKIE, J. L. (1977), *Ethics: Inventing Right and Wrong*, Harmondsworth: Penguin Books.

MALCOLM, N. (1984), *Ludwig Wittgenstein: A Memoir*, Oxford: Oxford University Press.

—— (1986), *Nothing is Hidden*, Oxford: Blackwell.

McCARTHY, T., and STIDD, S. C. (2001) (eds.), *Wittgenstein in America*, Oxford: Clarendon Press.

McDowell, J. (1994), *Mind and World*, Cambridge, Mass.: Harvard University Press.

McGinn, M. (1999), 'Between Metaphysics and Nonsense: Elucidation in Wittgenstein's *Tractatus*', *Philosophical Quarterly* 49: 491–513.

McGuinness, B. F. (1981), 'The So-Called Realism of the *Tractatus*', in I. Block (ed.), *Perspectives on the Philosophy of Wittgenstein*, Oxford: Blackwell; repr. in McGuinness (2002).

——— (1988), *Wittgenstein: A Life—Young Ludwig 1889–1921*, London: Duckworth.

——— (2002), *Approaches to Wittgenstein*, London: Routledge.

McManus, D. (1995), 'Philosophy in Question: *Philosophical Investigations* 133', *Philosophical Investigations* 18: 348–61.

——— (1999), 'The Rediscovery of Heidegger's Worldly Subject by Analytic Philosophy of Science', *The Monist* 82: 324–46.

——— (2000), 'Freedom, Grammar and the Given—*Mind and World* and Wittgenstein', *Journal of the British Society for Phenomenology* 31: 248–63.

——— (2002), ' "Bedingungen der Möglichkeit und Unmöglichkeit": Wittgenstein, Heidegger und Derrida', in A. Kern and C. Menke (eds.), *Philosophie der Dekonstruktion*, Frankfurt am Main: Suhrkamp Verlag.

——— (2003), 'Wittgenstein, Fetishism, and Nonsense in Practice', in C. J. Heyes (ed.), *The Grammar of Politics: Wittgenstein and Political Philosophy*, Ithaca, NY: Cornell University Press.

——— (2004*a*), 'Solipsism and Scepticism in the *Tractatus*', in McManus (2004*b*).

——— (2004*b*) (ed.), *Wittgenstein and Scepticism*, London: Routledge.

——— (forthcoming), 'Heidegger, Measurement and the "Intelligibility" of Science', *European Journal of Philosophy*.

Mill, J. S. (1973 [1843]), *A System of Logic*, in *Collected Works*, vii, Toronto: University of Toronto Press.

Monk, R. (1990), *Ludwig Wittgenstein: The Duty of Genius*, London: Vintage.

Moore, A. W. (1997), *Points of View*, Oxford: Oxford University Press.

——— (2003), 'Ineffability and Nonsense', *Proceedings of the Aristotelian Society*, suppl. vol. 77: 169–93.

Moore, G. E. (1903), *Principia Ethica*, Cambridge: Cambridge University Press.

Mounce, H. O. (1981), *Wittgenstein's* Tractatus: *An Introduction*, Chicago: University of Chicago Press.

Mulhall, S. (2001), *Inheritance and Originality: Wittgenstein, Heidegger, Kierkegaard*, Oxford: Oxford University Press.

——— (forthcoming), 'Words, Waxing and Waning: Ethics in/and/of the *Tractatus Logico-Philosophicus*', in G. Kahane, E. Kanterian, and O. Kuusela (eds.), *Wittgenstein and his Interpreters: Essays in Memory of Gordon Baker*, Oxford: Blackwell.

Nietzsche, F. (1997 [1888]), *Twilight of the Idols*, trans. R. Polt, Indianapolis: Hackett.

O'Brien, F. (1988), *The Third Policeman*, London: Paladin.

O'Neill, O. (2002), 'Instituting Principles: Between Duty and Action', in M. Timmons (ed.), *Kant's Metaphysics of Morals: Interpretative Essays*, Oxford: Oxford University Press.

Ostrow, M. B. (2002), *Wittgenstein's* Tractatus: *A Dialectical Interpretation*, Cambridge: Cambridge University Press.

Pears, D. (1987), *The False Prison*, vol. 1, Oxford: Clarendon Press.

—— (1997), 'Wittgenstein', in T. Mautner (ed.), *The Penguin Dictionary of Philosophy*, Harmondsworth: Penguin Books.

PITCHER, G. (1967), 'Wittgenstein, Nonsense, and Lewis Carroll', in K. T. Fann (ed.), *Ludwig Wittgenstein: The Man and His Philosophy*, New York: Dell Publishing Co.

POTTER, M. (2000), *Reason's Nearest Kin*, Oxford: Oxford University Press.

POTTS, T. C. (1980), *Conscience in Medieval Philosophy*, Cambridge: Cambridge University Press.

—— (1982), 'Conscience', in N. Kretzmann, A. Kenny, and J. Pinborg (eds.), *The Cambridge History of Later Medieval Philosophy*, Cambridge: Cambridge University Press.

PROOPS, I. (2001), 'The New Wittgenstein: A Critique', *European Journal of Philosophy* 9: 375–404.

QUINE, W. V. O. (1960), *Word and Object*, Cambridge, Mass.: MIT Press.

RAMSEY, F. P. (1923), 'Critical Notice of L. Wittgenstein, *Tractatus Logico-Philosophicus*', *Mind* 32: 465–78.

—— (1925*a*), 'The Foundations of Mathematics', in Ramsey (1990).

—— (1925*b*), 'Universals', in Ramsey (1990).

—— (1927), 'Facts and Propositions', in Ramsey (1990).

—— (1929), 'General Propositions and Causality', in Ramsey (1990).

—— (1990), *Philosophical Papers*, ed. D. H. Mellor, Cambridge: Cambridge University Press.

RECK, E. H. (2002) (ed.), *From Frege to Wittgenstein: Perspectives in Early Analytic Philosophy*, Oxford: Oxford University Press.

REID, L. (1998), 'Wittgenstein's Ladder: The *Tractatus* and Nonsense', *Philosophical Investigations* 21: 97–151.

RHEES, R. (1970), *Discussions of Wittgenstein*, London: Routledge & Kegan Paul.

RICKETTS, T. G. (1985), 'Frege, the *Tractatus* and the Logocentric Predicament', *Nous* 15: 3–15.

—— (1996), 'Pictures, Logic, and the Limits of Sense in Wittgenstein's *Tractatus*', in Sluga and Stern (1996).

RUSSELL, B. (1897), *An Essay on the Foundations of Geometry*, Cambridge: Cambridge University Press.

—— (1937 [1903]), *Principles of Mathematics*, London: Allen & Unwin.

—— (1980 [1912]), *The Problems of Philosophy*, Oxford: Oxford University Press.

—— (1984 [1913]), *Theory of Knowledge*, London: George Allen & Unwin.

—— (1917 [1914*a*]), 'On Scientific Method in Philosophy', repr. in *Mysticism and Logic*, London: George Allen & Unwin.

—— (1929 [1914*b*]), *Our Knowledge of the External World as a Field for Scientific Method in Philosophy*, 2nd edn., New York: W. W. Norton and Co.

—— (1918 [1914*c*]), 'The Relation of Sense-data to Physics', repr. in *Mysticism and Logic*, London: George Allen & Unwin.

—— (1956 [1918]), 'The Philosophy of Logical Atomism', in Russell (1956).

—— (1993 [1919]), *Introduction to Mathematical Philosophy*, London: Routledge.

—— (1921), *The Analysis of Mind*, London: George Allen & Unwin.

—— (1956), *Logic and Knowledge*, ed. R. C. Marsh, London: George Allen & Unwin.

RUSSELL, B. (1967), *Autobiography*, London: George Allen & Unwin.

_____ and WHITEHEAD, A. N. (1927), *Principia Mathematica*, vol. 1, 2nd edn., Cambridge: Cambridge University Press.

SCHOPENHAUER, A. (1969 [1844]), *The World as Will and Representation*, trans. E. F. J. Payne, New York: Dover Publications, Inc.

SEARLE, J. (1992), *The Rediscovery of the Mind*, Cambridge, Mass.: MIT Press.

SELLARS, W. (1956), 'Empiricism and the Philosophy of Mind', in H. Feigl and M. Scriven (eds.), *Minnesota Studies in the Philosophy of Science*, vol. 1, Minneapolis: University of Minnesota Press.

SLUGA, H. (1980), *Gottlob Frege*, London: Routledge.

_____ and STERN, D. G. (1996) (eds.), *The Cambridge Companion to Wittgenstein*, Cambridge: Cambridge University Press.

STERN, D. G. (1995), *Wittgenstein on Mind and Language*, Oxford: Oxford University Press.

STEVENS, G. (2005), *The Russellian Origins of Analytic Philosophy*, London: Routledge.

STONE, M. (2000), 'Wittgenstein on Deconstruction', in Crary and Read (2000).

SULLIVAN, P. M. (1996), 'The "Truth" in Solipsism, and Wittgenstein's Rejection of the *A Priori*', *European Journal of Philosophy* 4: 195–219.

_____ (2002), 'On Trying to be Resolute: A Response to Kremer on the *Tractatus*', *European Journal of Philosophy* 10: 43–78.

_____ (2003), 'Ineffability and Nonsense', *Proceedings of the Aristotelian Society*, suppl. vol. 77: 195–223.

_____ (2004), 'What is the *Tractatus* About?', in Kölbel and Weiss (2004).

WEINER, J. (1990), *Frege in Perspective*, Ithaca, NY: Cornell University Press.

WINCH, P. (1987), 'Language, Thought and World in Wittgenstein's *Tractatus*', in *Trying to Make Sense*, Oxford: Blackwell.

WITHERSPOON, E. (2000), 'Conceptions of Nonsense in Carnap and Wittgenstein', in Crary and Read (2000).

WITTGENSTEIN, H. (1984), 'My Brother Ludwig', in R. Rhees (ed.), *Recollections of Wittgenstein*, Oxford: Oxford University Press.

WRIGHT, G. H. von (1954), 'A Biographical Sketch', in Malcolm (1984).

_____ (1969), 'The Wittgenstein Papers', published in revised and expanded form in *PO*.

_____ (1994), 'To Hold Judgment over Himself was Part of Wittgenstein's Personality: Interview with K. O. Åmås and R. Larsen', in K. J. Johannessen, R. Larsen, and K. O. Åmås (eds.), *Wittgenstein and Norway*, Oslo: Solum Forlag.

Index

Mackie, J. L. 192
Malcolm, N. 35–36, 43, 57 n. 22, 124 n. 3
McGinn, M. 44 n. 4, 45, 50
McGuinness, B. F. 1 n. 1, 13 n. 12, 33, 36
  n. 8, 44 n. 5, 85 n. 9, 109 n. 12, 132 n. 4,
  178, 185–86, 205, 211, 234 n. 15, 256
McManus, D. 62 n. 33, 79 n. 4, 113 n. 23,
  116 n. 26, 252 n. 23
Meaningfulness, *see* Language, meaningfulness
  of *and* Intelligibility
Mill, J. S. 16, 18
Monk, R. 3 n. 3, 178, 212 n. 30
Moore, A. W. 137–38, 203 n. 19
Moore, G. E. 61, 78, 99 n. 10, 116 n. 25, 138,
  148, 164, 192, 238, 247 n. 18, 249
Mulhall, S. 50 n. 15, 132 n. 3, 176 n. 4
Mystical, the 116, 183, 209 n. 24, 223–27

(N-E), *see* Names
(N-P), *see* Names, and propositions
(N-S), *see* Names
Names 7–9, 29, 33–34, 65–69, 215
Names, and objects 34–35, 90–101, 104,
  216
Names, and propositions 33–34, 65–75,
  92–93, 99, 104, 142–44, 159, 215–16,
  221, 222 n. 3
Negation 150–52, 156, 237
Nietzsche, F. 227
Nonsense 26–28, 40–41, 43–64, 130,
  134–39, 243, *see also* Illogicality
Nonsense, 'austere' conception of 46–49, 60
  n. 29, 172 n. 12, 230
Notation, *see* Begriffsschrift
Notational reform, *see* Begriffsschrift

(O-E), *see* Objects, as substance of the world
(O-F), *see* Facts, and objects
(O-N), *see* Names, and objects
(O-S), *see* Objects, as simple
O'Brien, F. 70–71
Objects 7–9, 29–34, 119–28, 158–59
Objects, and analysis 9, 29–35, 124, 125
  n. 6
Objects, and facts, *see* Facts, and objects
Objects, and names *see* Names, and objects
Objects, as simple 31–33, 36, 119, 121–28,
  218–19
Objects, as substance of the world 31–33, 57,
  119, 121–28, 218–19, 256
O'Neill, O. 182 n. 11
Operations 166 n. 8, 213 n. 1
Ostensive definition, 107–8, 166, 227, 246
  n. 16
Ostrow, M. B. 44 n. 5, 93 n. 4, 95 n. 6, 163
  n. 2, 176 n. 4

Parts of speech 200–201, 221
Pears, D. 1, 33, 35 n. 7, 36, 117, 122, 131,
  141, 163 n. 3,
Personal identity 12–13, 229–30, 234, 256
  n. 27
Phenomenology 236 n. 2
Philosophical method 43–64, 72, 84,
  129–39, 240–56
Philosophical problems, nature of 3–4,
  20–22, 47, 49, 64, 73–75, 87–89,
  237–38, 247–56
Philosophy, essentialist concept of 247–56
'Picture' analogy 1, 8–9, 34, 65–75, 90–101,
  103, 143, 150–52, 201, 215–16, 222,
  239
Pitcher, G. 51 n. 18
Poetry 88–89
Potter, M. 13 n. 12
Potts, T. C. 182 n. 12
Proops, I. 45 n. 8, 48
Proposition 'shows its sense' 106–10, 216–17
Proposition, and definiteness or determinacy of
  sense 125–27
Proposition, and thought 105–6, 109–10
Proposition, as pictures, *see* 'Picture' analogy
Proposition, essentialist concept of 238–40
Proposition, general form of 10–11, 140–74,
  219–20, 240, 241 n. 10
Proposition, unity of 99 n. 10
Propositions, and names *see* Names, and
  propositions
Propositions, elementary and complex 10–11,
  33–34, 124–25, 140–74, 220–21
Psychologism 19, 27, 145

Quantification, *see* Generality

Ramsey, F. P. 44, 125 n. 4, 164 n. 4
Read, R. 44 n. 5, 113 n. 21
Realism 2, 5–6, 38, 40 n, 14, 98 n. 9, 110,
  115, 218, 236 n. 3
Reid. L. 50 n. 15
Relations, reality of 61, 125
Representation, form of, *see* Logical form
Representation, methods of, *see* Comparison,
  methods of
Representation, possibility of *see* Intelligibility
Resolute readings 7–8, 11, 43–51, 54–55,
  58–59, 112–13, 117 n. 27, 137–39, 150
  n. 6, 158, 176, 186, 195 n. 11, 204 n. 20,
  208, 232, 254–55
Responsibility 183–83, 191–94, 209–10,
  224, 226–29, 231–32
Rhees, R. 180 n. 8
Ricketts, T. G. 44 n. 5, 125
Rule-following considerations 171, 205 n. 21